JEWS IN ITALY UNDER FASCIST AND NAZI RULE

Jews in Italy under Fascist and Nazi Rule, 1922–1945, brings to light the Italian-Jewish experience from the start of Mussolini's prime ministership through the end of the Second World War. Challenging the myth of Italian benevolence during the Fascist period, the authors investigate the treatment of Jews by Italians during the Holocaust and the native versus foreign roots of Italian Fascist anti-Semitism. Each essay in this volume illustrates a different aspect of Italian Jewry under Fascist and Nazi rule. Areas of inquiry include the role of the Catholic Church with special reference to Pope Pius XII, Mussolini's attitude, and anti-Jewish persecution. Included also is an examination of cover images and articles from the Italian racist newspaper, *La Difesa della Razza,* intended to lay bare the influence of the Italian media on the general Italian public.

Joshua D. Zimmerman is an associate professor of history and the Eli and Diana Zborowski Professorial Chair in Interdisciplinary Holocaust Studies at Yeshiva University in New York City. He is the author of *Poles, Jews and the Politics of Nationality: The Bund and the Polish Socialist Party in Late Tsarist Russia, 1892–1914* (2004), and editor of *Contested Memories: Poles and Jews during the Holocaust and Its Aftermath* (2003).

Jews in Italy under Fascist and Nazi Rule, 1922–1945

Edited by

Joshua D. Zimmerman
Yeshiva University

CAMBRIDGE
UNIVERSITY PRESS

CAMBRIDGE
UNIVERSITY PRESS

University Printing House, Cambridge CB2 8BS, United Kingdom

One Liberty Plaza, 20th Floor, New York, NY 10006, USA

477 Williamstown Road, Port Melbourne, VIC 3207, Australia

314-321, 3rd Floor, Plot 3, Splendor Forum, Jasola District Centre, New Delhi - 110025, India

79 Anson Road, #06-04/06, Singapore 079906

Cambridge University Press is part of the University of Cambridge.

It furthers the University's mission by disseminating knowledge in the pursuit of education, learning and research at the highest international levels of excellence.

www.cambridge.org
Information on this title: www.cambridge.org/9780521145947

© Joshua D. Zimmerman 2005

First published 2005
Reprinted 2007
First paperback edition 2009

A catalogue record for this publication is available from the British Library

Library of Congress Cataloging in Publication data
Jews in Italy under Fascist and Nazi rule, 1922–1945 / edited by Joshua D. Zimmerman.
p. - cm.
Includes bibliographical references and index.
ISBN 0-521-84101-1 (hardcover)
1. Jews – Italy – History – 20th century. 2. Jews – Persecutions – Italy.
3. Holocaust, Jewish (1939–1945) – Italy. 4. Italy – History – 1922–1945.
5. Italy – Ethnic relations. I. Zimmerman, Joshua D. II. Title.
DS135.I8J48 2005
305.892′4045′09044 – dc22   2004024830

ISBN 978-0-521-84101-6 Hardback
ISBN 978-0-521-14594-7 Paperback

For Ruthi

CONTENTS

ACKNOWLEDGMENTS

This book was made possible by a generous grant from the Eli and Diana Zborowski Chair in Interdisciplinary Holocaust Studies at Yeshiva University. The majority of essays were first presented at the international Holocaust conference on Italian Jewry held at Yeshiva University in October 2002. My heartfelt thanks go to the participants, to the contributors to this volume, and to those who helped in organizing it, particularly my wife, Ruth Servi Zimmerman, who acted as conference secretary, as well as to professors Arthur Hyman and Jeffrey Gurock of Yeshiva University's Bernard Revel Graduate School of Jewish Studies.

For the preparation and selection of essays for this volume, I owe a particular debt of gratitude to Borden W. Painter, professor of history and director of Italian Programs at Trinity College, who generously gave of his time by agreeing to read and provide feedback on the entire manuscript. I am also grateful to the anonymous Cambridge outside readers who provided a valuable critique of the manuscript, as well as to Jonathan Steinberg, professor of history at the University of Pennsylvania, for his valuable comments and feedback. I would also like to thank, in particular, Sandro Servi, who gave freely and generously of his time in responding to questions on various aspects of Italian Jewish history and who provided valuable suggestions at the initial planning stages of the conference. In addition, Giorgio Fabre and Michele Sarfatti were extraordinarily helpful in their prompt and thorough replies to pointed questions on twentieth-century Italian history in general and on Italian Jewish history in particular.

Last but not least, I would like to acknowledge the exceptional work of Loredana M. Melissari, who translated chapters 3, 4, 9, 11, and 13 and a few passages from chapter 9, and of Antony Shugaar, who translated chapters 2 and 7, as well as the conclusion to chapter 13. Finally, Maurizio Molinari, Ruth Servi Zimmerman, and Cinzia Villani helped keep errors in the Italian to a minimum by kindly agreeing to proofread parts of the manuscript.

ABBREVIATIONS

CDEC	Center for Contemporary Jewish Documentation, Milan
Delasem	Delegation for the Assistance of Jewish Immigrants
PCI	Italian Communist Party
Questori	Provincial police chiefs
RSHA	Central Office for the Security of the German Reich
RSI	Italian Social Republic/Republic of Salò

LIST OF CONTRIBUTORS

Ruth Ben-Ghiat is associate professor in the Departments of Italian Studies and History at New York University. She is the author of *Fascist Modernities: Italy, 1922–45* (2001) and of many book chapters and articles on Italian Fascist culture and its memory. She is also coeditor, with Mia Fuller, of *Italian Colonialism: A Reader* (forthcoming, 2005). She is currently writing a book on Italian prisoners of war and the transition from dictatorship to be published by Princeton University Press.

Anna Bravo taught social history at Turin University and is currently an independent scholar living in Turin. Her research and writing deal with gender history, wartime armed and civil resistance, and deportation and genocide. She is co-author of *In guerra senza armi. Storia di donne 1940–1945* (2000) [In the War without Arms: A History of Women, 1940–1945] and has written numerous distinguished articles and book chapters on Italy and modern memory of the Holocaust.

Annalisa Capristo graduated in philosophy at the University of Rome "La Sapienza" and specialized in library management at the School of the Vatican Library. She obtained an annual scholarship from the Istituto Italiano per gli Studi Storici, founded by Benedetto Croce in Naples, and a triennial scholarship from the Accademia nazionale dei Lincei in Rome. She is currently librarian at the Center for American Studies in Rome. Capristo is the author of *L'espulsione degli ebrei dalle accademie italiane* (2002) [The Expulsion of Jews from the Italian Academies] and has published in *La Rassegna mensile di Israel.*

Frank J. Coppa is professor of history at St. John's University in New York, director of their University Symposium on Vatican Studies, and director of the university's doctoral degree in modern world history. Coppa is the author of a series of biographies, including *Pope Pius IX: Crusader in a Secular Age* (1979) and *Cardinal Giacomo Antonelli and Papal Politics in European Affairs* (1990). More recently he published the fifth and final volume in the Longman History of the Papacy, titled *The Modern Papacy* (1998), and in 1999 he served as editor-in-chief and contributor to *Encyclopedia of the Vatican and Papacy* and *Controversial*

Concordats: The Vatican's Relations with Napoleon, Mussolini, and Hitler. He has reviewed all the popes and anti-popes for the *Encyclopedia Britannica's* online references to the papacy and all the popes from the Renaissance through Gregory XVI for the new edition of *The Catholic Encyclopedia.* He has also served as general editor and contributor to *Great Popes Through History* (2002) and published *The Papacy Confronts the Modern World* (2003) in the Avil series.

Giorgio Fabre received his PhD in Italian literature at the University of Rome. He is a journalist and since 1990 has worked for the Rome-based *Panorama* magazine. He has published several books and essays that have focused on Italian intellectuals, the Jews, censorship, and the police, especially in the Fascist period. His most recent books are *L'elenco. Censura fascista, editoria e autori ebrei* (1998) [The List: Fascist Censorship, Publishing and Jewish Authors] and *Il contratto. Mussolini editore di Hitler* [The Contract: Mussolini, Hitler's Editor] (2004).

Roberto Finzi is professor of economic history at the University of Trieste. His research focuses on eighteenth-century economic thought, the history of agriculture and agronomy, the history of the climate, and the history of socialist movements and socialist thought. He is also interested in the Jewish problem under varied aspects and has published numerous essays, one of which was published in book form in English under the title *Antisemitism: From Its European Roots to the Holocaust* (1999). His book *L'università italiana e le leggi antiebraiche* (1997; 2nd ed., 2003) [The Italian University and the Anti-Jewish Laws] is the first comprehensive study of anti-Semitic persecution in the Italian universities. His works have been translated into French, English, Japanese, and Spanish.

Robert Katz is the author of twelve books and eight screenplays, including three adaptations from his own works: *Death in Rome, The Cassandra Crossing,* and *Days of Wrath.* A longtime resident of Italy, he has written extensively on Italian themes, particularly in the modern and contemporary periods, and maintains an Internet-based English-language reference work on Modern Italian history (www.theboot.it). He is the author of *Black Sabbath: A Journey Through a Crime against Humanity* (1969), a study of the roundup and deportation of the Jews of Rome. His latest book is *The Battle for Rome: The Germans, the Allies, the Partisans, and the Pope, September 1943–June 1944* (2003).

Fabio Levi is professor of contemporary history at the University of Turin. His first studies were devoted to the industrial development of modern Italy. Since the 1980s, Levi has focused on the history of Jews in Italy. He has published six books, including *L'ebreo in oggetto. L'applicazione della normativa antiebraica a Torino, 1938–1943* (1991) [The Implementation of Anti-Jewish Laws in Turin, 1938–1943], *L'identità imposta. Un padre ebreo di fronte alle leggi razziali di Mussolini*

(1996) [The Imposed Identity: A Jewish Father Faces Mussolini's Racial Laws], and *Le case e le cose. La persecuzione degli ebrei torinesi nelle carte dell'EGELI 1938–1945* (1998) [Real Estate and Objects: Persecution of the Jews of Turin in the Files of EGELI, 1938–1945], a study on confiscation of Jewish property during the Racial Laws.

Millicent Marcus is Mariano DiVito Professor of Italian Studies and director of the Center of Italian Studies at the University of Pennsylvania. Her specializations include Italian cinema and medieval literature. She is the author of *An Allegory of Form: Literary Self-Consciousness in the 'Decameron'* (1979), *Italian Film in the Light of Neorealism* (1986), *Filmmaking by the Book: Italian Cinema and Literary Adaptation* (1993), and *After Fellini: National Cinema in the Postmodern Age* (2002), as well as numerous articles on Italian literature and film. She is now conducting research on the recent surge of Italian films that deal with the subject of the Shoah and is working on a translation of the precursor text to Levi's *Survival at Auschwitz.*

Iael Nidam-Orvieto received her PhD in 2003 at the Hebrew University of Jerusalem, where she teaches Holocaust history at the Institute of Contemporary Jewry. She was a research Fellow at the Yad Vashem International Research Institute in Jerusalem in 2004, and, in 2005, will be a research Fellow at the University of Pisa and at the United States Holocaust Memorial Museum. Nidam-Orvieto has published numerous articles on Italian Jews during the Fascist period and on the rescue of children during the Holocaust as well as edited several Italian Jewish diaries and memoirs. She is preparing two books for publication: "The Villa Emma Children – a Story of Rescue During the Holocaust," and "Between Discrimination and Persecution: The Reaction of Italian Jewry to an Ever Increasing Crisis."

Liliana Picciotto was born in Egypt in 1947. She studied in Milan, where she received her PhD in political science at the State University. Since 1969 she has worked at the Center for Contemporary Jewish Documentation in Milan, where she is director of Historical Archives, and as a researcher in contemporary Jewish history, Fascism, the period of the German Occupation, and the Shoah in Italy. She also serves on the editorial board of *La Rassegna mensile di Israel*, the journal for Jewish studies of the Union of Italian Jewish Communities. She is the author of, among others, *L'occupazione tedesca e gli ebrei di Roma* (1979) [The German Occupation and the Jews of Rome]; *Il libro della memoria. Gli ebrei deportati dall'Italia 1943–1945* (1991; 3rd rev. ed., 2002) [The Book of Memory: The Jews Deported from Italy, 1943–1945], which was awarded the Acqui Storia prize and received special mention at the Premio Viareggio; *Gli ebrei a Milano. Persecuzione e deportazione 1943–1945* (1992) [The Jews of Milan: Persecution and Deportation], and editor of *Saggi sull'ebraismo italiano del Novecento in onore di Luisella Mortara Ottolenghi* (2003) [Essays on Twentieth-Century Italian Judaism in Honor of Luisella Mortara Ottolenghi] a special two-volume issue of *La Rassegna mensile di Israel.*

Michele Sarfatti is the author of several books and historical articles on Italian Fascist anti-Semitism. In 2002, Sarfatti became director of the Center for Contemporary Jewish Documentation in Milan. He is on the editorial board of *La Rassegna mensile di Israel* and was a member of the Government Commission of Inquiry into the Confiscation of Jewish Property in Italy, 1938–1945. His books include *Mussolini contro gli ebrei. Cronaca dell'elaborazione delle leggi del 1938* (1994) [Mussolini against the Jews: A Chronicle of the Elaboration of the 1938 Racial Laws], *Gli ebrei nell'Italia fascista. Vicende, identità, persecuzione* (2000) [The Jews in Fascist Italy: Identity and Persecution], and most recently, *Le leggi antiebraiche spiegate agli italiani di oggi* (2002) [The Anti-Jewish Laws as Explained to Italians Today].

Sandro Servi graduated from the University of Florence in the Department of Philosophy, where he completed a thesis on "Psychological Contributions to the Study of Antisemitism in Fascist Italy." Between the 1980s and 1995, he held annual seminars at the University of Florence on Judaism and anti-Semitism. Since 1995, Servi has been a Fellow of the Jerusalem Fellows Program (Mandel School of Jerusalem). In 1997, he founded *Rimmonim: Jewish Publishing and Communications*, dedicated to the dissemination of Jewish traditional texts and educational materials in the Italian language. He is recipient of two grants from the Memorial Foundation for Jewish Culture for his project to prepare an Italian edition of the *Sefer ha-Aggadah* by Bialyk and Rawnitski and is editor and co-translator of the first Italian edition of Adin Steinsaltz's introduction to Talmud, *Cos'è il Talmud* (2004). Servi is currently coordinator of educational projects for the Union of Italian Jewish Communities.

Alexander Stille is a distinguished author of three books. He graduated from Yale University in 1978 and received an MA from the Columbia School of Journalism in 1983. He was an assistant editor at Mondadori in Milan and, between 1990 and 1993, a freelance correspondent in Italy. He is the author of the prize-winning *Benevolence and Betrayal: Five Italian Jewish Families under Fascism* (1991), *Excellent Cadavers: The Mafia and the Death of the First Italian Republic* (1995), and, most recently, *The Future of the Past* (2002), a book about the ways in which technology both preserves and destroys the past.

Mario Toscano is associate professor of the history of political movements and parties at the University of Rome "La Sapienza." He has written widely on Italian Jewry. He is the author of, among others, *La Porta di Sion. L'Italia e* *l'immigrazione clandestina ebraica in Palestina, 1945–1948* (1990) [The Gateway of Zion: Italy and Illegal Jewish Immigration to Palestine, 1945–1948] and *Ebraismo e antisemitismo in Italia. Dal 1848 alla guerra dei sei giorni (2003)* [Judaism and Anti-Semitism in Italy from 1848 to the Six Day War] and the editor of *L'abrogazione delle leggi razziali in Italia (1943–1987). Reintegrazione dei diritti dei cittadini e ritorno ai valori del Risorgimento* (1994) [The Repeal of the Racial Laws in Italy, 1943–1987: Restoration of Law and Citizenship and the Return of the Values of the Risorgimento], *Stato nazionale ed emancipazione ebraica* (1992) [The National State and Jewish Emancipation], and *Integrazione e identità. L'esperienza ebraica in Germania e Italia dall'Illuminismo al Fascismo* (1988) [Integration and Identity: The Jewish Experience in Germany and Italy from the Enlightenment to Fascism]. Toscano serves on the editorial board of *Zakhor*, a journal devoted to Italian Jewish history, and he was appointed by the Italian president's council to serve on the Commission of Inquiry into the Confiscation of Jewish Property in Italy, 1938–1945.

Cinzia Villani was born in Bolzano, Italy. She received her degree from the University of Bologna, where she wrote a thesis on the history of the Jews in South Tyrol. Since 1988, Villani has been teaching at an Italian middle school in Bolzano. Her area of research includes racial persecution and the Final Solution in the provinces of Belluno, Bolzano, Trento, and Trieste as well as the history of the concentration camp of Bolzano. From September 1999 to January 2001, she worked for the Italian government's Commission of Inquiry into the Confiscation of Jewish Property in Italy, 1938–1945. She is the author of *Ebrei fra leggi razziste e deportazioni nelle province di Bolzano, Trento e Belluno* (1996) [Jews between the Racial Laws and Deportation from the Provinces of Bolzano, Trento and Belluno], which appeared in German as *Zwischen Rassengesetzen und Deportation. Juden in Südtirol, im Trentino und in der Provinz Belluno 1933–1945* (2003), and co-author of *Anche a volerlo raccontare è impossibile. Scritti e testimonianze sul lager di Bolzano (1999)* [It is Impossible Even If We Wanted to Tell it: Writings and Testimonies on the Concentration Camp of Bolzano].

Klaus Voigt is an independent scholar in Berlin. He received his PhD at the Free University in Berlin, where he wrote a thesis on Italian humanism. In the 1980s, Voigt headed a project on refugees in wartime Italy as a research Fellow at the University of Berlin. He has taught at the University of Nancy in France, Paris University, the University of Bologna, and the European University in Florence. He is the author of, among others, *Il rifugio precario. Gli esuli in Italia dal 1933 al 1945* [The Precarious Refuge: Exiles in Italy, 1933–1945] 2 vols. (1993–1996).

Joshua D. Zimmerman is an associate professor of history and the Eli and Diana Zborowski Professorial Chair in Interdisciplinary Holocaust Studies at Yeshiva

University in New York City. He is the author of *Poles, Jews and the Politics of Nationality: The Bund and the Polish Socialist Party in Late Tsarist Russia, 1892–1914* (2004), and editor of *Contested Memories: Poles and Jews during the Holocaust and Its Aftermath* (2003).

Susan Zuccotti received her PhD in modern European history from Columbia University. She is the author of *The Italians and the Holocaust: Persecution, Rescue and Survival* (1987); *The Holocaust, the French and the Jews* (1993); and, most recently, *Under His Very Windows: The Vatican and the Holocaust in Italy* (2000). Her first book won a National Jewish Book Award for Holocaust Studies in the United States and the Premio Acqui Storia – Primo Lavoro in Italy. Her most recent book received a National Jewish Book Award for Jewish-Christian Relations and the Sybil Halpern Milton Memorial Prize of the German Studies Association in 2002. Dr. Zuccotti taught the history of the Holocaust at Barnard College in New York and at Trinity College in Hartford, Connecticut.

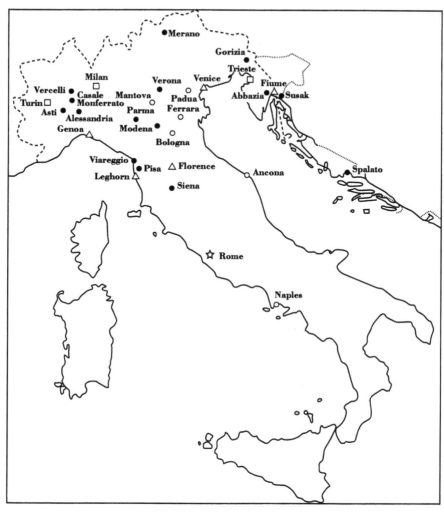

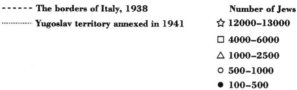

----- The borders of Italy, 1938
·············· Yugoslav territory annexed in 1941

Number of Jews
☆ 12000–13000
☐ 4000–6000
△ 1000–2500
○ 500–1000
● 100–500

MAP 1. The Jews of Italy, 1938.

- - - - - The borders of Italy, 1938

·············· Yugoslav territory annexed in 1941

▵ Internment camps between 1940 and 1943 with between 50 and 300 Jews.

□ Internment camps between 1940 and 1943 with at least 1600 Jews.

☆ Major destruction of synagogues between 1938 and 1943.

Regions in which labor and internment camps were planned but never built due to the collapse of Italy in July 1943.

MAP 2. Principal Centers of Anti-Jewish Persecution, 1938–1943.

Introduction

Joshua D. Zimmerman

> The Jews represent the only population which has never assimilated in Italy because it is made up of racial elements which are not European, differing absolutely from the elements that make up the Italians.
>
> *Manifesto of Racist Scientists*

> The [Gestapo] had our precise and up-to-date address, just as they had the address of every Jew, a gift from the "mild" Italian racial laws to the German allies.
>
> Aldo Zargani, *For Solo Violin: A Jewish Childhood in Fascist Italy*

Until recently, the subject of Italian Jewry under Fascist rule received little attention in English-language Holocaust historiography. A combination of factors, including the size of the community and the relatively small number of victims – about eight out of every ten Italian Jews survived the war – partly accounted for this neglect in the historical literature. With the third highest survival rate after Denmark and Bulgaria, a consensus emerged that Italian Fascist persecution of Jews was not only mild but that Mussolini, the Italian armed forces, Italian civilians, and many church officials consistently protected Jews throughout the war years. Many scholars do not dispute the fact that while Nazi Germany began its genocidal assault on European Jewry in June 1941, Fascist Italy, as long as it remained a sovereign state, became a haven of safety and security not only for Italian

I would like to thank Ruth Ben-Ghiat, Annalisa Capristo, Giorgio Fabre, Borden Painter, Michele Sarfatti, Sandro Servi, and Ellen Schrecker for their comments and suggestions on earlier drafts of the introduction.

1

Jews but for thousands of Jewish refugees fleeing Nazi persecution in both the peninsula as well as the Italian-occupied zones of France, Greece, and Croatia.[1]

Yet when the Germans occupied Italy in September 1943 and placed Mussolini at the head of a puppet Fascist state known as the Republic of Salò, tragedy struck Italian Jewry. In collaboration with Mussolini's republic, the Nazis implemented their Final Solution on Italian soil. Over the next twenty months, Italian and German authorities hunted down Jewish men, women, and children in German-occupied northern Italy, which led to the arrest of 8,529 Jews of whom an estimated 6,806 were deported to concentration and death camps.[2] Historians have not until recently drawn attention to the degree of Italian complicity in the implementation of Nazi Jewish policy on Italian soil. Rather, they highlighted the degree to which many officials of the Salò Republic, while outwardly and officially complying with Nazi demands, strove as much as possible to obstruct German roundup and deportation actions by warning Jewish communities in advance of impeding mass arrests. Thus, when comparing Italy with other European countries, historians of the Holocaust often characterized both the Italian government and the Italian people as shining examples of heroic resistance to Nazi barbarism.[3]

The decidedly positive evaluation of Italy during the Holocaust was articulated at a 1986 conference in Boston dedicated to Italian rescue efforts during the Holocaust. One historian maintained,

> the Holocaust is to a considerable extent a study in the potentialities of human evil and inhumanity. However, within all the horror, there were still sparks of good and hope.... Italy was one of these sparks which illuminated human good, compassion, and tolerance.... While the evil [of the Holocaust] cannot be forgotten, its darkness all the more serves to contrast with the light of the Italian response.[4]

An Italian-born Israeli historian earlier put forth the thesis that during the German occupation, "the Jews once more had an opportunity to experience the deep and courageous sympathy of the Italians, who did not hesitate to expose themselves to great peril to help the persecuted."[5] The U.S. Holocaust Memorial Museum's characterization is similarly representative: "Simple gestures of human decency were the hallmark of Italian rescue efforts even by Italian police officials who were forced to cooperate with the deportation."[6]

The favorable view of Italy rested, in part, on the tendency to use Nazi Germany as the only gauge against which Italy is measured, a method that has inevitably downplayed the gravity of Fascist Italy's own anti-Jewish persecution. By confining analysis to the period of the German occupation in 1943–5, which saw the deportation of Italian Jews to death camps, historians largely excluded from scrutiny a distinct phase in the persecution of Italian Jewry – the period of state-sponsored Italian anti-Semitism.

During the years 1938–43, prior to the loss of Italian sovereignty, Fascist Italy waged a debilitating campaign against its Jewish population. The passage of anti-Jewish laws, introduced primarily before the Second World War and without German interference, dealt a sharp blow to the Italian Jewish community. Soon after the *Manifesto of Racist Scientists* appeared, which attempted to prepare the public and provide a theoretical justification for the coming anti-Jewish campaign, a law of September 5, 1938, declared that Jews could no longer send their children to public or private Italian schools or be employed in any capacity in any Italian school from kindergarten to university;[7] a law of November 15, 1938, further decreed the immediate and permanent removal of all textbooks by Jewish authors from the Italian classroom.[8]

Two months later, the Council of Ministers passed a sweeping set of racial decrees. Signed by Mussolini, King Victor Emmanuel III, the minister of justice and others, the Royal Decree Law of November 17, 1938 – titled "Laws for the Defense of the Race" – decreed that intermarriages between "Aryans" and "non-Aryans" were henceforth illegal (Art. 1), a law that applied equally to Jews and blacks, or any other non-Aryan people, regardless of nationality, thus forming part of a larger racial policy in the wake of Italy's conquest of Ethiopia;[9] Jews could no longer perform military service in peace or wartime (Art. 10a); Jews were banned from being guardians of non-Jewish minors (Art. 10b); Jews were henceforth barred from any state employment and from owning or managing any business with more than one hundred employees or which received defense contracts (Art. 10c); Jews could no longer own land that had a taxable value of more than 5,000 lire or urban buildings worth more than 20,000 lire (Art. 10d, 10e); Jews were banned from employing domestic servants "of the Aryan race" (Art. 12); and Jews could lose legal parental control over children "who belong to a religion different from the Jewish religion, if it is demonstrated that they give them an education which does not correspond to their religious principles or to the national purpose" (Art. 11).[10] In addition, Italian citizenship granted to Jews after 1919 was henceforth revoked (Art. 23) and all foreign Jews – with the exception of those over sixty-five years of age or those married to Italian citizens – were ordered to leave the country within four months or be forcefully expelled (Art. 24 and 25).

Additional regulations to the "Laws for the Defense of the Race" sought the complete segregation of Jews from Italian society. On June 29, 1939, a new law banned Jews from the skilled professions, affecting some 1,599 Jewish doctors, lawyers, architects, journalists, dentists, and engineers.[11] Other additions included prohibitions on Jews frequenting popular vacation spots, on placing advertisements and death notices in newspapers, on owning a radio, on publishing books, on public lecturing, on having their names listed in telephone books, or on entering certain public buildings.[12]

On the eve of the racial laws in 1938, the Italian Jewish population of approximately 46,500[13] had been highly integrated into the general society, was overwhelmingly urban, and, on the whole, was solidly middle class. In the mid-1930s, 43.3 percent of Italian Jews worked in trade, 22.1 percent in industry, 11.6 percent in public administration, 8.8 percent in the liberal professions, 5.9 percent in credit and insurance, 3.6 percent in transportation and communications, and 1.5 percent in agriculture. In contrast, about half of the general population in 1936 was employed in agriculture, 8.2 percent in trade, 29.3 percent in industry, 0.6 percent in the liberal professions, 0.6 percent in credit and insurance, and 3.8 percent in transport and communications.[14] Despite the Italian Jews' overwhelmingly urban and middle-class character, there were significant regional, social, and religious variations. Most significant in this regard was the Jewish community of Rome, Italy's largest center with a Jewish population of 12,494 in 1938.[15] A significant portion of Roman Jews inhabited the old quarter of the former Jewish ghetto, were largely poor and working class, and had retained a high level of religious observance and social isolation. The contrast between the Roman Jews and other major Jewish centers can be illustrated by the divergent rates of intermarriage. Although the percentage of Jews marrying outside the faith in interwar Italy was 43.7 percent[16] as a whole and even higher in such large cities as Trieste (59 percent) and Milan (56 percent), only 8 percent of Roman Jews intermarried during the same period.[17] The Italian racial campaign, which effectively revoked the emancipation of Italian Jewry achieved during 1848–70, thus constituted a profound rupture in the modern history of Italy, interrupting a century-long pattern of growing social integration.

The immediate effect of the racial laws was the abrupt disruption of jobs and education. Within weeks of the racial laws, many Jews were fired from their jobs, including over 100 Jewish elementary school principals and teachers, 279 Jewish high school principals and teachers, 96 tenured professors, 133 university adjuncts, and several dozen part-time faculty.[18] At the same time, 1,500 university students (both Italian and foreign), 4,000 junior and high school students and 2,500 elementary school pupils were affected.[19] But the impact of three Jewish responses to the racial laws – conversion, withdrawal from the Jewish community, and emigration – permanently altered the character of the community. In an effort to circumvent the anti-Semitic decrees, it is estimated that between 4,528 and 5,429 Italian Jews formally left the Jewish community in the years 1938–41, either through conversion or officially removing their names from the registry books of the Union of Italian Israelite Communities, a number that reached close to 6,000 by the period 1943–5.[20] In addition, the permanent emigration of some 5,966 Italian Jews in the years 1938–41 depleted Italy of some of its most brilliant minds.[21] Thus, prior to the German occupation of northern Italy in 1943, Italy's anti-Jewish campaign had reduced the Italian Jewish population by a staggering one-fourth by conversion and emigration alone.

The first historian to draw attention to the severity of Italian race laws was the internationally renowned Italian scholar Renzo De Felice (1929–96).[22] De Felice's pioneering 1961 study, *The Jews in Fascist Italy: A History*,[23] was based on exhaustive research conducted in previously inaccessible Italian government archives of the Fascist period as well as of previously untapped Italian Jewish archives.[24] In this comprehensive account, a full and complex picture emerges of Italian Jewry under Fascism. Regarding the period 1943–5 – under the German occupation and Mussolini's puppet Fascist regime – De Felice argued that attempts to shift all responsibility for the murder of thousands of Italian Jews on the Germans alone was a distortion of the historical record and had to be revised. He documented not only the degree of Fascist complicity with Nazi Germany but also the widespread confiscation of Jewish property by Italian authorities during the German occupation.[25]

The vast majority of De Felice's study, however, was devoted to two distinct periods prior to the German occupation: Italian Jews under Fascism to 1938 and the dramatic deterioration of the Jewish position after the racial laws in 1938–43. Here, De Felice examined the nature and scope of Fascist racial policies and the motivations surrounding their introduction. He concluded that, while Mussolini and Italian Fascism bear much responsibility for the introduction of anti-Jewish laws in 1938, the ideological roots of racial anti-Semitism were foreign.[26] According to this line of interpretation, although Nazi anti-Semitism was the consequence of Hitler's profound ideological conviction, Mussolini was a cynical opportunist who used the race card solely to further a political agenda: to reenergize Fascism, to strengthen the alliance with Nazi Germany, and to regulate the interactions between Italians and natives in the African colonies. Based on the premise that Mussolini himself "did not personally harbor . . . any real prejudice against the Jews,"[27] De Felice argued that the transformation of Fascist Italy into a racial state derived primarily (but not exclusively) from the growing importance of the Axis alliance. The decision to introduce state-sponsored anti-Semitism, De Felice wrote, "stemmed from the belief that, in order to give credibility to the Axis, it was necessary to eliminate the most glaring difference in the policies of the two regimes."[28] De Felice also pointed to a complex of secondary causal factors in the period 1935–7, thus cautioning against reducing the shift in Italian Fascist racial policy to a single factor.[29] At least two factors were entirely domestic, including the anti-Fascist position of some Jewish individuals and Jewish organizations during the wars in Ethiopia and Spain, which led Mussolini to conclude that Jews were part of an international anti-Fascist campaign,[30] and the strongly anti-Semitic leanings of Mussolini's entourage. Due to Mussolini's own supposed lack of ideological conviction as well as his desire to distinguish Fascism from Nazism, De Felice argued that Mussolini consciously adopted a "non-biological approach" to the Jewish question in drafting racial laws.[31]

In contrast to the Italian government's adoption of institutionalized anti-Semitism, De Felice adamantly upheld the view that the Italian people as a whole rejected both the anti-Jewish campaign and the ideas behind it. Positing an almost absolute cleavage between the Fascist government and the Italian people, racial anti-Semitism was "alien to the Italian mentality and sensibility."[32] From the premise that biological anti-Semitism was a foreign import that found only a handful of genuine adherents in Italy, De Felice came to the conclusion that the Italian people and, for the most part, the Catholic Church rejected anti-Semitism and did their best to circumvent the laws. "It was clear," De Felice wrote, "that the initial measures and their underlying idea had been rejected by the overwhelming majority of Italians with such unanimity as to be, for once, truly 'totalitarian.'"[33] Nor, he held, did the period of institutionalized anti-Semitism in Italy make any impact on the collective psyche of the Italian people: "There is no doubt that, even in 1939–1943, the great majority of Italians remained . . . opposed to racism and anti-Semitism."[34] De Felice's book, which for many years was the only scholarly monograph on the topic, was curiously not translated into any foreign language until the English edition appeared in 2001. Thus the most comprehensive scholarly work on the topic was virtually unknown outside of Italy while its dissemination in the country remained confined to an elite group of intellectuals.

Nearly two decades after De Felice's book, the first full-length scholarly work on Italian Jewry under Fascism in English appeared.[35] Utilizing archives in

Germany, Israel, Italy, and Great Britain, Meir Michaelis examined the impact of German–Italian relations on the development of Fascist racial policy. Drawing heavily on files from the German foreign ministry archives, he demonstrated that Nazi Germany did not directly interfere in Italy's domestic Jewish affairs until the fall of Fascism in 1943. In contrast to De Felice, who argued that the transition to institutionalized anti-Semitism in Italy was the outcome of several interdependent factors of varying degrees of importance, Michaelis argued for the absolute primacy of the Axis alliance. Despite the absence of direct pressure from Nazi Germany, the passage of racial laws in 1938 was, according to Michaelis, "*solely* due to [Mussolini's] itch to emulate Hitler and his exaggerated sense of ideological solidarity with the Reich"[36] (emphasis mine). While acknowledging other forces in the years 1935–7 that generated a change in Mussolini's views (the conquest of Ethopia, the Spanish Civil War, Italian Jewish involvement in the anti-Fascist movement, and so on) these "minor" factors[37] nonetheless could not account for the Duce's "sudden conversion" to Nazi racial ideas, which he had earlier opposed.[38] "Mussolini," Michaelis maintained, "had all sorts of grievances against the Jews but only one reason for persecuting [Jews] as a 'race' – his ill-fated alliance with a Jew-baiter."[39] Despite their disagreements over the relative significance of factors behind Mussolini's change of policies, Michaelis and De Felice formed a consensus about the absence of a "Jewish question" in Italy during the years 1922–36.[40]

The coming of the fiftieth anniversary of the Fascist racial laws, commemorated in 1988, sparked a revival of interest in Italian Jewish history in general and in the history of Jews under Fascism in particular. A new postwar generation of scholars in Italy and abroad began to reevaluate the existing sources, uncover new ones, and raise new questions. The result of the revived scholarly activity was the appearance, beginning in the late 1980s, of sophisticated monographs on interwar and wartime Italian Jewry that have provided a new interpretative framework. These include a range of new studies on the impact of the racial laws, as well as on the circumstances surrounding the implementation of the Nazi Final Solution on Italian soil between 1943 and 1945.[41]

Several core works that have been fundamental in establishing the new interpretative framework for the study of Italian Jewry under Fascism have never appeared in English. First, in two major monographs, Michele Sarfatti revised the prevailing consensus by putting forth two theses: (1) that Mussolini supported the biological-racial type of anti-Semitism and (2) that anti-Jewish policies in Fascist Italy began earlier than had previously been accepted in the historical literature.[42] Second, Liliana Picciotto, in her now classic study, established that the effects of the deportations from Italy in 1943–5 on the Jewish community were similar, in percentage terms, as the rest of Western Europe.[43] And in his two-volume scholarly study, the German historian Klaus Voigt argued, for the first time, that the Italian regime's attitude toward Jewish refugees in 1933–45 was considerably less friendly than previous studies had claimed.[44]

Meanwhile, the heightened interest in Italian Jewry spread to American historians and writers. Particularly important in this regard was the appearance of Susan Zuccotti's *The Italians and the Holocaust: Persecution, Rescue, Survival*[45] and Alexander Stille's *Benevolence and Betrayal: Five Italian Jewish Families under Fascism.*[46] Taken together, these two American studies exposed the English reading public to a much more complex and ambivalent picture of Italian Jewry under Fascism. In *The Italians and the Holocaust*, based largely on published sources and documents from the Center for Contemporary Jewish Documentation in Milan, Zuccotti argued that the focus in the existing literature on tales of heroism and rescue in wartime Italy had distracted attention away from negative aspects of Italian–Jewish relations and had led to facile generalizations about the Italian national character. Although most Italians rejected Fascist racism and opposed German policies, there were a good many others who followed Mussolini and Hitler to the end, she maintained. An equally important aspect of Italian Jewry under Mussolini, Zuccotti argued, was the Fascist government's betrayal of its Jewish citizens before and during the German occupation. In her chapter titled, "The Italian Phase," Zuccotti documents the period when Italian Fascist guards, on their own and without assistance from the German occupying forces, arrested and interned thousands of Jews between November 1943 and February 1944 on orders from Mussolini.

Stille, in his extraordinary study of five Italian Jewish families under Fascist and Nazi rule, drew attention to the devastating material and psychological effects of the 1938 racial laws on Italian Jewry. Yet Stille, taking De Felice's lead, maintained that the application of the Italian racial laws, between 1938 and 1943, revealed "a fundamental lack of conviction" on the part of the Italian government.[47] Challenging the assumption that the Italian people overwhelmingly opposed anti-Jewish persecution, Stille revealed that acts of denunciation by fellow Italians during the German occupation led to deadly consequences for some members of each Italian Jewish family that he profiled. While revising some of the old views, these two works share many assumptions with previous studies about the uniqueness of the Italian Jewish experience, the degree of toleration in Italian society, and the willingness of Italians to engage in rescue efforts.[48]

✻

The present volume revolves around seven areas of inquiry that have given rise to controversy in the historical literature: (1) the native versus foreign roots of Italian Fascist anti-Semitism; (2) the extent and appearance of Fascist anti-Jewish policies prior to the racial laws; (3) Mussolini's attitude to the Jewish question as well as his personal role as ally and puppet of Hitler; (4) the character and aim of the Italian racial laws; (5) the attitude of the Italian masses to anti-Jewish persecution; (6) the Italian role in the roundup, deportation, and murder of Italian Jews to Nazi death camps in 1943–5; (7) and the attitude of the Catholic Church in Italy with special reference to Pope Pius XII.

Taken together, this collection of essays challenges the myth of Italian benevolence during the Fascist period. The chapters are divided chronologically and consist of both theoretical overviews and case studies. Alexander Stille and Mario Toscano examine the distinct features of Italian Jewry during the critical passage from nineteenth-century Liberal to early twentieth-century Fascist rule. Michele Sarfatti and Fabio Levi provide overviews of the character, aims, and impact of the Italian Fascist racial laws in 1938–43; Liliana Picciotto presents an overview of the fate of Italian Jews under the German occupation; and Frank Coppa analyzes the attitudes of Pope Pius XI and Pope Pius XII to Nazi and Fascist anti-Jewish persecution.

The majority of essays consist of case studies on the rise of racial persecution, its impact on Italian Jewry, and Italian Jewish responses. These include Giorgio Fabre's analysis of Mussolini's attitude to Jews and the Jewish question, Annalisa Capristo's study of the Italian academies' exclusion of Jews both before and after the racial laws, Sandro Servi's analysis of the image of the Jew in the Fascist anti-Semitic magazine, *La Difesa della Razza*, and Roberto Finzi's study of the reaction of the Italian universities to the racial laws both during and after the war.

With regard to Jewish reactions, Iael Orvieto examines the everyday life of Italian Jewry in 1938–43 through the lens of more than 1,000 Jewish letters to Mussolini and the royal monarch pleading for exemptions from the racial laws. Karl Voigt examines the individual and organizational response of Italian Jews to the plight of Jewish refugee in Fascist Italy before and after the German occupation. On the period of the German occupation, Robert Katz reexamines the October 1943 deportation of Roman Jewry in the light of newly declassified documents and Cinzia Villani offers new research on the fate of Italian Jewry in two northern occupation zones. With regard to the politically and emotionally charged issue of Pope Pius XII, Susan Zuccotti offers a dispassionate analysis of the latest literature. She concludes, from an examination of all the extant evidence, that Pius never issued a papal directive encouraging the rescue of Jews in Italy and other parts of Nazi-occupied Europe. Finally, Anna Bravo, Millicent Marcus, and Ruth Ben-Ghiat examine the problematic nature of modern Italian memory of fascist anti-Semitism through case studies of Italian film and public reaction to a recently published Italian rescuer's wartime diary.

Jews in Italy under Fascist and Nazi Rule, 1922–1945 provides a much-needed reconsideration of many assumptions in the English-language historical literature about the Jewish experience in Fascist Italy. It is my hope that this collection will bring to light a more balanced and historically accurate picture, reframe old debates, and set a new research agenda.

NOTES

1. On the treatment of Jews in Italian-occupied zones during the war, see Jonathan Steinberg's definitive work, *All or Nothing: The Axis and the Holocaust, 1941–1943*, 2nd ed. (London and New York: Routledge, 2002). See also Michele Sarfatti, "Fascist Italy and German Jews in South-Eastern France in July 1943," *Journal of Modern Italian Studies* 3, no. 3 (1998), 318–28; Michele Sarfatti, *Gli ebrei nell'Italia fascista. Vicende, identità, persecuzione* (Turin: Einaudi, 2000), 203–7; and Susan Zuccotti, *Under His Very Windows: the Vatican and the Holocaust in Italy* (New Haven: Yale University Press, 2000), chs. 8–9. For a critical examination of Steinberg's work, see Davide Rodogno, *Il nuovo ordine mediterraneo. Le politiche di occupazione dell'Italia fascista in Europa, 1940–1943* (Turin: Bollati Boringhieri, 2003), particularly pp. 432–84.

2. Liliana Picciotto, *Il libro della memoria. Gli ebrei deportati dall'Italia 1943–1945*, 3rd ed. (Milan: Mursia, 2002), 27. Of the 6,806 deportees, 6,007 were sent to Auschwitz. Only 363 returned (ibid., 31). In addition to Jews on the peninsula, 1,819 Greek Jews were deported from the island of Rhodes then under Italian control (ibid., 34).

3. See, for example, Michael Berenbaum, *The World Must Know: The History of the Holocaust as Told in the United States Holocaust Memorial Museum* (Boston: Little, Brown and Company, 1993), 166–9; Leni Yahil, *The Holocaust: The Fate of European Jewry*, transl. Ina Friedman and Haya Galai (New York and Oxford: Oxford University Press, 1990), 422–8; Michael R. Marrus, *The Holocaust in History* (New York: New American Library, 1987), 74–5; Yehuda Bauer, *A History of the Holocaust* (New York: Franklin Watts, 1982), 305; George L. Mosse, *Toward the Final Solution: A History of European Racism* (New York: Howard Fertig, 1978), 200; Nora Levin, *The Holocaust: The Destruction of European Jewry, 1933–1945* (New York: Schocken Books, 1973), 459–68; and

Raul Hilberg, *The Destruction of the European Jews* (Chicago: Quadrangle Books, 1961), 414–16.

4. Paul Bookbinder, "Italy in the Overall Context of the Holocaust," in *The Italian Refuge: Rescue of Jews during the Holocaust*, ed. Ivo Herzer (Washington, DC: Catholic University of America Press, 1989), 108.

5. Daniel Carpi, "The Origins and Development of Fascist Anti-Semitism in Italy (1922–1945)," in *The Catastrophe of European Jewry*, ed. Yisrael Gutman et al. (New York: Ktav, 1976), 297–8.

6. Berenbaum, *The World Must Know*, 169.

7. See Royal Decree Law, no. 1390 (September 5, 1938), "Provvedimenti per la difesa della razza nella scuola fascista," art. 1–3, reprinted in Michele Sarfatti, ed., *1938. Le leggi contro gli ebrei*, a special issue of *La Rassegna mensile di Israel* LIV, no. 1–2 (June–August 1988): 68–9. As Sarfatti demonstrates, the Royal Decree Law no. 1779 of November 15, 1938 [see *La Rassegna mensile di Israel* LIV, no. 1–2 (June–August 1938): 77–9], modified the September school law, stipulating that baptized children "of the Jewish race" would be allowed to enroll in private Italian primary and middle schools. See Sarfatti, *Gli ebrei nell'Italia fascista*, 195.

8. Royal Decree Law no. 1779 (November 15, 1938), "Integrazione e coordinamento in unico testo delle norme già emanate per la difesa della razza nella scuola italiana," Art. 4, cited in Giorgio Fabre, *L'elenco. Censura fascista, editoria e autori ebrei* (Turin: Silvio Zamorani, 1998), 126–7. For the original document, see *La Rassegna mensile di Israel* LIV, no. 1–2 (June–August 1938): 77.

9. A Jew was defined as a person born to two parents "of the Jewish race" regardless of religion or one who was half Jewish but was a member of the Jewish religious community on or before October 1, 1938. The racial definition of the Jew also included (a) a person who had one Jewish parent and one parent of foreign nationality, (b) a person with a Jewish mother and an unknown father, and (c) a person with one Jewish parent who possessed "indications of Jewishness" (*manifestazioni di ebraismo*). For the original document, see Art. 8 of the Royal Decree Law of November 17, 1938, reprinted in *La Rassegna mensile di Israel* LIV, no. 1–2 (June–August 1938), 72. For an English translation, see Renzo De Felice, *The Jews in Fascist Italy: A History* 1st English ed., transl. Robert L. Miller (1961; New York: Enigma Books, 2001), 701.

10. "Royal Legal Decree of November 17, 1938, no. 1728," reprinted in De Felice, *The Jews in Fascist Italy*, 702. For the full text of the law, see ibid., 700–705. The original is reprinted in *La Rassegna mensile di Israel*, no. 1–2 (June–August 1938): 72–6.

11. Sarfatti, *Gli ebrei nell'Italia fascista*, 47. For the original document, see *La Rassegna mensile di Israel* LIV, no. 1–2 (June–August 1938), 118.

12. De Felice, *The Jews in Fascist Italy*, 336.

13. Sarfatti, *Gli ebrei nell'Italia fascista*, 29.

14. Ibid., 46.

15. Sergio Della Pergola, "Precursori, convergenti, emarginati. Trasformazioni demografiche degli ebrei in Italia, 1870–1945," in *Italia Judaica. Gli ebrei nell'Italia unita 1870–1945* (Rome: Ministero per i beni culturali e ambientali, Ufficio centrale per i beni archivistici, 1993), 71.

16. De Felice, *The Jews in Fascist Italy*, 11.

17. Della Pergola, "Precursori, convergenti, emarginati," 64.

18. Sarfatti, *Gli ebrei nell'Italia fascista*, 195–6.

19. Ibid., 196, footnote 303; Susan Zuccotti, *The Italians and the Holocaust: Persecution, Rescue, Survival* (New York: Basic Books, 1987), 41–2.

20. See Della Pergola, "Precursori, convergenti, emarginati," 66; Filomena Del Regno, "Gli ebrei a Roma tra le due guerre mondiali: fonti e problemi di ricerca," *Storia contemporanea* 23, no. 1 (February 1992), 64–5; Dante Lattes, "Coloro che son partiti," *La Rassegna mensile di Israel* (August–September 1960): 347–50; and Sarfatti, *Gli ebrei nell'Italia fascista*, 209.

21. De Felice, *The Jews in Fascist Italy*, 355. In her autobiographical work, Natalia Ginzburg [*Family Sayings* (New York: Seaver Books, 1986), 117] recalled that "when the racial campaign started the Lopezes left for Argentina. All the Jews we knew were leaving Italy or preparing to go." Jewish émigrés from Italy during this time included the economist Franco Modigliani (1918–2003), later professor of economics at the Massachusetts Institute of Technology and recipient of the Nobel Prize for Economics in 1985; the physicist Emilio Segrè (1905–89), who was later a group leader in the Los Alamos Laboratory of the Manhattan Project, taught at University of California Berkeley and received the Nobel Prize in Physics in 1959; and the physicist Bruno Rossi (1905–93), who later helped develop the atom bomb at the Los Alamos Laboratory in New Mexico in 1943–6 and was subsequently professor of physics at the Massachusetts Institute of Technology.

22. The following discussion is a brief overview of the historiography of anti-Jewish persecution in Fascist Italy. I have therefore excluded from analysis several areas of inquiry, including the relations between Fascist Italy and Zionism as well as relations between the Fascist regime and the Italian Jewish communal leadership. On the legal status of the Jewish communities in Italy, see Guido Fubini, *La condizione giuridica dell'ebraismo italiano*, 2nd rev. ed. (Turin: Rosenberg & Sellier, 1998).

23. Renzo De Felice, *Storia degli ebrei italiani sotto il fascismo* (Turin: Einaudi, 1961). The first English edition (New York: Enigma Books, 2001) is a translation of the definitive fifth revised edition (Turin: Einaudi, 1988).

24. There has recently been a revival of interest in De Felice's classic work within the Italian scholarly community. See Michele Sarfatti, "Renzo De Felice e la storia della persecuzione antiebraica," in *Quale Storia* (forthcoming); Mario Toscano, "Fascismo, razzismo, antisemitismo: osservazioni per un bilancio storiografico," in Mario Toscano, *Ebraismo e antisemitismo in Italia: dal 1848 alla guerra dei sei giorni* (Milan: F. Angeli, 2003), 208–43; Emilio Gentile, *Renzo De Felice: lo storico e il personaggio* (Rome-Bari: Laterza, 2003); Pasquale Chessa, "Renzo De Felice e il volume sugli ebrei italiani sotto il fascismo," in *Nuova storia contemporanea*, 6, no. 2 (March–April 2002), 113–32; Paolo Simoncelli, *Renzo De Felice: la formazione intellettuale* (Florence: Le Lettere, 2001); Angelo Ventura, "Renzo De Felice: il fascismo e gli ebrei," in *Incontro di studio sull'opera di Renzo De Felice* (Rome: Giunta centrale per gli studi storici, 2000), 41–67; and Sergio Minerbi, "L'antisemitismo fascista negli scritti di De Felice e di altri storici, in Renzo De Felice: la storia come ricerca," *Annali della Fondazione Ugo Spirito* 10 (1998), 69–78.

I am grateful to Giorgio Fabre and Annalisa Capristo for bringing the latter sources to my attention.

25. See De Felice, *The Jews in Fascist Italy*, 445, where he concludes that "soldiers and functionaries of [Mussolini's republic] collaborated on a huge scale in the hunting down and, therefore, in the extermination of thousands of Jews." For the most updated reports on the confiscation of Jewish property, see Presidenza del Consiglio dei Ministri. Commissione per la ricostruzione delle vicende che hanno caratterizzato in Italia le attività di acquisizione dei beni dei cittadini ebrei da parte degli organismi pubblici e privati. *Rapporto generale* (Rome: Dipartimento per l'informazione e l'editoria, 2001), 535–6.

26. De Felice, *The Jews in Fascist Italy*, 21–2.

27. Ibid., 59.

28. Ibid., 231.

29. See Ibid., ch. 20.

30. In his 1938 "Declaration on Race," Mussolini wrote, "All anti-Fascist efforts can be traced back to a Jew; worldwide Judaism is, in Spain, on the opposite side." (Reprinted in De Felice, *The Jews in Fascist Italy*, 691.)

31. Ibid., 240. For an authoritative discussion on the character of the Italian race laws, see Sarfatti's chapter in this volume.

32. De Felice, *The Jews in Fascist Italy*, 25.

33. Ibid., 332.

34. Ibid., 372.

35. Meir Michaelis, *Mussolini and the Jews: German-Italian Relations and the Jewish Question in Italy, 1922–1945* (New York and Oxford: Clarendon Press, 1978). It should be noted, however, that Michaelis's book was the result of many years of research, some of which appeared in articles prior to the book. See, among others, Michaelis, "On the Jewish Question in Fascist Italy: The Attitude of the Fascist Regime to the Jews in Italy," *Yad Vashem Studies* 4 (1960), 7–41; and Michaelis, "The 'Duce' and the Jews: An Assessment of the Literature on Italian Jewry under Fascism (1922–1945)," *Yad Vashem Studies* 11 (1976), 7–32.

36. Ibid., 158.

37. For example, De Felice maintained that the influence of Mussolini's entourage on the transition to racialism was "considerable" (De Felice, *The Jews in Fascist Italy*, 227). Michaelis countered that Mussolini "was the head of the pro-German faction in the Fascist Party and the moving spirit behind the racial campaign" (Michaelis, *Mussolini and the Jews*, 187). As he would later write, De Felice had "exaggerated the importance of pressure from the pro-German extremists in Mussolini's entourage.... There was not a single Italian racialist or antisemite whom he did not encourage during the period under consideration" [cited in Meir Michaelis, "The Current Debate over Fascist Racial Policy," in *Fascist Antisemitism and the Italian Jews*, ed. Robert S. Wistrich and Sergio Della Pergola (Jerusalem: The Hebrew University, 1995), 82].

38. We should mention here that Mussolini's repeatedly contradictory and inconsistent statements have made it difficult to draw definitive conclusions about his views on Jews, the Jewish question, and Zionism. It is true that on several occasions Mussolini rejected

Nazi racial ideas: "Race!" Mussolini said in a 1932 interview, "It is a feeling, not a reality.... Nothing will ever make me believe that biologically pure races can be shown to exist today.... Antisemitism does not exist in Italy. Italians of Jewish birth have shown themselves good citizens, and they fought bravely in the war" (cited in Michaelis, "The Current Debate over Fascist Racial Policy," 52). Yet, as Giorgio Fabre demonstrates in his contribution to this volume, Mussolini's early writings were "interspersed with frequent antisemitic utterances" in articles in which he repeatedly referred to Jews "as a different race." While taking into account that the definition of race in pre-1938 Italy was closer to the idea of a "people" or "nation" rather than a fixed biological entity, the dichotomy Mussolini made between "Jews" and "Italians" in writings from the 1920s raises questions about the thesis of an abrupt and sudden conversion to the Jewish racial idea in the late 1930s.

39. Michaelis, *Mussolini and the Jews*, 125; Michaelis continues this line of interpretation in his most recent article. See Michaelis, "L'influenza di Hitler sulla svolta razzista adottata da Mussolini," *La Rassegna mensile di Israel* LXIX, no. 1 (January–April 2003): 257–66.

40. See Michaelis, *Mussolini and the Jews*, 3–9; Michaelis, "The Current Debate over Fascist Racial Policy," 439; and De Felice, *The Jews in Fascist Italy*, 21–2.

41. Among the most critical studies on Italian Jewry during the period of racial persecution, see the chapters by M. Sarfatti, F. Levi, T. Catalan, and S. Mazzamuto in the second volume of the exhaustive *Gli ebrei in Italia. Storia d'Italia*, ed. C. Vivanti (Turin: Einaudi, 1997), the first scholarly general history of Italian Jewry to appear since Attilio Milano's *Storia degli ebrei in Italia* (1963). For the most important regional study on the period of the racial laws, see Enzo Collotti, ed., *Razza e fascismo. La persecuzione contro gli ebrei in Toscana, 1938–1943*, 2 vols. (Rome: Carocci; Florence: Regione Toscana, Giunta regionale, 1999). On the contentious issue of the response of the Catholic Church to the racial laws, see Giovanni Miccoli, "Santa Sede e Chiesa italiana difronte alle leggi antiebraiche del 1938," in *La legislazione antiebraica in Italia e in Europa* (Rome: Camera dei Deputati, 1989), 163–274; Miccoli, "Santa Sede, questione ebraica e antisemitismo fra Otto e Novecento," in *Gli ebrei in Italia. Storia d'Italia*, 2: 1449–1574; Miccoli, *I dilemmi e i silenzi di Pio XII* (Milan: Rizzoli, 2000); Catherine Brice and Giovanni Miccoli, eds., *Les racines chrétiennes de l'antisémitisme politique (fin XIXᵉ–XXᵉ siècle)* (Rome: École française de Rome, 2003); Zuccotti, *Under His Very Windows*; and David Kertzer, *The Popes Against the Jews* (New York: Alfred A. Knopf, 2001). Recent monographs by contributors to this volume devoted to the period of persecution include Mario Toscano, *Ebraismo e antisemitismo in Italia. Dal 1948 alla guerra dei sei giorni* (Milan: Franco Angeli, 2003); Annalisa Capristo, *L'espulsione degli ebrei dalle accademie italiane* (Turin: Silvio Zamorani, 2002); Michele Sarfatti, *Le leggi antiebraiche spiegate agli italiani di oggi* (Turin: Einaudi, 2002); Sarfatti, *Gli ebrei nell'Italia fascista*; Fabre, *L'elenco. Censura fascista, editoria e autori ebrei*; Roberto Finzi, *L'università italiana e le leggi antiebraiche*, 2nd ed. (Rome: Editori Riuniti, 2003); Fabio Levi, ed., *Le case e le cose. La persecuzione degli ebrei torinesi nelle carte dell'EGELI, 1938–1945* (Turin: Compagnia San Paolo, 1998); Levi, *L'identità imposta. Un padre ebreo di fronte alle leggi razziali di Mussolini* (Turin: Silvio Zamorani editore, 1996); Cinzia Villani, *Ebrei fra leggi razziste e*

deportazioni nelle province di Bolzano, Trento e Belluno (Trento: Società di studi trentini di scienze storiche, 1996); Klaus Voigt, *Il rifugio precario. Gli esuli in Italia dal 1933 al 1945*, 2 vols. (Florence: La Nuova Italia, 1993–6); and Michele Sarfatti, *Mussolini contro gli ebrei. Cronaca dell'elaborazione delle leggi del 1938* (Turin: Zamorani, 1994); and [Fabio Levi, ed., *L'ebreo in oggetto: l'applicazione della normativa antiebraica a Torino, 1938–1943* (Turin: Silvio Zamorani, 1991). On Italian Jewry in 1943–5, see Picciotto, *Il libro della memoria*, and Robert Katz, *The Battle for Rome: The Germans, the Allies, the Partisans, and the Pope, September 1943–June 1944* (New York: Simon and Schuster, 2003). In addition, see the several new studies that have recently appeared in the special issue of *La Rassegna mensile di Israel* LXIX, no. 1 (January–April 2003), edited by L. Picciotto. For a recent comprehensive summary of the historiography, see Stefano Luconi, "Recent Trends in the Study of Italian Antisemitism under the Fascist Regime," *Patterns of Prejudice* 38, no. 1 (March 2004), 1–17.

42. Michele Sarfatti, *Mussolini contro gli ebrei. Cronaca dell'elaborazione delle leggi del 1938* (Turin: Zamorani, 1994); and Sarfatti, *Gli ebrei nell'Italia fascista. Vicende, identità, persecuzione* (Turin: Einaudi, 2000).

43. Liliana Picciotto, *Il libro della memoria. Gli ebrei deportati dall'Italia 1943–1945*, 3rd ed. (Milan: Mursia, 2002).

44. Klaus Voigt, *Zuflucht auf Widerruf. Exil in Italien 1933–1945*, 2 vols. (Stuffgart: Klett-Cotta, 1989–93). Italian translation: *Il rifugio precario. Gli esuli in Italia dal 1933 al 1945*, 2 vols. (Florence: La Nuova Italia, 1993–6).

45. (New York: Basic Books, 1987; reprint, Lincoln: University of Nebraska Press, 1996).

46. (New York: Summit Books, 1991; reprint, New York: Picador, 2003). Both books appeared in Italian translation shortly after their publication in English.

47. Stille, *Benevolence and Betrayal*, 75.

48. It should also be noted that several literary works available in English have significantly contributed to our understanding of the Italian Jewish experience under Fascism. These include, among others, Primo Levi's *Survival in Auschwitz* (New York: Collier Books, 1986), *The Reawakening* (New York: Collier Books, 1986), and *The Drowned and the Saved* (New York: Summit Books, 1988), which have educated a generation of English readers through extraordinarily lucid, evocative, and moving stories of an Italian Jewish Holocaust survivor; Giorgio Bassani's *The Garden of the Finzi-Continis* (New York, 1965) and the celebrated 1970 film that followed, which provided a moving portrayal of an Italian Jewish family during the period of Fascist and Nazi anti-Jewish persecution; and Natalia Ginzburg's *Family Sayings* (New York, 1988), an extraordinary memoir detailing the experience of one Italian Jewish family under Fascism.

PART ONE

ITALIAN JEWRY

FROM LIBERALISM

TO FASCISM

1 The Double Bind of Italian Jews: Acceptance and Assimilation

Alexander Stille

The study of Italian Jews has significantly progressed since the mid-1980s when the subject began to attract more serious attention. In the United States, interest in the Italian Jews received an important stimulus by the publication in the mid-1980s of the works of Primo Levi, starting with the *Periodic Table* (1984) and *If Not Now, When?* (1985). At the time, the initial response was enthusiastic but somewhat naïve, typified by the remark made by one of the characters in Levi's novel *If Not Now, When?* who, on meeting Italian Jews for the first time, expresses surprise and disbelief, "Italian Jews? How can that be?" he said, thinking that all Italians were Catholic. At early conferences dedicated to the Italian Jews, one often heard remarks like that and the fact that they continued to get a laugh was an indication of the paucity of general knowledge as well as historical work done on the subject.

At the time, there were a few good books on the Italian Jews, but many of them were already quite dated. On the subject of the Jews during Fascism, there were the works of Renzo De Felice and Meir Michaelis, which were mostly concerned with documenting the relations between Mussolini's Fascist regime and the leadership of Italy's Jewish community.[1] Vast areas of Italian Jewish life and thousands of important individual stories remained undocumented. Much remained to be said and written about the redaction and application of the racial laws that were passed in 1938, about the relation between the Vatican and the Jews, and about the nature of the deportation of the Jews that took place nearing the end of World War II among other things.

As the theme of Italian Jewry, particularly during Fascism, was first taken up, it was often discussed in relatively naïve and simplistic terms. The tendency was to emphasize – following De Felice's lead and without close analysis – the difference of the Italian case, in particular its difference from Nazi Germany. The fact that the vast majority of Italian Jews survived the war was generally attributed to the fundamental goodness of the Italian people and their tendency to bend, ignore, or defy the law with a decidedly unteutonic spirit. Documentary films such as Joseph Rochlitz's "The Righteous Enemy" (1991) emphasized the courage and humanity of Italian soldiers and diplomats in the territories occupied by Italian troops – in particular Yugoslavia and Southern France – who steadfastly refused to hand over Jews under their control for deportation to Germany. Although these stories were true enough, lost in this wave of enthusiastic discovery of the Italian case were many other facets of the Italian Jewish experience under Fascism. Much of the very good scholarship and literature that has been produced in the past fifteen years has offered us a considerably more nuanced portrait of Italy's Jews – even though the Italian experience does remain a unique and exceptional one in many ways.

As the works of Michele Sarfatti and others have shown, the Italian racial laws were hardly mild, were applied with considerable severity, and had devastating effects on Italian Jewry.[2] In certain respects, as Sarfatti shows, aspects of the 1938 laws went beyond the harsh restrictions of Germany's Nuremberg laws. The immediate banishment of Jewish children and teachers from Italian public schools; the expropriation of most Jewish businesses; and the ban on Jewish professionals, lawyers, doctors, and dentists wiped out thousands of families, making many feel like strangers at home and forcing a sizeable chunk of the community to emigrate overseas. Although it is not comparable to genocide, it is hardly a chapter of which Italy can be proud.

In her *Libro della memoria*, Liliana Picciotto, who traced the destinies and listed one by one the approximately 8,000 Jews who were deported from Italy, offered a somewhat darker picture than the accounts that placed Italy right next to Denmark among the countries in which Jews fared the best under Nazi occupation.[3] When the several thousand Jews who fled the country are subtracted, the claim that 85 percent of Italians Jews survived the war – about the same percentage as Denmark – does not hold up. According to Picciotto's calculations, just over 7,000 of approximately 33,000 Jews were deported or killed, which brings their percentage up to just over 20 percent. When the Jews in the islands of the Greek Dodacanese, which were Italian territory at the time – nearly 1,800 Jews on the Island of Rhodes, almost the entire community, were deported – are also counted, then the statistics get much worse: more than 8,500 deported or killed out of about 35,000, which brings us up to about 25 percent.

Although it is certainly true that many Jews who looked for help found it among the Italian population, it is also true that without the racial laws, the lists they compiled of the Italian Jewish communities, and the obligatory *di razza ebraica* that was stamped on Jews' identity cards, it would have been much, much harder for the Germans to track down the country's Jews. Moreover, the notion that only the Germans deported Jews, whereas Italians tried to help them, is a gross simplification. In the roughly 4,500 arrests that have been documented, more than 43 percent were carried out by Italians and Italians alone.[4] The percentage is somewhat higher if you take into account the instances in which Italians of Mussolini's Republic of Salò (RSI) and Germans worked together. At a moment when former volunteers of the Republic of Salò are in the current Italian government there is a tendency to romanticize it as a noble if desperate cause, an attempt to defend the fatherland even when the battle was clearly lost. Before we go much further toward romanticization, it would be good for many Italians to look closely at this particular chapter of the RSI.[5]

David Kertzer and Susan Zuccotti have, in their most recent books, sharpened the focus of discussion about the Vatican's relations with the Jews and its responsibility for their persecution.[6] Kertzer pretty well shoots holes through the Vatican commission's report on the Holocaust, which apologized for the Church's anti-Jewish preaching in the distant past, but excused itself from any responsibility in the Holocaust by making a broad distinction between anti-Jewish theology and twentieth-century biological anti-Semitism. The distinction, however, does not hold up to close scrutiny. As Kertzer points out, the Church played a major role in the late nineteenth century and early twentieth century in forging the idea of a Jewish conspiracy for world domination and in painting the Jews as a dangerous subversive minority, a social parasite sucking the healthy life out of the body politic. Although this was not biological racism, the Church certainly practiced powerful political anti-Semitism and its many arguments and metaphors were taken up by those combined with doctrines of racial superiority. Zuccotti and John Cornwell have documented the particular role Pius XII played in negotiating a concordat with Hitler's Germany to the complete absence of any record of his acting to help the Jews, despite his being one of the better informed people in Europe about the nature and extent of the mass extermination.[7]

But while the cliché of *italiani, brava gente* ("The Good Italian") has been gradually replaced with a much more complex portrait, there is much that is distinctive about the Italian experience. Although this is difficult to quantify, individual interviews with Jews suggest that the great majority did not feel themselves to be living in a hostile environment, even as their rights were cruelly stripped away. Saul Steinberg, the great illustrator and cartoonist, frequently called Italy *nostro paradiso perduto* ("our paradise lost"), speaking of that brief parenthesis for many German and Eastern European Jews who left their native countries after Hitler came to power in 1933 and until they were forced to leave Italy in 1938. My own father and aunt, who had grown up in Italy, were extremely reluctant to leave the country even though their position was extremely precarious. It was only my grandfather, who had grown up in Tsarist and Soviet Russia and had witnessed pogroms as a young man, knew that things could get much, much worse than they were in Italy in 1941.

Part of my family's reluctance was the atmosphere of solidarity with which they were surrounded. My father recalled a Sunday afternoon shortly after the proclamation of the racial laws when the family received a completely unexpected visit from a family of farmers they knew from Formia, where my family had lived for a while and continued to visit during the summer. These simple working people, who were hardly in the habit of visiting Rome, appeared on my grandparent's door as if it were the most natural thing in the world. They all sat down to tea and talked of various things. With a delicacy of soul worthy of the most refined aristocrats, my father said, the peasant family let my family know that if they should need help in the times to come, they could count on them.

My own family received help from people like Gabriele D'Annunzio, the soldier-poet of Fascism, who signed a patently false document to help my family gain citizenship or from a well-known Fascist senator who helped my family even after the regime had turned against them. When I asked my father about these bizarre contradictions, he would shrug and say that one had to be in Fascist Italy to understand. In that atmosphere, he said, these things were normal.

The Historical Legacy: The Era of the Ghetto

The experience of Italian Jews under Fascism and during World War II is riddled with paradox and ambiguity, as I tried to express in the title of my book, *Benevolence and Betrayal.*[8] Italy went from being one of the most backward countries in Europe, with its Jews confined to ghettoes until 1870, to one of the most enlightened, in which Jews were able to aspire to the highest levels of society, including the office of prime minister, a tradition continued by Mussolini during his first sixteen years in power until his about-face in 1938. Italy was a virtually unique case in Europe, a country where Jews were often Fascists and where Fascists often helped to save Jews.

These paradoxes I argue are embedded in the 2,000-year history of the Jews in Italy, which has always been marked by oscillations between tolerance and persecution. Even in ancient Roman times, there was tolerance for differing religious customs followed by moments of reaction against the stubbornness of the Jews in sticking to their traditions.

As the center of the Catholic world, Italy was a source of religious persecution. But the presence of the Vatican generally ensured that this persecution did not reach the violent excesses of the murderous pogroms that marked much of the rest of Europe. The Renaissance city-states often welcomed Jewish merchants to stimulate trade and became major centers of Jewish learning and culture. At the same time, the institution of the ghetto is an Italian invention, begun in 1516 in Venice.

Understanding the nature of the ghetto provides us with a highly instructive model for understanding the dynamic between the Jewish minority and the Italian majority in later periods, especially the Fascist era. Through extremely elaborate legislation, the Catholic majority defined exactly what a Jew could do and be. In many ghettoes, Jews were prevented from owning real estate or engaging in trade except in secondhand goods. But unlike their Christian brothers, Jews were allowed to lend money. Renaissance Italy was in a difficult bind: burgeoning trade required capital for investment but papal laws against usury prevented Christians from lending money at interest. By keeping Jews out of the traditional occupations (law, commerce, agriculture) and leaving them money lending as the only alternative, Italian society accomplished several purposes. It eliminated competition for Catholic merchants and supplied needed capital for economic growth. But it served a useful ideological purpose. It placed Jews in a separate, immediately recognizable, category apart from their Christian brethren. By marking them physically, making them wear a red or yellow strip on their clothing, by making them practice the hated and sinful trade of usury, the ghetto laws helped demonize the Jews. When times were good, the Jews were valued bankers. And when times were bad, they were perfect scapegoats: public anger during moments of famine or hardship could be directed at the wretched usurer – a rootless, landless creature who produced nothing and seemed to have a special attachment to money. When one reads the ghetto legislation, it seems almost as if it sought to create the figure of Shylock in Shakespeare's *Merchant of Venice*.

The ideological uses of the Jews increased with the Counter-Reformation in the middle of the sixteenth century. With the infamous Papal Bull, *Cum Nimis Absurdum* of 1555, the Vatican's much more strict laws of punitive segregation were codified and broadened and then imposed throughout the Italian peninsula.

Before 1555, the Jews of Rome had been as free and as flourishing a community as existed in Europe. Although some occupations were closed off to them, they were active as bankers, doctors, and silk merchants; they were able to own real estate and live where they chose. The Jewish doctors were world famous during the Middle Ages and the Renaissance and often acted as the attending physicians to the pope himself.

During the sixteenth century, however, the Catholic Church responded to the rise of the Protestant Reformation by lashing out furiously against religious heterodoxy in all forms. Although the popes were powerless to halt the spread of Lutheranism in Northern Europe, within their own territory they could force the Jews to knuckle under to the most rigid conformity. Declaring the absurdity of allowing Jews to live freely among Christians, Pope Paul IV (1555–9) confined the Jews of Rome to a single walled area of the city and regulated and restricted almost every aspect of their lives.

The scope of the ghetto system in Rome went far beyond insulating Christian society from the pernicious influence of the Jews. As the wayward people whose conversion to Christianity would crown the Final Judgment, the Jews occupied an important place within Catholic theology. The ghetto was to be a theatre for the great drama of Christian redemption. In Rome the Jews were forced to attend weekly sermons meant to convert them to the true faith. Indeed it was a form of popular entertainment for the rabble to jeer and throw objects as they watched the Jews file off to church. The Jews were forced to participate in public foot races at carnival time, a practice ended only when the community agreed to pay a tribute of 300 scudi to the pope to be delivered each year in the capitol above the old Roman forum. With the crowning of each new pope, elders of the Jewish community were compelled to pay tribute to the pontiff, kissing his foot before the symbol of their humiliation, the Arch of Titus.

Lest the populace think that the wages of sin were high, the Jews of Rome were systematically stripped of all their resources. Forced to sell whatever real estate they owned and saddled with all manner of taxes and tributes, they were also gradually excluded from all but the most humble and degrading occupations. Banned from practicing medicine, banned from lending money, banned even from selling firsthand clothing, they were eventually permitted no other livelihood than repairing and selling secondhand clothes.[9] The important larger lesson in this history is that the nature of the Jewish community was determined by political needs of the larger society. As a weak, barely tolerated minority, the Jews were a sort of negative mirror for the majority: every society gets the particular kind of Jew it needs. At one moment a wealthy, cultured banker and at another a wretched, ignorant rag picker.

And yet, in another paradox, Italy moved rapidly into an era of liberal tolerance that has almost no equal in that age.

Out of the Ghetto: From the Risorgimento to Fascism

There were three Jews elected to the first Italian parliament in 1861. In 1874, there were eleven Jewish deputies and in 1894, their number reached fifteen – the highest level in Italian history. Moreover, Jews achieved positions of genuine responsibility. Luigi Luzzati became prime minister in 1910. And Sidney Sonnino, who was half-Jewish and a protestant by religion, was prime minister in both 1906 and 1909–10. The Italian minister of war and the tutor to the Italian royal family, Giuseppe Ottolenghi, was a Jewish general – this at a time when France was still arguing over the case of Captain Dreyfus.

There were specific historic reasons for this. In Italy, the struggle for the creation of the united modern Italian state and the struggle for emancipation of Italian Jews were virtually synonymous. It is an important historic accident that the forces of reaction in Italy – the Austrian Hungarian Empire (which dominated most of Northern Italy), the Papal States (which occupied central Italy), and the Spanish Empire (which controlled southern Italy) – were also the main opponents to Italian unity. And it is highly significant that King Carlo Alberto, the head of the Savoy dynasty, which would become Italy's royal family, literally signed the decree granting religious freedom to the Jews in 1848 on the battlefield of Voghera before going off to fight Austrian troops. Thus, the Italian cause and the battle for Jewish freedom were exactly contemporaneous. Naturally, Jews dedicated themselves to the cause of Italian unification with particular enthusiasm. Eight of the famous 1,000 soldiers that Giuseppe Garibaldi sailed off with to liberate Sicily from Bourbon domination were Jewish.

The Italian Jews were in an unusually strong position to jump from the ghetto into the emerging Italian middle class. At the time of Italian unification most Italians could neither read nor write, whereas literacy in the Jewish community was nearly 95 percent.[10] Moreover, unlike most other European Jews who spoke a separate language – Yiddish or Ladino – Italian Jews spoke the local dialect of the city they lived in.[11]

This marriage of the causes of Jewish emancipation and national union made Italian Jews unusually patriotic citizens during World War I, with many identifying with Fascism before the racial laws. Mussolini's religious politics were, as in almost every area, contradictory and highly expedient: he had begun his career as a firebreathing anti-Catholic but during his drive for power reversed himself shamelessly, proposing to make Catholicism the official state religion.

With respect to the Jews, Mussolini tailored his statements to suit the needs of the moment so that in his writings and speeches one can find almost every possible position – and its opposite. In 1917, Mussolini briefly blamed the Russian Revolution on "Jewish vengeance" against Christianity, saying "Race does not betray race ... Bolshevism is being defended by the international plutocracy. That is the real truth." A few weeks later, he did a 180-degree turn: "Bolshevism is not, as people believe, a Jewish phenomenon," he wrote. "The truth is that Bolshevism is leading to the utter ruin of the Jews of Eastern Europe."[12]

Although not a biological racist, Mussolini was a great believer in national traits and made sweeping generalizations about the Jews as a people (unusually intelligent, drawn to money, tendentially subversive and democratic). But he had similarly stereotypical ideas about almost everyone – the Russians, the French, the English, and so on. With an alternating mix of resentment and admiration, Mussolini frequently used the terms "Jewish finance," "Jewish international" or "the international plutocracy" to refer to a vaguely defined cabal of Jewish interests. Because he believed more in the idea of *nation* than in *race*, he regarded the Italian Jews as Italian; he was suspicious, however, of Zionism because of its connections to the "Jewish International." Mussolini's anti-Jewish sentiments resembled his opposition to freemasonry, which both implied a secret loyalty independent of Fascism and echoed some of the late-nineteenth-century terminology used by the Catholic Church.

And yet Mussolini's remarks about the "Jewish International" notwithstanding, Mussolini had warm relations with Jews at various levels. His first cabinet included Aldo Finzi, an early Jewish supporter who became undersecretary of the interior. His mistress and official biographer in that period, Margherita Sarfatti, was also Jewish.

In this sense, Mussolini reflected many of the contradictions of Italy's history with the Jews and the ambivalent attitude of the Church. For although the Church did engage in anti-Semitism, it also played a moderating role throughout the centuries, saving the Jews from physical harm and preventing pogroms.

That Italy could again turn so quickly from full acceptance to renewed persecution shows that the integration of the Jews in liberal Italy was a conditional one; it was based on a kind of tacit pact that the Jews would be fully accepted as long as they fit in and did not make too much of a fuss about being Jews.

Religion, at least Jewish religion, was considered to be a private affair and as long as Jewish worship was discreet and out of the way, it could be well tolerated. But it was better not to be too emphatic.

Fascism was always highly suspicious of Zionism, for example. In a certain sense, this was not dissimilar to its persecution of freemasonry that was also seen to be an allegiance to an international power potentially beyond the control of the Italian state.[13] During the Fascist period, Italian Jews were repeatedly put on notice that they had to demonstrate – with actions and not just words – that they actively condemned both Zionism and anti-Fascism, giving them a higher threshold for citizenship than other Italians. Several of the key anti-Semitic tracts of the late 1930s, in particular by Roberto Farinacci and Telesio Interlandi, repeated the theme consistently. Farinacci, using the arrest of several Jewish anti-Fascists as a pretext to attack Italian Zionists, wrote the following in 1934:

> We do not exclude the possibility that there are good Jews, but it is also our right to demand clarity. Does there or does there not exist a Zionist movement in Italy? To deny it would be to lie. The existence of a newspaper in Florence [the Zionist magazine, *Israel*] should cut short any discussion. And so these others who claim to be anti-Zionists, what are they doing to fight the other Jews who believe they have another Fatherland that is not Italy? So far, nothing.
>
> Therefore, it is necessary to decide. We have reached a point at which everyone must take a position. Because he who declares himself Zionist has no right to hold any responsibilities or honors in our country.[14]

A significant number of Italian Jews accepted the premise of this position, namely that their standing as "good" Italian Jews depended on their conduct and their willingness to show that they had one and not a multiple identity.

The founding of the magazine *La Nostra Bandiera* ("Our Flag"), by Ettore Ovazza in Turin, was needed, he explained, to counteract the negative and unpatriotic image of Jews created by the Zionists' newspaper, *Israel*. "We clearly reject the Zionists who live ... with one eye looking to Rome and the other to Jerusalem," Ovazza wrote, calling Zionism "the greatest ally of racist policy."

Following the logic of Farinacci, Ovazza demanded that all Italian Jews clarify their position and declare their "full and absolute adhesion to the Fatherland." Finally he insisted that whoever does "not feel the sacred and obligatory love for the Fatherland where he is born should remove himself from his own country."

This extreme position – almost advocating the expulsion of Zionist Jews from Italy – went far beyond anything Fascism had ever articulated. Ovazza and the *bandieristi* divided the Italian Jews into bitterly warring camps precisely at a time they faced an extremely dangerous common threat.

The situation, however, was highly confusing. Publicly Mussolini and the regime never uttered an anti-Semitic word, and occasionally expressed words of support, whereas those who attacked the Jews appeared to act on their own. This barrage of conflicting messages put Italy's Jews in what studies on schizophrenia have called the "double-bind." The Italian Jews became increasingly disoriented by a society that simultaneously reassured and attacked them.

The Fascist Jews tried everything to please Mussolini, giving increasingly large sums of money to help develop the new Italian colonies and renouncing all ties to the international Jewish community. The Turinese Jews began a second major offensive against the Jewish establishment. They prepared a booklet, published by *La Nostra Bandiera*, called "For the Fulfillment of Jewish Duty in Fascist Italy," which proposed to radically reform Italian Judaism along Fascist lines. It proposed ousting the current leadership, setting up a new centralized governing body with authoritarian power, prohibiting contacts with Jewish groups overseas, and limiting religious observance to its purely ritual functions. Absorbing much of the rhetoric of anti-Semitism, the booklet even accused the official Jewish leadership of "old Masonic roots" and "international links" with subversive, anti-Italian elements. In many instances, as I discovered in the state archives, *La Nostra Bandiera* was frequently criticized by the government for some of its attacks on international Jewish organizations – during the periods Mussolini was trying to use them for his own political aims.

Thus, the *bandieristi* found themselves being whipsawed from the other side. After Mussolini had joined Hitler in sending troops to fight in the Spanish Civil War, Farinacci's newspaper, *Il Regime Fascista*, attacked the Jewish Fascists viciously for failing to act against their subversive Zionist brethren:

> Why do they do nothing concrete to disassociate themselves from all other Jews in the World, the ones whose only goal is the triumph of the Jewish International?... There is a growing feeling that all Europe will soon be the scene of a war of religion. Are they not aware of this? We are certain that many will proclaim: we are Jewish Fascists. That is not enough. They must prove with facts to be fascists first and then Jews.[15]

In May 1937 – as Fascist and Nazi officials shuttled back and forth between Rome and Berlin preparing a German–Italian alliance – anti-Jewish propaganda took a quantum leap forward. An important Fascist publicist, Paolo Orano – a member of parliament and rector of the University of Perugia – published an attack on Italian Jews thinly disguised as a disinterested scholarly analysis. More disturbing was the fact that virtually all the Italian papers, including Mussolini's own *Popolo d'Italia*, used Orano's book, *The Jews of Italy*, as a pretext to raise the so-called "Jewish question."

The book helped create a specifically Italian Fascist brand of anti-Semitism, based not on biology and eugenics, but on historical, religious, and national considerations. Orano, while speaking warmly of several individual Jews (particularly Ettore Ovazza), argued that the Jews were a fundamentally subversive, revolutionary people who inevitably sought to control and undermine the nations in which they settled. He dedicated an entire chapter to Ovazza, incorporating his critique of Zionism and then extending it to apply to all Jews. While calling Ovazza "the most frank" of the Italian Jews, Orano accused him of suffering from some of the worst traits endemic to his race: "vanity, pride, sense of superiority ... presumption of belonging to a chosen people."[16]

Even as he was preparing the psychological terrain for the Jewish persecutions, Orano never failed to demonstrate affection and respect for Ovazza and his family in their private correspondence. Incredibly, their friendship survived the publication of Orano's book with no loss in cordiality. That a leader of the Jewish community should be on close personal terms with one of the country's leading anti-Semites is highly emblematic of the paradoxical and contradictory nature of the relationship between Jews and Fascist Italy. I cannot help thinking that this reproduces the structural relationship of the Church and the Jews through the centuries, which acted as a center of both persecution and physical protection.

This notion that the status of Italian Jews depends on their good conduct is still present in some Italian thinking. Just a few years ago, the prominent author, Sergio Romano, published the book titled, *Lettera ad un amico ebreo*[17] ("Letter to a Jewish Friend"), which reminded me in many ways of Paolo Orano's *Jews of Italy*. Its thesis is essentially that the Jews should stop writing and talking about the Holocaust because they are going to provoke a new wave of anti-Semitism. Other articles often write that Jews must disassociate themselves from the politics of Israel or they will provoke waves of anti-Semitism. The logic is essentially that of Orano and Farinacci: that anti-Semitism is something that the Jews bring about or prevent through their own behavior. Lost in this reasoning is the notion that Jews are individuals with the same rights as anyone else who should think and act as their conscience sees fit rather than a monolithic block to be judged en masse, guests who will receive a report card of either a passing or a failing grade. This logic is closely tied to the difficulty Italy has had with the notion of a double or multiple identity, due to the centrality of Catholicism to Italian identity. This ignores, of course, the fact that during the period when the Vatican did not recognize the legitimate existence of the Italian state – between the unification of Italy in 1870 and the Concordato of 1929 – the double identity that did represent a genuine problem was that of being both an obedient Catholic and a good Italian.

This double bind – of acceptance on condition of assimilation – helps to explain why the seeming contradictions between Italy's treatment of Jews – from extremes of persecution and tolerance – are less contradictory than they might appear. But I do not want to overemphasize this point, for the sense of acceptance that most Italian Jews felt was not pure illusion.

The Jewish Experience in Fascist Italy: Distinctive Features

What distinguished the story of Italian Jews from that of the rest of Europe was the long coexistence between Jews and Fascists in Mussolini's Italy. Italian Fascism was in power for sixteen years before it turned anti-Semitic in 1938. Until then, Jews were as likely as other conservative-minded Italians to be members of the Fascist party. This singular fact altered the entire moral and existential equation for Italy's Jews.

The close bond between Fascist Italy and its Jews had a whole series of important consequences – both positive and negative – in the lives of individuals. It changed the Jews' sense of national and religious identity and it affected the decisions they made about whether to stay or emigrate after 1938. During the German occupation, it altered their perceptions of the dangers they faced and the way they reacted to them. After the war, it influenced the decision of most Italian Jews to remain in Italy rather than emigrate to Israel or the United States, as most German and Eastern European Jews did.

The lack of a tradition of biological racism and the assimilation of the Jews into the wider population made Italians less receptive to the policy of persecution when it arrived. This is not to say that Italy was free of anti-Semitism, but Italian anti-Semitism was decidedly different from the German (and perhaps also Polish and Russian) variety. I was struck in a memoir I recently read by Aldo Zargani in which the narrator, who was a small boy during the war, tells about a Piedmontese peasant woman who hid Zargani's family during the last months of the war, sharing both hardship and danger with them.[18] After the war, the old woman asked the author's mother how it was that nice people like them could kill Christian children and use them for the Passover ritual. Thus, the old woman had absorbed and evidently believed the old blood libel myth of ritual murder, preached by the Church with energy for centuries and not erased from official Church doctrine until the papacy of John XIII in the 1950s. And yet, at the same time, she clearly saw and treated these people as people to be helped.

I myself collected a number of personal stories that echo Zargani's story of the peasant woman who hid Jews whom she thought engaged in ritual murder. I interviewed an Eastern European Jew who was living in Italy at the time who told me the following story. He wanted to take a vacation on the Adriatic coast, but the racial laws forbade Jews from going to seaside resorts, out of fear that they might communicate with submarines off shore. So this gentleman wrote to the proprietress of a little *pensione*, saying "You should know that I am Jewish, so let me know if this poses a problem." The woman wrote back: "It doesn't matter if you are a Jew or a Christian, as long as you are a member of the Aryan race."

Emanuele Pacifici is fond of repeating that for every Jew who survived there is a non-Jewish Italian who helped him. Many Italian police were not particularly eager to carry out the arrests of Jews and warned them beforehand so that they might flee. This, indeed, happened to Pacifici and his family at one point.[19]

It has often been pointed out that it was much easier for Italians to help Jews than, say, Poles, who were living under a ferocious Nazi occupation for five years in which aiding Jews was publishable by death. And yet precisely because it was easier, the Italian case is interesting because it was a place in Europe where choice was possible and one can learn a lot about human nature in observing the choices that people made. In some parts of Europe, even small help to the Jews required genuinely heroic courage, which is almost always in short supply. I think Italy is such a singular and interesting example to study because it occupies what Primo Levi described as the "grey zone," an area of choice and complicity.

Although it is important not to fall victim to national stereotypes or cultural or racial generalizations, one should also not fall into moral relativism either. The conduct of the few does not absolve the sins of the many. The stark contrast between the behavior of most Italian and German soldiers – that emerges clearly from scores of interviews and close study – makes it legitimate to reflect on the cultures in which they were raised.

Many of the people who were interned in the Italian transit camp of Fossoli described the dramatic change that came about when the camp passed from Italian into German hands. Franco Schonheit, for example, described the terrifying incident that occurred when the prisoners were out on a work detail one day. The group was being supervised by a German officer who had just arrived in

Italy, spoke no Italian, and did not have an interpreter with him. At one point, he barked an order to a Roman Jewish man, who did not understand and turned left rather than right. The young German officer simply took out his pistol and shot the man dead.[20]

Although I think it is legitimate to think about the nature of Italian culture, national character, and the nature of Italy's attitude toward the Jews, this sort of discussion leaves out a very important dimension: politics. The fact that when we speak about Italy we often speak about individual stories of Italians hiding or saving Jews ignores the political responsibility of those who left the salvation of the persecution up to private, individual initiative.

Although the courageous behavior of thousands of Italians in helping or saving Jews deserves every kind of recognition, it is also important to think about the larger historical picture. The military alliance between Mussolini and Hitler was of enormous help in furthering Hitler's expansionist and murderous designs. It is questionable whether Hitler would have felt emboldened to take on the rest of Europe without the support, or at least guaranteed neutrality, of his Italian partner.

The fact that the life and death of Jews was left to individual choice and courage and private initiative raises an important political point. Belgium, Holland, and Poland were invaded through no fault of their own. The same is not the case of Italy.

There has been a tendency in Italian historiography, begun by Renzo De Felice and accelerated by the political need to reintegrate former members of the neo-Fascist party, Il Movimento Sociale Italiano, into mainstream Italian politics, to engage in a rather superficial historical revisionism. Prime Minister Silvio Berlusconi has tried to underline the difference between the "good" period of Fascism and the "bad" period marked by the alliance with Hitler and the war. It has become standard practice to acknowledge that the anti-Jewish racial laws, the alliance with Hitler, and the war were wrong. But the eagerness to separate the good from the bad in Fascism has created an artificial divide between the period 1922–38 and what followed, as if the racial laws and the war were a deviation from the true course of Fascism that could have been easily avoided. I consider this view wrongheaded and ahistorical. The alliance with Hitler and the war was the very natural result of a long progression of events and the desire to recreate the Empire, the glory, and even positive, revivifying effects of war.

Mussolini began to speak frequently of the need to mold the undisciplined Italian people into a warrior nation and to view war as a form of education for the soft bourgeois class. The war in Spain, the Duce said, would give the middle class "a sound kick in the shins...and when that's done, I'll invent something else so that the character of the Italians forms itself through war."[21]

The wars in Ethiopia and Spain prepared the terrain and created a de facto alliance between Italy and Germany. After beating war drums for nearly two decades and portraying himself as the new Caesar, Mussolini could hardly back away from the struggle when the war began – particularly when France lay prostrate at his feet.

Moreover, the Italian experience during the war demonstrates the fundamental weakness of authoritarian regimes. Having stamped out and discouraged all dissent, Mussolini only heard his own voice echoing back to him in the official propaganda of the period. Although perhaps initially invented for public consumption, Mussolini, as solitary leader, began to believe his own rhetoric that England was a hopelessly decadent nation of people who wore slippers and could not live without their five o'clock tea. He gradually came to believe that he was an invincible man chosen by destiny and that the Italians stood ready with their eight million bayonets to destroy any adversary. He could not hear the words of caution expressed by his own generals who informed him clearly that they were nowhere near ready for war. And although the great majority of Italians had little interest in fighting a second world war, the totalitarian system he created gave no channel to that sentiment. The passivity of most Italians in front of the racial laws cannot be separated from the passivity and indifference with which they watched during the 1920s the fragile framework of Italian democracy dismantled piece by piece.

Thus, to conclude, while I believe that the history of Italian Jews offers a chance to reflect on the particular relationship between Italy and its Jews, the particular nature of Italian anti-Semitism and Jewish integration also contains valuable lessons about the importance of systems that protect us against what is worst in all us.

NOTES

1. Renzo De Felice, *Storia degli ebrei italiani sotto il fascismo* (Turin: Einaudi, 1961); Meir Michaelis, *Mussolini and the Jews: German-Italian Relations and the Jewish Question in Italy, 1922–1945* (Oxford: Clarendon Press, 1978).

2. *La persecuzione degli ebrei durante il fascismo. Le leggi del 1938, Camera dei deputati* (Rome: Camera dei deputati, 1998). Liliana Picciotto Fargion, *Il Libro della memoria. Gli Ebrei deportati dall'Italia (1943–1945)* (1991; reprint, Milan: Mursia, 2002). Michele Sarfatti, *Gli ebrei nell'Italia fascista. Vicende, identità, persecuzione* (Turin: Einaudi, 2000). Michele Sarfatti, *Le leggi antiebraiche spiegate agli italiani di oggi* (Turin: Einaudi,

2002). Michele Sarfatti, *Mussolini contro gli ebrei. Cronaca dell'elaborazione delle leggi del 1938* (Turin: Zamorani, 1994). Michele Sarfatti (a cura di), "1938 le leggi contro gli ebrei," special issue of *La Rassegna mensile di Israel*, vol. LIV, nos. 1–2 (January–August 1988).

3. Picciotto Fargion, *Il libro della memoria*.

4. Ibid.

5. Alexander Stille, "Italy's Kinder, Gentler Fascism," *New York Times*, September 28, 2002.

6. Susan Zuccotti, *Under His Very Windows: The Vatican and the Holocaust in Italy* (New Haven, CT: Yale University Press, 2000); David I. Kertzer, *The Popes against the Jews: The Vatican's Role in the Rise of Modern Anti-Semitism* (New York: Knopf, 2001).

7. John Cornwell, *Hitler's Pope: The Secret History of Pius XII* (New York: Viking, 1999).

8. Alexander Stille, *Benevolence and Betrayal: Five Italian Jewish Families under Fascism* (New York: Penguin, 1993).

9. Attilio Milano, *Il ghetto di Roma* (Rome: Carucci editore, 1988), 156–74. Per capita income in the Rome community, which had been a fairly florid 250 scudi a year before the imposition of the ghetto, had shrunk to a paltry 15 scudi a year by the year 1800. In the last decades of the ghetto, a third of Rome's Jews depended almost entirely on the charity of their fellow Jews.

10. Susan Zuccotti, *The Italians and the Holocaust* (New York: Basic Books, 1987), 16.

11. Cecil Roth, *The History of the Jews of Italy* (Philadelphia: Jewish Publication Society of America, 1946); Attilio Milano, *Storia degli ebrei in Italia* (Turin: G. Einaudi, 1963).

12. Stille, *Benevolence and Betrayal*, 44.

13. But there is also a tendency in Italy to see the Jews as citizens of divided loyalty, which today is manifest in the Italians' frequent confusion of Jews and Israelis, so that demonstrations against Israeli government policy begin, appropriately, in front of the Israeli embassy and end up, inappropriately, in front of the Rome synagogue.

14. Stille, *Benevolence and Betrayal*, 51.

15. Ibid., 62.

16. Ibid., 65–6.

17. (Milan: Longanesi, 1997).

18. Aldo Zargani, *Per violino solo. La mia infanzia nell'Aldiqua, 1938–1945* (Bologna: Il Mulino, 1995); English: *For Solo Violin: A Jewish Childhood in Fascist Italy, A Memoir* (Philadelphia: Paul Dry Books, 2002).

19. Stille, *Benevolence and Betrayal*, 223–78.

20. Ibid., 279–314.

21. Galeazzo Ciano, *Diario 1937–1943* (Milan: Rizzoli, 1946).

2 Italian Jewish Identity from the Risorgimento to Fascism, 1848–1938

Mario Toscano

Examining the question of Italian Jewish identity from the Risorgimento to Fascism entails a number of steps. We must identify and document dates, crucial junctures, transitions, and solutions offered by Italian Jews to the problems created by emancipation. We must identify and clearly describe the various external and internal components that influenced Italian Jewry in its process of modernization. We must also attempt to address the question of whether it is proper to speak of the experience of emancipated Judaism in Italy as unique in Europe, one accompanied by a specific cultural and political program that in turn engendered a particular identity possessing distinct characteristics that set it apart from other Western European experiences of the Diaspora. We must further establish links and relationships between this collective historical identity and the manifold individual accounts and identities that characterized the historical experience of so small a minority, small at least in strictly numerical terms. The Jewish population in Italy is estimated at 34,000 in 1800, out of a total Italian population of more than 18 million, and about 48,000 in 1938, out of more than 43 million Italians.[1] Yet Italian Jewry constitutes a minority with a rich and multifaceted history extending back into antiquity.

In this chapter I attempt to provide some answers to the questions posed above by offering hypotheses and interpretations of recent historiographic debates, by summarizing the results of research I have previously conducted,[2] and by drawing attention to topics still awaiting investigation.

Research into the history of contemporary Italian Jewry has made substantial progress over the past twenty years. This is due to the efforts of a new generation of scholars who have learned from the methods of more advanced schools of historians working in parallel fields (especially in the United States, Israel,

France, and Germany). It is also due to a shift in the broader cultural climate, encouraging greater attention to these topics in publishing and academia, as well as reexamined work on old and new sources. Much remains to be done. However lively and stimulating these discussions have been, they have occasionally been influenced, regrettably, by an overpoliticized analysis of historical events that tend to link them to current events.

The cultural and historical debate has veered in the past between two opposing approaches, strongly influenced by contingent demands of Jewish identity. On the one hand, we find a simplistic and moralistic view that long interpreted the history of postemancipation Italian Jewry as an unbroken process of assimilation, marked by a loss of national, historic, and even religious identity.[3] On the other hand, a positive interpretation emerged of the process of Jewish emancipation and integration in Italy as paradigmatic. This view took the Risorgimento as a crucial element of emancipated Jewish identity, a criterion for the interpretation of subsequent events, with a particular reference to the anti-Fascist Resistance, understood as a "second Risorgimento."[4]

For many years, in fact, only scattered attention was paid to problems bound up with the dialectic of integration and assimilation, to reconstructing the processes of acculturation, to efforts to define the religious attitudes of Italian Jews, or to the relationship between Jewish religious tradition and Italian national identity. Certainly, the lack of sources – especially statistical sources[5] – has made it all the more difficult to reconstruct these aspects of the question. Available documentation, however, allows us to develop the broad outlines of the political and cultural processes typical of Italian Jews in the various phases of emancipation. This can be seen in the most recent research that has moved beyond merely supplying important information and evidence by offering sometimes radical (and questionable) attempts to provide innovative interpretations.[6]

As a point of departure in any attempt to evaluate the processes of Jewish emancipation, integration, and acculturation in Italy and to reconstruct the self-image that Italian Jews developed in that context, I would begin with a theory set forth in 1933 by Arnaldo Momigliano of "parallel nationalization"; that is, the simultaneous formation of a national consciousness among Jewish and non-Jewish Italians during the Risorgimento. As I have observed on other occasions, it is necessary to distinguish between Momigliano's thesis and the interpretation of that viewpoint offered by Gramsci, who derived from it an absence of anti-Semitism in unified Italy.[7]

We must also establish a few basic points of reference in Italian and Jewish history between the last three decades of the eighteenth century and the end of the Risorgimento (1870). We may thus ascertain the meanings and implications of Momigliano's theory of parallel nationalization, which, as I myself wrote,

> represents not merely an historical and political interpretative indication, but an encouragement to evaluate the processes of acculturation that characterized Italian Jewry between the seventeenth and nineteenth centuries, identifying 1848 as the culminating moment of a process that we must break down into its political, juridical, cultural, economic, and religious component parts, each intersecting and interacting with the others; we should also take care to note the European references and remember the aspects of modernization of Italian society in general and Jewish society in particular.[8]

The nationalization of Italian Jews is thus configured as a synthesis of a longer-term historical process, marked by the effort of modern states to establish their own power over private bodies and separate powers and by the development of relationships between state and church. In particular, from the final three decades of the eighteenth century, both the jurisdictional policies and measures of tolerance of Habsburg enlightened absolutism, even in its own Italian dominions, as well as the Jacobin triennium (1796–9) and Napoleonic rule engendered processes of transformation and modernization among Jewish communities that had different effects depending on the differing historical conditions of the Jews in the various states of the Italian peninsula. Aside from the limitations and duration of these processes (first emancipation), a new situation was beginning to emerge, reshaping the image of the Jew and driving a transformation of the economic and social profile of certain elite communities.[9]

Recent research thus leads us to attenuate the strict distinction between the first (1796–9 and 1800–14) and the second (1848–70) emancipation periods and to underscore the more significant elements of continuity introduced by the process of transformation. For that matter, if the effects of the Napoleonic era on the Italian history of the Risorgimento must be viewed over the long term, a similar hypothesis can be formulated as well for the historic events of Italian Jews who certainly emerged from the brief but dizzyingly euphoric experience of liberty – shared with the elites of the Italian peninsula – completely transformed. For Italian Jewry, the Napoleonic experience also entailed a first encounter with the national ideals of a united Italy. The idea of an Italian nation emerged in close conjunction with the demand for broader liberties and with the full freight of rights that sprang from the entire span of the revolutionary movement. As a result, in contrast with the situation in other European countries, that idea did not seem destined to derive any significant and lasting antinational stereotypes of the emancipated Jew from the French bestowal of rights upon the Jews. At the same time, the processes of aggregation that culminated in the creation of the Kingdom of Italy (1805) shaped even the life of Italian Jewish communities within the context of new national prospects.[10]

Alongside the developing processes of socioeconomic modernization and acculturation, we should consider the transformation of Italian Jewish cultural and religious life that emerged in those years in connection with the larger transformations that, in the same years, were sweeping through other central and eastern European communities, taking on specific aspects that would in time engender important consequences. As Lois Dubin has clearly shown, from the end of the eighteenth century, the renewal of Jewish culture encouraged by the Haskalah penetrated to Italy through the filter of Trieste,[11] although cleansed of its more disturbing and subversive impulses. "Generally Italian Jews heard the Haskalah's education message as a supplement to their own traditions," Dubin writes, "not as a substitute or radical overhaul."[12] She continued:

> Wessely's Italian allies were neither passive recipients nor imitators. They selected carefully ... affirming values and methods that seemed familiar but rejecting that which struck them as radically new.... their tradition of acculturation ... enabled Italians to find Wessely's message familiar and ultimately compatible with their own outlook. Later, the drive for inclusion in the emerging Italian nation-state did not entail a Jewish debate about acculturation; its absence was in fact the distinguish[ing] characteristic of Jewish modernization in Italy. Despite the ghetto, the Italians ... had an ongoing tradition of cultural openness.... It was a legacy at work among all respondents, even those from areas not affected by Enlightened absolutist policies.... That cultural legacy helped prepare Jews for integration, i.e., to make the transition out of the ghetto, which reduced the potential conflict between tradition and modernity. Italian supporters of Haskalah were not a peripheral coterie of radical intellectuals but the rabbinic and communal elite.[13]

In this context, we should also mention the work of the Rabbinical College of Padua, established in 1829 by the communities of Lombardy-Venetia[14] in compliance with the Hapsburg regulations (1820) concerning the education of Jews and the preparation of rabbis, intended to keep pace with changing times but also with the new needs to make Jews into faithful subjects.[15] Because of the work of Shemuel David Luzzatto (1800–65) and Lelio Della Torre (1805–71),[16] the strict formulation of rabbinical studies made it possible to incorporate the encouragement provided by the *Wissenschaft des Judentums* (Science of Judaism) to a scholarly approach in the study of traditional Jewish culture without yielding to assimilationist impulses and to reformist demands.[17] The college played a fundamental role in the education of a new generation of rabbis (for the communities of Lombardy-Venetia and subsequently for those of the Kingdom of Italy), influenced by a pastoral vision of Catholic derivation, but open to demands of cultural renewal stripped of the more radical reformist impulses through solid traditional training.[18]

Despite the fact that some of the rabbis trained at Padua were inclined to favor religious reform, in Italy that reform was limited to external aspects of worship that in no way affected the essence of Jewish tradition.[19] The true instrument of the transformation and modernization of the Jewish condition was Italianization. That process was implemented as well through a reorganization of traditional Jewish schools, which in many locations progressively opened up to modern Italian culture.[20] The (Italian) acculturation preceded the process of juridical and civil emancipation of the Jews, which by this point appeared as a claim of particular freedom in the context of the liberal and national program pursued by the political and cultural elites of the Italian peninsula.

The debate in Italian culture on the Jewish question between the end of the eighteenth century and the first half of the nineteenth century has been thoroughly studied. In this context, leaving aside the hostilities against the Jews and the opposition to Jewish civic equality that persisted in conservative, Catholic, and reactionary milieus, suffice it to say that from the 1830s on, there was a rising orientation in favor of full Jewish emancipation on the part of supporters of liberalism, democracy, and liberal Catholicism.

Although some had initially subordinated Jewish emancipation to expectations of conversion or of Jewish civic and moral self-improvement, support for Jewish emancipation increasingly grew closely linked to the movement of national emancipation, which could hardly neglect the issue of Jewish equality if it truly claimed to support liberty.[21] The awareness of several leading figures in the Risorgimento of the Jewish condition was also heightened by the common use of biblical references in the creation of an Italian national myth.[22] That awareness also fit into the context of a clear political understanding of the liberal and democratic contents of the national idea, as was true of Cavour and Mazzini, and it possessed economic and moral aspects, as in the case of Carlo Cattaneo. Beginning in the latter half of 1847, these views emerged with growing clarity in the journalistic and political debate, as the links between national and liberal goals on the one hand and the emancipation of Italy's Jews on the other became increasingly evident.[23]

At the same time, the debate over the shape of the coming emancipation also involved several leading Italian Jewish figures. Some among them, accepting demands from outside the Jewish community for self-improvement, supported the need for radical change in the economic, social, and moral structure of Jewish society, especially in the poorer and more depressed sector of the community. There were others who suggested a willingness to accept substantial religious reforms, but others still vigorously demanded equality without concessions if the emancipation of the Jews was going to be an essential element of the Risorgimento movement.[24]

The decisive turning point in this process came in 1848, a genuine "springtime" for Italian Jews,[25] not merely because of the achievement of a juridical and civil emancipation destined to endure after the end of the revolutionary period of 1848 only in Piedmont, but also because of both the clear support of liberal public opinion for Jewish emancipation and the component of Italian nationalism added to Jewish identity by the Italian rabbinate, thus sanctioning a lengthy process of acculturation. It was in that very year that Shemuel David Luzzatto (1800–65) emphasized that "the Israelites have no other homeland than the one in which they were born, or where they permanently reside."[26] In February, in a speech delivered in the temple of Leghorn, Elia Benamozegh (1822–1900), the other great master of nineteenth-century Italian Judaism, encouraged his listeners to love Italy with all their "heart," all their "soul," and all their "faculties" without renouncing their Jewish identity.[27] These statements were accompanied by the activity of many rabbis of the Padua school in support of emancipation and the Risorgimento movement.[28]

Between 1848 and 1870 the process of emancipation affected the whole of Italian Jewry, with the exception of Trieste, which was part of the Hapsburg empire. With it came a rapid process of integration, clearly marked by the liberal content of the national idea of the Italian Risorgimento, by the importance of the preceding process of acculturation of Italian Jews, by the concrete experiences of the Risorgimento years that had helped to define the self-image of Italian Jews. All of these elements were powerful influences upon the development of the identity of postemancipation Italian Jewry and its progress up to the racial laws under Fascism.

In the wake of the achievement of national unification, Italian Jews, and especially the intellectual, economic, and social elites, enjoyed a situation that was especially favorable for their integration. In social terms, the concomitant formation of the Italian state and a middle class ensured equal opportunity of social advancement.[29] In juridical terms, from the 1848 *Statuto Piemontese* (the constitution that extended to the Italian Kingdom in 1861) to the 1871 Law of Guarantees, which regulated relations between Italy and the Holy Sea, this period saw the gradual acceptance of the idea of the equality of all faiths under the law.[30] In political terms, there was no foundation in newly unified Italy for an effective political utilization of anti-Semitism. Jews were few in number and they enjoyed a deep-rooted tradition of historic and social stability along with a solid process of acculturation. The visible features of their religious diversity were limited and confined to the home.[31] Their participation in the general effort to build a new state was based on their allegiance to the values of a religion of the liberal Savoy fatherland.[32] Anti-Semitism remained basically alien to the political views of the bourgeoisie and the ruling classes. The main anti-Jewish demonstrations in this phase emerged from Catholic milieus. Bound up with theological motives, Catholic anti-Semitism in those years took on new political motives in the context of the dispute pitting the Vatican and the Catholic world against the Italian state, as well as the spread of anticlericalism, secularism, and freemasonry. It did not result in a political phenomenon of any importance due to the detachment or hostility of the Catholics toward the liberal state,[33] although its presence helps one to understand the difficulty, as the historian Roberto Finzi writes, "– aside from any personal beliefs – that the liberal ruling class encountered in considering a nationalistic utilization of anti-Semitism,"[34] even though serious and disturbing disputes did take place in the first decades following unification.[35]

On the whole, however, these episodes did not represent significant obstacles to the process of integration. Keenly aware of their contribution to the cause of the Risorgimento, reinforced by a solid process of acculturation, and strengthened by their awareness of the liberal values of the new state and ruling class as well as Catholic opposition to that state and ruling class, Italian Jews felt they were part of the Italian middle class, engaged in the construction of the new state.[36] Accordingly, they developed, in the context of these conditions, their own integrationist program that entailed the replacement of their aspiration to a mythical homeland set sometime in the future with the concrete reality of a European homeland[37] and the limitation of Judaism to the strictly religious dimension. These values informed their lives, in keeping with a self-image that, alongside various sources of strength, presented certain structural factors of weakness. The narrow confines of liberal-national public opinion and the hostility of the Catholic world to the liberal state, which at this point represented important factors in the Jewish image and self-image as a component of the Italian middle class, would reveal their negative consequences when Catholics entered the political life of the state and the explosion of mass society helped to engender a crisis in the state founded in the Risorgimento and the idea of nation that had driven it.

Despite the pressures emerging from the context for a disregard of Jewish tradition, following unification the integrationist approach of postemancipated Italian Jews did not necessarily entail a renunciation of Jewish identity. In December 1875, *Il Vessillo Israelitico*, long considered a supporter of assimilation trends, set forth its platform, proclaiming "Neither isolation, nor fusion."[38] *Il Vessillo Israelitico* supported a confessional Judaism that tried to combine the national identification of its future with the universalistic vocation of its values and tradition.

Research on these topics does not yet provide a complete reconstruction of the religious orientations and attitudes, or of the relationship with tradition, of Italian Judaism in the last third of the nineteenth century. In any case it seems possible to deduce from the studies and documents now available that, until the turn of the twentieth century, observance of the rites of passage was largely respected, that the preference for marrying within the religion had not yet been broadly undercut by the spread of mixed marriages,[39] and that the social and economic life of Italian Jews largely took place within the context of a traditional family network.[40]

Certainly, participation in a new social context did much to undercut respect for religious practice. Yet Italian Judaism, as has been authoritatively observed, managed to reduce its religious observance without eliminating the content of its tradition,[41] preserving a heritage of values and culture that remained available and could always be recovered once the crisis had passed. Consequently, what we should investigate is not so much a decline in religious observance, but rather the causes of what was seen as the growing inadequacy of the available Jewish religious identity in the face of the progress of processes of integration and acculturation.

It is in this context that we should reconsider the growing denunciations of the decline of religious feeling and the crisis of Italian Jewish identity at the end of the nineteenth century. A reading of the Jewish press and pamphlets of the period offers above all an image of Judaism in crisis, a Judaism that had lost its absolute value. These contemporary Jewish writings also reveal a nostalgia for a world that was vanishing and condemnation of those abandoning traditional forms of social behavior in the face of the temptations of a lay and secular modernization, following different paths in the various economic, social, geographic, and sexual contexts of the time. All of these contexts, however, betrayed the same sense of disquiet that derived from the apparent inadequacy of Jewish religious identity that was available. This uneasiness involved cultural and political personalities, Italian Jewish women who were prominent in the struggle for the emancipation of women,[42] but also the middle and lower-middle classes who were profoundly integrated into the economic and social life of the country. The problem becomes a matter of identifying the difficulties assailing an identity that had long modeled itself on the forms of Catholic worship as practiced by the Italian middle class, exemplified by the monumental synagogue-cathedrals built at the end of the nineteenth century.[43] This crisis of identity was now challenged by the ideas and concerns of freethinkers, rationalists, socialists, and the criticisms of a culture that stigmatized Judaism and the Jews as holdovers of an archaic identity rendered obsolete by the progress of reason and science.

In order to understand the late-nineteenth-century crisis of Italian Jewish religious identity, we must call upon the larger context of dominant cultural references upon which Jews relied as well. At the end of the nineteenth century, Italy was still a country with a weak tradition of anti-Semitism. Secular culture was nevertheless increasingly pervaded with a bitter, corrosive critique of Judaism, often based on the stereotypes of the Enlightenment's antireligious polemic. This critique, underlined by the negative image and low esteem accorded to Judaism, one that a number of Jews internalized, exerted further pressure on Jews to abandon Judaism.[44] Powerful voices in the larger cultural debate on positivism, scientism, agnosticism, and faith in progress only increased the pressure, culminating in an aspiration to a higher form of religious feeling, a synthesis of traditional religions that would render them obsolete.[45] In some cases this path leading away from Judaism found its final destination in freemasonry.[46]

Certainly, this reconstruction of the Italian Jewish identity emphasizes certain aspects of the process of integration, selectively viewing social strata and focusing on the attitudes of political and cultural personalities, white-collar and intellectual middle class, rather than the vast numbers of small shopkeepers and the poor and proletarians found especially in Rome and Leghorn. The latter were often bound up with a more traditional identity and relied upon the charitable and educational structures of the Jewish community for their day-to-day survival.[47] All the same, this reconstruction seems basically sound and substantially indicative of the views of most Italian Jews.

Significantly, Arnaldo Momigliano wrote, "It is my impression that the transition from the ghetto to the upper classes took place more frequently among

Jewish families through entry into civil service and the university than through any successful practice of business."[48] This is an important and significant observation that would require the support of proper statistical evidence but that is partially confirmed by recent studies that document modalities and typologies of the identification of Italian Jews in the nation state.[49] Examples are offered not only by the figures of politicians, but also by the vast array of military people, public officials, school teachers, and university professors that populated the Jewish communities following emancipation. The Jewish press trumpeted the latter figures as evidence and models of the process of integration, characterizing them as representative images of the Jewish condition and the Jewish destiny.[50] These personalities and functions took on in some circumstances an emblematic value, as in the case of Shemuel David Luzzatto's pupil and friend Graziadio Isaia Ascoli (1829–1907), who became the founder of modern Italian linguistics,[51] or Ludovico Mortara (1855–1937), son of the chief rabbi of Mantua,[52] who was the first chief justice of Italy's highest court (the Court of Cassation), a minister of justice and of religions, and subsequently deputy prime minister of the Kingdom of Italy (1919–20).[53] Mortara was just one emblematic figure among the many jurists of Jewish descent who contributed to the foundation of the legal system in postunification Italy.[54] Italian Jews thus played central roles in building the two crucial pillars of the idea of the nation and the construction of a state: language and law.

These phases in the process of Jewish integration into the life of the Italian state and society helped to define and reinforce the idea of the Jewish self as part of a national bourgeoisie that had been central to the period of the Risorgimento. These events encouraged Jewish participation in the construction of the state, as well as an energetic participation in political currents and cultural movements, the ideal trends of Italian society. One long-term effect of this development was to restrict Jewish religious identity to a private practice. The decisive problem for Italian Judaism, fifty years after emancipation, was constructing a new and vital identity, capable of fitting into the program of nationalization entailed by emancipation and also compatible with the demands of a modern society and culture. From this point of view, the appearance of Zionism was decisive in Italy as well. In 1848, modernization was synonymous with Italianization. Fifty years later, when Italian Jewry risked even a total loss of identity, Zionism could offer a way out of the crisis in a Jewish context.

When it first became popular in Italy, Zionism, because of its philanthropic nature and its goal of rescuing the persecuted Jews of Eastern Europe who lacked a "fine and noble" country like Italy, appealed to many members of the Italian

Jewish professional and entrepreneurial middle class as a tool that could assist in the modernization of Jewish identity without undercutting allegiance to the homeland.[55]

Il Corriere Israelitico, an Italian-language newspaper published in Trieste by Dante Lattes (1876–1965), a major figure in the history of Zionism and Jewish culture in Italy, noted the fundamentally political nature of Zionism and its importance in restoring Jewish identity.[56] Soon enough, through the involvement of various intellectual and social elites, Zionism began to offer a number of solid responses to the crisis of Jewish religious identity in Italy. Zionism also worked to undercut the self-image that emancipated Italian Jewry had constructed for itself.

In fact, in the first fifteen years of the twentieth century, a revival of Jewish life and culture took shape in Italy, and its importance far outweighed the limited numbers of its participants. This revival was based in Florence, the new site of the Italian rabbinical college from 1899. It boasted the presence of such teachers as Hirsch Perez Chajes (1876–1927), and Shmuel Zvi Hirsch Margulies (1858–1922), supporters of Zionism and proponents of a solid Jewish culture. It was encouraged by the vigorous rebirth then underway of Jewish journalism, with such periodicals as Lattes's *Il Corriere Israelitico* and *La Settimana Israelitica*, founded in Florence in 1910. It also involved a substantial and significant group of young intellectuals, beginning with the students of the college. They focused on the function of Zionist ideology as an incentive for a return to Judaism, as a way to win back Jewish culture (history, language, and tradition) and thus Jewish identity.[57] In particular, *La Settimana Israelitica* issued an appeal to young people and urged them to discover their own (confused) Jewish awareness[58] and acknowledge that they were "a living force, not an anachronism; an active virtue, not a prejudice."[59]

The message launched by the youth movement, which was presented to the placid but stagnant waters of emancipated Italian Jewry, acquired a shattering value of rupture and renewal. These young people took concrete action in the form of three conferences (October 1911, December 1912, and February 1914), which opened up new opportunities for social interaction and provided important forums for cultural discussion on an array of Jewish topics. All this was conducted in the context of cultural Zionism and, for some, integral Judaism, offering a place in the limelight for several of the most representative figures, from Dante Lattes to Alfonso Pacifici (1889–1983).

The role that the so-called youth movement played was to change the function of Zionism in Italy from a philanthropic instrument to an ideology for the renewal of Jewish identity and the recovery of Jewish culture. Historically, Zionism's function appears to have been essential, even though its boundaries were limited and its members an elite. Moreover, the effervescence these initiatives triggered was dampened by the outbreak of war in Europe in 1914 and the subsequent entry of Italy into the war in May 1915. Italy's entry into World War I absorbed the psychic and physical energies of the nation at large, as well of course as the Jewish community.

As I have argued in earlier studies, World War I marked a decisive break in the history of Italian Jewry too. The majority of Italian Jews responded to the country's entry into war with feverish demonstrations of patriotism, filling in the shortcomings of their religious identity with the content of a national identification powerfully marked by the values and forms of the Risorgimento and an allegiance to the Savoy monarchy, which had provided equality and liberty. Participation in World War I was thus experienced as a moment of consecration in the process of Italianization, sealed by the blood shed on the field of battle. National and patriotic identification became the prevalent content of identity that restricted the space available for a Jewish identity conceived increasingly as a secondary and private religious practice.

The leading figures of the youth movements in favor of Jewish and Zionist renewal were also loyal supporters of their nation in wartime. These young Zionists nonetheless did not fail to point out in the general context of wartime tragedies the more specific tragedies that befell the Jews, who had been summoned to participate in a war against their brothers and to support with weapons even nations that would deny them the most basic rights. In keeping with this viewpoint, several of these personalities encouraged activities in favor of equal rights for the oppressed Jews of eastern Europe, progressively involving as well a number of Italian Jewish leaders. These Italian Jews gradually expanded their plans, finally attempting to link the objectives of Zionism to Italian aspirations for a more active role in the Mediterranean and the Near East.[60]

Aside from the question of their substance, these projects are clear indicators of the modifications under way in terms of the identity and values of Italian Judaism, modifications that had been significantly supported by the youth movement and accelerated by the outbreak of war, with all its implications. As one moderate member of the Italian Jewish leadership put it, the period following the Balfour Declaration and World War I brought plenty of new developments for Italian Jews as well, requiring them to reconcile Jewish "national feeling" and "religious observance."[61]

The setting of this new phase of the eternal debate over Jewish identity was nonetheless quite different from the context in which the emancipation and integration of the Jews in Italy had taken place. The crisis that swept away the liberal state in the years following the First World War dissolved values and structures that had accompanied the process of emancipation. This was clearly indicated by the growing political and cultural power of the nationalist movement, driven by certain anti-Semitic impulses as early as 1911, and marked by an idea of nation that sharply contrasted with the liberal one of the Risorgimento. The same period also saw the growing political integration of the Catholics who founded a party that sought to reconstitute Italian society in a Democratic and Christian context.[62]

Certainly, in the Italian crisis of the period immediately following the war, anti-Semitism played no political role. It did not form part of the original Fascist ideology. Italian Jews generally behaved like their fellow citizens, supporting the various parties on the right and left. They did find it necessary, however, to consider their own identity in relation to the new condition of Judaism in the world and to the new situation in Italy, one marked by the dismantling of the liberal state and the incipient construction of an authoritarian state. While most of Italian Jewry continued its life with no particular concern, there were significant attempts to form responses to these new demands. A quest for new forms of Jewish identity characterized the fourth youth assembly, held in Leghorn in 1924, ten years after the last assembly. Different options were considered in the course of that assembly during a passionate and heated discussion: Alfonso Pacifici, from an integral Jewish standpoint, proclaimed the need to return to divine law, in order to find a Jewish solution to the many problems facing them, and expressed a turning inward in the face of the generalized violence of Italian society; Enzo Sereni (1905–44) pointed the way to a Zionist and socialist rebirth in Palestine, a path that he would personally pursue three years later; Nello Rosselli (1900–37) drew a link between the values of his Jewish identity and the need to struggle for liberty; Joseph Colombo (1897–1975) pointed out the imperative to prepare for the defense of the Jews' cultural and educational heritage in view of the assimilationist and Palestine-centric orientation of Italian Zionists at a time when the liberal state was being demolished and a return to confessional orientations loomed on the horizon.[63]

These differing viewpoints were to constitute the framework upon which Italian Jewish life and thought would develop over the years that followed; that is, in a lively, intense, and finally dramatic exchange of views which extends beyond the chronological boundaries of this chapter.

It is, in any case, important to emphasize that, despite the absence of anti-Semitism in the ideology and the behavior of the new Fascist regime, Italian Jews were obliged to rethink their position in the larger national context. As new studies and documents show, by the mid-1920s, these problems were at the center of the concerns of a number of rabbinical and community leaders, especially

Angelo Sacerdoti, the chief rabbi of Rome. These leaders tried to develop a strategy for adapting to the new regime, which foresaw Jewish collaboration in Fascist Mediterranean policy without sacrificing their dignity or Zionist aspirations while taking advantage of the Fascist government's reorganization of the state, with its ecclesiastic and religious policies, to encourage a reform of the juridical regulation of Jewish communities. Such reforms would make it possible to provide a solution to the organizational and administrative problems that remained unsolved following unification.[64]

In terms of the development of the contents of Jewish identity, this ambitious project, which is still only barely hinted at in recent studies, seems to have been prompted by the desire to both preserve a Jewish identity rooted in Italian culture and in the Italian state, without renouncing Zionism's new lessons, which appealed by now to at least a part of the Jewish leadership. This was an intriguing plan in the Italy of this period, indicative of the transformations under way, but based on an insufficient evaluation of the new developments of Fascism and its ideological and cultural stratifications. Certainly, in the years in which the authoritarian state was constructed, this project might have posed, alongside the risk of conflict, at least some possibilities of seconding the interests of Fascist politics. That possibility was swept away by the accelerating process of constructing the totalitarian state in the second half of the 1930s. It was at this time that the Jew became the negative model par excellence in the creation of the new Fascist Italian, and Jewish identity, stripped of its rich variety, was reduced by law to the least common denominator of biological affiliation. The Fascist regime thus undertook the eradication of the rich and variegated identity that had been created by Italian Jews over the course of a centuries-long process of original acculturation.

Translated from the Italian by Antony Shugaar

NOTES

1. S. Della Pergola, "La popolazione ebraica in Italia nel contesto ebraico globale," in *Storia d'Italia: Annali 11 Gli ebrei in Italia*, Vol. 2 (Turin: Einaudi, 1997), 905 (Henceforth cited as *Gli ebrei in Italia*). In the first case, 0.2 percent; in the second, 0.1 percent.

2. For this aspect of my research, see M. Toscano, *Ebraismo e antisemitismo in Italia. Dal 1848 alla guerra dei sei giorni* (Milan: Franco Angeli, 2003), 316. I shall refer very often to this work in this chapter.

3. See P. Bernardini, "The Jews in nineteenth-century Italy: Towards a reappraisal," *Journal of Modern Italian Studies*, vol. 1, no. 2 (Spring 1996), 292. Useful information

about these years can be found in A. Milano, "Gli Enti culturali ebraici in Italia nell'ultimo trentennio (1907–1937)," *La Rassegna mensile di Israel*, vol. XII, no. 6 (February–March 1938), 253–4, and "Un secolo di stampa periodica ebraica in Italia," *La Rassegna mensile di Israel*, vol. XII, no. 7–9 (April–June 1938), 96–133, which depicted the postemancipation period as a dull time, devoid of inspiration and basically stripped of identity, exemplified by the experience of *Il Vessillo Israelitico*; a different interpretation of the role played by this periodical was recently ventured by B. Di Porto in his "Il giornalismo ebraico in Italia. Un primo sguardo d'insieme al *Vessillo Israelitico*," *Materia Giudaica*, vol. 6, no. 1 (2001). A. Milano, *Storia degli ebrei italiani* (Turin: Einaudi, 1963), 362, 370, in any case was also responsible for the delineation of the new characteristics acquired by the history of the Jews following the emancipation of 1848–70 and for many years constituted the only point of reference available for any interpretative and methodological discussion. A. M. Canepa, "Emancipazione, integrazione e antisemitismo liberale in Italia. Il caso Pasqualigo," *Comunità* 174 (June 1975), 191, described the period following emancipation as the "history of a progressive ethnic and cultural, though not religious, self-extinction."

4. For more on this interpretation, see S. Foà, *Gli ebrei nel Risorgimento italiano* (Assisi-Rome: Carucci, 1978), 76; A. Momigliano, "Recensione a Cecil Roth, Gli Ebrei in Venezia," in *Pagine ebraiche*, ed. A. Momigliano, foreword by S. Berti (Turin: Einaudi, 1987), 237–9, and the discussion I set forth in M. Toscano, "Risorgimento ed ebrei: alcune riflessioni sulla 'nazionalizzazione parallela,'" *La Rassegna mensile di Israel*, vol. LXIV, no. 1 (January–April 1998), 59–70 (now in Toscano, *Ebraismo e antisemitismo*, 13–23, from which I took the passages shown here and the bibliographic references).

5. Concerning the lack of statistical data, see A. M. Canepa, "Emancipazione, integrazione e antisemitismo," 191–4; some interesting figures on dissociations and abjurations from 1857 to 1942 in F. Del Regno, "Gli ebrei a Roma tra le due guerre mondiali: fonti e problemi di ricerca," *Storia contemporanea*, vol. 23, no. 1 (February 1992), 62–7.

6. For more on this line of interpretation, see Bernardini, "The Jews in nineteenth-century Italy," p. 295, and the observations that I set forth in Toscano, *Ebraismo e antisemitismo*, pp. 14–15 and in M. Toscano, Introduction to Toscano, ed., *Integrazione e identità. L'esperienza ebraica in Germania e Italia dall'Illuminismo al fascismo* (Milan: F. Angeli, 1998), 11–20.

7. Gramsci's observations appear, among other places, in A. Momigliano, *Pagine ebraiche*, 241–242. To set this issue against its background, see F. Sofia, "Su assimilazione e autocoscienza ebraica nell'Italia liberale," in *Italia Judaica. Gli ebrei nell'Italia unita 1870–1945* (Rome: Ministero per i beni culturali e ambientali, Ufficio centrale per i beni archivistici, 1993), 33, and F. Izzo, "'I Due Mondi' Tatiana Schucht, Antonio Gramsci e Piero Sraffa sulla questione ebraica," *Studi Storici*, vol. 34, no. 2–3 (April–September 1993), 657–85.

8. See Toscano, *Ebraismo e antisemitismo*, 16; Momigliano, *Pagine ebraiche*, 237–239. Concerning the relationship between acculturation and the national integration of Italian Jews, see L. Dubin, "Trieste and Berlin: The Italian Role in the Cultural Politics of the Haskalah," in *Toward Modernity: The European Jewish Model*, J. Katz, ed. (New Brunswick and Oxford: Transaction Books, 1987), 209. See also E. Artom, "Per una storia

degli ebrei nel Risorgimento," *Rassegna Storica Toscana*, vol. XXIV, no. 1 (January–June 1978), 138–9.

9. See P. Bernardini, "The Jews in nineteenth-century Italy," 292–3; M. Toscano, *Ebraismo e antisemitismo*, 17; M. Caffiero, "Tra Chiesa e Stato. Gli ebrei italiani dall'età dei Lumi alla Rivoluzione," in *Gli ebrei in Italia*, vol. 2, 1092–3, 1129–30.

10. Toscano, *Ebraismo e antisemitismo*, 18. Cfr. inoltre P. Bernardini, *La sfida dell'uguaglianza. Gli ebrei a Mantova nell'età della rivoluzione francese* (Rome: Bulzoni, 1996), 251–4; Bernardini, "The Jews in nineteenth-century Italy," 293–4; R. Romeo, *Italia mille anni* (Florence: Le Monnier, 1981), 39; A. Scirocco, *L'Italia del Risorgimento* (Bologna: Il Mulino, 1990), 8, 9, 26, 27; Toscano, introduction to *Integrazione e identità*, ed. Toscano, 15–18.

11. Dubin, "Trieste and Berlin," in *Towards Modernity*, 190. Speaking about the Jews of Trieste, Gorizia, and Gradisca, she writes: "Their horizons, like those of other Italian Jews in the eighteen and ninteenth centuries, included Western Europe and the Mediterranean. But their location 'on the German-Italian frontier' gave these northerners a special role, [a] conduit between Central Europe and Italy. Geographic proximity, direct Habsburg rule, economic and family ties brought them within the Central European orbit, while language and culture reinforced their extensive family and economic ties to Italian communities. Thus, culturally Italian and politically Austrian, the Jews of Trieste and environs show in microcosm the interaction between Italian-Jewish traditions and realities, and Central European policy and ideologies."

12. Dubin, "Trieste and Berlin," in *Towards Modernity*, 203.

13. Ibid., 209. Dubin, pp. 193–4, notes that Trieste established contact with Berlin on themes of the Enlightenment, for the organization of state-supported Jewish schools, in compliance with rules established by Hapsburg policy in 1781. On the subject of the Jewish school, see also T. Catalan, *La Comunità ebraica di Trieste (1781–1914)* (Trieste: LINT, 2000), 148–55 and S. Foà, *Gli ebrei nel Risorgimento italiano*, 35–36, who underscores the importance of the study of Italian history and literature in the Collegio Foà of Vercelli, between the late twenties and the early thirties. See also M. Del Bianco Cotrozzi, *Il Collegio Rabbinico di Padova*, Introduction by P. C. Ioly Zorattini (Florence: L. S. Olschki, 1995), 55, which discusses an age-old tradition of the coexistence of Jewish studies and secular culture.

14. Cotrozzi, *Il Collegio Rabbinico di Padova*, 32, 109; A. Milano, *Storia degli ebrei italiani*, 375 and 621.

15. Cotrozzi, *Il Collegio Rabbinico di Padova*, 25–6, 61, 66–7.

16. G. Luzzatto Voghera, "Aspetti della cultura ebraica in Italia nel secolo XIX," in *Gli ebrei in Italia*, vol. 2, 1215–17.

17. Ibid., 1219. See also Cotrozzi, *Il Collegio Rabbinico di Padova*, 46–9, 57–8; concerning the personality and the role of I. S. Reggio, see Cotrozzi, 86, 90–1, 93–103; on Shadal see Cotrozzi, 216–27.

18. Cotrozzi, *Il Collegio Rabbinico di Padova*, 147–8, 151–2.

19. Ibid., 275.

20. Cfr. Foà, *Gli ebrei nel Risorgimento italiano*, 35–6; and Momigliano, *Pagine ebraiche*, 134–6.

21. Cfr. F. Della Peruta, "Gli ebrei nel Risorgimento fra interdizioni ed emancipazioni," in *Gli ebrei in Italia*, vol. 2, 1135–67.

22. See F. Sofia, *Reminiscenze bibliche del Risorgimento italiano*, report to the Conference "Tra Stato multinazionale e Stato nazionale: ebrei in Austria e in Italia (1848–1918)," Trent, November 6–7, 1997 (typescript).

23. F. Della Peruta, "Gli ebrei nel Risorgimento fra interdizioni ed emancipazioni," in *Gli ebrei in Italia*, vol. 2, 1154, 1156–62.

24. A. M. Canepa, "L'atteggiamento degli ebrei italiani davanti alla loro seconda emancipazione: premesse e analisi," *La Rassegna mensile di Israel*, vol. XLIII, no. 9 (September 1977), 419–36, according to which, after unification, the assimilationist positions triumphed. But see also the views of P. Bernardini, "The Jews in nineteenth-century Italy," 299.

25. See the recent contributions by T. Catalan, "La 'primavera degli ebrei.' Ebrei italiani del Litorale e del Lombardo Veneto nel 1848–1849," and by C. Ferrara degli Uberti, "La questione dell'emancipazione ebraica nel biennio 1847–1848: note sul caso livornese," both of which appear in *Zakhor*, vol. 6 (2003), respectively on pages 35–66 and 67–91.

26. Cited in R. Di Segni, *Le origini del sionismo in Italia*, Introduction by Sandro U. Servi (Florence: Centro giovanile ebraico di Firenze, 1972), 10–11; G. Luzzatto Voghera, *Il prezzo dell'eguaglianza. Il dibattito sull'emancipazione degli ebrei in Italia (1781–1848)* (Milan: Angeli, 1998), 96; M. Procaccia, "Maggioranza e minoranza: dialettica storico-culturale nelle carte private: il caso dell'archivio di Samuele David Luzzatto," in *Il futuro della memoria*, (Rome: Ministero per i Beni culturali e Ambientali, 1997), 582.

27. C. Ferrara degli Uberti, "La questione dell'emancipazione ebraica," 87–8. In the same line, Benamozegh wrote, in a letter to Isacco Artom, Cavour's secretary, dated May 18, 1876, that the Piedmontese statesman was the "Italian Moses." Cited in F. Del Regno, "Un archivio ottocentesco: le carte di Isacco Artom presso il Centro Bibliografico," *La Rassegna mensile di Israel*, vol. LXIV, no. 1 (January–April 1998), 22. Regarding Benamozegh, see Voghera, "Aspetti della cultura ebraica in Italia," 1226–8.

28. A. Ravenna, "La scuola rabbinica di Padova e il Risorgimento italiano," *La Rassegna mensile di Israel* vol. XXXIII, no. 7 (July 1957), 315–16; and Cotrozzi, *Il Collegio Rabbinico di Padova*, 249, 250, 254, 256, 270–1, 289–90.

29. See M. Meriggi, "Bourgeoisie, Burgertum, borghesia : i contesti sociali dell'emancipazione ebraica," in *Stato nazionale ed emancipazione ebraica*, F. Sofia and M. Toscano, ed. (Rome: Bonacci, 1992), 157; F. Sofia, "Su assimilazione e autocoscienza ebraica nell'Italia liberale," 35; F. Sabatello, "Trasformazioni economiche e sociali degli ebrei in Italia nel periodo dell'emancipazione," in *Italia Judaica*, 120.

30. See C. Ghisalberti, "Sulla condizione giuridica degli ebrei in Italia dall'emancipazione alla persecuzione: spunti per una riconsiderazione," in *Italia Judaica*, 19–31.

31. R. De Felice, *Storia degli ebrei italiani sotto il fascismo* (Turin: Einaudi, 1993), 21–2; A. M. Canepa, "Cattolici ed ebrei nell'Italia liberale (1870–1915)," in *Comunitá* (April 1978), 43–53; M. Toscano, "Gli ebrei in Italia dall'emancipazione alle persecuzioni," *Storia contemporanea* 17, no. 5 (October 1986), 916.

32. M. Toscano, "L'uguaglianza senza diversità: Stato, società e questione ebraica nell'Italia liberale," in Toscano, *Ebraismo e antisemitismo*, 26–7.

33. See De Felice, *Storia degli ebrei italiani sotto il fascismo*, 29, 31–43; Canepa, "Cattolici ed ebrei nell'Italia liberale," 54–5, 61, 106; R. Moro, "L'atteggiamento dei cattolici tra teologia e politica," in *Stato nazionale ed emancipazione ebraica*, Sofia and Toscano, eds., 321–2, 325, 326–9, 331, 335, 338. and Toscano, *Ebraismo e antisemitismo*, 27.

34. R. Finzi, "Gli ebrei nella società italiana dall'unità al fascismo," *Il Ponte*, vol. XXXIV, no. 11–12 (November–December 1978), 1392.

35. Toscano, *Ebraismo e antisemitismo*, 27–33.

36. D. V. Segre, "L'emancipazione degli ebrei in Italia," in *Integrazione e identità*, ed. Toscano, 106–9.

37. J. Eisenberg, *Une histoire du peuple juif* (Paris: Fayard, 1974), 462.

38. F. Servi, "Ai nostri lettori," *Il Vessillo Israelitico* (December 1875), 353: "The sociability of Judaism is written in indelible characters in the inspired pages of the Bible; the Mosaic religion has principles and a morality that does not shrink in the face of the most advanced civilization, the most elevated forms of progress. But these principles must be carried out, diffused . . . , but this handful of believers in the One God, bound to a covenant, certainly of the moral triumph toward which it is advancing, feels a need for its dogmas to be known, along with its history, the life that it leads in the midst of the peoples of which it forms part, and to which invisibly, amazingly it blazes a path of industriousness, hard work, and the indomitable strength that withstands time, martyrdom, and achieves that which it wishes."

39. Useful information on these subjects is provided by L. Allegra, "La comunità ebraica di Torino attraverso gli archivi di famiglia," in Comunità Israelitica di Torino ed., *Ebrei a Torino. Ricerche per il centenario della sinagoga 1884–1984* (Turin: Allemandi, 1984), 34. See also the account of A. Rosselli, *Memorie*, M. Calloni, ed. (Bologna: Mulino, 2001), 52, 69, 84, 92, 119–20, 124, 127–30; and *Il Bat Mitzwà nelle Comunità Italiane* (Rome: Litos, 2001), 24.

40. See I. Pavan, *Il comandante. La vita di Federico Jarach e la memoria di un'epoca* (Milan: Proedi Editore, 2001), 35, 58–60, 75–6, 77–8; G. Sapelli, "Sulla presenza ebraica nell'economia italiana. Note metodologiche," in Toscano, ed., *Integrazione e identità*, 41, 66.

41. Milano, *Storia*, 374; H. Stuart Hughes, *Prigionieri della speranza. Alla ricerca dell'identità ebraica nella letteratura italiana contemporanea*, trans. Valeria Lalli (Bologna: Mulino, 1983), 16–18, 24, 189. [Original English: *Prisoners of Hope: The Silver Age of the Italian Jews, 1924–1974* (Cambridge, Mass.: Harvard University Press, 1983).]

42. On the subject of Italian Jewish women, see M. Miniati, *Les "Emancipées": Les femmes juives italiennes aux XIX° et XXe siècles (1848–1924)* (Paris: Honoré Champion, 2003), 152–67.

43. R. Bonfil, "La Sinagoga in Italia come luogo di riunione e di preghiera," in *Il Centenario del Tempio Israelitico di Firenze* (Florence: Giuntina, 1985), 36–44.

44. M. Toscano, *Ebraismo e antisemitismo*, 29–38.

45. R. De Felice, "Stato, società e questione ebraica nell'Italia unita," in *Stato nazionale*, 427–8.

46. B. Di Porto, "Dopo il Risorgimento, al varco del Novecento. Gli ebrei e l'ebraismo in Italia," and A. A. Mola, "Ebraismo italiano e massoneria," in *La Rassegna mensile di Israel*, vol. XLVII, no. 7–12 (July–December 1981), respectively pp. 22–4 and 120–2.

47. E. S. Artom, *La scuola ebraica in Italia. Relazione letta al 2° Convegno giovanile ebraico (Torino, 24 dicembre 1912)* (Florence: Giuntina, 1913), 13; M. Toscano, "Ebrei ed ebraismo nell'Italia della grande guerra. Note su una inchiesta del Comitato delle comunità israelitiche italiane del maggio 1917," in *Israel "Un decennio" 1974–1984 Saggi sull'ebraismo italiano*, F. Del Canuto, ed. (Rome, 1984), now in Toscano, *Ebraismo e antisemitismo*, 144, 148–9.

48. Momigliano, *Pagine ebraiche*, 138.

49. Aside from the essays by T. Catalan and C. Ferrara degli Uberti cited in note 26, interesting observations on the subject have been made by I. Pavan, *Il comandante*. Aside from these references, it should be pointed out that the subject of the contents of postemancipation Italian Jewish identity is present in much of the history and memoirs produced in recent years.

50. In this connection, the views expressed in *Il Vessillo Israelitico* seem emblematic, as A. Milano critically noted in his "Un secolo di stampa periodica ebraica in Italia," *La Rassegna mensile di Israel* (April–June 1938), 108.

51. Procaccia, "Maggioranza e minoranza," 581.

52. Cotrozzi, *Il Collegio Rabbinico di Padova*, 256.

53. S. Satta, "Pagine autobiografiche di Lodovico Mortara," in Salvatore Satta, ed., *Quaderni del diritto e del processo civile* (Padua: Cedam, I, 1969), 34–65.

54. See S. Mazzamuto, "Ebraismo e diritto dalla prima emancipazione all'età repubblicana," in *Gli ebrei in Italia*, vol. 2, 1767, 1822.

55. See "I nostri ideali," *L'Idea Sionista*, January 31, 1901; Toscano, *Ebraismo e antisemitismo*, 65, 67; S. Della Seta, "La comunità ebraica italiana dal sionismo alla rinascita d'Israele," in *Gli Ebrei, l'Italia e Israele*, "Quaderni de Il Risorgimento," Milano, undated, pp. 29–30.

56. T. Catalan, "Società e sionismo a Trieste fra XIX e XX secolo," in *Il mondo ebraico*, G. Todeschini and P. C. Ioly Zorattini, eds. (Pordenone: Studio tesi, 1991), 470.

57. M. Toscano, "Fermenti culturali ed esperienze organizzative della gioventù ebraica italiana (1911–1925)," *Storia contemporanea*, 13, no. 6 (December 1982), 915–61, reprinted in Toscano, *Ebraismo e antisemitismo*, 69–109.

58. "Appello ai giovani," in *La Settimana Israelitica* (July 14, 1911).

59. "Il Convegno giovanile," in *La Settimana Israelitica* (July 28, 1911).

60. See M. Toscano, "Gli ebrei italiani e la prima guerra mondiale (1915–1918): tra crisi religiosa e fremiti patriottici," *Clio* (January–March 1990), 79–97; also see "Ebrei ed ebraismo," both reprinted in Toscano, *Ebraismo e antisemitismo*, 110–22 and 123–54.

61. A. Colombo, "Facciamo gli ebrei," and "Facciamo gli ebrei. Il problema della scuola," *Il Vessillo Israelitico*, respectively December 15–31, 1917, and October 15–31, 1918.

62. E. Gentile, *Fascismo e antifascismo* (Florence: Le Monnier, 2000), chs. 1–2.

63. Toscano, *Ebraismo e antisemitismo*, 99–107.

64. M. Sarfatti, *Gli ebrei nell'Italia fascista* (Turin: Einaudi, 2000), 66–8, 70–1; Toscano, *Ebraismo e antisemitismo*, 166, 168–70; A. Calò, "La genesi della legge del 1930," *La Rassegna mensile di Israel*, vol. LI, no. 3 (September–December 1985), 334–402.

3 Mussolini and the Jews on the Eve of the March on Rome

Giorgio Fabre

European anti-Semitism at the beginning of the twentieth century is widely known. One need only cite the Dreyfus case, Vienna's mayor Karl Lüger, and the 1903 Kishinev pogrom. When analyzing the situation in Italy, however, there is one important factor we must bear in mind: although anti-Semitic groups and leanings did exist in those years, no such overt instances of anti-Semitism occurred in Italy in the nineteenth or early twentieth centuries. Nor was Italy's ruling class basically anti-Semitic.

The case of Mussolini was different.

I would like to cite, first, two hitherto unknown episodes. The first occurred in 1922. Between the November 26 and 30 of that year, Mussolini – who at the time was both prime minister and foreign minister – received a report from the embassy in Budapest. It said that the Hungarian ambassador to Rome, Albert Nemes, had intimated that Fascism would not be "strong and lasting" and would end up by endangering the monarchy. Mussolini wrote in the margin of the report, in French: "c'est un juif et idiot par dessus le marché" ("He is a Jew and an idiot to boot"). The remark was of no small consequence. The handwritten jotting is still there, in the margin of the report, and was therefore read by foreign ministry officials.[1] Mussolini was training his diplomatic service to become accustomed to his anti-Semitic leanings. The March on Rome had taken place only four weeks earlier.

The second episode took place a few months later at the end of August 1923[2] and involved the interior ministry. Mussolini had received a letter by a director of an important company, the Consorzio commerciale italiano. Its content was absolutely anti-Semitic. The author claimed to have some "very secret information" concerning the Communist government in Russia, indicating that it was "fighting against Fascism": the leader of this "silent action" was the "Great Rabbi" Judah Magnes, the founder of Yichud; also, the "chief agents" of Magnes were some well known "Jewish financiers" from different countries, namely Zacharov, Stinnes, and Toeplitz. Mussolini deemed the letter reliable and sent it to the chief of police, general Emilio De Bono, together with a note in which he wrote, "All the same, you should indicate that Stinnes is not a Jew, and Zakarov is a war profiteer, and belongs to the Orthodox Church." De Bono wrote on that same note, by way of instruction: "tenere presente" (keep for future reference). Thus, other ministry officials were sure to sense that Fascist leaders had a problem with Jews. At the same time, Mussolini was intimating that the question of Jews was one he knew how to handle properly. He could tell (supposedly, or rather let it be thought that he could) who was a Jew and who was not.

Actually, Mussolini had been a good anti-Semite since the end of the first decade of the century, when he was a young socialist. He continued to be an anti-Semite, and more openly, when he left the Italian Socialist Party (PSI) in 1914 at the age of thirty-one. There are few archival documents, but the articles he wrote – and not just those that are already widely known – are interspersed with frequent anti-Semitic utterances, as Angelo Ventura has pointed out.[3] These are even more numerous if one adds the articles not written by him but published in the newspaper he edited. Some of those sentences, as we will see immediately, are very gross indeed.

One instance is his well-known essay on the superman, written in 1908, with the long and notorious passages in which he railed against the "pallid Judeans" who "wrecked" the Roman Empire.[4] To Mussolini, Rome was at the time already a highly valued myth, and Jews – according to his theory – had brought about its ruin with their moral quibbling. Or, we would say nowadays, with their "decadent" ideas. The essay was written in polemical response to Claudio Treves, a socialist (and Jewish) member of parliament, who had excoriated Nietzsche's superman.

Another writing I would like to examine is a short story (yes, Mussolini wrote even short stories) in which he portrayed an appalling character who lived in a "ghetto" and had "the hooked nose of the true Semite." This was in 1909.[5] There is more. In July 1910, Mussolini insulted Prime Minister Luigi Luzzatti because of an excessively prudish directive on pornography he had issued. "He is old and he is Jewish" declared the young journalist: Jewish because (like the Jews of ancient Rome), he was beset by "moral concerns" and was ready to turn political somersaults.[6] In September 1913, Mussolini had progressed in his career. He was now editor of the socialist daily *Avanti!* In the pages of that important newspaper he again took up the motif of Jews and of the havoc they had wrought in ancient Rome.[7] But this time there was something new, expressed in the following sentence: "The immigration of Orientals causes the degeneration of the race, weakens it, prostrates it before new gods." Here he had added the notion of race.

True, this was cultural or ideological anti-Semitism. One must bear in mind, however, what Robert Michels, the scholar of political parties and politics, and Georges Sorel wrote at that time.[8] In their writings (which were well known to Mussolini) they both pointed to a serious problem within the European socialist parties: the great number of Jews in the socialist elite. Sorel, who was an anti-Semite, found that the problem was present in the Italian Socialist Party. In his view, Jewish leaders were far too influential and dangerous. According to Michels, this presence had led to anti-Semitic strife. What it amounted to, actually, was simply a struggle for power among the various leadership groups.

Mussolini's personal history as a socialist seems to have followed a similar pattern. He too was embroiled in a violent clash for power within the party, was defeated, and at the end of 1914 went on to found another newspaper, *Il Popolo d'Italia*. Some of his political enemies were Jews: Claudio Treves, Emanuele Modigliani, Elia Musatti, and even Alceste Della Seta. And were not, after all, the so-called "Jewish Bolshevik leaders" he reviled after the October Revolution[9] also part of European socialism?

As long as he remained a socialist, however, personally Mussolini did not openly display his anti-Semitism in his political skirmishes (the article in *Avanti!* seems to be an exception). This is easily understood. There were Jews in his faction as well. And quite influential ones at that, such as Angelica Balabanoff and the Sarfattis, husband and wife. In Italy, the anti-Jewish surge had not started as yet (it would begin four years later). If Mussolini had flaunted his anti-Semitism, he would have been ostracized.

His anti-Semitism surfaced instead in his new daily, *Il Popolo d'Italia*. Let me point out some instances. When the occasion arose, Mussolini did not hesitate to call the foreign minister Sonnino, a Jew, by the name of "Shylok" (March 1915).[10] In that same month of March 1915 there was the well-known quarrel with Claudio Treves, which ended in a furious duel with swords. The quarrel arose from an anti-Semitic insult, although of an extremely tortuous kind. The main point in Mussolini's attacks against Treves was the use of an undoubtedly offensive sobriquet: "palancagreca."[11] The meaning of the word is not entirely clear, but it somehow alluded to Treves's alleged greed for money of which Mussolini had supposedly been a witness. It was, in short, the traditional allegation against

Jews. Mussolini had reached the stage of the racist slur and invective. The stage of politics would be reached a few months later when the actual Fascist movement was founded in March 1919 and then grew into a political party.

There is one aspect I would like to elucidate at this point. In Italy Fascist anti-Semitism – as well as the anti-Semitism of the Nazis in Germany, of István Friedrich's National Christian Party in Hungary, and of Maurras's and Daudet's Action Française – received a crucial impulse, before and after the First World War, from the emergence of the issue of minorities in international politics. This issue then combined, in the various European nations, with other factors: the sense of having been wronged by the peace treaties, the violently contentious climate stirred up by war veterans' associations and movements that went under the name of "combattentismo," and a new and keen social and political awareness born in the trenches.

All political clashes on the issue of minorities revolved around the patchwork of races and religions that existed in the four empires, most prominently in the lands under Hapsburg rule, but also in the German, Russian, and former Ottoman empires. The rights of minorities were embraced and brandished mainly by those whose purpose was the dissolution of those empires. Mussolini himself, first as a journalist and then as editor-in-chief of the socialist daily *Il Popolo*, in Trento, and later in his book on the Trentino region, wielded the notions of race, racism, and minorities. It should be recalled indeed that in the Hapsburg Empire, Italians too were a minority. But, on the other side, we must consider that his ideas of "race" were conditioned by the conceptions of "classic racists" like Houston S. Chamberlain and Joseph Arthur de Gobineau, who had in mind an *ethnic* and *genetic* idea.[12]

After the end of the World War I those problems seemed to have found a solution mainly as a result of the intervention of President Wilson. Wilson brought pressure to bear on European states to obtain some guarantee on this point. He succeeded in the Treaty of Saint Germain, signed on September 10, 1919 by the Italian authorities too, which concerned the countries of the former Austrian empire. This international document mentioned – although in connection with only some of the countries formerly under Hapsburg rule – safeguards for the various "races," and did so by using precisely the term "race."

The balance among races was a typical American concern, and now an attempt was made to transfer it to Europe. In Europe – and in Italy too – were penetrated, in particular in some intellectual circles, conceptions of "race" elaborated by the classic racists. A different idea dominated those treaties, one that linked race to the conceptions of "people" and "nation." But, essentially, a subtle ambiguity remained between the two meanings in intellectual and political opinion, particularly in relation to the Jews.

Basically, the new balance among races in Europe amounted to this: a majority (whether racial, religious, or otherwise) and minorities were identified within each state, and the latter were granted safeguards. The majorities, however, provided tangible protection – legal, economic, and otherwise – to those minorities in other countries that were linked to them (Hungarians in Hungary, for instance, protected Hungarians in Romania, and so forth).[13]

Those treaties, although flawed in many ways, had a strong impact on European public opinion. And in Italy too; although it was a nation that was not regulated by any of those treaties, as winner of the war it had signed them in relation to the losing countries. And the themes of minorities in Italy were known very well. King Victor Emanuel III, for example, in an important speech before the Italian parliament on December 1, 1919, spoke explicitly of acting in "defence of populations of Italian race and language."[14] Mussolini expressed his approval. As we have seen, Mussolini knew well (and approved) the "genetic" meaning of the word "race," but in this period he preferred to use the "political" one, which, after the treaties, had imposed itself.

Among the minorities mentioned in the treaties were the Jews. They were, however, a minority that did not amount to a majority in any one country. Therefore, and mostly due to the efforts of President Wilson and of American Jews, the question of a Jewish National Home in Palestine, a settlement where Jews in theory could become a majority, began to be discussed concretely. Political Zionism thus attained formal international recognition. At the same time, the old idea took hold that Jews in the various nations were a "race" apart from the rest of the population.

In the geopolitical order that followed the war, Fascism (which was born in Italy and only some years later spread to other countries) too had to tackle the problems of minorities and of race. On these issues, and particularly on the issue of the "Italian race," it had been preceded by some groups of intellectuals, nationalists, and futurists. Eventually, however, Fascism appropriated the issue entirely and made it into its banner. Mussolini himself said so when he outlined the political program of the new party (July 1921).[15] The new issues in the order of the day were the "crucial problems of race" and "Italian expansion in the world."

This, then, is the complex context in which the issue of Jews was placed at this stage. The same word "race" had different meanings, a strong ambiguity that applied to the Jews as well. Moreover, this ambiguity was even stronger in Mussolini, who, since he was young, had known and accepted a "genetic" and "ethnic" (that is, "biological") concept of race, even if in the postwar period he flirted with the "nationalistic" concept of "people" and "nation." Anyway, to him the problem had an easy solution in Italy and with a reference to the treaties: indeed, Italy, in comparison with other European countries, had very slender minorities and, overall, "assimilated" ("assimilate"). "Between all the nations in the world Italy is the one more 'clearly' identified, from all points of view (. . .). Inside, 'alien' groups are very small and were assimilated."[16]

In this sense for Mussolini on the one hand Italian Jews could have been "Italian." On the other hand – and this was his real strong or, better, preconceived idea – they were a "different race," a concept he repeated many times. "Men of other race and of other mentality" in front of "a people like ours": in this way he defined the Jews in an article of July 1922.[17] In his first speech in the parliament, June 21, 1921, he was even sharper: if Palestine had transformed itself into a state, all the Jews living in other countries, Italy included, should have become "immediately" "foreigners."[18] Other minorities could be considered only "alien" groups, not the Jews. In his mind they had this double identity.

Within the Fascist movement and since its very beginnings, Mussolini had full authority on the subject. Even his first speech as a member of parliament was largely dedicated to Palestine and the Jews. He, and he only, dictated the Fascist party line. His considerations about (or against) the Jews therefore carried a compelling weight.

When Mussolini in *Il Popolo d'Italia* on June 4, 1919, published his famous piece ("The Accomplices," "I complici") against Jewish Bolshevik leaders whom he claimed had been financed by Jewish American bankers, the most notorious anti-Semite of the Fascist era, Giovanni Preziosi, was not yet a Fascist (he would become one only a year later, in May 1920) and not even an anti-Semite. Only when he joined the Fascist movement, in the middle of 1920, did Preziosi assume an openly anti-Semitic stance, on the advice of the liberal economist Maffeo Pantaleoni and, from a political point of view, probably of Mussolini himself. Thus, anti-Semitism spread from Mussolini to Preziosi, not the other way around. On the other hand, when Preziosi's magazine, *La Vita Italiana*, was transformed into an anti-Semitic publication, this took on for the Fascist movement and then for the National Fascist Party (PNF) a heavily anti-Jewish significance, which was reinforced when the magazine was joined by another anti-Semitic periodical, the *Rivista di Milano*. Robert Michels, sharp-eyed as usual, pointed this out immediately in December 1922.[19] Nor was he the only one to do so. The newspaper of the small and democratic Republican Party (the party inspired by Giuseppe Mazzini) made a very similar comment.[20] The symbolic climax in this anti-Jewish operation came a little later, on March 1, 1923, when the anti-Semite Pantaleoni was appointed senator under the first Mussolini-led government and at Mussolini's wish.[21] For the very first time in Italy, a party had an official or semiofficial anti-Semitic wing. When something similar had happened before the war in the Nationalist Association – a small "nationalist association" which, after the war, set up a real influent party – the "association" had split in two.[22]

Mussolini himself impressed a personal anti-Jewish mark upon Fascism: his devastating hostility against the Jewish political elite, first and foremost against the elite of the socialist or communist "enemy." Michels's intuition, that anti-Semitism was the result of a struggle within the socialist leadership, was borne out by Mussolini's course of action after he left the socialist party and founded a movement that was in some respects a competitor of the former. I will cite just two examples. The first is an article in *Il Popolo d'Italia* that followed a well-known leading article in the same paper about Bela Kun and the Jews typically supporting communism (October 19, 1920). *Il Popolo d'Italia* published some comments on this editorial, some written by Jews who were seething with rage. But there was also an alarming editorial comment (October 21) published in a column signed with a pseudonym sometimes used by Mussolini, "il fromboliere" (the slinger). It contained a list of socialist and communist leaders who were or were believed to be "Israelites": Treves, Modigliani, Ottolenghi, Musatti, and Della Seta. After stating, "they are mostly against Italy" and therefore un-Italian, the anonymous writer concluded, "Even without drawing antisemitic conclusions (. . .) it's worth giving it some thought."

Maybe Mussolini did not write these words, but they certainly were published with his permission. According to a document found by Michele Sarfatti, it was about that time, after all, that Mussolini informed Dante Lattes, the Italian Zionist leader, that those very socialist leaders, by giving their support to the communist revolutions, had offended his "racial pride as an Italian."[23]

The same ideas are to be found in the second article. Although this article is similarly anonymous and is not included in his *Opera Omnia* (Collected Works), it can nevertheless be attributed to Mussolini.[24] It is dated September 1, 1921, and in it Mussolini commented on the Zionist conference at Karlsbad, which had been attended by Dante Lattes and other Italian delegates. Alluding to them, Mussolini wrote that there were "Jews who are fed up with living [in Italy], which is something that does not trouble us in the least." The "anonymous" writer of *Il Popolo d'Italia* then added, If Italian – so-called Italian! – Zionists were to move elsewhere and take with them the whole pack of Treveses, Modiglianis, Musattis, Momiglianos, Sacerdotis (Genosse), Passiglis and that fine Mr. Ottolenghi who has regaled Italy with several strikes of the postal service, it would afford us great pleasure to expedite this 'exodus.'"[25]

Mussolini, as we have seen, had evinced against some Jewish political leaders an animosity based on race. This does not mean that he intended to impose a sweeping mass anti-Semitism. Mussolini was well aware that Italian Jews – many of whom had fought valiantly in the war – formed a highly regarded if small community (a great deal smaller than the communities living in Germany or in Hungary). And he also knew that it was deeply integrated. Moreover, he was trying to project an image of Fascism as a peace-bringing political force. For these reasons he proclaimed repeatedly, as early as this, that Fascism would not raise a "Jewish question." In another article, on October 19, 1920,[26] he wrote, "Italy knows no antisemitism and we believe that it will never know it." But he added – and this is far more significant – "Let us hope that Italian Jews will continue to be sensible enough so as not to give rise to antisemitism in the only country where it has never existed."[27]

It is true that Mussolini was not encouraging anti-Semitism in the above-cited article. But he nonetheless did not rule out that it might arise. On the one hand, there was an ongoing war against the Jewish political elite that Mussolini considered hostile. On the other, he rejected social anti-Semitism. This rejection, however, was not complete and did not hinder occasional anti-Semitic gestures. And the Jewish elite that needed to be fought tended somehow to expand very rapidly. In August and October 1922, *La Vita Italiana*, by now an ultra-Fascist and anti-Semitic publication, maintained that the "enemies" were to be found not just in political circles, but also in the higher echelons of state bureaucracy, among the academic intelligentsia and in prestigious public places.[28]

Three considerable problems remain to be considered: Jews in the Fascist leadership, Jews in the world of finance, and Zionism and the Zionists.

Mussolini and his minions tackled the first of these issues, Jews on the top levels of the Fascist leadership, shortly before the March on Rome. On September 23, 1922, on the first page of *Il Popolo d'Italia*, a press release appeared by the Direzione, that is, the executive of the PNF in response to an article in *Avanti!*[29] The socialist newspaper had pointed out a difference between Italian Fascism and the Hungarian Fascist movement of István Friedrich: whereas the Hungarian movement was exclusively anti-Semitic, "among the leaders" of Fascism, wrote *Avanti!*, there were also "men of the Jewish faith," such as Aldo Finzi and Dino Philipson. It might have been taken as a favorable comment. *Il Popolo d'Italia* chose instead to be affronted. The PNF press release denied what it called a "panzana colossale" (monstrous whopper). "Not one member of the party executive and almost none of the Fascist members of Parliament is Jewish, and of the two Italian MPs named by the said newspaper one [this referred to Philipson] is not even a Fascist."

On the issue of the "leaders" who were both Fascist and Jewish, then, the outlook was not at all reassuring. And, as a matter of fact, no Jew had ever held a truly leading post in the party. Gino Arias, the famous nationalist economist, who was a Jew and would receive the party membership card on May 1, 1923, was in fact invited to the momentous Fascist congress held in Naples on October 25, 1922.[30] But he was quite definitely only a guest. Mussolini himself wrote an extremely chilly and disconcerting letter concerning his invitation, saying that his participation was "not impossible."[31] Margherita Sarfatti's situation, around that time, was in many ways similar. Maybe she was indeed Mussolini's mistress. And in any case, her being a woman complicated things. In January 1922, when she had in fact a post of some importance, as the editor of the cultural review *Gerarchia* (of which Mussolini was the editor in chief), her name did not appear. She officially appeared as "direttore responsabile" (that is solely as the person legally responsible in front of authorities) only in February 1925.

Some Jews had indeed had a hand in launching the Fascist movement in 1919, but by 1922 the situation had changed. The most prominent among the "Jewish founders" of 1919, Piero Jacchia from Trieste, had left the party about a year earlier, for reasons that are not entirely known.[32] Two other prominent Jews who had been among the early followers of the Fascist movement had also left: the well-known entrepreneur Oscar Sinigaglia[33] and (probably) Nello Rosselli.[34] Both Rosselli and Jacchia died in the 1930s as anti-Fascists.

Many other Jews joined the movement before and after the founding of the PNF, which took place in November 1921. It was around this time, however, that the problem arose within a movement and a party which, for the first time in Italian history, included an official or semiofficial anti-Semitic wing. And there were those who would not forget the strong personal anti-Jewish stance of Mussolini himself.

The second issue related to the so-called "Jewish finance," that is, Italian Jewish financiers and bankers. According to *La Vita Italiana* and particularly to Pantaleoni, Jewish financiers were the greatest evil of all. And yet, surprising as it may seem, Mussolini never launched an all-out war against them. Toward Italian Jewish financiers and bankers (unlike toward their American counterparts, as we have seen) he was cautious. He almost certainly considered them untrustworthy, but he also believed that he could draw them over to his side.

One major problem was that of Banca Commerciale. This bank had come under heavy attack from several quarters during the war, because it was believed to be German and managed by Germans and therefore potentially a traitor. After the war, those very same "Germans," such as Giuseppe Toeplitz (who was actually Polish), became "Jews" and were attacked for taking part in the "Jewish conspiracy." Toeplitz, by the way, had been christened in 1890.

It is not yet clear if Commerciale had financed Mussolini during or after the First World War. It is possible that this was the case.[35] This much is certain, however: up to 1921, Commerciale advertised frequently in *Il Popolo d'Italia* as well as in Mussolini's personal magazine, *Gerarchia,* from January until July 1922. More important still, the newspaper always refrained from attacking Commerciale, even at the time when the famous confrontation between the bank and the Perrone brothers for the ownership of Ansaldo, the great metallurgic company, was at its peak. However, Mussolini's distrust toward Toeplitz and Commerciale was well known and was displayed quite openly on two occasions (his note to the chief of police, De Bono, as we have seen, is a further and secret instance). About the time of the March on Rome and then again in June 1923, Mussolini's newspaper – probably at his personal request – accused Commerciale for the lira's bad performance in the exchange market.[36] And yet, once those crises had blown over, when in 1924 it became necessary to find a financial institution that would grant a huge loan to Poland, Mussolini's choice fell on Commerciale, of all banks. True, the deal involved a considerable risk. On the other hand Toeplitz, who was Polish, as we have seen, was particularly interested in the deal, which carried an important public recognition.

With regard to the third issue, Zionism and Zionists, Mussolini had denounced Italian and non-Italian Zionists alike in his comment on the Karlsbad Conference of September 1, 1921. "Zionism has brought war and bolshevism to formerly untroubled territories; has unleashed opposition in the Arab and in the Christian world and, in the damnable event that it should reach its aims, it will in fact result in a new legal status for Jews in the western nations." Once he sat in parliament, Mussolini decided, in regard to Palestine, to align himself with the international policy of the Roman Catholic Church and to be hostile toward the British Empire. By the time he assumed office as prime minister in October 1922 he was therefore totally opposed to a Zionist settlement in Palestine. And yet when he met with Chaim Weizmann, two months after assuming power (on January 3, 1923), although he did express this hostility, he also showed himself willing to negotiate if concessions were made to Italy.[37]

To sum up, when Mussolini rose to power his position on the various issues was multifaceted. He was against Jews being in high places whether in politics or elsewhere – most of all, of course, within the PNF. He was however fully aware that some Jews possessed a strong sense of belonging to the nation. He was hostile to Zionism in general, but was ready to come to terms with it. He was accommodating with "Jewish" business enterprises that could be useful to him. Finally, he was basically opposed to a sweeping anti-Semitism, although he did not entirely rule it out.

The result was necessarily ambiguous. Mussolini's anti-Semitic leanings were strong and plainly discernible, but his action was erratic: this would remain so in the following years as well. On the one hand, Mussolini was exhibiting, even in his now official capacity, a deep hostility against Jews; on the other, while declaring his intention to hold in check the most virulent anti-Semitism, he did not disdain some aperture toward its blander varieties. This attitude was in many respects, especially if compared to the previous situation, both disconcerting and menacing.

Let me mention the following last episode. On assuming power, Mussolini was congratulated by the rabbi of Genoa. In his polite answer he wrote, "I rely on all those who love, in deed, Italy"; the emphasis was on those words "in deed," which clearly – and ominously – implied a request for some actual deeds.[38] Beneath an apparent balance, the static was precarious to say the least. It needed only a minimal shift to upset it and change the situation for the worse.

Mussolini's ideas on the subject were well known in Europe. The growth and rise to power of Fascism were an inspiration to several European anti-Semitic political parties. From France to Germany and Hungary, right-wing extremist and anti-Semitic movements hailed Mussolini's rise and his accession to power as a victory against Jews. But when in 1923 Hitler from Germany, at the time of the putsch, and Friedrich from Hungary appealed to Mussolini for help or even just for some kind of sign, they were both met with a curt refusal. Now that he was prime minister, Mussolini acted in foreign politics as he had in domestic affairs and refused to lend support to political anti-Semitism. This caused, after 1923, some resentment against him among other European racists, most notably in Alfred Rosenberg.[39]

That refusal was of little use. It took Hitler another ten years, but eventually he rose to power, always looking to Mussolini as his guiding light. Something similar happened in Hungary and in France. But in 1923 the leader of Fascism had indeed opposed these movements. Once again he had chosen caution: he had preferred to keep an open dialogue with the persons ruling those countries (who in some cases, such as Count Bethlen in Hungary, were themselves anti-Semites), rather than rush into awkward adventures with ragtag opposition parties that at the time seemed to have no future.

With his rise to power Mussolini had shown to the world that the anti-Semitic movement could be successful. He was considered an authority on this. And he continued to be one, despite his decision to reach a modus vivendi with Jews. From this point of view one can claim that, although he officially restrained excesses, he and Fascism were a solid prop for European anti-Semitism.

I shall conclude with a quote:

> Mussolini did not personally harbor, even after rising to power, any real prejudice against the Jews; he did not view them with either sympathy or antagonism; (. . .) he was not immune to anti-semitic remarks and prejudices, but this was not important; (. . .) This traditional antisemitism had no practical consequences for him (. . .). The Mussolini of the "origins" and of the years up to the racial campaign would never adopt the extreme views of Preziosi, who never had any real influence [on him].

The author of these sentences is the Italian historian Renzo De Felice, who wrote them in his well-known *Storia degli ebrei italiani.* I quote from the English translation by Robert Miller, *The Jews in Fascist Italy: A History.*[40] I believe, after what I have written above, that De Felice's sentences contain a great many errors and that things went quite differently.

Translated from the Italian by Loredana M. Melissari

NOTES

1. Archivio Ministero Affari Esteri, Affari Esteri, Affari Politici 19–30, folder 1745.

2. Archivio Centrale dello Stato (ACS), Interno (MI), Pubblica Sicurezza (DGPS), 1924, folder 13, file Russia. Rappresentanti dei Soviets Russi.

3. Angelo Ventura, "La svolta antiebraica nella storia del fascismo italiano," in *Antisemitismo in Europa negli anni trenta. Legislazioni a confronto,* Anna Capelli and Renata Broggini, eds. (Milan: Angeli, 2001), 229.

4. Benito Mussolini, "La filosofia della forza (Postille alla conferenza dell'On. Treves)," *Il pensiero romagnolo,* December 6, 1908, then in B. Mussolini, *Opera Omnia (O.O.)* (Florence: La Fenice; Rome: Volpe, 1951–80), I: 177.

5. Benito Mussolini, "Convegno supremo," *Il Popolo,* February 24, 1909; *O.O.,* II: 17.

6. "Miscellanea," *La Lotta di Classe,* July 9, 1910; *O.O.,* III: 143.

7. M. [Benito Mussolini], "Come perirono gli dei di Roma," *Avanti!*, September 6, 1913; *O.O.*, V: 279.

8. Roberto Michels, *La Sociologia del Partito Politico nella Democrazia Moderna* (Turin: Utet, 1912), 274–80; original ed. 1910; Georges Sorel, "Gli ebrei," *Il divenire sociale*, July 16, 1910, 198.

9. "Il Napoleone della viltà," *Il Popolo d'Italia (PdI)*, December 3, 1917; *O.O.*, X: 110.

10. Mussolini, "Pedate ai neutri," *PdI*, March 26, 1915; *O.O.*, VII: 285.

11. "Palancagreca!" and so on, *PdI*, March 19, 24, 26, 28, 1915; *Avanti!*, March 23, 27, 1915; *O.O.*, VII: 268–9, 278, 281–9, 483–7.

12. Benito Mussolini, "Il pangermanismo," *Pagine libere*, September 15–October 1, 1910, 389–400.

13. The bibliography about these treaties and the problem of the races is very complex. Anyway, see Nathan Feinberg, *La question des minorités de la Paix de 1919–1920 et l'action juive en faveur de la protection internationales des minorités* (Paris: Rousseau, 1929); in Italy: Mario Toscano, *Le minoranze di razza, di lingua, di religione nel diritto internazionale* (Turin: Bocca, 1930), esp. 55–156.

14. "Il discorso del re," *PdI*, December 2, 1919. See, on the same issue, his "Commento," *O.O.*, XIV: 163.

15. Mussolini, "In tema di pace," *PdI*, July 2, 1921; *O.O.*, XVII: 21.

16. "Fra tutte le nazioni del mondo l'Italia è quella che è più "nettamente" individuata, da tutti i punti di vista (. . .). All'interno, i gruppi "allogeni" sono piccolissimi e sono stati assimilati." See Mussolini, "Per le frontiere di pace. Alle Alpi Giulie!," *PdI*, February 22, 1920; *O.O.*, XIV: 335–6.

17. "Noi e il Partito Popolare," *PdI*, July 27, 1922; *O.O.*, XVIII: 318.

18. "Il primo discorso di Mussolini al Parlamento italiano," *PdI*, June 28, 1921; *O.O.*, XVI: 431–46, esp. 438–9.

19. R. Michels, "Der Aufstieg des Fascismus," *Neue Zürcher Zeitung*, December 29, 1922.

20. "Fascismo ungherese," *La Voce Repubblicana*, September 21, 1922.

21. "Mussolini ha la fissazione di volerci," "Mussolini has the fixed idea to want us [as Senators]," wrote Pantaleoni to his friend Vilfredo Pareto on December 5, 1922. See the letter in Vilfredo Pareto, *Lettere a Maffeo Pantaleoni. 1890–1923. III (1907–1923)*, Gabriele De Rosa, ed. (Rome: Banca Nazionale del Lavoro, 1960), 389.

22. Francesco Perfetti, *Il movimento nazionalista in Italia (1903–1914)* (Rome: Bonacci, 1984), 123–5, 292–3; Tullia Catalan, "L'antisemitismo nazionalista italiano visto da un ebreo triestino. Carlo Morpurgo ed il 'caso Coppola,'" *Qualestoria*, April–August 1994, 95–118.

23. Michele Sarfatti, *Gli ebrei nell'Italia fascista* (Turin: Einaudi, 2000), 54.

24. "Un convegno sionista a Carlsbad," *PdI*, September 1, 1921. About the sure attribution to Mussolini, see G. Preziosi, "Mussolini e l'ebraismo prima della Marcia," *La Vita Italiana*, September 15, 1940, 242.

25. In the original Italian: "Se i sionisti italiani – sedicenti italiani! – se ne andassero altrove e si portassero con loro lo stock dei Treves, dei Modigliani, dei Musatti, dei Momigliano, dei Sacerdoti (Genosse), dei Passigli e di quel bel signor Ottolenghi che

ha regalato all'Italia le delizie di parecchi scioperi postelegrafonici, vorremmo darci il piacere di facilitare questo 'esodo.'"

26. M. [Benito Mussolini], "Ebrei, Bolscevismo e Sionismo italiano," *PdI*, October 19, 1920; *O.O.*, XV: 271.

27. In the original Italian: "Speriamo che gli ebrei italiani continueranno ad essere abbastanza intelligenti, per non suscitare l'anti-semitismo nell'unico paese dove non c'è mai stato."

28. g. pr. [Giovanni Preziosi], "Gli ebrei nelle amministrazioni dello Stato italiano," *La Vita Italiana*, August 15, 1922, 106–11; Pilo Bandini, "Gli ebrei nell'Amministrazione dello Stato Italiano," *La Vita Italiana*, October 15, 1922, 306–10.

29. "Il Fascismo italiano e le sue imitazioni all'estero," *PdI*, September 23, 1922; about *Avanti!* see Ral, "Il fascismo in Ungheria," *Avanti!*, September 21, 1922.

30. "Gli importanti lavori del Convegno Fascista a Napoli," *PdI*, October 26, 1922.

31. ACS, MI, Demografia e razza (DGDR), fascicoli personali, folder 42, file 3653. Arias Gino.

32. ACS, MI, DGPS, Casellario Politico Centrale, folder 2606, file 58310. Jacchia Giusto Pietro fu Eugenio.

33. Lucio Villari, *Le avventure di un capitano d'industria* (Turin: Einaudi, 1991), 50. ACS, MI, DGDR, fascicoli personali, folder 27, file 2046. Dis. Sinigaglia Oscar.

34. Marina Giannetto, ed., *Un'altra Italia nell'Italia del fascismo: Carlo e Nello Rosselli nella documentazione dell'Archivio centrale dello Stato* (Città di Castello: Edimond, 2002), 87–8.

35. But see Giorgio Fabre, "Mussolini e le sovvenzioni della Comit," *Quaderni di storia*, no. 60 (January–June 2003), 281–99.

36. "Ribalderia," *PdI*, October 28, 1922; "Avvertimento per i cambi," *PdI*, June 29, 1923.

37. Meir Michaelis, *Mussolini and the Jews* (Oxford: Clarendon Press, 1978), 25–6.

38. "Mussolini al Rabbino prof. Sonnino," *Il Vessillo Israelitico*, November 15– December 31, 1922, 332.

39. Alfred Rosenberg, "Deutschland und Italien," *Völkischer Beobachter*, June 17–18 1923. See M. Michaelis, 36.

40. Renzo De Felice, *The Jews in Fascist Italy: A History* (New York: Enigma Books, 2001), 59.

PART TWO

RISE OF RACIAL

PERSECUTION

4 Characteristics and Objectives of the Anti-Jewish Racial Laws in Fascist Italy, 1938–1943

Michele Sarfatti

In 1978, the great German American historian, George Mosse, characterized Mussolini's attitude to the Jewish question in the following passage:

> In October 1938 Mussolini had proclaimed his racial laws, which forbade mixed marriages and excluded Jews from military service and large landholdings, but *he* immediately *exempted* from the law all those Jews who had taken part in the First World War or in the Fascist movement. Moreover, Mussolini himself put out the slogan: "Discrimination and not persecution." [...] Mussolini *was no* racist.[1]

In the last years of his life, Mosse amended his view, writing the following in 1999:

> By 1936 Mussolini *had embraced* racism. [...] We shall never know whether Mussolini himself became a convinced racist, but *he did increase* the severity in the draft of the racial laws which had been submitted to him. [...] Mussolini may have embraced racism out of opportunism [...], or to give Fascism a clearly defined enemy [...], to give a new cause to a young generation.[2]

Mosse offered insight into his revised view of Mussolini in a 1997 interview with *Corriere della Sera*. "On antisemitism and racism," Mosse declared, "I do not wholly agree with De Felice, also because in the meantime new material on Mussolini has come to light. At the time of the racial laws the dictator was enthusiastic, not a sceptic."[3] In fact, George Mosse's mistake in 1978 had been to rely on the book published in 1961 by the great Italian historian Renzo De Felice.

The crux of the matter lies in one particular aspect of the Fascist anti-Jewish laws, that is, that which goes under the Italian term *discriminazione*. In the anti-Semitic parlance of Italian Fascism, a "discriminated" person referred to a Jew who was treated better than other Jews. Jews could be "discriminated" if they had acquired "merits" in wartime, through politics, in business, or in culture. Mosse wrote in 1978 that "Mussolini was no racist" because he believed that "discrimination" meant total exemption from persecution and, therefore, that Mussolini had decided in 1938 to persecute only some Jews, not all of them. One has to admit that such a persecution cannot be termed racist.

In fact, the document approved on October 6, 1938 by the Grand Fascist Council (Gran Consiglio del Fascismo) titled "Declaration on the Race" ("Dichiarazione sulla Razza") did say that "discriminated" Jews would suffer no persecution, with the single exception of teaching in schools. And in his book, De Felice had affirmed that the entire declaration such as it was had been converted into law,[4] adding: "There is no doubt that the famous slogan 'discriminate, but do not persecute' reflected Mussolini's true intentions,"[5] thereby suggesting that the laws had maintained the nonracist approach set out in the declaration.

A closer examination reveals that the Fascist laws of November and December 1938 dictated that "discriminated" Jews as well would be excluded from all public employment, from military service, from the National Fascist Party (Partito Nazionale Fascista), from banks, and so forth. They were, in short, exempted from just a few of the persecutory measures; Italian Fascist anti-Jewish laws, consequently, were clearly based on a racist approach.

This is De Felice's error, which Mosse followed unsuspectingly in 1978 and amended twenty years later.

Characteristics of the Italian Fascist Racial Laws

In Italy today, a debate continues on whether the racial laws were of the biologically racist or of the spiritually racist type; that is, whether they were based on blood or on immaterial traits.

To answer this question, one must focus on a particular section of that legislation that specified the persons at which it was aimed, who were its intended victims.[6] The evidence is clear. Italian anti-Jewish laws were not aimed just at anti-Fascist or non-Fascist Jews or only at people who were members of a Jewish community; they were aimed at all those who were termed "of Jewish race." Those defined as being "of Jewish race" included every person whose parents were both "of Jewish race" even if he or she belonged to the Christian faith. In other words, this meant that whatever their religious or cultural choices, people could not change what had been automatically bequeathed to them by their parents. This is undoubtedly biological – not spiritual – racism. One should add that some commentators gave this biological approach a spiritual veneer: this, however, pertained to the image of Fascist racism and not to its essence.[7]

The parents' "race" was determined according to their own parents' "race," and so on, going back in time up to the point when there were no more birth registers, when it was assumed that a person belonging to the Jewish faith was automatically "of the Jewish race." This method is totally unscientific, but then racism is always unscientific. In the case of so-called "racially mixed marriages," the "race" of the children was determined according to their actions: whether they were christened or belonged to a Jewish community, whether they were married to a person "of Jewish race" or to one "of Aryan race," and so on. Again, it is an entirely unscientific method, but this is the way racist minds work. Following these criteria, all those who had three grandparents classified as "of Jewish race," a substantial minority of those who had two grandparents classified as "of Jewish race," and a tiny minority of those who had one grandparent classified as "of Jewish race," were themselves classified as "of Jewish race." The biological criterion was also applied to people belonging to the Jewish faith but born of two "Aryan" parents: they were invariably classified as being "of Aryan race."

The Italian Racial Laws in Comparative Context

To situate the Italian racial laws in the wider context of European anti-Jewish persecution, one has to distinguish between the period before and after the beginning of World War II. Moreover, after 1939, there were specific aspects of racial laws linked with the war that varied greatly from one country to the other, as did the chronology.

As far as the period from January 1933 to August 1939 is concerned, one can affirm that only the anti-Jewish laws in Nazi Germany and Fascist Italy were of the biologically racist type. The three other countries that passed anti-Jewish laws prior to World War II – Romania, Hungary, and Slovakia – took into consideration either the original citizenship of Jews or the date when children of two Jewish parents had been christened.[8] This does away with the assumption that, during the period between 1938 and the outbreak of World War II, the weaker the country, the readier it was to import Germany's biological racism.

It goes to prove that the Italian Fascist passage of racial laws in 1938 was the decision of a strong country acting on its own.

The difference between Berlin and Rome, therefore, lies not in the character of their anti-Jewish laws but rather in the chronological progression of that policy and in the presence of a widespread, extreme violence in Germany along with the legislative measures.

A careful comparison of all anti-Jewish laws enacted in various countries from 1933 to 1945 brings to light numerous, if sometimes minor differences, which suggest some quite interesting considerations. Take for example the use of the biologically racist classification (two parents "of Jewish race" will automatically produce a child "of Jewish race"). In the various countries (including, in some respects, even in Nazi Germany) this classification is always contained in later laws. Only in Italy does it appear in the very first group of laws. Moreover, this classification was everywhere added in connection with the prohibition of new racially mixed marriages, with the exception of Vichy France, which at no time outlawed such marriages. These two comparisons clearly show that Mussolini had chosen drastic action and that his confrontation with the Holy See was entirely of his own making and had not been forced on him by anyone.

Just how drastic Italian Fascist anti-Semitism in 1938 was also emerges from a technical comparison between legislation in Berlin and Rome. Taken as a whole, the former was certainly more persecutory than the latter. Nonetheless, if we analyze Fascist anti-Jewish laws issued between September and the beginning of November 1938, we discover that, even for a few weeks, Mussolini was a step ahead of Hitler in some areas of legislation, such as the general exclusion of Jewish pupils from state schools, the expulsion of foreign Jews from the country, and the limitations imposed by law on the ownership of enterprises and real property. In short, Fascist Italy acted on its own.

The use of antisemitic violence in Fascist Italy never attained the level it reached in Nazi Germany. When comparing the two regimes, however, one must take into account more than anti-Jewish violence alone. The truth of the matter is that by the second half of the 1920s Mussolini was determined to build up a system of government based on harsh preventive control and swift repression by the state, as he strove for consent among the population, limiting "material violence" as much as possible. So, while Hitler opened the camp at Dachau, Mussolini sent his opponents to Eboli.[9] The extremely low level of Fascist anti-Jewish violence in the years 1938–43 was in accordance with this general policy. In this context, actually, the ravaging of the synagogues in Ferrara,

Trieste, and Spalato (Split)[10] in 1941 and 1942 takes on a very grim significance indeed.

The Meaning of Anti-Jewish Persecution in Fascist Italy

Although it resembled in some respects the racist shift which had taken place in 1936–37 against the subjects in Italy's African colonies, the anti-Jewish persecution enacted in 1938 differed from it, in so far as it was directed against people who were citizens of the state. It meant therefore a breach of the pact of equal citizenship entered into during the Risorgimento and negated the liberal principles of the nineteenth century.

While it is true that from 1938 to 1943 Italy did not pass any law stripping Italian Jews of their Italian citizenship, one should bear in mind that it did exclude them, in a sweeping and definitive manner, from the armed forces, from the National Fascist Party, and from the entire life of the nation. In other words, in 1938 the historical and national epoch that had begun with the Risorgimento came to an end. My great-grandfather, the art historian Paolo D'Ancona, wrote in 1939: "Suddenly, all my pursuits as a citizen and as a scholar have been broken off: I have been expelled from the army, from my chair [at the university in Milan], even from schools through [the banning of my] textbooks and must look on as everything which gave meaning to my life is undone."[11] Thus 1938 caused a rupture in Italian history whether at the time its victims or the other Italians were aware of it or not.

Anti-Jewish laws affected Italy as a whole, not just its political, social, economic, or cultural life. From the Fascist point of view, they had brought about a sweeping and permanent reform. Mussolini had decided that Fascism and Italy as a whole were to be Aryan and anti-Semitic. And both became or at least set out to become so. It was inevitably a process of gradual change, gaining ground continuously, although not evenly. In some sectors the process had not yet been completed by the end of the war; in others, it progressed at great speed. In order to understand the impact of the racial laws, however, one must view it within the Italian context of the time.

The Aim of Fascist Anti-Jewish Persecution

From 1938 to 1943 Fascist Italy was determined to eliminate all Jews, whether Italian or foreign, from Italian soil and from Italian society.

Between September and November 1938 the government banned foreign Jews from entering the country for the purpose of taking up residence and ordered all those who had become residents of Italy after 1918 to leave the country within a few months. In August 1939, Jews from central Europe were banned from entering Italy for obtaining *soggiorno* (temporary residence) and, in May 1940, even for transit.

When Italy entered the Second World War on June 10, 1940, the government decreed that all foreign Jews still living in the country were to be interned in small towns and villages or even in actual internment camps until the end of the war, when they would be expelled. The government also interned in various Italian towns, villages, and camps some groups of Jews who happened to be in other Italian territories in the Mediterranean. Although internment was in itself an anti-Semitic measure, there were no acts of anti-Semitic violence in the camps. Internment was accompanied by a strict ban on individual entries into the country and by the expulsion of all those who had somehow managed to enter illegally.

As far as Italian Jews were concerned, the government at first endeavored to persuade them to emigrate voluntarily.[12] It also revoked the Italian citizenship of those Jews who had become naturalized after 1918. Regarding these actions, one should bear in mind that had the government decided to strip all Italian Jews of their citizenship, thereby making them stateless, and to expel them, such a policy would certainly have backfired by causing neighboring countries to close their frontiers.

In 1940–1 the government started to work on a law that would expel Italian Jews once and for all and officially communicated this intention to the Union of Italian Jewish Communities (Unione delle Comunitá Israelitiche Italiane).[13] The plan was soon put on hold, however, no doubt because with the war spreading to so many geographical areas the possibilities for emigration were by now practically nil.

From 1940 to 1943 measures were taken which extended internment and forced labor to Italian Jews as well. Over the years, as military defeat followed military defeat, these measures became increasingly sweeping and persecutory.[14]

One should bear in mind that the aim of the Italian Fascist regime in those years was to eliminate Jews from the country, not to eliminate the country's Jews. Thus between the end of 1942 and the beginning of 1943 Rome reached an agreement with Berlin (similar to those reached by many other European capitals, whether neutral or in sympathy with the Axis) that Italian Jews should be repatriated from the areas where the Third Reich was by now carrying out its policy of eliminating the Jews of Europe.[15]

As a way of achieving this final aim of creating an Italy without Jews, Fascism harassed Jews with a myriad of prohibitions covering all aspects of a person's life. In a series of crushing decrees from 1938 on, Jews were banned from state schools, from the entertainment industry (theatre, music, film, etc.), from cultural and sports associations, from publishing, from public employment, and increasingly from private employment as well, and so on.

These measures served to implement on the one hand the policy of persecuting Jews, and on the other that of separating them from non-Jews. Both were necessary preconditions for the intended policy of expulsion from the country.

I have already mentioned that Italian Fascism also intended to "aryanize" Italian society. These policies of expelling Jews from the various sectors of employment, education, and social life and of separating them from non-Jews, therefore, served also the purpose of de-Judaizing and of racializing the country, which increasingly took on the character of an Aryan and racial state.

The Implementation of Fascist Anti-Jewish Laws

Historiography is a constant process of revising previous constructions and judgments. But no scholar has ever proved that Italian racial laws were implemented at a slower pace or with less resolve than other laws in Fascist Italy. Should somebody succeed in proving this on the basis of scientific evidence, I shall be happy to change my mind. But evidence, and scientific evidence at that, will be required for this to happen. Obviously, racist prejudices against Italians cannot be considered scientific evidence.

Anti-Jewish laws met with consent from many – far too many – quarters of Italian society. King Victor Emmanuel III of Savoy signed each and every law. Pope Pius XI protested publicly – by means of an article in the *Osservatore Romano* – only against the rule forbidding the "trascrizione" (that is, the recording in the marriage registers by Italian state authorities) of racially mixed marriages celebrated with Roman Catholic rites. His successor, Pius XII, never made any public protest whatsoever. The great majority and sometimes the totality of the noblemen and high-ranking army officers who sat in the Senate voted in favor of the anti-Jewish laws.

Students and young Fascist intellectuals zealously supported and publicized them. Older intellectuals decided to remain members of the aryanized academies.

Low- and high-level officials of the National Fascist Party applauded the new laws and acted as propagandists. The newspapers belonging to the Fascist party cheered while the so-called independent press joined the chorus.

The laws were applied equally to Fascist, anti-Fascist, and non-Fascist Jews; to those belonging to the Jewish faith, the Roman Catholic faith, or to no faith at all; to Zionists and anti-Zionists; to high-ranking army officers and to peddlers; to Jews in Rome and in Trieste; to children, adults, and the elderly.

Undoubtedly, persecution was made possible by the fact that Italy was ruled by a dictatorship, which, by the way, some Jews had helped to set up. But the implementation of the anti-Jewish laws was in itself proof that the Fascist dictatorship was no joke and that it had succeeded in compelling an ample consent among the Italian population.

Translated from the Italian by Loredana M. Melissari

NOTES

1. George L. Mosse, *Toward the Final Solution: A History of European Racism* (New York: Howard Fertig, 1978), 200 (emphasis mine). Italian translation: *Il razzismo in Europa dalle origini all'Olocausto* (Rome-Bari: Laterza, 1980), 214–15.

2. George L. Mosse, *The Fascist Revolution: Towards a General Theory of Fascism* (New York: Howard Fertig, 1999), 36 (emphasis mine).

3. George Mosse in an interview by Alessio Altichieri, *Corriere della Sera*, November 20, 1997 ("Su antisemitismo e razzismo non seguo De Felice fino in fondo, anche perché intanto è venuto alla luce nuovo materiale su Mussolini. Al momento delle leggi razziali il dittatore fu entusiasta, non scettico").

4. Renzo De Felice, *Storia degli ebrei italiani sotto il fascismo* (Turin: Einaudi, 1961), 350, 393, 401 [4th Italian ed. (1988), 307, 344, 351; English translation: De Felice, *The Jews in Fascist Italy* (New York: Enigma Books, 2001), 294, 331, 338–9].

5. De Felice, *Storia degli ebrei italiani*, 296 [(1988), 256; (2001), 240] ("Non vi è dubbio che il famoso slogan 'discriminare non perseguitare' rispecchia le vere intenzioni di Mussolini"). Cf. also Michele Sarfatti, *Le leggi antiebraiche spiegate agli italiani di oggi* (Turin: Einaudi, 2002), 51–2.

6. On Italian anti-Jewish laws see Michele Sarfatti, *Gli ebrei nell'Italia fascista. Vicende, identità, persecuzione* (Turin: Einaudi, 2000); by the same author, "Documenti della legislazione antiebraica. I testi delle leggi," in: by the same author (Ed.), *1938. Le leggi contro gli ebrei*, special issue of *La Rassegna mensile di Israel*, LIV, nos. 1–2 (January–August 1988): 49–167.

7. For the most concise work on the basic principles of Italian Fascist racism in the years 1938–43, see Mauro Raspanti, "I razzismi del fascismo," in Centro Furio Jesi, ed., *La menzogna della razza. Documenti e immagini del razzismo e dell'antisemitismo*

fascista (Bologna: Grafis, 1994), 73–89. Also see Mauro Raspanti, "Le correnti del razzismo fascista," in Anna Capelli and Renata Broggini, eds., *Antisemitismo in Europa negli Anni Trenta. Legislazioni a confronto* (Milan: Franco Angeli, 2001), 238–51; Giorgio Israel and Pietro Nastasi, *Scienza e razza nell'Italia fascista* (Bologna: Il Mulino, 1998); Roberto Maiocchi, *Scienza italiana e razzismo fascista* (Florence: La Nuova Italia, 1999); and Aaron Gillette, *Racial Theories in Fascist Italy* (London and New York: Routledge, 2002).

8. For a comparison between European anti-Jewish laws, see Renata Broggini and Anna Capelli (Eds.), *Antisemitismo in Europa negli anni Trenta. Legislazioni a confronto* (Milan: Franco Angeli, 2001).

9. Carlo Levi, *Cristo si è fermato a Eboli* (Turin: Einaudi, 1946) [English translation: *Christ Stopped at Eboli* (Harmondsworth: Penguin, 1982)].

10. Sarfatti, *Gli ebrei*, 202–3.

11. Paolo D'Ancona, *Ricordi di famiglia. Note personali*, typescript, 1939.

12. Sarfatti, *Gli ebrei*, 176–7.

13. Ibid., 163–4, 177–9. The proposed bill stated, "Residence in the Kingdom is forbidden to all persons of whichever nationality or citizenship...of the Jewish race" ("La residenza nel Regno è vietata alle persone di qualunque nazionalità o cittadinanza... appartenenti alla razza ebraica.") The text of the law is reprinted in Sarfatti, *Le leggi antiebraiche spiegate agli italiani di oggi*, 85–7.

14. Sarfatti, *Gli ebrei*, 181–7. The last legal step was the establishment in June 1943 of four labor camps for all Italian Jews between eighteen and thirty-six years old. The project, though, was not realized due to Mussolini's dismissal on July 25, 1943.

15. On the complex and fluctuating Italian policy toward Italian and foreign Jews outside of Italy, see Liliana Picciotto Fargion, "Italian Citizens in Nazi-Occupied Europe: Documents from the Files of the German Foreign Office, 1941–1943," in *Simon Wiesenthal Centro Annual* 7 (1990), 93–141; Davide Rodogno, *Il nuovo ordine mediterraneo. Le politiche di occupazione dell'Italia fascista in Europa (1940–1943)* (Torin: Bollati Boringhieri, 2003); Jonathan Steinberg, *All or Nothing: The Axis and the Holocaust 1941–1943* (New York and London: Routledge, 1990); Klaus Voigt, *Il rifugio precario. Gli esuli in Italia dal 1933 al 1945* (Florence: La Nuova Italia, 1996), vol. 2, 1996 (original ed. *Zuflucht auf Widerruf. Exil in Italien 1933–1945*, Klett-Cotta, Stuttgart, vol. 2, 1993). Also see Daniel Carpi, *Between Mussolini and Hitler: The Jews and the Italian Authorities in France and Tunisia* (Hanover and London: Brandeis University Press, 1994); Daniel Carpi, "The Rescue of Jews in the Italian Zone of Occupied Croatia," in Yisrael Gutman and Ephraim Zuroff, eds., *Rescue Attempts during the Holocaust: Proceedings of the Second Yad Vashem International Historical Conference, April 1974* (Jerusalem: Yad Vashem, 1977), 465–525; Jasa Romano, *Jevreji Jugoslavije 1941–1945. Zrtve genocida i ucesnici nor* (Belgrade: Saveza Jevrejskih Opstina Jugoslavije, 1980), 151–4, 199, 581; Zvi Loker, "The Testimony of Dr. Edo Neufeld: The Italians and the Jews of Croatia," in *Holocaust and Genocide Studies*, vol. 7, no. 1 (Spring 1993); Aleksandar Matkovski, "The Destruction of Macedonian Jewry in 1943," *Yad Vashem Studies* 3 (1959); Daniel Carpi, "Notes on the History of the Jews in Greece during the Holocaust Period: The Attitude of the Italians (1941–1943)," in *Festschrift in Honor of Dr. George S. Wise*

(Tel Aviv: Tel Aviv University Press, 1981); Daniel Carpi (ed.), *Italian Diplomatic Documents on the History of the Holocaust in Greece (1941–1943)* (Tel Aviv: Tel Aviv University Press, 1999). Also see Sarfatti, *Gli ebrei*, 179–81, 203–7, and my "Fascist Italy and German Jews in South-Eastern France in July 1943," *Journal of Modern Italian Studies*, 3, no. 3 (Fall 1998): 318–28.

5 The Exclusion of Jews from Italian Academies[1]

Annalisa Capristo

With the passage of anti-Jewish racial laws in Italy between September and November 1938, the Fascist regime banned Jews not only from public schools and universities, but also from academies and learned societies. Almost overnight, Italian Jews were completely eliminated from the Italian cultural milieu. Although in the past decade new research has documented the impact of the racial laws on Jewish teachers, professors, and writers, this chapter examines the position of the Italian academies on admittance of Jewish members before and after the racial laws to the onset of racial persecution in Fascist Italy.[2]

In the world of the academies, as well as in universities and schools, enforcement of governmental directives was quick, effective, and accompanied by a "deafening silence"[3] of members of the institutions concerned. Acquiescence, active consent, and concern about exclusion from the cultural milieu made – with a few exceptions – the ban of Jewish intellectuals substantially accepted.

Academies were a major element of Italian cultural organizations.[4] They included many different types: some had a long and well-established tradition, whereas others had been founded more recently, such as societies for historical studies as well as some scientific societies specializing in different subject areas. These academies, institutes, and societies constituted an organizational benchmark that served as sites for cultural exchanges. Their publications (serials, collections, papers, and conference proceedings) functioned as a means of cultural and scientific diffusion.

Italian Academies and the Jews in the Early 1930s

During the 1930s, prior to the racial laws, government policy toward these institutions was characterized by progressive centralization and "an authoritarian planning" of their activities.[5] In particular, a 1933 decree introduced a revision that would take effect by the end of 1934 that all members of Italian academies under state supervision swear allegiance to the Fascist regime, something that had been required of university professors since 1931.[6] Only a few scholars, among them Benedetto Croce, Gaetano De Sanctis, Lionello Venturi, and Vito Volterra, refused to take the oath and were consequently expelled.

Governmental intervention in the field of high culture entered a new phase in 1926, when Mussolini founded the Accademia d'Italia "to promote and coordinate the intellectual Italian movement in the field of sciences, humanities and arts, to preserve its pure national character according to the genius and the traditions of the race and to sustain its expansion and influence beyond the borders of the State."[7] According to its features and mission, the new academy was under strict government control: the political appointment of its members and higher echelons, the large endowment fund granted by the state (which included the annual allowance for the academy members), and the lack of foreign members were all elements assuring that control. The activity of the Accademia d'Italia was solemnly inaugurated on October 28, 1929 – the seventh anniversary of the March on Rome – after three years of delicate work to select the first thirty members.

As far as the anti-Semitic action in the cultural institutions is concerned, the case of the Accademia d'Italia represented a meaningful precedent. In fact, no Jewish scholar was ever appointed to this institution,[8] even though many authoritative candidates, such as Gino Arias, Giorgio Del Vecchio, Federigo Enriques, Carlo Foà, Tullio Levi-Civita and Cesare Vivante, had been presented through the years.[9] As early as 1929, antifascist *émigrés* in Paris maintained that this exclusion was deliberate and attributable to the anti-Semitic bias of the Italian prime minister, Mussolini himself, who had the power to appoint academy members.[10]

This opinion was raised by the journalist Emil Ludwig in an interview with the Italian dictator. Conducted between March and April 1932, and subsequently published as *Talks with Mussolini*,[11] the Duce strongly denied any bias, noting that the illustrious archaeologist Alessandro Della Seta – a Jew – had recently been proposed as a candidate for the academy.[12] This reply, however, was only telling one part of the story; as a matter of fact, Mussolini had rejected Della Seta's candidacy just a few days before the interview. As Ugo Ojetti revealed in his posthumously published diary,[13] this happened precisely because he was a Jew. The archaeologist was rejected again in 1933, despite the fact that, also in this case, he was ranked first for his subject.

Evidence of anti-Jewish prejudice and a veto – referable undoubtedly to Mussolini – on appointments of Jewish members in the most representative cultural institution of the regime can be found in several documents, including the minutes of academy meetings and the personal notes of President Guglielmo Marconi, who marked the names of Jewish candidates with an "E," the initial letter of the Italian word "Ebreo" ("Jew").[14]

The case of the Accademia d'Italia constitutes important evidence of the existence in Italy of a creeping anti-Semitism well before 1938, when it was made public and official by the racial legislation. That case constitutes rare evidence of a little visible and even discontinuous process; indeed, after March 1932, some Jewish personalities continued to hold important public offices.[15]

In this regard the remarks of Guido Lodovico Luzzatto, Piero Treves, and Piero Sraffa may be recalled. In an article from December 1938 (when anti-Jewish persecution was already in full progress) titled "The Emergence of Anti-Semitism,"[16] Luzzatto spoke of "the devious progress of anti-Semitism" since the Fascist regime's inception; he argued that the decision to introduce anti-Semitic measures in Italy was not the result of an unexpected change in Mussolini's policy. In defense of this view, Luzzatto mentioned the case of the Accademia d'Italia as outstanding evidence of that discriminatory intention. In 1981, Treves similarly asserted that an anti-Semitic climate existed well before 1938, especially in the field of high culture, once again bringing the ban on the admission of Jewish scholars to the academy as a significant example.[17] On another occasion he spoke of "warning signs" with reference to the "systematic exclusion of the Jewish *intelligentsia* from the Accademia d'Italia."[18] In a letter of December 1931, Piero Sraffa similarly affirmed that "they [the Italian Jews] are excluded, *de facto* if not *de jure*, from some offices; so it is well known that Jews are not admitted to the Accademia d'Italia (some of them, who are Fascists and scholars of international renown, were excluded)."[19]

The Racial Laws and their Impact

With the onset of the racial laws, the exclusion of Jews, which had been previously unofficial and confined to the Accademia d'Italia, was inscribed into law and extended to all academies and learned societies. Moreover, the application of discriminatory laws to such prestigious institutions represented, on the one hand, "the coronation of the tendentially totalitarian policy of the regime"[20] toward these institutions and, on the other hand, the final stage in the process of their substantial acquiescence to the authoritarian policy of the government.

Exclusion implied two aspects: the expulsion of existing Jewish members of such cultural institutions and the prohibition of future admission. Evidence of measures to remove Jews from academies can be found in legislation.

The policy of open exclusion with regard to Italian Jews can be dated back to September 5, 1938, when a Royal Decree Law (RDL) decreed inter alia that "Jews shall cease to be members of academies and learned societies as from October 16, 1938." A second decree, dated November 15, 1938, specified that "academies and learned societies shall not admit Jewish members."[21] By these and other measures, the minister of national education, Giuseppe Bottai, demonstrated his strong will to achieve a "complete Aryanization" in his field of competence.[22]

The RDL of September 1938 decreed that all Jewish members had to be expelled from academies by October 16, 1938 – that is, before the reopening of the academic year and the resumption of cultural activities.[23] To enforce the expulsion, Jewish members had to be identified. To this end, Minister Bottai – "anticipating with circulars the laws still at the drafting stage"[24] – had already instructed the competent ministry directorate to organize a thorough census at institutions involved in "Aryanization." As early as August 19, 1938, the General Directorate for Academies and Libraries had issued *Circular no. 11836* to regulate the census of academy members and require completion of the survey by September 30. In spite of many organizational obstacles – most societies included in their rolls hundreds, even thousands, of members, residents in many different cities, and the survey took place in the summer when academic activities were suspended and it was more difficult to find people at their usual address – the secretariats of most institutions completed the racial census and prepared the lists of Jewish members in compliance with the ministerial requirements. Some institutions, however, did not carry out the procedure in time and complied with the directive over the following months.

Institutions had to forward to their members a form to be filled out with personal and professional details. They had to declare whether their father, mother, and spouse were of Jewish stock, whether they were registered at the Jewish community, whether they professed Judaism, or if they had converted to Roman Catholicism. Then the institutions had to readdress the completed forms to the ministry along with a schedule with the results of the census, indicating the number and names of the members that had to be considered Jews by law.[25]

According to the ministerial circular, the forms for the racist survey had to be sent to Italian members only. Foreign members (if Jews) had to be expelled as well – with little stir, however: therefore, academies had to collect confidential information relating to the "race" of their foreign members and then report back to the ministry. To gather this information, some institutions (for example, the Accademia dei Lincei) turned to the Italian embassies abroad; others, such as the Italian Society of Dermatology, contacted their German counterparts, which had already been required by German regulations to carry out a similar purge. Other institutions, such as the Accademia di Santa Cecilia, used publications listing the most outstanding Jews in specific sectors (such as music[26]). Sometimes, however, institutions sent the form also to foreign scholars residents in Italy, and their replies are still kept in the archives. The Accademia dei Lincei, for instance, sent the census form to professors Jérôme Carcopino,[27] Ludwig Curtius,[28] and Franz Cumont,[29] who lived in Rome. Carcopino and Curtius returned the form duly filled out, with negative replies to questions concerning their belonging to the "Jewish race" and specifying that they professed Catholicism; Cumont instead addressed a note to the academy president on September 3, 1938 to stress that there was not even "one drop of Jewish blood in my veins."[30] Among Jews, the Austrian conductor and musicologist, Rudolf Cahn-Speyer, a resident of Florence since 1933, refused to fill out the form. Instead, he sent a letter to the president of the Florentine Academy of Music, stating that he was of "the purest Jewish race."[31]

The number of institutions involved in the racial survey was large. According to a list from the files of the General Directorate for Academies and Libraries there were at least 140 such institutions.[32] There were, however, surely many more, including for instance the Deputazioni di storia patria, that is, the regional historical societies located in the major Italian cities.

Many scholars – constituting a significant share of the small Italian Jewish community – were stripped of their academy membership. On the basis of documentation known to date (which is still incomplete, however), at least 672 Italian Jews were expelled from such instututions. These included leading intellectuals, musicians, and professionals. One only need mention figures such as Guido Castelnuovo, Mario Castelnuovo Tedesco, Federigo Enriques, Ugo Fano, Guido and Eugenio Fubini, Tullio Levi-Civita, Giorgio Levi Della Vida, Bruno Rossi, Emilio Segrè, and Vito Volterra to illustrate the caliber of individuals who fell victim to this intellectual purge of Italian cultural life.[33]

Many Jewish academy members disputed the racist approach of the questionnaire by deleting from their forms the expression "person belonging to the Jewish race" and replacing it with "person professing the Jewish religion" or "person belonging to an Italian family of Jewish religion." Others proclaimed their patriotic merits, writing of their participation in the First World War and of military honors received. The exclusion was even more traumatic for those who had adhered with conviction to Fascism and that in most instances were also Catholic converts (such as Gino Arias, university professor and member of the Italian parliament[34]). It should be noted that even in the cases of Catholic converts no exceptions were made, for family ancestry was the pivotal element.

Regarding foreigners, some resigned their membership in protest against the discriminatory laws enacted in Italy. Such individuals include Albert Einstein (a member of the Accademia dei Lincei in Rome) and the historian Cecil Roth (a member of the Società Colombaria in Florence and of the Deputazione di storia patria in Venice)[35]; others were officially expelled, like the musicians Guido Adler, Ernest Bloch, and Arnold Schönberg (members of the Accademia di Santa Cecilia in Rome) and the aeronautical engineer and mathematician Theodor Kármán and the philosopher Henri Bergson (members of the Accademia delle Scienze in Turin).

Both academies and non-Jewish scholars played an important role in the completion of the census. On the one hand, institutions were active – and in many cases even zealous – in collecting and transmitting personal data on their members. On the other hand, the large majority of non-Jewish scholars did not oppose the survey and completed the ministerial form. In addition to the identification of Jewish members for the purpose of expulsion, the racial survey thus achieved a second remarkable objective: it served to verify how widespread the support was within the Italian intellectual *élite* for the Fascist regime's anti-Semitic policies. Indeed, the census carried out at academies was even more significant in that regard than the similar one conducted on the public administration personnel (which included school teachers, university professors, and libraries staff). In the latter case, fear of dismissal from employment strongly conditioned people in their replies, although the highest risk for the academy members refusing to comply with the ministerial circular was expulsion, namely loss of a purely honorary appointment which was usually not remunerated (the Accademia d'Italia was an outstanding exception to this rule). Moreover, many academy members were not (or no longer, as for retirees) public employees and their economic and social standing would have allowed them to disagree with the survey.

A remark by Vittorio Foa well captures the attitude of the majority of non-Jewish Italians toward the racist campaign:

> Indifference was the most evident fact.... There was no noticeable protest by intellectuals, not even by those who shortly afterwards would have been outstanding champions of democracy and Communism. That silence is serious for postwar intellectual antifascism.... The fault of intellectuals – secular or religious, communists or democrats – was precisely not to understand that severe and irremediable harm derives from the indulgence for still little and remediable harm.[36]

In this regard, the testimony of Ernesta Bittanti, widow of the patriot Cesare Battisti,[37] can also be recalled. In her diary, she wrote:

> The legislation is a reagent, which makes the basest instincts of Aryans come to the surface and points out deficiencies and ignorance; it revives superstitious hatred.... Italian Aryans' response: One, *public*: no protest... supine obedience to orders to wipe Jews out of cultural, study and business associations, in short out of any association. Coming out from a meeting of a high-culture institution in which the names of illustrious Jewish scholars had been cancelled, a professor said: "yet we were all opposed." When we asked why they had done that, he replied: "we are all [like] sheep" (reduced to this condition after sixteen years of absolutist regime).[38]

The extraordinarily long list of those who answered the call of the regime includes many prominent personalities in the Italian culture and society of that time. These included, as well, young scholars who were destined for a brilliant scientific career. Among those who returned their completed forms, some held public offices (ministers, senators, rectors, bankers, executives) and others were intellectuals openly aligned with the Fascist regime (such as the philosopher Giovanni Gentile) or scientists and journalists who supported the racial campaign. There were even clergymen. Noticeably, the questionnaire was also compiled by exponents of the former liberal regime, people who later held outstanding positions (such as the president-to-be of the Italian Republic, Luigi Einaudi) or declared themselves opponents of Fascism.

Notwithstanding the substantial consensus in favor of racial discrimination, responses demonstrate a rather large range of attitudes, spanning from formal compliance with ministerial regulations, to denial of any Jewish "contamination" in one's genealogy (many punctiliously claimed their aristocratic descent, their Catholicism, or other Christian denominations), to strong adhesion to the racist policy.

Many people added anti-Semitic remarks quite superfluously, as for instance "absolute Aryan," "nothing of Jewish descent," "Aryan family without any con-tamination," "one hundred per cent Aryan and Catholic," "pure Aryan race," and so on. Senator Antonio Taramelli shouted that he was returning the ques-tionnaire "with profound joy, as for a national memorable event. We might be faced with hard times, but these will be overcome by the usual courage of us Italians if we will free ourselves from this Jewish intrusion which was about to stifle us."[39] However, a figure like Marquis Aldobrandino Malvezzi de Medici refused to fill out the questionnaire and polemically resigned from all institutions to which he belonged. His attitude, however, was not driven by solidarity with Jewish members; it was instead determined by a feeling of outrage for having been requested to state the obvious, that is, that he was not Jewish.

Criticism of anti-Semitic persecution was very limited. Provided that instances of "silent dissent" cannot be excluded, on the basis of extant documents the only two scholars who refused to fill out the form were the philosopher Benedetto Croce and the historian Gaetano De Sanctis.

It will be recalled that both Croce and De Sanctis had been expelled from academies to which they belonged in 1934 due to their refusal to swear an oath of allegiance to the Fascist regime required by the revised statutes. Some institutions, however, had not deleted them from the members' rolls and in 1938 sent them the racial survey form.

Benedetto Croce's support for Jewish scholars was outspoken. On September 21, 1938, he sent a letter to Luigi Messedaglia, president of the Venetian Institute of Sciences, Letters and Arts, explaining that he would have preferred to be expelled rather than return the form completed, as he did not intend to perform the "hateful and at the same time ridiculous act of claiming that I am not a Jew just as that people are being persecuted."[40] Messedaglia acknowledged this negative answer, but he did not notify the ministry, as he wanted to avoid having to expel such a famous scholar. Croce's letter is very important because it is, to date, the only evidence of unequivocal dissent from the persecutory initiative.[41] His firm refusal shows a full awareness of the implications of supporting the government policy: as a matter of fact, answering and signing the questionnaire was equivalent to endorsing persecution and to assuming joint responsibility for it by a small but meaningful action.

On September 6, 1938, De Sanctis replied to the president of the Institute for Etruscan Studies in Florence, refusing to fill out the form and at the same time resigning his membership. In his letter, however, he did not explain the reasons for his decision, just specifying "to avoid any misunderstanding" that "those reasons have nothing to do with my genealogy, as I belong from both maternal and paternal side to families always professing Catholic religion."[42]

In the end, the Minister for National Education, Giuseppe Bottai, fully achieved his aim: in fact, on the basis of the "criterion of racial separation" all Jewish fellows were expelled from the Italian academies and learned societies.[43]

✳

After the Second World War, research into the history of Italian Jewry under Fascism held that the anti-Jewish persecution began in 1936–7 as a consequence of Italy's progressive alignment with Nazi Germany. The present research, and particularly the reconstruction of the exclusion of Jews from the Accademia d'Italia, requires a revision of this view. As a matter of fact, in the case of the academy, documentary evidence demonstrates that Jews were systematically excluded – solely because they were Jews – from membership into Italy's most prestigious cultural institution as early as 1932–3. Indeed, there is evidence that exclusion dated back to its inception in 1929. Thus, anti-Jewish persecution in the field of high culture began well before the time commonly accepted, even before the Nazi party rose to power.

The present chapter also confirms that Fascist anti-Jewish persecution in the realm of Italian culture was really totalitarian. That is, it aimed to completely eliminate Jews from the Italian intellectual milieu without leaving any niche for them. Jews were excluded not only from schools, universities, newspapers, and publishing, but even from scientific societies and reading centers. Thus, as a target of Fascist anti-Semitism, culture was hit first and thoroughly.

Joint consideration of the two remarks above opens up an interesting field of inquiry, which can be reduced to the following questions. First, why did this remarkable persecutory anticipation take place just in the cultural milieu?[44] Second, why was it so radical? Finally, and most critically, was the elimination of Jews from the heart of the Italian intellectual *élite* initially conceived as a limited action with a strong symbolic meaning or rather as the first step of a full exclusion of Jews from Italian society? On these important questions research is still open.

ABBREVIATIONS

DBI: *Dizionario biografico degli italiani* (Rome: Istituto dell'Enciclopedia italiana, 1960–<2002>).

DSB: *Dictionary of scientific biography*, edited under the auspices of the American Council of Learned Societies (New York: Scribner's Sons, 1970–90).

EI: *Enciclopedia italiana di scienze, lettere e arti* (Rome: Istituto della Enciclopedia italiana, 1929–<2000>).

Grove: *The new Grove dictionary of music and musicians*, Stanley Sadie, ed. (London and New York: Macmillan, 1995).

NOTES

1. This chapter presents for the first time in English the main findings of two studies previously published in Italian: "L'esclusione degli ebrei dall'Accademia d'Italia," *La Rassegna mensile di Israel*, 67, no. 3 (2001), 1–36; and *L'espulsione degli ebrei dalle accademie italiane* (Turin: Zamorani, 2002). On this occasion, textual quotations were also added and bibliographical references updated.

2. On the exclusion of Jews from Italian public schools and universities see *Conseguenze culturali delle leggi razziali in Italia* (Rome: Accademia nazionale dei Lincei, 1990); Michele Sarfatti, "La scuola, gli ebrei e l'arianizzazione attuata da Giuseppe Bottai," in *I licei G. Berchet e G. Carducci durante il fascismo e la resistenza*, D. Bonetti, R. Bottoni, G. Giargia De Maio, and M. G. Zanaboni, eds. (Milan: Liceo classico statale G. Carducci, 1996), 37–66; Michele Sarfatti, "L'espulsione degli ebrei dall'università italiana," *Italia contemporanea*, 209–10 (December 1997–March 1998): 253–7; Roberto Finzi, *L'università italiana e le leggi antiebraiche* (1997; 2nd rev. ed., Rome: Editori Riuniti, 2003); Angelo Ventura, "La persecuzione fascista contro gli ebrei nell'Università italiana," *Rivista storica italiana* 109, no. 1 (1997), 121–97; Giorgio Israel and Pietro Nastasi, *Scienza e razza nell'Italia fascista* (Bologna: Il Mulino, 1998); *La cattedra negata: dal giuramento di fedeltà al fascismo alle leggi razziali nell'Università di Bologna*, eds. Domenico Mirri and Stefano Arieti (Bologna: Clueb, 2002). On the action against Jewish authors and books, see Giorgio Fabre, *L'elenco: censura fascista, editoria e autori ebrei* (Turin: Zamorani, 1998). On Italian academies, see Annalisa Capristo, *L'espulsione degli ebrei dalle accademie italiane* (Turin: Zamorani, 2002).

3. On the "silence of intellectuals" toward the anti-Semitic persecution in Italy see Finzi, *L'università italiana e le leggi antiebraiche*, 39–48; Israel and Nastasi, *Scienza e razza nell'Italia fascista*, 261, 286; Angelo Ventura, "Sugli intellettuali di fronte al fascismo negli ultimi anni del regime," in *Sulla crisi del regime fascista, 1938–1943: la società italiana dal "consenso" alla Resistenza. Atti del convegno nazionale di studi, Padova, 4–6 novembre 1993*, Angelo Ventura, ed. (Venice: Marsilio, 1996), 365–86; Angelo D'Orsi, *Intellettuali nel Novecento italiano* (Turin: Einaudi, 2001), 27–8; Gabriele Turi, *Lo stato educatore: politica e intellettuali nell'Italia fascista* (Rome-Bari: Laterza, 2002), 142–6.

4. Gabriele Turi, "Le accademie nell'Italia fascista," *Belfagor* 64, no. 4 (1999): 403–24, and Gabriele Turi, *Lo stato educatore*, 104–20. See also Albertina Vittoria, "L'organizzazione degli intellettuali nel primo Novecento," in *Cultura e società negli anni del fascismo* (Milan: Cordani, 1987), 473–98.

5. Mario Isnenghi, *Intellettuali militanti e intellettuali funzionari: appunti sulla cultura fascista* (Turin: Einaudi, 1979), 85–6. By the same author, also see *L'educazione dell'italiano: il fascismo e l'organizzazione della cultura* (Bologna: Cappelli, 1979), 66–83.

6. Royal Decree Law (RDL), September 21, 1933, no. 1333, "Provvedimenti per le Accademie, gli Istituti e le Associazioni di scienze, lettere ed arti" ["Measures for Academies, Istitutions and Societies of Sciences, Letters and Arts"], articles 1 and 3 in *Gazzetta ufficiale del Regno d'Italia*, no. 249, October 25, 1933. On the oath of allegiance in the universities, see Renzo De Felice, *Mussolini il duce: gli anni del consenso, 1929–1936* (Turin: Einaudi, 1974), 109–10; Helmut Goetz, *Der freie Geist und seine Widersacher: die Eidverweigerer an der italienischen Universitäten im Jahre 1931* (Frankfurt am Main: Haag und Herchen, 1993); Angelo Ara, "L'università italiana e il giuramento del 1931," in *Per ricordare Giorgio Errera: il rifiuto del giuramento fascista* (Pavia: Università degli studi, 1998), 7–12; and Giorgio Boatti, *Preferirei di no: le storie dei dodici professori che si opposero a Mussolini* (Turin: Einaudi, 2001). On the academies, see Capristo, *L'espulsione degli ebrei*, 14–16.

7. RDL January 7, 1926, no. 87, Art. 2 ("L'Accademia d'Italia ha per scopo di promuovere e coordinare il movimento intellettuale italiano nel campo delle scienze, delle lettere e delle arti, di conservarne puro il carattere nazionale, secondo il genio e le tradizioni della stirpe e di favorirne l'espansione e l'influsso oltre i confini dello Stato"). See *Annuario della Reale Accademia d'Italia* 1 (1929–VII), 297.

8. See Annalisa Capristo, "L'esclusione degli ebrei dall'Accademia d'Italia," *La Rassegna mensile di Israel*, 67, no. 3 (2001): 1–36 and "Tullio Levi-Civita e l'Accademia d'Italia," *La Rassegna mensile di Israel* 69, no. 1 (2003), 237–56. See also Judith R. Goodstein, "The rise and fall of Vito Volterra's world," *Journal of the History of Ideas*, 45, no. 4 (1984), 607–617.

9. Gino Arias (1879–1940) was professor of political economy at Rome University and a member of the Italian parliament. He adhered to Fascism in 1923 and converted to Catholicism in 1932. After the promulgation of the racial laws, he left Italy and settled in Argentina. He taught political economics at the University of Córdoba, where he died in 1940. Biography in DBI.

Giorgio Del Vecchio (1878–1970) taught philosophy of law at Rome University. A Fascist since 1921, he was rector (1925–7) and dean (1930–8) at Rome University. During World War II he converted to Catholicism. Biography in DBI.

Federigo Enriques (1871–1946) was professor of geometry at Rome University. Biography in DBI and DSB. See also *Federigo Enriques scienziato e filosofo*, Raffaella Simili, ed. (Bologna: Cappelli, 1989).

Carlo Foà (1880–1971) was professor of physiology at Milan University. A Fascist since 1924, he converted to Catholicism in 1938. After the promulgation of the racial laws he left Italy and settled in Brazil, subsequently returning to Italy. Biography in DBI.

Tullio Levi-Civita (1873–1941), see note 33.

Cesare Vivante (1855–1944) was professor of corporate law at Rome University. Biography in EI.

10. "Les Juifs en Italie," *Italia*, bulletin d'informations édité par la Concentration antifasciste italienne, Direction: Filippo Turati (Paris, 1er juin 1929), 5.

11. Emil Ludwig, *Colloqui con Mussolini* (1932; reprint, Milan: Mondadori, 1950), 72. English edition: Emil Ludwig, *Talks with Mussolini* (London: Allen & Unwin, 1932); American edition: Emil Ludwig, *Talks with Mussolini* (Boston: Little, Brown, 1933).

12. Alessandro Della Seta (1879–1944) was professor of archaelogy at Rome University and director of the Italian Archaeological School in Athens, Greece. Biography in DBI.

13. Ugo Ojetti, *I taccuini: 1914–1943* (Florence: Sansoni, 1954), 385–6, 391.

14. Capristo, "L'esclusione degli ebrei dall'Accademia d'Italia," 14–18.

15. On this point see Giorgio Fabre, "Mussolini e gli ebrei alla salita al potere di Hitler, *La Rassegna mensile di Israel* 69, no. 1 (2003), 187–236, as well as Fabre's *Il contratto: Mussolini editore di Hitler* (Bari: Dedalo, 2004).

16. Guido Lodovico Luzzatto, "L'avvento dell'antisemitismo," *Il nuovo Avanti*, December 17, 1938, reprinted in *Scritti politici: ebraismo e antisemitismo*, Alberto Cavaglion and Elisa Tedeschi, eds. (Milan: Franco Angeli, 1996), 86.

17. Piero Treves, "Formiggini e il problema dell'ebreo in Italia," in *Angelo Fortunato Formiggini, un editore del Novecento,* Luigi Balsamo and Renzo Cremante, eds. (Bologna: Il Mulino, 1981), 66–7. See also Meir Michaelis, *Mussolini and the Jews: German-Italian Relations and the Jewish Question in Italy, 1922–1945* (Oxford: Clarendon Press, 1978), 51; and Michele Sarfatti, *Gli ebrei nell'Italia fascista: vicende, identità, persecuzione* (Turin: Einaudi, 2000), 81–2.

18. Piero Treves, "Preface to the 1988 edition" in *Le interdizioni del Duce: a cinquant'anni dalle leggi razziali in Italia,* Alberto Cavaglion and Gian Paolo Romagnani, eds. (1988; 2nd ed. rev., Turin: Claudiana, 2002), 6.

19. Piero Sraffa, *Lettere a Tania per Gramsci,* ed. Valentino Gerratana (Rome: Editori Riuniti, 1991), 42 (my translation). See also Francesca Izzo, "I due mondi: Tatiana Schucht, Antonio Gramsci e Piero Sraffa sulla questione ebraica," in *Cultura ebraica e cultura scientifica in Italia,* Antonio Di Meo, ed. (Rome: Editori riuniti, 1994), 173–209.

20. Turi, *Lo stato educatore,* 129.

21. RDL September 5, 1938, no. 1390 "Provvedimenti per la difesa della razza nella scuola fascista" ["Measures for the Defense of the Race in the Fascist School"], Art. 4 ("I membri di razza ebraica delle Accademie, degli Istituti e delle Associazioni di scienze, lettere ed arti, cesseranno di far parte delle dette istituzioni a datare dal 16 ottobre 1938-XVI"); RDL November 15, 1938, no. 1779, "Integrazione e coordinamento in unico testo delle norme già emanate per la difesa della razza nella Scuola italiana" ["Consolidated Rules for the Defense of the Race in the Italian School"], Art. 2 ("Delle Accademie, degli Istituti e delle Associazioni di scienze, lettere ed arti non possono far parte persone di razza ebraica"), reprinted in Michele Sarfatti, "Documenti della legislazione antiebraica. I testi delle leggi," in *1938: le leggi contro gli ebrei,* special issue of *La Rassegna mensile di Israel* 54, no. 1–2 (1988), [66] and [77].

22. Sarfatti, *Gli ebrei nell'Italia fascista,* 194.

23. The racist survey took place also in public schools and universities, where it started even earlier than in academies, by a separate circular (no. 12336 of August 9, 1938, promulgated by the General Directorate for Higher Education). Pursuant to RDL September 5, 1938, no. 1390, Jewish teachers of public schools and Jewish professors of universities were suspended from their duties from October 16, 1938. According to the RDL November 15, 1938, no. 1779, they were finally dismissed. See Ventura, "La persecuzione fascista contro gli ebrei nell'Università italiana," 127–8.

24. Ventura, "La persecuzione fascista contro gli ebrei nell'Università Italiana," 125. On the use of circulars, see also Michele Sarfatti, "Documenti della legislazione antiebraica. Le circolari" in *1938: le leggi contro gli ebrei,* 169–71.

25. For instance, a person who was the child of two Jewish parents was considered a Jew even if he or she had converted to Roman Catholicism. Sons of mixed marriages were considered Jews not only if they had remained Jewish by faith, but also if they had declared to be agnostics or if the non-Jewish parent was a foreigner. In other words, sons of mixed marriages were exempted from persecution only if they were Catholics and their non-Jewish parent was Italian. See Sarfatti, *Gli ebrei nell'Italia fascista,* 154–64.

26. The Accademia di Santa Cecilia (an old and prestigious academy of music sited in Rome) referred to the book *Judentum und Musik: mit dem ABC jüdischer und nichtarischer*

Musikbeflissener, H. Brückner, ed. (München: H. Brückner-Verlag, 1938), still kept in the academy library.

27. Jérôme Carcopino (1881–1970) was professor of Roman history at Sorbonne University in Paris. In 1937 he was appointed director of the École Française in Rome. See http://www.academie-francaise.fr/immortel (November 30, 2003).

28. Ludwig Curtius (1874–1954) was a specialist in the ancient art of Greece, Rome, and Egypt. He was professor at Erlangen and Heidelberg universities and director of the Deutsche Archäologische Institut (German Archaeological Institute) in Rome, 1928–38. See *Archäologenbildnisse: Porträts und Kurzbiographien von Klassischen Archäologen deutscher Sprache,* Reinhard Lullies, and Wolfgang Schiering, eds. (Mainz am Rhein: Verlag Philipp von Zabern, 1988), 186–7.

29. Franz Cumont (1868–1947) was a historian of religions and antiquity, philologist, archeologist, and epigrapher. See *Biographie nationale publié par l'Académie royale des sciences, des lettres et des beaux-arts de Belgique* (Bruxelles: E. Bruylant, 1976), 39, Suppl., t. XI: 211–222 and http://www.academiabelgica.it (November 30, 2003).

30. Archivio storico dell'Accademia nazionale dei Lincei, Rome. Posizione 4, fascicolo [file] 1938. Razza ebraica, Censimento.

31. Archivio Centrale dello Stato, Rome. Ministero della Pubblica Istruzione, Direzione Generale Accademie e Biblioteche (1926–1948), busta [folder] 113, posizione 13, Notifiche importante interesse. Censimento Razza ebraica, fascicolo [file] R. Accademia del R. Conservatorio di musica "Luigi Cherubini," Florence.

32. Archivio Centrale dello Stato, Rome. Ministero della Pubblica Istruzione, Direzione Generale Accademie e Biblioteche (1926–1948), busta [folder] 109, Posizione 13, Censimento Razza ebraica, Affari generali, fascicolo [file] Statistica della razza, reproduced in Capristo, *L'espulsione degli ebrei dalle accademie italiane,* 398–404.

33. Guido Castelnuovo (1865–1952), mathematician, taught analytical and projective geometry at the University of Rome. Biography in DBI.

Mario Castelnuovo Tedesco (1895–1968) was a pianist and composer. In 1939 he moved to the United States, where, along with other European composers in exile, he turned his hand to film music. He died in Los Angeles. Biography in DBI and Grove.

For Federigo Enriques (1871–1946), see note 9.

Ugo Fano (1912–2001), an atomic physicist, fled with his family to the United States in 1939 to escape Fascist Italy. He worked in Washington from World War II through the 1960s, his tenures including the National Bureau of Standards, the Washington Biophysical Institute, the Carnegie Institute, and the U.S. Army Ballistic Research Laboratory. From 1966 he was professor at the University of Chicago. http://physics.uchicago.edu/fano.html (November 30, 2003).

Guido Fubini (1879–1943) was professor of mathematical analysis at the Turin Polytechnic. In 1939 he fled to the United States and taught at Princeton and in New York. Biography in DBI and DSB.

Eugenio Fubini (1913–97), engineer, scientific consultant to the U.S. Army and Navy in the European theater in 1943–4, assistant secretary of defense (1963–5), and vice president of IBM. See Edoardo Amaldi, "Il caso della fisica," in *Conseguenze culturali delle leggi razziali in Italia* (Rome: Accademia nazionale dei Lincei, 1990), 107–33 and http://www.nae.edu (November 30, 2003).

Tullio Levi-Civita (1873–1941), prominent mathematician of international renown, was professor of rational mechanics at Padua and Rome universities. Biography in DSB and EI. See also *Tullio Levi-Civita: Convegno internazionale celebrativo del centenario della nascita (Roma, 17–19 dicembre 1973)* (Rome: Accademia nazionale dei Lincei, 1975).

Giorgio Levi Della Vida (1886–1967), orientalist, was professor of Hebrew and Semitic languages at the University of Rome. He was one of the few Italian professors who refused to take the oath to the Fascist regime in 1931. As a consequence, he lost his chair. In 1938 he fled to the United States and taught at the University of Pennsylvania in Philadelphia. Biography in EI. See also his autobiography: Giorgio Levi Della Vida, *Fantasmi ritrovati* (Venice: Neri Pozza, 1966).

Bruno Rossi (1905–93) was professor of physics at Padua University. After dismissal in 1938, he spent short periods in Copenhagen, Manchester (England), and Chicago, joining the faculty of Cornell University in 1940. From 1943 to 1946 he was on the staff of the Los Alamos Laboratory in New Mexico, where the atomic bomb was developed. Then he was professor of physics at the Massachusetts Institute of Technology. Biography in EI. See also his autobiography: Bruno Rossi, *Moments in the Life of a Scientist* (Cambridge: Cambridge University Press, 1990).

Emilio Segrè (1905–89), prominent physicist, moved to the United States in 1938. He taught at the University of California Berkeley. From 1943 to 1946 he was a group leader in the Los Alamos Laboratory of the Manhattan Project. In 1959 he was awarded the Nobel Prize in Physics. Biography in EI. See also his autobiography: Emilio Segrè, *Autobiografia di un fisico* (Bologna: Il Mulino, 1995).

Vito Volterra (1860–1940), mathematician of international renown, senator, former president of the Accademia dei Lincei and of the National Research Council (Consiglio Nazionale delle Ricerche, CNR), was professor of mathematical physics at the University of Rome. In 1931 he refused to swear allegiance to the Fascist regime and was dismissed. In 1934 he was also expelled, for the same reason, from the Accademia dei Lincei. Biography in DSB and EI. See also *Vito Volterra e il suo tempo (1860–1940): mostra storico-documentaria*, Giovanni Paoloni, ed. (Rome: Accademia nazionale dei Lincei, Consiglio nazionale delle ricerche, Archivio centrale dello Stato, 1990) and *Convegno internazionale in memoria di Vito Volterra (Roma, 8–11 ottobre 1990)* (Rome: Accademia nazionale dei Lincei, 1990).

34. See note 9.

35. Also the mathematician Solomon Lefschetz resigned his membership from the Academy of Sciences, Letters and Arts in Padua.

36. Vittorio Foa, *Questo Novecento* (Turin: Einaudi, 1996), 150–1 (my translation).

37. Cesare Battisti (1875–1916), Italian patriot, was born in Trento, now seat of the Italian Trentino province, then part of Austria-Hungary. Socialist and irredentist, in 1911 he was elected to the diet (parliament) in Vienna. In 1914, at the beginning of World War I, he left Austria for Italy where he became very active in promoting an Italian war against Austria. Later, when Italy entered the war against Austria in May 1915, Battisti enlisted in the Italian Alpine Corps. Captured, he was executed at the castle Buon Consiglio in Trento, together with Fabio Filzi. Biography in DBI.

38. Ernesta Bittanti-Battisti, *Israel-Antisrael. Diario 1938–1943*, Antonino Radice, ed. (1984; 2nd ed., Trento: Manfrini, 1986), 63–4 (my translation).

39. Archivio dell'Istituto nazionale di studi etruschi e italici, Florence [Archive of the National Institute for Etruscan and Italic Studies, Florence, Italy]. Posizione 3, Membri, fascicolo [file] Censimento degli accademici di razza ebraica, letter of Antonio Taramelli to the president of the Institute for Etruscan Studies in Florence, Antonio Minto, September 4, 1938. Antonio Taramelli (1868–1939) was senator and superintendent emeritus to antiquities of Sardinia.

40. Biblioteca civica di Verona [Municipal Library, Verona, Italy]. Carteggio [Correspondence] Luigi Messedaglia, busta [folder] 1014, letter of Benedetto Croce to Luigi Messedaglia, president of the Venetian Institute for Sciences, Letters and Arts (Venice), September 21, 1938. See Luigi Messedaglia, "Benedetto Croce e l'Istituto veneto: ricordi e documenti," *L'arena di Verona*, December 17, 1952; Giuseppe Gullino, *L'Istituto veneto di scienze, lettere ed arti dalla rifondazione alla seconda guerra mondiale (1838–1946)* (Venice: Istituto veneto di scienze, lettere ed arti, 1996), 167–8; *Carteggio Croce-Messedaglia*, Carlo De Frede, ed. (Bologna: Il Mulino, 1999), 9–10; Capristo, *L'espulsione degli ebrei*, 38–40.

41. On Croce's stand against persecution of Jews both in Germany and in Italy see *Le interdizioni del Duce*, 275–92; Alberto Cavaglion, "La posizione di Croce e del pensiero liberale," *Qualestoria* 17, no. 1 (1989), 67–74; Gennaro Sasso, *Per invigilare me stesso: i Taccuini di lavoro di Benedetto Croce* (Bologna: Il Mulino, 1989), 148–49; and Turi, *Lo stato educatore*, 141. On his intervention regarding a sequestration of books by Jewish authors published by Laterza, see Fabre, *L'elenco*, 286–8, 464.

42. Archivio dell'Istituto nazionale di studi etruschi e italici, Florence [Archive of the National Institute for Etruscan and Italic Studies, Florence, Italy]. Posizione 3, Membri, Varie [loose sheet of paper]. It is interesting to mention the fact that in De Sanctis's memoirs posthumously published the following different response is reported: "I am Catholic indeed, but I do not want to make a statement of Catholicism when this just serves to reinforce the injustice according to which in Italy only Catholics are allowed to be members of scientific institutions." See Gaetano De Sanctis, *Ricordi della mia vita*, Silvio Accame, ed. (Florence: Le Monnier, 1970), 155–7.

43. Archivio Centrale dello Stato [Central Archive of State, Rome, Italy]. Ministero dell'Interno, Direzione Generale Demografia e Razza, Affari diversi (1938–1945), busta [folder] 2, fascicolo [file] 11, Questioni varie. 5) Membri ebrei di sodalizi ariani: "Gli ebrei, in omaggio al principio della separazione delle razze, sono stati eliminati da tutti i sodalizi aventi carattere culturale, morale, sportivo, sociale, ecc." ("Jews, due to the criterion of racial separation, have been eliminated from all institutions – cultural, moral, social, sports clubs, etc."). See Michele Sarfatti, "Documenti della legislazione antiebraica. Le circolari" in *1938: le leggi contro gli ebrei*, 193.

44. For some considerations on this point, see Turi, *Lo stato educatore*, 121–46.

6 The Damage to Italian Culture: The Fate of Jewish University Professors in Fascist Italy and After, 1938–1946

Roberto Finzi

The Cultural Background

On May 23, 1933, an Italian youth, while in Germany attending his studies, wrote home to a close friend about the problem of the anti-Semitic policies adopted by the newly established Nazi government. He maintained that in Germany there was "a very serious Jewish question which existed *in itself*" above and beyond the fact that "practically all the Jews were the enemies of the 'revolution.'" Despite "statistical lies" characterizing Jews as a negligible minority, "they actually dominated the finance, the press, political parties and, in Berlin, represented the majority even in some professions." Neither "religious differences nor *racial prejudices* are sufficient to explain why co-existence is impossible." The point – he then remarked – is that German reality is totally different from the Italian one:

> In Italy we are used to considering the Jews as *survivors of history* to whom we [do] not deny our respect and do not feel offended if some of them are proud of their origins. Our policy, based not on tolerance but on understanding, has yielded the best possible results, and it will continue to do so until the moment, not so far ahead, when the tradition of Jewish dealers will be considered on an equal footing with that of ancient maritime republics, just one of the many traditions the Italians, one single, indivisible people, are proud of.

The situation in Germany was "completely different." In that country "the Jewish question existed" and "showed no sign of finding a spontaneous solution." "Whether the surgical approach could have been replaced by a firm and wise policy that could have led to slower but more desirable developments" was something debatable and anyway left to the judgment of history.

According to the letter's author, the reason that prompted "the Aryans to give almost unanimous support for the antisemitic struggle" was not "the romantic racial theory," but

> the existence of that stupid and offensive thing called Jewish na-
> tionalism. Most German Jews were not Europeanized, or, in this
> case, Germanized. That may be due to the continuous inflow of
> fanatics from the Eastern ghettoes – this is at least the most com-
> monly provided explanation. The fact is that the Jews asserted
> their separation from the Germans in almost the same vigorous
> ways the Germans did, except for some useless attempts at con-
> ciliation made at the last moment, when the storm was already
> approaching. It is inconceivable that a country of 65 million can
> accept being guided by a minority of 600,000, who openly de-
> clared they wished to become a separate nation. Some say that
> the Jewish issue would not exist if the Jews knew how to keep
> their mouths shut.

The letter's author concludes that "the situation of the Jews is not as dire as it appeared abroad." For he argued that exemptions granted to exservicemen from the new anti-Jewish race law were keeping many employed and "in certain categories they amount to two thirds of the total." And, he commented, "it should not be forgotten that under the empire only converted Jews could be employed as civil servants. The majority of those who ran businesses of their own were not at all affected by the changes, with very few exceptions." Therefore,

> on the whole, the future of German Jews can be considered
> with some optimism, although complete integration with the
> rest of the population will be delayed as a consequence of re-
> cent events. Such events, however, may indirectly bring about
> positive developments if they are able to curb the dangerous
> Jewish immigration from the primitive communities of Slavic
> countries, most particularly Poland. It is just among such new
> immigrants that we find trouble-making rabbis who are said
> to welcome persecutions because they unite their people, who
> would otherwise risk disintegration, if living peacefully together
> with other peoples. It's always the same old story. But irre-
> spective of what the immediate future has in store for us, we
> can expect that civilization will eventually succeed both in
> Germany and in those other countries where a Jewish issue
> exists.

The reading of this already disquieting text becomes even more disconcerting with our understanding today of just how tragically civilization indeed failed. All the more so, once we identify the author and addressee. The author was Ettore Majorana whose mysterious – and to a certain extent theatrical – vanishing, at the end of March 1938, was to elicit a long, and still continuing debate, about the true meaning of his "giving up life." The addressee was Emilio Segrè, a Jew who was forced to emigrate from Italy after the racial laws and whose brilliant career as a physicist was crowned by a Nobel Prize in 1956.[1]

Majorana and Segrè had been friends since their childhood. They both worked with Enrico Fermi in Rome during that fateful year of 1933. Both belonged to that mythical group of scientists known thereafter as the "boys of via Panisperna." This is not at all a negligible piece of information. Indeed that group kept regular contacts with foreign countries, with Germany in particular, and many Jews were among its members and scholars who were later to be affected by the 1938 racial laws. Moreover, the two most prominent representatives of the Roman school of physics, Enrico Fermi and Franco Rasetti, left Italy in protest against Fascist dictatorship. Fermi – a member of the Accademia d'Italia, and as such well aware that "believers of other religions" were discriminated against in gaining access to that scientific institution since the beginning of the 1930s[2] – left because he felt directly hit by that legislation, his wife being a Jew, and Rasetti, an "Aryan" without any Jewish relations, emigrated to show his abhorrence of laws he considered reprehensible.

There is evidence suggesting that a serious rupture between Fermi's group and the Fascist regime occurred in 1935.[3] Fermi's group of scientists considered the Italian aggression in Ethiopia unjustifiable in both political and economic terms. This act of aggression had revealed an aspect of the regime that they had not perceived – or maybe had refused to see – before. No matter what was claimed in all later autobiographic essays, their non-negative evaluation of the regime until the Ethiopian adventure was at least *partly* reflected in their approach toward the rise of the Nazi dictatorship, including its policy with the Jews, which was only later to reveal its cruel design of genocide. The presence of an authoritative and non-Nazi portion of German scientists, such as Max Plank and Werner Heisenberg,[4] with whom Majorana was working at the time he wrote his letter to Segrè, certainly supported such an approach.

Was Majorana an anti-Semite, as was later claimed? Judging from his letter, the only answer is yes, although his dislike of the Jews was not founded on the biologically based racial theories of those times.[5] It is therefore more accurate to say that Majorana held anti-Jewish attitudes. Such an indisputable and apparently simple judgment is made less simple by the fact that he was writing to a *Jewish* friend.

As far as we know, the letter did not cause friction or any difficulty in the friendship between the two young physicists. We can therefore assume that Segrè considered it "normal" and acceptable, either because he himself shared that line of thinking or because he considered it as the expression of commonly shared feelings of people who were not particularly hostile to the Jews, especially in Italy. Majorana's letter is a mixture of prejudices about the Jews and the "Jewish question," very common among Italian intellectuals of the time, who sometimes adopted racist attitudes against "colored" people and who were later attracted by modern biological racist ideas that were also present in democratic countries.[6]

Ettore Majorana came from a Sicilian family who had already given prominent personalities to the pre-Fascist Italian political and scientific community. Moreover he lived in Rome among the most influential intellectual bourgeoisie. He had absorbed the widely held attitude and common sense that accepted, developed, and disseminated anti-Jewish stereotypes – something also adopted by the most radical and fanatic anti-Semites of the time – according to which the Jews were not only the enemies of the Christian religion but also the enemies of law and order. Needless to say, such ideas were much more powerful than "statistical lies"[7] would declare, everywhere and always in league among themselves. As Gioacchino Volpe wrote at the end of World War II in a text aimed at absolving the Italian academic community – all Italians nourished "the vague and disquieting perception that wherever a Jew appeared, many others would follow."[8] Such Pavlovian reflexes permeated the whole Catholic world.[9]

A clear example is given by the words that Pope Pius XI – who was later to take a clear stand concerning the Nazis and who, had death not prevented him, would have openly declared the Holy See against Hitler's anti-Semitic policy – uttered to Mussolini in 1932, as reported by the dictator to King Vittorio Emanuele III:

> I have just received the 36th volume of the Russian anti-religious library. It also contains the anti-Christian attitude of Judaism. Indeed, in Warsaw, I noticed that in all Bolshevik regiments the civilian commissioner was a Jew.
>
> Soon afterwards, however, the Pope reportedly added: "Italian Jews, though, are an exception."[10]

Such positions were not confined to the Church hierarchy but were spread throughout society by means of liturgy, catechism, sermons, and the like. They accounted for the great success enjoyed by the book *Storia di Cristo* by Giovanni Papini,[11] "in whose numerous antisemitic passages the main theme is the connection between Judaism, gold and satanic worshipping."[12] Moreover, Majorana, who had received a Jesuit education,[13] shared the Catholic positions that similarly foresaw a progressive (and rather quick) moderation of the Nazi regime.[14]

Majorana's full acceptance of the position on the "Jewish question" taken by the majority of the intellectuals of his time came with his belief, then prevailing among the cultural elite, of assimilation as the only "rational" and "progressive" solution to the "Jewish problem." Such an idea was common to all great nonconfessional universalistic ideologies of the nineteenth and early twentieth centuries. It was a notion that did not correspond to the solution of the "Jewish question" suggested by some authoritative Catholic representatives, that is, a "friendly segregation." But this notion was not opposed to one of the basic concepts of Christian anti-Judaism: conversion as the final solution, as the "getting over" (or better, rejecting) of one's own Jewish identity. It is not a coincidence that a few years later, at the onset of persecution against Italian Jews, Benedetto Croce, himself neither a clerical, a Fascist, nor an anti-Semite, proposed as a model Antonius Galateus's letter in defense of the Jews and most particularly of neophytes. The letter is a passionate peroration in favor of the "older brothers" as well as a clear indication of the right direction to take. Indeed, the great humanist claimed the lawfulness of the marriage between the son of a noble Christian and a *converted* Jewish girl. Therefore, while defending the Bible's great message and claiming the Jewish origin of Christ and his mother, Galateus clearly showed Jews the right way to go: first conversion and then assimilation through marriage to a Christian.[15] Despite the fact that he himself was horrified by anti-Semitism, Croce remained faithful to this assimilationist position even in the postwar period after the Nazi Final Solution became known. Not only did he initiate a polemic on the solution of the "Jewish problem" whose roots, for him, were in the millennial separatism of Jews,[16] but he put forth moral justifications for questionable political positions and government decisions.[17]

This was the cultural background that produced contempt and criticism toward eastern Judaism and toward what Majorana refered to as "the existence of that stupid and offensive thing called Jewish nationalism." The same contempt and criticism were also common among socialists as well as among German Jews themselves.[18] Majorana combined the stereotypes he received from his Catholic upbringing with the solution supported by the nonconfessional liberal tradition, thus becoming himself a synthesis and an example of an attitude that was very common and dominant among the cultural elite of the 1930s, when anti-Semitic

laws were introduced in Italy. Such laws, as it will be discussed later, had a particular impact on universities and, in more general terms, on all cultural institutions.
This is why I have studied the subject at length: I wanted to demonstrate in vivo
how the upper, cultivated classes automatically took many anti-Judaic prejudices
for granted, as if they were real facts. For them it was as if all the Jews were – as
we can read in the *Dictionnaire des idées recues* by Gustave Flaubert – "peddlers
selling *lorgnettes*,"[19] that is, mean[20] but, above all, ambiguous, greedy, and not
to be trusted.[21]

The adoption of consolidated stereotypes about "hard-headed" Jews, the "survivors from history," destined to blend with and eventually disappear into the
ocean of universal progress, was not necessarily detached from (but neither necessarily attached to) tolerance and "understanding." It was a kind of soft anti-
Judaism, one that did not encourage violence and might even disapprove of legal
discrimination – as was the case of a minority in Italy in 1938. It could also,
however, understand, that is, accept and justify, actions interpreted as aiming
at speeding up the unavoidable absorption of the Jewish anomaly. This might
sometime include some deprivations of civil rights intended to limit exaggerated
manifestations of Judaism, which "trigger[ed] off anti-Judaism," as Mussolini
put it on December 31, 1936 in *Il Popolo d'Italia*.

The Reactions of Italian Universities to the Racial Laws

Such a mental attitude – an abyss of ignorance that affected even the shrewdest
and most cultivated minds – was the main cause accounting for the deafening silence with which the universities met each step leading to legal anti-
Jewish discrimination and the 1938 laws, enforced in educational and cultural
institutions and most particularly in Italian universities. Then, of course, cow-
ardice, opportunism, and cynical professional calculations also came to play
their role.[22] The actions after the racial laws were all justified with the notion
that it was too dangerous to oppose any decisions taken by the dictatorship.
In theory this is always true in regimes that have abolished political freedoms.
But in practice things are different. There is no evidence of any really repressive measures taken in those few cases when mild but clear solidarity[23] was
given to the persecuted or when anti-Semitic laws were openly criticized. Perhaps the modest reaction was due to the fact that dissent was very limited.[24]
Whatever the reason, it is clear that whoever protested, even if in ambiguous ways, did not suffer serious consequences. The most significant case was
that of *Vita universitaria*, the official journal of Italian universities. It stated

that expelling Jewish professors from Italian universities would cause serious vacancies that could hardly be filled for many years because of the lack of adequately qualified people. It was therefore advisable to leave those chairs vacant to avoid the risk of giving permanent jobs to unworthy and unqualified people.[25]

There is no doubt that the journal meant to strongly attack the Italian government's anti-Semitic policy, which impoverished – as openly stated by the journal – the scientific and didactic resources of Italian universities. There is no evidence that the editors of the magazine bore any consequence for their ideas openly published in the journal following the passage of anti-Semitic laws. On the whole, however, the university world remained silent. Faced with so many unexpected and coveted vacant jobs, it behaved as if nothing had happened. All told, to quote Majorana's words on Nazi Germany, it looked as if in universities "the persecution of the Jews made the Aryan majority happy."[26]

It should be noted that the evidence largely contradicts the above-cited statement, particularly the testimony of Jews who reported widespread solidarity on the part of their Italian colleagues. But a closer analysis reveals two significant elements that emerge from these documents. The first is that dissent was usually declared *in private*. Many – even though not as many as was intended to demonstrate later on – privately gave support to their persecuted colleagues, continued to see them, and remained friends with them. Such things provided strong psychological support to men and women who were suddenly deprived of their civil rights. However, this cannot make us ignore the behavior of the vast majority who, *in public*, fully acquiesced to the anti-Semitic measures, failing to take any advantage of the albeit narrow opportunities to offer some resistance, even a passive one, to the regime's racist policy.

The second element regards the emphasis that the witnesses have placed on the solidarity Italians offered to the Jews.[27] The above-mentioned psychological element here plays an important role: when everything around is crumbling to the ground, any support takes up great importance. But the role of hindsight is also a factor of some significance. Witnesses gathered in the postwar period, after the persecution of lives that was part of the "Final Solution" and that hit also Italian Jews between September 8, 1943 and April 25, 1945. So in recalling all the events that occurred in 1938 as well as between 1938 and 1943, the witnesses were biased both by what Italian Jews, like all European Jews, had to suffer as a consequence of the "Final Solution" and by the behavior of many Italians after the armistice and the establishment of the Italian Social Republic under German control. It was a behavior that helped save many lives and that gave the Jews the feeling of generalized help and support, which was not the case, despite the fact that many among the population defied the Germans' and Salò Fascists' rage in order to help Italian and foreign Jews.

Vita universitaria had indicated a viable solution. Even though anti-Semitic laws made the expulsion of Jewish teachers unavoidable, the universities still kept their autonomy in deciding how to fill in those vacancies. But in practice just the opposite happened: universities dealt with those vacant jobs according to the usual academic practice, or, in an even more cynical way, as if all those new jobs were an extra bonus offered them by the government. And a dainty dish indeed it was, as we shall see.

At this point, it is useful to note that, no matter how shameful it may rightly appear now, the behavior of the Italian academic world in 1938 should not actually be a surprise to us. The justified disdain we feel about it stems from our ideal vision of what universities should be, of their mythical dimension, which *luckily enough* has not vanished and is still present in our minds – according to which universities cannot be but absolutely free, for freedom is the indispensable prerequisite for the progress of human knowledge. However, the real world is not so rosy, and in the 1930s the universities of European Fascist countries were far less than ideal. In 1933, the German academic world accepted with little resistance the despicable and devastating racist policy of the regime.[28] And before that, in 1931, in Italy, the vast majority of university teachers – including those who were to be defined as Jews by the racial laws of 1938 – had gone as far as shamefully agreeing to a pledge of loyalty "to the King, to his Royal successors and to the *fascist Regime.*"[29]

The reaction of universities to the 1938 laws was shrewdly foreseen by one of the most coherent opponents of Fascism, Ernesto Rossi. From prison, in 1938, Rossi wrote to his mother: "Quite a number of university chairs will be vacant all at once: a godsend for all the candidates that will run in flocks to sit for the entrance exams in order to get them."[30] And a godsend they really were.

The Fate of Jewish University Teachers, 1938–1943

After fifteen years of intense research begun in 1988 on the occasion of the fiftieth anniversary of the Italian anti-Semitic laws, we now have a clearer idea about how these laws affected many university employees, even though the exact number will never be known. In fact we will never be able to count how many students or young graduates who had intended to pursue academic carriers were prevented from doing so: such information could only be obtained in direct interviews of people that the inexorable passing of time has already taken away from us; their memories are buried with them forever.

The present state of research suggests that practically all universities and all disciplines were involved. If we take into account all levels of university posts, 7 percent of the teaching staff, equal to some 390 people, were expelled; these included as many as 96 professors (curiously enough they too represented 7 percent of that category).[31] Such figures give us a more precise view of the Jewish presence in Italy, a population that, according to official statistics of the Fascist authority, was said to account for *one per thousand* of the Italian population.

But the actual damage to universities was even worse and more pervasive than the statistics suggest. The development of many young talents was curbed forever. In many university departments, most particularly in medical schools, the expulsion of the professor was soon followed by that of his collaborators, even those who were not Jews. The case of the pediatrics clinic at the University of Bologna is a good example in terms of methods used and the duration of its effects that are still felt today.[32] Thus, the supply of human resources that were to guarantee a turnover in the teaching profession was impoverished.

Young Jews indeed were denied access to universities (as well as to all levels of public education), although, after some hesitation, those who had already entered were allowed to conclude their studies (Primo Levi was among those who benefited from this provision). Some of those who attended university, or wanted to enter, migrated elsewhere: now it is impossible to know how many of them came back or how many started a university career in other countries. We know definitely that such cases existed. Let me share one such case, in a discipline I am familiar with. Franco Modigliani, who was granted the Nobel Prize in 1985, left Italy as a student in 1938, returned to Italy after the war to complete his degree, immediately left again, and developed his whole career in the United States.

Persecution dried up another potential resource of the Italian academic world: the presence of foreign Jewish students. The unclear attitude Mussolini displayed toward the Jews in the 1930s, prior to 1938, led to an opening of Italian universities to Jewish students coming from the numerous countries, such as Poland, where quotas severely limited their chances of attending university. Early in 1938 foreign Jewish students were quite numerous in Italy: 1,344 (i.e., 1.7–1.8 percent of the total number of university students) according to the data gathered by the Ministry of Education, mainly concentrated at universities in Pisa and Bologna.[33] When the storm was approaching, many preferred not to renew their registration, to prevent expulsion.[34] In this way, talented minds that could have enriched Italian universities left the country and brought nourishment to other educational and research systems. An example is found in the field of economics. Alfred Otto Hirschmann, a German, had come to the University of Trieste, where he received his degree in 1938, after a stay in France. Due to forced emigration, however, his great critical skill enriched the United States.

But in an era of globalization, when, at least since World War II, people, goods, and ideas circulate rapidly, does all this have any importance? I still believe it does. In universities, the presence of highly qualified personalities possessing high standards in professional ethics bears a strong impact on the quality of teaching, on research, and on the training of young researchers. This is why the damage caused in 1938 had permanent effects that could not be remedied in 1945.

The Attempt to Reintegrate Jewish University Teachers, 1944–1946

The history of the coming back to life of Italian Jews is only a recent field of study.[35] Things turn out not to be as simple, or as happy, as it was assumed until now. What happened within universities is one clear piece of evidence.

Because of space limitations, I will not dwell on the rather astonishing fact that in some cases Jews were tried in courts with the charge of being former Fascists. One such case even had a tragic ending: Tullio Terni, an anatomic pathologist in Padua, committed suicide when he was expelled from the Accademia dei Lincei, one of the most important cultural institutions in Italy, as an ex-Fascist.[36] One other protagonist of such events, Giorgio Del Vecchio, stated that "the new persecution against a victim of the persecution" was absurd.

> It is utterly illogical to suspect that, after suffering from a vile and cruel persecution, any Jews can remember the former regime with nostalgia instead of being loyal to the new State that has given them back their civil rights. Which other Italians can feel a greater horror towards fascism, now a synonym with Nazism? Is it not unfair and *paene ridiculum* [grotesque] to subject them to epuration?[37]

I shall therefore only briefly describe the reintegration of Jewish teaching staff into the universities from which they were expelled. One would expect a smooth reintegration and, from the point of view of their careers, the acknowledgement of all those years of *forced* absence from university. That seemed to be the case at the beginning, but then things changed. I will confine my remarks to the two legal provisions that created the context for a rather complex issue,[38] whose practical repercussions have not yet been completely retraced.[39]

The story of readmission of Jewish university teachers – or teachers of Jewish origin – in postwar Italy revolves around two crucial pieces of legislation. On October 19, 1944, law no. 301 (*Decreto Legislativo Luogotenenziale*) provided that teachers expelled from Italian universities "because of political or racial reasons" must be reintegrated, reacquiring their original chairs. On May 27, 1946, however, law no. 535 (*Regio Decreto Legislativo*), consisting of just one article, stated that those who were reintegrated as university teachers after being expelled for political or racial reasons must be "assigned to temporary chairs established on purpose." According to the new law, these newly created "temporary chairs" would be eliminated when the holders had retired or had transferred to another university.[40]

Another significant change had to do with calculating years of university service. The law of 1944 had stipulated that the years of forced absence would be counted toward the teachers' length of service. In this way, the Ministry of Education sought to avoid what would have clearly been an unacceptable situation. As the 1944 law stated: "Unless [the reintegrated teachers] are assigned the seniority they would have been entitled to were they not forcibly driven away from their posts, they will find themselves under the direction of those who were their assistants at the moment of expulsion. It would be a very queer situation, an evident aberration."[41] However, the policy of compounding the years of service from the persecution and postwar periods was soon abolished. Thus, at the beginning, the victims of persecution were given priority, while later, priority was given to those who benefited from their expulsion.

I cannot but reiterate what I stated years ago, when I argued that following the law issued in May 1946, those who had benefited from (or even taken advantage of) the Jews' expulsion from universities kept their roles and powers unchanged, while the status of the reintegrated professors was radically different from what it was in 1938. As I wrote in my 1997 book,

> No longer full-fledged professors, responsible for the teaching of one discipline, they became the equivalent of assistants, occupying a post doomed to disappear. This made a considerable difference among the teaching staff of the time [...]. Reintegration in the previous role was not guaranteed by the law, and could only be possibly regained if an individual teacher was sufficiently strong from the academic, psychological and political points of

view. Some of them were in such a position. Many others were
not. It is no surprise that many Jewish professors refused to return
to Italy![42]

Why did this happen? Franco Modigliani draws a picture of the unfavorable
situation for Jewish academics after the war. In his memoirs, Modigliani explained
how, until 1946, he and his wife considered returning to Italy. They subsequently
changed their minds and decided to stay abroad:

> News coming from Italy reported a very quick return to old atti-
> tudes, to the worst habits of the past. Within universities the situ-
> ation had not gotten any better: public competitions for teaching
> posts were rare and decided beforehand, with available jobs al-
> ready allotted to the protégés of the powerful. So we decided to
> stay and apply for American citizenship.[43]

Indeed the Italian situation tended to rapidly shift toward a moderate position,
supported by upper, more powerful classes, to which most academic professors
belonged. Rather than protest against the 1938 racial laws, this same upper
stratum of Italian society had taken advantage of them. However, this is not, by
far, the whole story.

Until 1946, when the Christian Democrats began to dominate educational
policy and would continue to do so for a half century, the Italian Ministry of
Education was governed by officials with a nonconfessional background who
were strongly under Croce's influence. They were undoubtedly convinced that
the solution to the Jewish problem had to be and could not be other than
assimilation; such conviction was further supported by the great momentum
of Zionism soon after the war, an idea that went against what they considered
the only solution to the problem of the Jews, that is, the elimination of their
"century old separatism."[44]

The reintegration process was also complicated by providing evidence that
many Jews were compromised with Fascism and therefore did not deserve favorable treatment. The anti-Semitic laws were in some respects ambiguous, and
purposely so, in order to provide some escape through arbitrary interpretation by
the involved administrations.[45] As the head of the Political Intelligence Department stated, the majority of the Italians developed the belief that for the Jews "it
was enough to have the personal support of some influential politician in order
to challenge the laws."[46] At the same time, the ambiguous possibilities of being
exempted from persecution reinforced the myth among Jews according to which

"[racial] laws were dictated by the desire to be compliant with Hitler and Nazism, but they were actually contrary to Mussolini's Latin, honest thinking: therefore they would never be really enforced, at least not in their harsher parts." So – as Enzo Levi[47] writes – "the argument used to justify 'honest' fascists became the false hope for many of the persecuted."[48] This generated a great confidence in "discriminations" (exempt status) so that the "rush" to get it "became even frantic; differentiation had to be obtained at all costs, with all means, including bribery – and all this in order to get [...] advantages that later turned out to be useless."[49]

So, too many Jews, including university professors, had been Fascists until 1938, had justified the abolition of political freedoms, had pledged loyalty to the regime, and had supported the wars in Ethiopia and Spain. This Fascist background was very important in postwar Italy, when one's past for or against Fascism was what made the difference. This was considered further evidence that such people were compromised by Fascism and therefore did not deserve any favorable treatment. Such a view applied also to the Jewish community during the twenty years of Fascism: too many Jews, including university professors, had been Fascists until 1938.

Conclusion

To make a full appraisal of why the reintegration of Jewish professors in Italian universities proved rather humiliating, it is necessary to add one further element to those already described in this chapter. There was one shortcoming among those groups who were building a new Italy: the failure to understand the strategic value that a radical change of the school and university system could have had. The new postwar leadership thought that it was enough to eliminate (in a more or less formal way) Fascism from the education system and to reintroduce, into a structure largely shaped by Fascism, the blessed freedom of teaching. But in the meantime the world had completely changed. Suffice it to cite Edoardo Amaldi's remarks concerning the years immediately following World War II: "Research in high and low energy nuclear physics was moving from the traditional scale of university laboratories to that of semi-industrial enterprises."[50]

Giving priority to and understanding the strategic importance of this sector would have attracted back to Italy the professors expelled during the Fascist period, brilliant minds who had made important international contributions. Although Italy was very dear to the hearts of its émigré university professors, it remained for them only a sentimental dream, just like one's country of birth always is for immigrants.[51] Thus the damage to Italian culture became a permanent one, and its extent has yet to be fully understood.

NOTES

1. See Ettore Majorana, "Lettera a Emilio Segrè," May 22, 1933, reprinted in E. Recami, *Il caso Majorana* (Rome: Di Rienzo, 2000), 171–3. For the publishing history of Recami's book see R. Finzi, *Ettore Majorana: Un'indagine storica* (Rome: Edizioni di Storia e Letteratura, 2002), 8; 11, footnote 1. The letter, first thought to be lost, was published by Emilio Segrè on the fiftieth anniversary of Majorana's vanishing in *Storia Contemporanea* 19 (1988), 107–11. Segrè also included it in his autobiography. See E. Segrè, *Autobiografia di un fisico* (Bologna: Il Mulino, 1995), 173–5. For the English version, see *The Mind Is Always in Motion: The Autobiography of Emilio Segré* (Berkeley and Los Angeles: University of California Press, 1993). Italics mine.

2. See A. Capristo, "L'esclusione degli ebrei dall'Accademia d'Italia," *La Rassegna mensile di Israel*, LXVII, 3 (Tishrì – Tevet 5762, September–December 2001), 1–36.

3. Cf. L. Fermi, *Atomi in famiglia* (Milan: Mondadori, 1954), 123 [English: L. Fermi, *Atoms in the Family: My Life with Enrico Fermi* (Chicago: University of Chicago Press, 1954)] and E. Segrè, *Enrico Fermi, fisico. Una biografia scientifica* (Bologna: Zanichelli, 1987), 90 (I quote this edition instead of the 1971 one, because an interesting documentary section accompanies the later edition making it more complete) [English: E. Segré, *Enrico Fermi: Physicist* (Chicago: University of Chicago Press, 1970)].

4. See John L. Heilbron, *I dilemmi di Max Planck, portavoce della scienza tedesca* (Turin: Boringhieri, 1988) 125, 127, 129 [English: J. L. Heilbron, *The Dilemmas of an Upright Man: Max Planck as Spokesman for German Science* (Berkeley and Los Angeles: University of California Press, 1986)]; David C. Cassidy, *Un'estrema solitudine. La vita e l'opera di Werner Heisenberg* (Turin: Boringhieri, 1996), 343.

5. As stated above, in his letter to Segrè, the author writes the reason that "prompted the Aryans to give an almost unanimous support to the antisemitic struggle" is not "to be found in the romantic race theory." Such theory does not enjoy an exaggerated support, and what reasonably spread is rather a moderate tendency to ban the Jews from public offices. The adjective "romantic" is given its exact interpretation in a letter Majorana wrote to Giovanni Gentile Jr. not much later, on June 7: "unable to find in its culture and in its history sufficient elements in order to create a feeling of unity among German speaking populations, Germany is compelled to resort to that *stupid ideology of race* that has not apparently found enough echo in Austria" (Recami, *Il caso Majorana*, 173, 178). Italics mine.

6. Regarding Italy, see R. Maiocchi, *Scienza Italiana e razzismo fascista*, (Scandicci [Florence]: La Nuova Italia, 1999). For Nazi Germany, see part II of J. Olff-Nathan, ed., *La science sous le Troisième Reich* (Paris: Seuil, 1993). For the example of a democratic country, see P. S. Colla, *Per la nazione e per la razza. Cittadini ed esclusi nel "modello svedese* (Rome: Carrocci, 2000).

7. The article about Hungarian Judaism published in *La Civiltà Cattolica* in July 1938 is exemplary. See R. Taradel and B. Raggi, *La segregazione amichevole. "La Civiltà Cattolica" e la questione ebraica 1850–1945* (Rome: Editori Riuniti, 2000), 131–4. On the same subject, see the remarks by R. Moro in his *La Chiesa e lo sterminio degli Ebrei* (Bologna: Il Mulino, 2002), 98.

8. Quotation from P. Treves, "Formiggini ed il problema dell'ebreo in Italia," in L. Balsamo and R. Cremante, eds., *A.F. Formiggini: A Publisher of the 20th Century* (Bologna: Il Mulino, 1981), 66. In February 1932, a note to Mussolini stated the need for the Duce to issue clear directives for the appointment of new members to the Italian Academy "in order to obviate the inconveniences of electoralism." The question was raised whether it was advisable to grant "those Jews who had gained a prominent position particularly in physical and mathematical disciplines a proper representation, without exaggerating though, so as to prevent the risk of the lively Semitic proselytism" (quoted from Capristo, *L'esclusione degli ebrei*, 12).

9. See G. Miccoli, "Santa Sede, questione ebraica e antisemitismo fra Otto e Novecento," in *Gli ebrei in Italia. Storia d'Italia Annali 11, 2 Dall'emancipazione ad oggi*, C. Vivanti, ed. (Turin: Einaudi, 1997), 1371–1574.

10. "Mussolini a Vittorio Emanuele III. Colloquio col Papa. Ore 11 del giorno 11 febbraio 1932 in Vaticano" enclosed to A. Corsetti, "Dalla preconciliazione ai Patti del Laterano. Note e documenti," in Biblioteca Civica di Massa, ed., *Annuario 1968*, p. 224.

11. Centro Furio Jesi, ed., *La menzogna della razza. Documenti e immagini del razzismo e dell'antisemitismo in Italia* (Bologna: Grafis, 1994), 177.

12. Moro, *La chiesa e lo sterminio degli ebrei*, 62–3.

13. Recami, *Il caso Majorana*, 195.

14. See S. Zuccotti, *Il Vaticano e l'Olocausto in Italia* (Milan: Bruno Mondadori, 2001), 29. [English: *Under his Very Windows: The Vatican and the Holocaust in Italy* (New Haven, CT: Yale University Press, 2000)]

15. "Si quis ex iudaeo vere christianus effectus, nonne est laude dignior, quam nos qui in alieno, loco sati, in aliena stirpe tamquam neophyti, hoc est novelli surculi insiti sumus" ("Un'epistola del Galateo in difesa degli ebrei," reproduced in 1938 in *La critica* and now in Alberto Cavaglion and Gian Paolo Romagnani, eds., *Le interdizioni del Duce. A cinquant'anni dalle leggi razziali in Italia (1938–1988)* (Turin: Meyner, 1988), 238).

16. See, for example, B. Croce, *Storia d'Italia dal 1871 al 1915* (Bari: Laterza, 1967), 97–8 and B. Croce, *Storia d'Europa nel secolo decimonono* (Bari: laterza, 1961), 277.

17. For all this, see my "Croce. Lettera sul 'popolo eletto,'" in *Il Corriere della Sera* (June 29, 1998), 25; "Che gli Israeliti si controllino . . . !," in *Il diario della settimana*, III, 29, (July 22–28, 1998), 74–7; "Da perseguitati a "usurpatori" per una storia della reintegrazione dei docenti ebrei nelle università italiane," in *Il ritorno alla vita. Vicende e diritti degli ebrei in Italia dopo la seconda guerra mondiale*, M Sarfatti and Fondazione Centro di Documentazione Ebraica Contemporanea, eds. (Florence: Giuntina, 1998), 95–114; "Nel LX anniversario delle leggi razziali," in *Il ponte*, LV, 4 (April 1999), 92–9; "Bisogna che gli israeliti che ritornano si controllino," in Enrica Basevi, *I beni e la memoria, L'argenteria degli ebrei. Piccola "scandalosa" storia Italiana* (Soveria Mannelli [Catanzaro] Rubettino, 2001), 9–23. All such works are unclear only to those who do not want to understand.

18. "It is just the most conservative among the Jews that are now migrating from the East to the highly developed West. The first consequence is that the assimilation process of the western Jews is hindered. The second is that antisemitism thrives on that [...] At the same time, Judaism is undergoing a rupture: very often the well-off, cultivated and almost assimilated Jews of the West are not that enthusiastic about the arrival of their poor and ignorant *Yiddish* brothers from the East, towards whom they often have a feeling that could be defined as antisemitism within Judaism" (Karl Kautsky, "Rasse und Judentum (1914)" italian trans. in Massimo Massara, ed., *Il marxismo e la questione ebraica* [Milan: Edizioni del Calendario del Popolo, 1972], 461–2). Apart from Kautsky's quotation, see for example Walter Boehlich's interview by Gert Mattenklott in 1988: "In the German empire German Jews themselves too always had prejudices against Eastern Jews. The more they were culturally integrated and assimilated, the more they believed they could live in freedom. The Eastern Jews were exactly the opposite" (G. Mattenklott, *Ebrei in Germania. Storie di vita attraverso le lettere* [Milan: Feltrinelli, 1992], 135–6 [original German version: 1988]).

19. G. Flaubert, *Dizionario dei luoghi comuni*, Italian translation by J. Rodolfo Wilcock (Milan: Adelphi, 2000), 47, item "Jew" (a contribution by Edmond La Porte, the writer's neighbor).

20. "Regarder, voir passer le petit bout de la lorgnette," meaning "avoir un espritétroit."

21. Etymology alone explains well the meaning of this definition. The name of this "petite lunette d'approche dont la forme [originally] ètait telle, qu'on pouvait voir d'un coté différent de celui vers le quel on presentait le visage" (Littré) derives from "lorgner" which means to glance furtively, stealthily. It means not only to steal a greedy look at a beautiful woman, but above all it means to have an evasive look, not straight in the face of someone. It means longing for other people's property, and therefore, it is the synonym for a lack of sincerity or hypocrisy which are thought to infect all those who buy the "lorgnettes" from the Jews.

22. See A. Capristo, *L'espulsione degli ebrei dalle accademie italiane* (Turin: Zamorani, 2002), 22–46.

23. One example of open opposition to the racial laws in the universities was Arrigo Serpieri, the rector of the University of Florence. See G. Turi, "Ruolo e destino degli intellettuali nella politica razziale del fascismo," in Camera dei Deputati, *La legislazione antiebraica in Italia e in Europa* (Rome: Camera dei Deputati, 1989), 107.

24. In this connection see R. De Felice, *Storia degli ebrei italiani sotto il fascismo* (Turin: Einaudi, 1961), 302, 357–8, 443; R. Bianchi Bandinelli, *Dal diario di un borghese ed altri scritti* (Milan: Il saggiatore, 1962), 71 (concerning this text it is worthwhile to remember the remarks made by A. M. Vinci about Luzzatto Fegiz's diary [P. P. Luzzatto Fegiz, *Lettere da Zabodaski. Ricordi di un borghese mitteleuropeo 1900–1984* (Trieste: Lint, 1984)]: "it certainly is a corrected and revised diary" [A. M. Vinci, *Storia dell'università di Trieste: Mito, progetti, realtà* (Trieste: Lint, 1997), 261]; A. Asor Rosa, "Bontempelli Massimo" in *Dizionario biografico degli italiani*, vol. XII (Rome: Istituto dell'Enciclopedia Italiana, 1970), 423; L. Pardo, "La scienza non ha confini. Universitari stranieri a Bologna tra le due guerre," in *Strenna storica bolognese* (1987), 329; U. Santarelli, "Un illustre e appartato foglio giuridico, La rivista di diritto privato

(1931–1944)," in *Quaderni fiorentini per la storia del pensiero giuridico moderno*, 16 (1987), 701; N. S. Onofri, *Ebrei e fascismo a Bologna*, Crespellano [Bologna], Grafica Lavino, 1989), 126; P. Nastasi, "Leggi razziali e presenze ebaiche nella comunità scientifica" in A. Di Meo, ed., *Cultura ebraica e cultura scientifica in Italia* (Rome: Editori Riuniti, 1994), 121.

25. "Come coprire i vuoti," in *Vita universitaria*, October 5, 1938.

26. Majorana's letter to his mother, dated May 5, 1933, is reprinted in Recami, *Il caso Majorana*, 170.

27. Cf. F. Chabod and A. Momigliano, *Un Carteggio del 1959*, G. Sasso, eds., with a conclusion by R. Di Donato (Bologna: Il Mulino, 2002), 105.

28. See S. Friedlander, *Nazi Germany and the Jews: The Years of Persecution 1933–1939* (New York: Harper Collins, 1997); J. Olff-Nathan, ed. *La science sous le Troisiéme Reich*; A. D Beyerchen, *Gli scienziati sotto Hitler* (Bologna: Zanichelli, 1981) [original English edition: *Scientists under Hitler* (New Haven, CT: Yale University Press, 1977)].

29. A. Acquarone, *L'organizzazione dello stato totalitario* (Turin: Einaudi, 1965), 179, where the full text of the oath is reprinted. On the same matter, see H. Goetz, *Il giuramento rifiutato. I docenti universitari ed il regime fascista* (Milan: La Nuova Italia, 2000) [original German version: *Der freie Geist und seine Widersacher*, Frankfurt am Main: Haag + Herchen Verlag GmbH, 1993]; G. Boatti, *Preferirei di no. La storia dei dodici professori che si opposero a Mussolini* (Turin: Einaudi, 2001).

30. E. Rossi, *Elogio della galera. Lettere 1930–1943* (Bari: Laterza, 1968), 444.

31. For these figures, see R. Finzi, *L'università italiana e le leggi antiebraiche* (Rome: Editori Riuniti, 1997), 109–14; M. Sarfatti, "La scuola, gli ebrei e l'arianizzazione attuata da Giuseppe Bottai," in *I licei G. Berchet e G. Carducci durante il fascismo e la resistenza*, D. Bonetti, R. Bottoni, G. Gargia De Maio, eds. (Milan: Liceo Classico Statale "G. Carducci," 1996), 56–60; and A. Ventura, "La persecuzione fascista contro gli ebrei nell'università italiana," in *Rivista storica Italiana*, CIX (1997), I, 148, 149, 161, 192–7.

32. Finzi, *L'Università italiana e le leggi antiebraiche*, 68–75.

33. G. P. Brizzi, *Silence and Remembering: The Racial Laws and the Foreign Jewish Students at the University of Bologna* (Bologna: CLUEB, 2002), 13. All general reference data come from ISTAT, *Sommario di Statistiche storiche 1926–1985* (Rome: ISTAT, 1986).

34. R. Finzi, "Undici 'vacanze' nel DCCCL annuale della fondazione dell'Università di Bologna," in *Lo studio e la città. Bologna 1888–1988*, W. Tega, ed. (Bologna: Alfa, 1987), 353 (see also Brizzi, *Silence and Remembering*, 26).

35. See, for example, M. Toscano, ed., *L'abrogazione delle leggi razziali in Italia (1943–1987)* (Rome: Senato della Repubblica, 1988); Fondazione Centro di Documentazione Ebraica Contemporanea and Sarfatte, ed., *Il ritorno alla vita*; I. Pavan and G. Schwarz, eds., *Gli ebrei in Italia. Tra persecuzione fascista e reintegrazione post-bellica* (Florence: Giuntina, 2001).

36. R. Levi Montalcini, *Elogio dell'imperfezione* (Milan: Mondadori, 1987), 62–3.

37. Giorgio Del Vecchio, *Una nuova persecuzione contro un perseguitato. Documenti* (Rome, 1945), 11–12.

38. I traced back the events through their various stages in Finzi, "Da perseguitati a 'usurpatori' per una storia della reintegrazione dei docenti ebrei nelle università italiane," in *Il ritorno alla vita*, 95–114.

39. The above-described events have been thoroughly investigated by Francesca Pelini in "Appunti per una storia della reintegrazione dei professori universitari perseguitati per motivi razziali," in Pavan and Schwarz, eds., *Gli ebrei in Italia*, 113–39.

40. Toscano, ed., *L'abrogazione delle leggi razziali in Italia (1943–1987)*, 124–54.

41. A. G. Ricci, ed., *Verbali del Consiglio dei Ministri, luglio 1943 – maggio 1948. Edizione critica III (Governo Bonomi, 18 giugno 1944–12 dicembre 1944)* (Rome: Archivio Centrale dello Stato, 1995), 407–8.

42. Finzi, *L'Università italiana e le leggi antiebraiche*, 105.

43. F. Modigliani, *Avventure di un economista. La mia vita, le mie idee, la nostra epoca*, Paolo Peluffo, ed. (Rome-Bari: Laterza, 1999), 53–4.

44. B. Croce, *Nuove pagine sparse* (Bari: Laterza, 1966), 345.

45. "The institution of 'differentiation' and 'aryanization' gave rise to all sorts of intrigues [. . .]. It is reported that a differentiation could cost as much as 500 thousand lire [a huge sum for those times]" (E. Enriques Agnoletti, "Il nazismo e le leggi razziali in Italia," in L. Arbizzani and A. Caltabiano, eds., *Storia dell'antifascismo italiano* (Rome: Editori Riuniti, 1964), I, 140–1).

46. G. Leto, *OVRA Fascismo, antifascismo* (Bologna: Cappelli, 1952), 192.

47. Lawyer in Modena, father of well-know journalist Arrigo, grandfather of Ricardo Franco, first spokeman of Romano Prodi, the former European Commission president.

48. E. Levi, *Memorie di una vita (1889–1947)* (Modena: STEM Mucchi, 1972), 88.

49. F. Coen, *Italiani ed ebrei: come eravamo* (Genova: Marietti, 1988), 65.

50. E. Amaldi, "Il caso della fisica," in *Conseguenze culturali delle leggi razziali in Italia*, Accademia Nazionale dei Lincei, ed. (Rome: Accademia dei Lincei, 1990), 116.

51. Examples in this connections can be found in B. Rossi, *Momenti nella vita di uno scienziato* (Bologna: Zanichelli, 1987), 28, 32, 83; and Segrè, *Autobiografia di un fisico*, 386.

7 Building a Racial State: Images of the Jew in the Illustrated Fascist Magazine, *La Difesa della Razza*, 1938–1943[*,1]

Sandro Servi

In the context of the Fascist racial press campaign (1937–43), one of the regime's most intense efforts took the form of the publication and distribution of a new illustrated magazine devoted entirely to the pursuit of a new racial consciousness among the Italian populace. *La Difesa della Razza*, published biweekly from August 5, 1938, to June 20, 1943, had a very large print run and was distributed extensively throughout Italy. Its foundation was closely linked with the publication of the so-called *Manifesto of Racist Scientists*, the chief goal of which was to establish a biological approach – as opposed to a political approach – to the "Jewish question" in Italy.[2] The text of the *Manifesto* appeared for the first time in an unsigned article ("Fascism and the Race Problems") in *Il Giornale d'Italia* on July 15, 1938, and was subsequently cited or reprinted by all the national newspapers.[3] Ten days later, a *Comunicato* (Communiqué) of the National Fascist Party dated July 25, 1938,[4] provided a version of how it had come about and listed the names of its supposed authors: ten scientists, for the most part young assistant lecturers. Both the version supplied in the *Comunicato* and the reconstruction attempted by De Felice,[5] however, should now be revised because of information provided by a document that has since surfaced about which De Felice knew nothing. This document reveals the true origin of the *Manifesto*, the primary role played by Mussolini, and the role of skillful and zealous agent played by Guido Landra. From a letter by Landra, a young lecturer in anthropology at Rome University, and one of the signatories of the *Manifesto*, to Mussolini,[6] we learn for certain:

---

[*] Sandro Servi retains the copyright in this chapter and has granted only nonexclusive publication rights for its inclusion in the present volume.

1) That in February 1938 Guido Landra was summoned, at the personal behest of Mussolini (who had read a few memos Landra had written), to an audience with minister of popular culture Dino Alfieri, who ordered him to "put together a scientific committee to plan and implement the racial campaign;"

2) That on June 24, 1938, Benito Mussolini gave audience to Landra and commanded him to "establish a special research office in the ministry [of popular culture]" allowing him freedom to choose his own staff, "so that within five or six months the basic points could be determined in order to launch the racial campaign in Italy." During that audience, Mussolini "had spoken to him at length about the race problem, examining every aspect;"

3) That, on the same day (June 24), Alfieri had instructed Landra to "outline in writing the basic points" of Mussolini's thoughts;

4) That Landra had performed the task, "assembling, in a sort of Decalogue," Mussolini's directives;

5) That "this was how the Manifesto of Italian Racism (or *Carta della Razza*) had come about, as it was later printed, with only the slightest changes;"

6) And that, therefore, the above-cited article, "Fascism and the Race Problems," was written by Guido Landra.

Because Landra's letter was written personally to Mussolini, and we may assume that he cast himself in the best possible light, he certainly could not have misstated the essential facts concerning the origin of the *Manifesto* and on the role that Mussolini had played in its inception. The timing of events – Mussolini's "lecture" to Landra on racism on June 24; on July 15, the anonymous publication of the *Manifesto* written by Landra according to Mussolini's instructions; on July 25 the *Comunicato* of the National Fascist Party, which gave credit for the *Manifesto* to a group of ten scientists; on August 5 the publication of the first issue of *La Difesa della Razza*, with a graphic reproduction of the *Manifesto* on the title page; on August 6 a series of circular letters from the minister of national education went out to university rectors, principals, directors of education, and other officials recommending that *La Difesa della Razza* be distributed in public schools, universities, and libraries[7] – proves that the project had been undertaken and planned in such a way as to give *La Difesa della Razza* a leading role in the Fascist regime's racial and anti-Semitic campaign.

Telesio Interlandi, a journalist and the editor of *Il Tevere* and *Il Quadrivio*, was appointed editor of the magazine. His responsibilities were shared by an editorial committee consisting of Guido Landra, Lidio Cipriani, Leone Franzì, Marcello Ricci, and Lino Businco. Another name was officially added to the committee, beginning with the fourth issue: that of the assistant editor Giorgio Almirante.[8] The team that edited the magazine was not representative of all the sectors of Italian racism. At the same time, it was closely linked to Mussolini himself.

Interlandi's *Il Tevere* was generally thought to be directly inspired by Mussolini. When Mussolini wrote for *Il Popolo d'Italia*, he remained cautious and diplomatic. When he wrote for *Il Tevere*, on the other hand, he unleashed much wilder language.[9] We have already discussed Guido Landra's close collaboration with Mussolini in the composition of the *Manifesto*. As the founding director of the *Ufficio Razza*, or Race Bureau at the Ministry of Popular Culture, from its establishment in August 1938 until February 1939, he directly supported the magazine. The operation of *La Difesa della Razza* was, in fact, undertaken directly by the Ministry of Popular Culture from its debut (August 1938) until November 1940, when it was handed over to the publisher Tumminelli.

Kept off the editorial staff were leading members of other currents of racism, such as Nicola Pende, Sabato Visco, and Giacomo Acerbo, who belonged to the so-called national school of racism (the first two had been signatories of the *Manifesto* and, because of their disagreement, tried to distance themselves from the Manifesto itself[10]). Also excluded were such figures as Giovanni Preziosi and Julius Evola, who could be classed as an esoteric and traditionalist of racism, or Paolo Orano and Gino Sottochiesa, representatives of a Catholic-based anti-Semitism.[11] The February 1939 replacement by Sabato Visco as director of the Race Bureau (*Ufficio Razza*) (which changed its name in April 1939 to *Ufficio Studi e Propaganda sulla Razza* or Bureau for Racial Research and Propaganda) is indicative of a certain modification in the regime's official policy on race. Visco was in turn replaced in May 1941 by Alberto Luchini, and this further change of personnel coincided with a revival of the Fascist regime's propaganda activity.

La Difesa della Razza was presented in the guise of a journal of popular science. In fact, it featured contributions from anthropologists, zoologists, demographers, medical ethicists, physicians, biologists, sociologists, statisticians, and so on, as well as historians and authors. The level of debate, however, was anything but academic, and anti-Semitic tirades were the real *Leitmotiv*. For this purpose, all sorts of anti-Semitic material was employed ranging from classical pagan anti-Judaism to Christian anti-Jewish themes and from medieval legends to modern economic prejudices.

La Difesa della Razza was designed to foster pride in the "Italian race" while combating the feeble racial awareness of Italians in the African colonies and especially mixed marriages and "crossbreeding." It criticized "demo-plutocratic" powers (such as France, Great Britain, and the United States), which it accused of weakness, femininity, racial mingling, and sterility.

We should point out that anti-Semitism was not the magazine's only theme. A considerable number of articles were devoted to eugenics, folklore, national traditions, and the celebration of the Italian race and the races of allied nations (Germany, Hungary, and Japan), as well as to the denigration of the populations of enemy nations and nations peopled with "inferior" races.

The magazine had a print run of 140,000–150,000 copies for the first issues, but with the passage of time, and especially once the war had begun, that print run dropped to 19,000–20,000 copies in the final period of publication by the Ministry of Popular Culture (July–November 1940), when at least 9,000 copies were mailed by subscription to institutional recipients and about 4,000 copies were actually sold. Probably, print runs and sales were even smaller in the last period of publication (November 1940–June 1943) when the magazine was operated by the publisher Tumminelli. The number of pages also dropped in later issues (forty pages + front and back cover for the first issue, and usually forty-eight pages in the issues that followed, or occasionally as many as fifty-six or sixty-four pages), and the quality of paper stock also declined, probably as a result of the war.

The magazine received funding from banks, insurance companies, and manufacturers.[12] The publisher Tumminelli, aside from publishing the magazine, also brought out a series of books on racism that sometimes contained collections of articles reprinted from the magazine.[13]

The Cover

La Difesa della Razza (Plate A) featured a two-color cover with striking modern graphics as well as extensive use of photographs, diagrams, caricatures, and photomontages. The cover illustration remained unchanged (only the background color changed) for the first three issues, after which it was used as a logo, under the masthead, in all issues of the publication. It depicted a *gladium* (the typical Roman short sword), gripped by a white hand, separating a classical head from a Semitic head and the head of a young black woman. The message was unmistakable, and it summarized the ten points of the *Manifesto of Racist Scientists* with a clear reference to the concept of *romanità* or "Roman-ness."[14] Beneath the word *razza* in the masthead appeared the legend "scienza documentazione polemica" ("science, documentation, polemic"), to which was added, from the fourth issue (September 20, 1938) on, the word "questionario" (in fact, beginning with the fourth issue, the magazine featured a column with an exchange of questions and answers from the readers). Each issue carried the year and issue number, and the date, with day, month, and year of the Fascist era (the first issue, for instance, carried the date "5 August XVI," as if to emphasize that it was practically useless to state the year 1938, given the momentous date of 1922, the dawning of the "Fascist revolution"). The first issue presented a quote from Dante (see Plate A, upper left-hand corner): "*Sempre la confusion delle persone / principio fu del mal della cittade* (It has always been a fact that confusion of blood/has been a source of evil to city-states)" (Dante, *Paradiso* XVI, 67–8). By the second issue, and for all the issues that followed, the quote was replaced by another: "*Uomini siate, e non pecore matte, / sì che' l Giudeo di voi tra voi non rida!* (Be men, not mad sheep, lest the Jew among you find cause to point his finger in derision)" (Dante, *Paradiso* V, 80–1).[15]

As further evidence of the link between the *Manifesto* and *La Difesa della Razza*, we may point out that this first issue of the magazine featured articles by all the signatories of the *Manifesto* (Lino Businco, Lidio Cipriani, Leone Franzì, Guido Landra, Marcello Ricci, Arturo Donaggio, Franco Savorgnan, and Edoardo Zavattari),[16] with the exception of Nicola Pende and Sabato Visco, who at first attempted to distance themselves.

The Magazine and the *Manifesto of the Racist Scientists*

Just twenty-one days after its publication in *Il Giornale d'Italia* and eleven days after the appearance of the party's *Comunicato*, the *Manifesto of Racist Scientists* was reprinted in a very visible format below the masthead of the first issue of the magazine (Figure 1). Although its scientific validity was negligible,[17] and it was characterized by a succession of pseudo-scientific claims, alternating with political, social, historical, cultural, and ideological observations, the *Manifesto* was an attempt to provide a scientific and ideological platform for Italian racism in general and anti-Semitism in particular. It was broken down into ten points, each of which consisted of a heading and a short explanatory text:

1) Human races exist.
2) There are great races and little races.
3) The concept of race is a purely biological concept.
4) The population of present-day Italy is of Aryan descent and its civilization is Aryan.
5) The influx of great masses of men in historical times is a myth.
6) There is now a pure "Italian race."

1. *La Difesa della Razza*, I, 1 (August 5, 1938). The infamous "Manifesto of Racist Scientists" appeared on the front-page of the magazine's inaugural issue. Point 9 reads: "The Jews do not belong to the Italian race".

7) The time has come for the Italians to declare themselves openly racist.
8) It is necessary to make a clear distinction between Mediterranean peoples of Europe (westerners) on the one hand and Africans and "easterners" on the other.
9) The Jews do not belong to the Italian race.
10) The purely European physical and psychological features of the Italians must be altered in no way.

Point 9, the only one that specifically referred to the Jews, presented the following text beneath the heading:

> Of the Semites who, over the course of the centuries, landed on the sacred soil of our Fatherland, for the most part, nothing has survived. Even the Arab occupation of Sicily left nothing behind but the memory of a few names. For that matter, the process of assimilation was always exceedingly rapid in Italy. Jews are the only people who were never assimilated in Italy, because they comprised non-European racial elements, entirely different from the racial elements from which the Italians take their origin.

The magazine made extensive use of photographs and illustrations to present the government's new policy of racism. A diagram published in the second issue of the second year (November 20, 1938) (Figure 2) explained in an "amusing" manner that, in compliance with the new laws, Jews could no longer "serve in the military, act as legal guardians, own companies with roles in the national defense, own lands or buildings, employ 'Aryan' domestic help, and that foreign Jews would be expelled from the country." Of course, all the Jews in the drawing are portrayed with a stereotypical Jewish nose.

Stereotypes of Christian Anti-Judaism

Although *La Difesa della Razza* sought to present itself as a forum for the popularizing of modern biological racism, it did not hesitate to make use of all the centuries-old baggage of anti-Jewish prejudices of every sort, beginning, of course, with those of the never-vanquished Christian anti-Judaism. Articles and illustrations in almost every issue made use of Christian legends and depictions, both medieval and modern, that accused the Jews of horrible crimes against the Christians. Clearly, the source of all these myths is the accusation of deicide committed by the Jews against Jesus, one of the foundational beliefs of Christian churches until the second half of the twentieth century. In this sense, while we

2. *La Difesa della Razza*, II, 2 (November 20, 1938), p. 24. A cartoon showing the legal prohibitions against the Jews following the Grand Fascist Council's deliberations.

may perhaps agree with the statement that "the Shoah was the work of a typical neo-pagan modern regime,"[18] any analysis of the text and illustrations of *La Difesa della Razza* cannot help but confirm that the Fascist anti-Semitic campaign (like its Nazi counterpart), which served as a foundation and accompanied the discrimination, the persecution, and ultimately the extermination of the Jews, could only have been implemented due to the rich anti-Judaic heritage built over the centuries by the teachings of the Christian churches.[19]

Among the countless examples that we could reproduce here, a double-page spread from *La Difesa della Razza* dated October 20, 1939, under the headlines "Jewish Rituals" (Figure 3) featured a list of so-called ritual murders taken, according to the magazine, from a novel written by a converted Jew.[20] Accompanying the article are two illustrations. On the left the 1882 "death of a young girl murdered by Jews" at Tisza-Eszlar in Hungary is depicted (the Jews are immobilizing the young girl, naked, while they collect in a basin the blood that flows from a wound in her neck).[21] On the right page, a similar, alleged murder of a Christian child is represented, which supposedly took place in Munich in 1285.[22] Here the Jews are stabbing the little boy, tied naked to a table, in order to draw off his blood. Next to the table, two Jewish children gaze with smiles at a basin filled with blood. All around, as evidence that this is a public ritual and certainly not a private murder, numerous men and woman stand watching the scene. The victims of ritual murder were male children, whose purity and innocence symbolized Jesus Christ, crucified by the Jews (*giudei*), or young women, always shown naked, upon whom the Jews performed their typical perversion.

The frequent appearance in the magazine of articles and illustrations related to the accusation of ritual murder merits some reflection on the meaning and purpose of such references, especially if we consider the degree to which such accusations were no longer credible and clearly anachronistic.[23]

The Christian accusation against the Jews of ritual murder should be considered as an example of the more general blood libel, linked therefore with charges of desecration of the Host, and utilization of Christian blood for medical or magical purposes, for cannibalism and vampirism.[24] In an attempt to reinforce orthodox beliefs concerning the dogma of the Eucharist, a dogma that in the twelfth century had been the subject of debate between Catholic supporters of transubstantiation and supporters of consubstantiation,[25] the theory later accepted by Martin Luther and the Protestant movement, the Church fought bitterly against any possible heterodox belief by condemning all magical practices involving blood and the consecrated Host. The Jews were the innocent and unwitting victims of this battle.[26]

3. *La Difesa della Razza*, II, 24 (October 20, 1939), pp. 38–39. "Jewish Rituals".

In reality the rite of the Eucharist constitutes an allegorical reinterpretation of the Jewish paschal sacrifice (*Korban Pesach*), in which the flesh and blood of Jesus [*Ecce agnus Dei, ecce qui tollit peccatum mundi* – Behold the Lamb of God, which taketh away the sin of the world. (John 1:29)] are consumed by the faithful in the form of Host and wine,[27] in place of the lamb of the ancient biblical sacrifice. Jews, accused of piercing the Host with a sharp object and of consuming Christian blood (using it, in fact, to make unleavened bread for *Pesach*, or Passover), and therefore of performing a grotesque and terrible caricature of the controversial Christian ritual, served as an external scapegoat upon which to project the doubts that afflicted the Christian believers concerning the dogma of the Eucharist.

The accusation of ritual murder, which had visited such atrocious suffering upon the Jewish population in medieval Europe,[28] was recycled and updated by the Fascist regime for various reasons we shall attempt to analyze here. First of all, the diffusion of that accusation by traditionalist Christian circles had not actually occurred that long before[29] and, in all likelihood, many readers had been educated according to those legends. Second, the reference to blood had always been a powerful tool in the spread of the racial myth in question.[30] Blood had constantly been associated with the concept of race: the sixth point of the *Manifesto* stated, "There is now a pure 'Italian race.' This statement is not based on any confusion of the biological concept of race with the historical and linguistic concept of people and nation. Rather, it is based on the exceedingly pure *blood relations* that join the Italians of today with the generations that have populated Italy over past millennia. This *ancient purity of blood* is the greatest title of nobility that the Italian nation can boast." (Italics mine) In his article in the first issue of *La Difesa della Razza*, Landra devoted a section to blood, writing, "The concept that the blood of one human race is different from the blood of another race is commonly held, even among relatively unlettered individuals: this belief is based upon solidly scientific facts which were sensed by ordinary people before being known to scientists."[31] In the third issue of the magazine (September 5, 1938) there appeared an article titled, "Blood and Race," which offered scientific data on blood, along with some very unscientific hypotheses on the link between race and blood.[32]

But the blood libel accusation lent itself very well to use in the Fascist propaganda campaign, in part because several of its features converged with the new doctrine on race. In fact, alongside a certain "theological" content, the charge carried with it two features that fit especially well with modern, state-driven anti-Semitism: a biological definition of Jewish difference and a conspiracy theory.

If we examine the uses of Christian blood that the blood libel accusation laid to the Jews, we find that many of these uses entail a biological difference of Jews. The blood was used by the Jews (aside from other ritual uses) in order to remove the *foetor judaicus* (the typical and distinctive odor of Jews); to cure the wound of circumcision; to cure a number of diseases that irremediably afflicted Jews, such as scabies, ringworm, certain foot ulcers, and eye problems; and as a cure for menstrual problems (which it was believed affected Jewish men as well).

Another part of the blood libel was the detail that ritual murder was committed in turn by the various Jewish communities, which then sent out the blood that they had obtained to all the other Jewish communities of the Diaspora. There was, in other words, a "Jewish plot," a secret that was zealously concealed and handed down from generation to generation.[33]

The cover of *La Difesa della Razza* from January 20, 1942 reproduces another image of ritual murder (Plate B). This depiction is a detail from a renowned fifteenth-century German woodcut, by the German painter and engraver Michael Wohlgemuth (1434–1519), showing the "martyrdom of the Blessed Simon of Trent."[34] The Trent case (1475) and the trial that followed is one of the best documented episodes of ritual murder. There are documents and a rich bibliography concerning the case, including a manuscript with the trial proceedings now in the possession of the Yeshiva University Archives in New York.[35] This illustration is both artistically powerful and striking (Wohlgemuth was the teacher of Albrecht Dürer, who served as an apprentice in Wohlgemuth's workshop in Nuremberg) and it features another especially unsettling aspect of the blood libel. The child is portrayed standing, to further identify him with Jesus being crucified. The Renaissance iconography (in contrast with the Byzantine, Romanesque, or Gothic iconography) often depicted the Baby Jesus naked, his male organ visible, in order to symbolize the "humanity" of the Messiah and Savior and his participation in and transcendence of humanity's sensual nature.[36]

The scene shown in the engraving (both in the original and in the detail reproduced in *La Difesa della Razza*) is composed in such a way as to attract the viewer's attention to the torture performed by the Jews on the child's male organ (located in the geometric center of the image); in the magazine this emphasis is accentuated powerfully by adding the color red for the blood pouring from the wound and filling up the basin. The scene unquestionably succeeds in arousing horror in the viewer with a reference to the rite of circumcision and the linked fear of castration. In his essay, "Moses and Monotheism," Freud suggested that the Jewish custom of circumcision could be used to whip up anti-Semitic sentiments by reminding non-Jews of the "feared idea of castration" with its

4. *La Difesa della Razza*, III, 16 (June 20, 1940), p. 39. The illustration's caption (lower left) reads, "Jews Poisoning Wells".

terrifying connotations.[37] Freud considered the initiation rite of circumcision as a ritual compromise in which the father and God Himself, while renouncing the punitive castration of the son, settle for the *pars pro toto* – the part for the whole. Otto Fenichel claims that this practice triggered in non-Jewish populations the sensation that there is something unsettling about the Jews.[38] The practice of circumcision is strange and yet familiar in the depths of the subconscious, and it is especially well suited to render the Jew the object of a diabolic projection. C. G. Schoenfeld[39] claims that, since circumcision, on a subconscious level, is usually identified with castration, it can easily lead one to abhor all that is Jewish. Henry Loeblowitz-Lennard[40] explicitly links the medieval accusation of ritual murder to the reaction of anguish at the idea of castration caused by the practice of circumcision upon Jewish children. All of this, of course, should be studied in greater depth in the light of interpretations of anti-Semitism that link the origins of monotheism with the development of the Oedipal conflict, suggesting an analogy between the function of the father in the family and the role of the monotheistic God. Just as the father imposes upon the son social and family taboos, so does the monotheistic God impose the Ten Commandments, triggering frustration and therefore aggressivity,[41] but this line of inquiry would lead us far afield of the theme and the limitations of this chapter.

Accompanying an article bylined "C.B." (possibly Carlo Barduzzi) about "Jews (*giudei*) and Arabs in Medieval Spain," in issue number 16, year III (June 20, 1940), there appeared, without any explicit relationship to the text, an illustration with the caption, "Jews (*giudei*) Poisoning Wells" (Figure 4). The accusation that Jews poisoned wells spread in France during an outbreak of the plague.[42] The Jews, inspired by the devil and in cahoots with the Moors of Granada, supposedly made a pact with the lepers to destroy Christians by infecting well-water by tossing little bags of blood, urine, herbs, and consecrated Hosts into them. The result was a series of pogroms, trials, and massacres, ranging as far afield as Switzerland and Germany. This accusation also reinforced the idea of a Jewish conspiracy.

A lengthy article by Fernando Porfiri ("Saint Thomas and the Jews") in the issue of May 20, 1940[43] (Figure 5), illustrated with pictures of Saint Thomas Aquinas done by great Renaissance painters (Fra Angelico, Taddeo Gaddi, Gentile da Fabriano, and others), reconstructs the *Philosophia perennis* of the Catholic Church toward the Jews through quotes from the great Father of the Church, while pointing out that "lest we commit serious errors and anachronisms, the point of departure, Saint Thomas's overriding motive (...) was not, of course, political, ethnic, or if you like, racial in nature, but rather religious, ethical, and social." Quoting from the *Summa Theologica* and from the *De Regimine*

5. *La Difesa della Razza*, III, 14 (May 20, 1940), pp. 35–35–36. Double page from an article titled, "Saint Thomas and the Jews".

Judaeorum of the *doctor angelicus*, a number of scrolls featured phrases about the Jews: "Jews (*giudei*) are devoted to idolatry," "Jews (*giudei*) are cruel and devoted to greed," and (on the following page) "The Jews are condemned to servitude" and "The Jews profit only through robbery and theft."

Through articles like this, accompanied by the publication of books devoted to classical Christian anti-Judaism, the product primarily of the Catholic-driven school (Gino Sottochiesa, Mario Lolli), the Fascist regime meant to demonstrate the convergence of Fascist anti-Semitism with the traditional teachings of the Church, denouncing the "Jewish peril," and to show the legitimacy and necessity of the repressive measures adopted by the regime.

Stereotypes of Biological Racism

A double-page illustration in the third issue of the magazine[44] (Figure 6) contains a collage of images comparing the beauty and harmony of a mother belonging to the Italian "race," here represented by Domenico Ghirlandaio's Renaissance painting, *Virgin Mary with Christ Child*, with the supposed ugliness and vulgarity of mothers and children belonging to non-European peoples. The illustration does not accompany any article and so the message is entirely entrusted to the visual impact of the photographs and the short captions that provide commentary. The caption reads, "Mothers and Children of All Races." Surrounding the central image, a legend states, "Italian Motherhood. Ghirlandaio's Madonna." Next to one photograph, the text reads, "The indecent pose with which a Negress from Rhodesia offers her breast to her child," while another states, "The savage expression of a mother from Tierra del Fuego." A third caption states, "When motherhood means debasement: the bastards of Rehoboth, a hybrid between Negroes and Dutchmen."

Issue 10 of the third year (March 20, 1940) is a special number: it is sixty-four pages long (instead of the usual forty-eight pages) and it is entirely dedicated to so-called "crossbreeding," featuring articles on "The Bastards of Rehoboth," "The Mulattoes of Jamaica," "Half-breeds of the Rhineland," "Half-breeds of the Americas," "Hybrids between Chinese and Europeans," "Half-breeds of Polynesia," "Crossbreeding in South America," "Negro-Chinese Hybrids," and more. It should be remembered that Fascist racism also constituted a historic choice of the regime at a time of colonial conquest as a response to the problems that emerged from relations between white colonists and the indigenous population.[45] Separating two articles in the magazine is a full-page photograph (Figure 7), which depicts "Jews, Negroes, and half-breeds fraternizing in an

6. *La Difesa della Razza*, I, 3 (September 5, 1938), pp. 24–25. "Mothers and Children of All Races."

7. *La Difesa della Razza*, III, 10 (March 20, 1940), p. 31. The caption (lower right) reads, "Jews, Negroes, and half-breeds fraternizing in an American nightclub."

American nightclub."[46] The message (it should be remembered that most Italians of the time had never actually seen black men or women, but only photographs of African natives) is simple and complex at the same time: the United States is a degenerate nation, where the mingling of the races, combined with the general moral decadence, leads to crossbreeding, abetted by the modern music particularly of Jazz, a Jewish-Negro product. Or put in other words, if a white hand and a black hand are joined, a flower will wilt (Plate C): an allegorical interpretation of the concept of infertility attributed to mixed marriages.[47]

Political and Economic Anti-Semitism

Factors in the economic anti-Semitism utilized in Fascist propaganda constituted the following elements: the envy caused by professional competition, the resentment felt by economically subordinated social categories toward those who wielded economic power, and the conscious or subconscious ambivalence toward the wealthy.

A French caricature from 1898[48] in the issue of March 5, 1939, was used to illustrate an article by Francesco Scardaoni titled, "Jewish Scandals in Paris"[49] (Figure 8). This illustration carries a clear message: before the French Revolution, only the aristocracy oppressed the unfortunate peasants; afterward, bureaucracy and bourgeoisie, Socialists and Freemasons, and, above them all, a capitalist with the usual exaggerated Jewish features. In Paris, "a completely Judaized city," there are numerous economic scandals – according to the author – involving Jews, since their "interests can only be gained by either the accumulation of wealth, or the destruction of the wealth of others." Of course, Jewish crime was not limited to the economic sphere, but included pornography and corruption. Here, too, we find the conspiracy motif, since the Jewish criminal Bernard Tannenzaft, later Bernard Nathan, did not act alone, but worked with a network of Jewish accomplices involved in banking, the stock exchange, and the political world.

Another article, also by Scardaoni, "The Judaic Shadow over France,"[50] explained the dastardly influence of Jews in France, beginning with the bestowal of the rights of citizenship upon them in the Constituent Assembly of September 27, 1791. During the French Revolution, the Jews "specialized in carrying out the most frightful massacres. . . . The blood-thirsty Marat, after all, was himself a Jew." The article was illustrated with a caricature of a Jew, with a hooked nose and

PERCHÈ FU FATTA LA RIVOLUZIONE FRANCESE

8. *La Difesa della Razza*, II, 9 (March 5, 1939), p. 23. "Why the French Revolution took place: before and after." A cartoon taken from the French magazine *Caran D'Ache* (1898).

9. *La Difesa della Razza*, I, 3 (September 5, 1938), p. 34. "The Judaic Shadow Over France."

10. *La Difesa della Razza*, I, 6 (October 20, 1938), p. 52. Turning the cartoon upside down, the reader learns that Bolshevik and Jew are one in the same.

curly hair (Figure 9) drawing a spider web over France. In the magazine's iconography, Jews were often associated with dangerous and repulsive animals, such as snakes or insects. In a cover from February 1939, the strong hand of Fascism is shown throttling a number of snakes, forming a Star of David (Plate D).[51]

The Soviet Union was often the target of attacks in the magazine. An article from October 1938 titled "Jewish-style Bolshevism," by Aldo Bomba, identified the Soviet regime entirely with the Jews:

> The Christian land of the Czars has become a veritable feudal
> holding of the Israelites. We may safely conclude, then, with-
> out fear of error, that the Bolshevik Hydra, which threatens the
> world, is Jewish by nature, that all of the instruments suitable
> for laying the foundations of world revolution are Semitic, and
> that if we wish to defend ourselves from Moscow and its death-
> dealing doctrine, we must first and foremost preserve ourselves
> with any and all means possible from the Zionist infiltration into
> our national life.[52]

The article is illustrated with a number of pictures. One shows "the leaders of Jewish Communism," whose portraits form a Star of David and a cartoon reproduced here (Figure 10) which shows, beyond the shadow of a doubt, that Bolshevik and Jew amount to the same thing.

11. *La Difesa della Razza*, V, 7 (February 5, 1942), p. 40. An article and illustration explaining "How the Jews (*giudei*) dragged the US into the war."

With the entry of the United States into the war, a new enemy appeared alongside France and Great Britain. Here, too, of course, it was "the Jews" (*giudei*) who had dragged the United States into war (Figure 11).[53] In fact, beginning with the outbreak of war in September 1939, Fascism had attempted to place blame for hostilities on the Jews.[54] Great Britain was also, of course, Judaized: an efficacious caricature[55] (Figure 12) showed the true face of "England in the Mirror."

Art and Science

Albert Einstein was the most spectacular example of the so-called modern Jewish science that was being attacked by the magazine. One page from 1939 (Figure 13)

12. *La Difesa della Razza*, IV, 18 (July 20, 1941), pp. 16–17. "England in the Mirror."

13. *La Difesa della Razza*, II, 17 (July 5, 1939), p. 20. A satirical commentary on Einstein's personality and theory used in the struggle against the supposed Jewish domination of science and society.

PLATE A. *La Difesa della Razza*, I, 1 (August 5, 1938). Cover page.

PLATE B. *La Difesa della Razza*, V, 6 (January 20, 1942). Cover page.

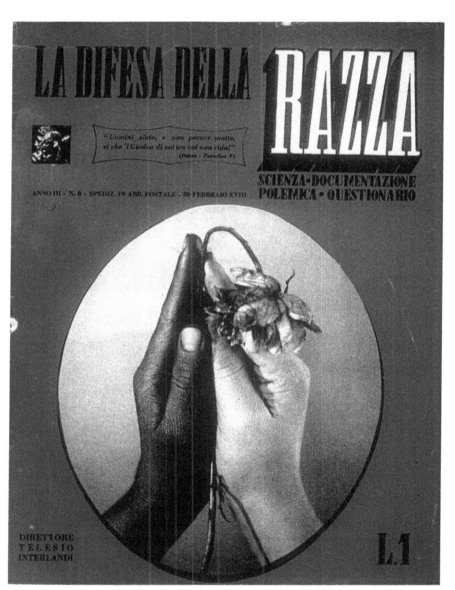

PLATE C. *La Difesa della Razza*, III, 8 (February 20, 1940). Cover page.

PLATE D. *La Difesa della Razza*, II, 8 (February 20, 1939). Cover page.

maintained that Judaism dominated society.[56] Captions, surrounding a photograph of Albert Einstein, state, "The most delicate sectors of education monopolized by Jews," "Internationalism under the guise of 'pure science,'" and "Destructive Theories: Sterile Cerebralisms." These statements served as commentary to the great Jewish physicist. The Italian school of nuclear physics, comprised for the most part of Jews (and led by Enrico Fermi, who had married a daughter of the Jewish admiral Augusto Capon), emigrated to the United States, contributing to the production of the atom bomb, which finally ended the war.[57] In an article from September 1938, Sigmund Freud, Karl Marx, and Cesare Lombroso (Figure 14) were denounced as "proponents of Jewish materialistic culture in the nineteenth century."[58]

Julius Evola (1898–1974), a philosopher who was initially anti-Christian,[59] anti-modern,[60] and anti-Semitic, even before the anti-Semitism of the Fascist state,[61] became the master of so-called "esoteric traditionalist" racism and was an agent in the espionage service of the SS in Italy.[62] In an article published in February 1940, Evola explored the subject of "Jews and Mathematics,"[63] attempting to demonstrate that Judaism is the antithesis of "Aryan civilization," and attacking, as examples of the Semitic mindset, "Pithagorism," "the Kabbalah and the Zohar," and "Jewish dualism" while wondering whether "mathematics is an objective science." The article was illustrated with a number of pictures, including Spinoza, Einstein, and a Jew meditating between a Masonic square and compass. (Figure 15)

In general terms, we cannot attribute to Fascism the negative view of modern art that was so typical of Nazism. The fact that many members of the Italian Futurist movement joined the Fascist party soon after its formation led, especially in the early years, to a certain degree of artistic innovation. All the same, the anti-Semitic polemic did not spare the work of Jewish artists, probably for an as-yet undisclosed German influence. One instance is found in an article, signed by G. Dell'Isola, in a 1939 issue of the magazine.[64] The author criticizes rationalism in architecture with attacks against Le Corbusier, Walter Gropius, and Erich Mendelsohn but blames a group of Jews, foreigners (the Hungarian Faludi), and Italians (Levi Montalcini), faulting them for the diffusion of this rationalism in Italy.[65] The chief crime of these architects was the use of iron, which Italy had to import. As Dell'Isola wrote, "While [these architects] claimed they wanted to become 'modern,' the iron, imported for no good reason, has brought that much more gold dropping into the pockets of the international plutocracy." The article was illustrated – with little relation to the text – by two sculptures by Jacob

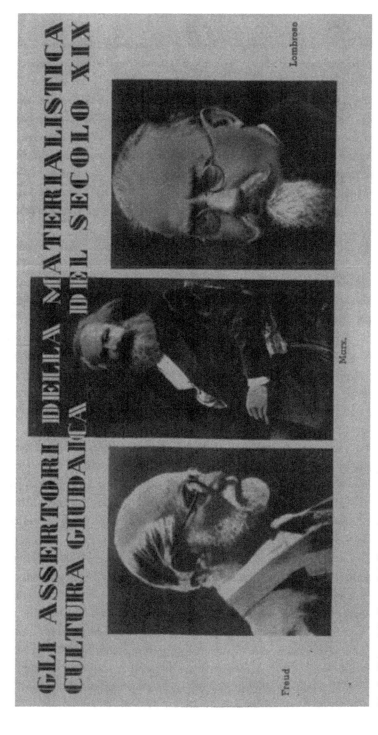

14. *La Difesa della Razza*, I, 3 (September 5, 1938), p. 32. An attack against three representative of "Jewish materialistic culture."

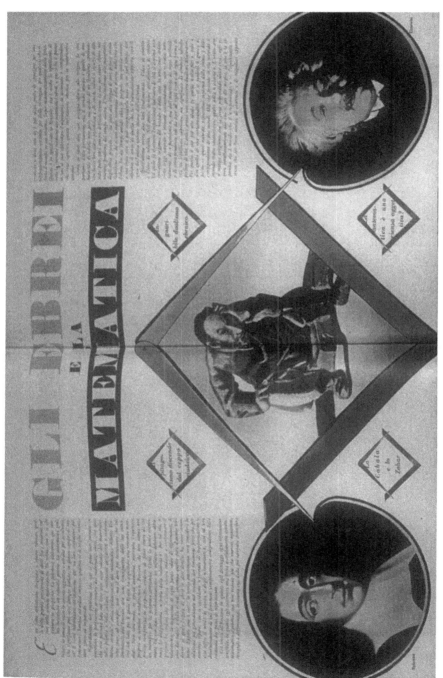

15. *La Difesa della Razza*, III, 8 (February 20, 1940), pp. 24–25. An article by Julius Evola conflating and denigrating simultaneously Jews, mathematics and Freemasonry.

16. *La Difesa della Razza*, II, 17 (July 5, 1939), pp. 16–17. Two examples of "Jewish degenerate art" (Epstein and Chagall) used to illustrate an article against internationalism and the industrialization of modern architecture.

17. *La Difesa della Razza*, II, 10 (March 20, 1939), pp. 34–35. An article contrasting international feminism and the Italian woman.

Epstein (Figure 16), a famous Jewish sculptor born in New York and active in England, as well as a painting by Chagall.

Antifeminism and Sexuality

The Fascist movement's exaltation of the roles of the Fascist wife and mother inevitably led to polemics against the modernist tendencies of the more advanced societies, especially in the United States. An article titled "Feminism and the Italian Woman" contrasted three pictures (Figure 17, from left to right): "The Communist Jewess Rosa Luxemburg, who led the bloody Spartacist movement in Germany," "A quaint group of girl scouts in the United States," and a happy Italian mother.[66] A conference of Zionist women in America (Figure 18) was, obviously, a very odd picture for the Italian reader.[67]

The cover of *La Difesa della Razza* from April 5, 1939 contains an image (Figure 19)[68] that reproduced the traditional iconography of the episode of "Susannah and the Elders,"[69] a subject that was quite frequent in the sixteenth and seventeenth centuries in the works of famous artists like Anthony Van Dyck, Albrecht Altdorfer, Lorenzo Lotto, and Rembrandt.[70] The protagonists of the ancient story were, of course, all Jews. But here, while the chaste Susannah is depicted with European features, the two elders are replaced by two caricatures: one with stereotypical Jewish features, the other, black features with devil horns.

18. *La Difesa della Razza*, IV, 6 (January 20, 1941), p. 27. "Zionist Women participating in a Congress in America."

19. *La Difesa della Razza*, II, 11 (April 5, 1939) Cover page.

If we return for a moment to what we maintained about the relationship between anti-Semitism and the Oedipal conflict, then we will clearly touch, as one historian of anti-Semitism put it, "directly the psychological, 'Oedipal' truth about anti-Semitism, whereby only the male Jew is dangerous and horrendous. In fact, the castrating father could only be virile. As she has no penis, the Jewish woman is not subject to the 'curse of the race.' Rather, indeed, her innocence makes her

20. *La Difesa della Razza*, III, 3 (December 5, 1939), p. 40.

especially desirable."[71] Moreover, the episode of Susannah, when deftly reinter-
preted, serves as training material for the accusation against the Jews of sexual
corruption of Aryan women. The theme became common with the emancipation
of the Jews in Europe and their integration into society in numerous anti-Semitic
cartoons published in England (beginning in the last decades of the eighteenth
century), France, and Germany.[72] The theme recurred in Fascist and Nazi anti-
Semitic propaganda. The projective aspect of the accusation (it is neither the
truth nor the falsehood of the accusation that constitutes the qualifying element
for the anti-Semite, as much as the psychological motivations of the accusation itself) is demonstrated by the fact that the accusation against the Jews of
sexual immorality was relatively scarce in contemporaneous America (where
anti-Semitic prejudice was hardly lacking). This is probably due to the presence in the United States of another object, better suited as the target of such
projections: black males.[73] In *La Difesa della Razza* as well as in Fascist propaganda in general, the accusation of sexual immorality was directed against Jews,
and it was not until the later years of the war that cartoons and posters appeared
that addressed the topic of the rape of white women by black enemy soldiers.
On this cover, the Jew and the black are associated in the accusation, even though
the black man, identified with the devil, seems to have a largely symbolic value.
As a matter of fact, the racial laws concerned both Jews and the natives of the

colonies. Indeed, on the title page of the same issue of the magazine is portrayed a sieve from which falls a Jew with a large nose and goatee and a half-naked savage-like black man.

Fortunately, as shown in this cartoon from 1939 (Figure 20), a brave young man armed with a truncheon (an allegory of Fascism?), knows how to give this Jew-headed snake its just desserts.[74]

Conclusions

By presenting this gallery of images with commentary, we have attempted to show how *La Difesa della Razza* was something much more than merely a new publication. Rather it was a government-sponsored undertaking closely linked with the launching of state-sanctioned racism. The timing of the episode of the *Manifesto*, the very close ties between Mussolini and the leading figures involved, the role attributed to the magazine in the campaign of anti-Semitic propaganda, and the Fascist promotion of the magazine all point to the central and important status of *La Difesa della Razza*.

The selection of images presented here was meant to cover, to the greatest degree possible, the broad range of anti-Semitic themes (with the occasional extension to racism against people of color). Therefore, in *quantitative* terms, they are not wholly representative. For example, caricatures of hook-nosed Jews were certainly much more common than photographs of Zionist congresses. We must keep this in mind lest we gain a mistaken idea of the magazine from the set of images shown here. All the same, the most important currents of anti-Semitic propaganda (Christian anti-Judaism; biological anti-Semitism; political and economic anti-Semitism; and science-related, arts-related, and sexually driven anti-Semitism) have been presented and commented upon.

It would be boastful to think that, at this point, we could offer any definitive conclusions. We would need to study all the images in *La Difesa della Razza* as well as analyze and classify them in a scholarly manner. We do believe, however, that we could offer some interpretative hypotheses and that we can now suggest some food for thought, especially concerning one question: how effective was the Fascist government's anti-Semitic press and propaganda campaign? Before we attempt to answer the question, we must define the *goal* the Fascist regime hoped to attain by adopting anti-Semitism. And that is not an easy question to answer. For instance, we cannot accept Michele Sarfatti's argument that "Fascism intended to eliminate Italian Jews from the territory of the Italian peninsula."[75] In our view, that was only *one of the results* that Fascism, *in a particular phase of the persecution*, aimed to achieve.

Although in Italy the anti-Semitic movement never mobilized the masses on its behalf, inciting them to commit lynchings or pogroms (nor had this ever been the intention of the movement's promoters), the regime nonetheless utilized anti-Semitism as an important instrument of national unity. Anti-Semitic propaganda, while it may have prompted some reactions among people of conscience, still played a substantial role – specifically through its relentless press campaign – in bringing Italians together around the imperialistic idea of Fascism. The blood myth was designed to give every Italian the mystical confidence that he or she belonged to a superior people and had a homeland worth sacrificing and even dying for. At the same time, that myth was meant to indicate – with no half-measures or uncertainties – everything that those Italians should not be, identifying the Jew as the essence of all sin and vice. And this educational aspect, if you will, should not be underestimated.[76] The Aryan model that the Fascist regime wished to set up for all Italians to imitate lacked any concrete scientific or cultural foundation (and Mussolini knew this as well as, or better than, anyone else, as is shown by many quotes prior to the *Manifesto*[77]). In reality, that model could be defined only by its negative, only by the polemic against all that which is Jewish. In a situation like that found in Italy, where the Jews – a minor, peaceful, well-integrated minority – presented no danger at all to the nation, the "Jewish problem" was raised and utilized primarily to teach the Italians *what they should not be*, using the Jew as a personification of the most complete antithesis.[78]

And all of this took place at a specific moment in the history of Fascism. The anti-Semitic legislation, which some view as a pure "German import product,"[79] (but which modern historians view, at best, as an undertaking that counted among its many motivations that of showing compliance with Nazi Germany and facilitating cooperation between the two dictatorships) was adopted in a historic phase in which the war of conquest in Ethiopia and the Spanish Civil War had pushed Italy into isolation, forcing it into closer cooperation with Germany, its only possible ally. It also took place at a time when international economic sanctions were having sharp repercussions upon the quality of life of the Italian people and at a time when, therefore, consensus toward the Fascist regime (which had probably reached its high point in the years 1935–7[80]) was progressively weakening.

From the picture painted here, meant to delineate the true aim of Fascist state anti-Semitism, it should now be easier to address the question earlier posed: How effective was this racial and anti-Semitic propaganda?

We believe that the propaganda was very effective because, in the face of just a few, illustrious dissenters, it served as a powerful tool of national cohesion. It made available to everyone a handy process of transference whereby it was possible to shift the legitimate hostility of the lower classes toward the Fascist regime onto an innocent and helpless minority. Aimed at the Italian people, who had few militaristic ideals, it helped, to a certain degree of success, to consolidate the myths of Duce and Empire, for which the populace was now summoned to fight.

In the narrowest sense (that is, if we limit ourselves to anti-Semitism), if we wished to measure, in a rigorous scholarly manner, the efficacy of the anti-Semitic campaign of *La Difesa della Razza*, it would have been necessary to subject a representative sampling of the Italian population to an anti-Semitism test[81] prior to the campaign and then repeat the test on the same sampling again in 1943 (in addition, we would have to ascertain whether that sampling had been exposed to other influences). Obviously, this is something that we cannot do. But we can take certain other facts into consideration.

La Difesa della Razza enjoyed a massive distribution by the standards of the Italy of the time. The magazine also received extensive coverage from all the vehicles of the press and propaganda. In particular, through the efforts mentioned above on the part of the ministries of National Education and Popular Culture, it was distributed extensively in public schools, universities, libraries, and all cultural institutes; in all local party branch offices; and in all national companies. Given its style and the language that it used, and its cost, *La Difesa della Razza* did not reach the homes of the millions of Italian peasants who were still semi-illiterate, but it was read in the homes of the ruling class, the homes of the middle and lower-middle classes, the homes of all head clerks, and the homes of schoolteachers who often brought copies to class. It was used as material with which to organize school exhibits and for neighborhood organizations. It constituted a biweekly appointment for journalists and writers in the provinces, perhaps in a province where there were no Jews, but where from time to time the local press would feature overwrought articles about the "Jewish peril."

Considering the degree of integration attained by the Italian Jewish community from the unification of Italy in the nineteenth century to the 1930s (and without underestimating the persistence of anti-Judaic prejudices of Catholic origin), certain manifestations of anti-Jewish hatred, which later found expression in the public positions taken by well-known personalities, in the work of informers, in the active participation in the persecution and deportation of the Jews, but also in the indifference with which the broad majority of the Italian population[82] witnessed the oppression of the helpless and defenseless Jewish minority, all the way up to the "Jew hunt" – well, let us say that these manifestations of hatred seem surprising and unpredictable. But things that might have seemed impossible in 1936 actually took place a few years later: what had changed in the interval? Certainly not the inner structures of the average Italian personality; perhaps a number of general political and economic conditions had worsened (as described above), but above all, the mass anti-Semitic propaganda had had a chance to do its work. The shift in the attitude of the average Italian citizen toward his or her Jewish neighbor (or toward the abstract idea of the Jew, but which nonetheless led all the same to the denigration or physical harming of a flesh-and-blood human being) was the product, basically, of the efficacy of the anti-Semitic propaganda machine set into operation by the Fascist regime in the years 1937–8. *La Difesa della Razza* was an important cog in that machinery.

Translated from the Italian by Antony Shugaar

NOTES

1. All the images presented here come from our personal collection, except for Figure 15 and Figure 16, which we photographed from the collection of the CDEC in Milan, whom we thank gratefully.

Upon reviewing the English translation of our article (and we want to thank here the translator, Antony Shugaar, for his competent and sensitive work), we were informed about the appearance of an e-book dedicated to the magazine *La Difesa della Razza* by Valentina Pisanty titled *Educare all'odio: la Difesa della razza (1938–43)*, Motta online (www.Mottaeditore.it) 2002. The work is an annotated anthology of excerpts and illustrations taken from the magazine and presents systematically (although without deep analytic insights) various aspects of the review (from eugenics to the myth of the race, from the description of different races to anti-Semitism, etc.). It constitutes a very comprehensive survey of Fascist racism, and we strongly recommend it to those interested in the subject.

Finally we want to express our gratitude to the organizer of the conference in New York and editor of this book, Dr. Joshua Zimmerman, for his stimulating suggestions and critiques.

2. The *Manifesto* does not have an official name and is therefore referred to in documents, in addition to the above-used form, both as *Manifesto del Razzismo Italiano* ("Manifest of Italian Racism") or *Carta della Razza* ("Charter on the Race"). For the sake of accuracy, we will use the various terms according to the form employed in the documentation.

3. The text of the article is roughly identical to the one that was later published in *La Difesa della Razza* (see below), but it condensed the ten articles into three sections, with the headlines "Difference of the Races: art. 1–3," "Aryan Italy: art. 4–7," and "Necessary Distinction: art. 8–10." The ten articles were followed by a brief editorial that announced a coming "action that would in time 'profoundly affect our way of life' and create a certain

attitude in the Italian people concerning the question of race" and then went on to clarify the meaning of the terms *Aryan, Italian race,* and *Nordic.*

4. See Document 17 in Renzo De Felice, *Storia degli ebrei italiani sotto il fascismo* (Turin: Einaudi, 1961). [English edition: Renzo De Felice, *The Jews in Fascist Italy: A History* (New York: Enigma Books, 2001.]

5. We should point out that De Felice rightly noted the protests of the two most respected signatories, Nicola Pende and Sabato Visco.

6. Letter to Benito Mussolini, Rome, September 27, 1940, Archivio Centrale dello Stato, Segreteria particolare del Duce, Carteggio Ordinario 1922–1943, b. 476, fasc. 183506, cited in Centro Furio Jesi, *La menzogna della razza* (Bologna: Grafis Edizioni, 1994), 367–8.

7. Archivio Centrale dello Stato, Min. Int., Dir. Gen. Demografia e Razza (1938–1943), b. 4, fasc. 15, Direttive dei ministeri in materia di razza.

8. Almirante had worked for Interlandi at the newspaper *Il Tevere.* In the period following World War II, he represented the neo-Fascist Movimento Sociale Italiano in the Italian parliament from 1948. He served as the secretary of the party several times and then as its chairman until his death in 1988.

9. A. Lyttelton, *La conquista del potere, il fascismo dal 1919 al 1929* (Bari: Laterza, 1974), 642–3. [English: Lyttelton, *The Seizure of Power: Fascism in Italy, 1919–1929,* 2nd ed. (Princeton, NJ: Princeton University Press, 1987)].

10. See De Felice, *Storia degli ebrei italiani,* 275–7.

11. We are using here a classification of different groups of anti-Semitic writers that differentiates among various approaches toward the "Jewish problem". This terminology is not, and could not be, a rigorously scientific one and is similar to that used in the already quoted book: Centro Furio Jesi, *La Menzogna della razza,* where different chapters are dedicated to "Il razzismo biologico," "Il nazional-razzismo," "Il razzismo esoterico-tradizionalista," and "Antigiudaismo cattolico e antisemitismo fascista."

12. Funding came from, among others, Credito Italiano, Banca Commerciale Italiana, Banco di Sicilia, Istituto Nazionale delle Assicurazioni, R. A. S., Breda, and Officine Villar Perosa. For information on print runs and funding, see "La Difesa della Razza" (Amministrazione) Archivio centrale dello Stato, Ministry of Popular Culture, fasc. "La Difesa della Razza" (rivista), quoted in Centro Furio Jesi, *La menzogna della razza,* 231.

13. The volumes that were published include T. Interlandi, *Contra Judaeos* (Rome and Milan: Tumminelli, 1938); I. B. Pranaitis, *Cristo e i cristiani nel Talmud* (Rome and Milan: Tumminelli, 1939); and G. Preziosi, *Come il giudaismo ha preparato la guerra* (Rome: Tumminelli, 1940).

14. See Arturo Donaggio, "I caratteri della romanità," in this first issue of *La Difesa della Razza,* 22–3.

15. Quotations from Dante, *The Divine Comedy,* trans. John Ciardi (New York: W. W. Norton, 1977). In the first quotation, Dante was referring to the fact that many families of the surrounding countryside were moving into the city of Florence; in particular he mentioned the Cerchi, who were the leaders of the White Guelphs, and the Buondelmonte, who had been the first to cause the division of the population into Guelphs and Ghibellines (see Giovanni Villani, *Storie Fiorentine,* Book Five, chapters 38–9). In the

second quotation, Beatrice, speaking to Dante, exhorted Christians to observe both Old and New Testaments, so that the Jews, who recognized only the Old Testament, should be given no reason to scorn them. Neither of the two quotes from Dante, then, had a content that would support racism or anti-Semitism. Indeed, the second quotation contained something approaching a compliment for the Jews (Benvenuto de' Rambaldi of Imola [1338–1390], commenting "sì ch'l Giudeo," wrote: "*qui habet solum Vetus Testamentum et optime servat praecepta legis antiquae* [who has only the Old Testament and observes excellently the precepts of the ancient law] [Epist. XI, 4]." But this last verse also had the advantage of containing the word *giudeo*, a term for Jew that had been common in Dante's time, but which had taken on over time a more negative connotation than the other Italian terms for Jew, such as *ebreo* or *israelita*. That is precisely why Fascism demanded that the term *giudeo* be used in the press. It is clear that, even though they had been unable to find any anti-Judaic statements in Dante, the editors of *La Difesa della Razza* had wished, all the same, to quote the greatest Italian poet in order to ennoble their undertaking with a reference to the most fundamental work in the Italian language and culture.

16. The first five were also members of the magazine's editorial board.

17. It is interesting to note that in the entry "Race" in the *Enciclopedia Italiana* (the great Italian encyclopedia, completed in 1936, commissioned by the Fascist Regime and produced under the supervision of Giovanni Gentile, we read: "There is no Italian race, therefore, but only an Italian people and an Italian nation. There is neither a Jewish race nor nation, but only a Jewish people; and, the most serious error of them all, there is no Aryan race, but only an Aryan civilization and Aryan languages." [Gioacchino Sera, Professor of Anthropology at the University of Naples, section "Human Races," entry "Race," *Enciclopedia Italiana*, vol. 27 (Rome: 1935).]

18. As is stated by a recent document of the Catholic Church; see Commission for Religious Relations with the Jews, *We Remember: A Reflection on the Shoah* (Rome, March 16, 1998).

19. And we can hardly help but be surprised that even today the Catholic Church, at the same time that it performs a "*a reflection on the Shoah*," should wonder: "But it may be asked whether the Nazi persecution of the Jews was not made easier by the anti-Jewish prejudices imbedded in *some* Christian minds and hearts" (Italics ours) (Commission for Religious Relations with the Jews, *We Remember*) and that the answers supplied to this question should be evasive and tending toward absolution. If the authoritative members of the commission were to peruse the pages of *La Difesa della Razza* (or of *Der Stürmer*), they would certainly have been unable to reach such a conclusion.

20. The supposed author was a converted Jew named Algranati who, under the pseudonym of Rocca d'Adria, published a novel titled *Nella Tribù di Giuda*.

21. The source indicated was a popular Romanian print.

22. Engraving by Raphael Sadeler (1584–1632) in Matthäus Rader's history of the saints, titled *Bavaria Sancta* (Munich, 1624). The false accusation in Munich led to a pogrom in the course of which the 180 Jews living in the city took refuge in the synagogue where they were burned alive. We have been able to identify specifically this and the following engraving (about which, as was its practice, *La Difesa della Razza*

provided no information or only scanty information) through the vast collection of images contained in Heintz Schreckenberg, *Die Juden in der Kunst Europas. Ein Bildatlas* (Göttingen: Vandenhoeck & Ruprecht, 1996) [English version: *The Jews in Christian Art: An Illustrated History* (London: SCM Press, 1996)].

23. August Rohling, a Catholic priest and theologian, a professor in Münster (Germany) and Prague (1839–1931), and the author of *Der Talmudjude* (Münster, 1871), a book containing anti-Judaic accusations, was condemned by the ecclesiastical authorities in 1899 and obliged to quit teaching. His book was banned by the Church. In 1882 Rohling had testified that it was an actual Jewish practice to make human sacrifices in the trial of Tisza-Eszlar (the subject of the picture in *La Difesa della Razza*). In 1925 Vincenzo Manzini, a professor at the University of Padua, published a book titled *La superstizione omicida e i sacrifici umani, con particolare riguardo alle accuse contro gli ebrei* (Padua: Cedam, 1925, 2nd expanded ed., 1930) that reported hundreds of cases of accusations of Jewish ritual murder, proving that they were all false (including the two cases, at Tisza-Eszlar and Munich, to which the two pictures in the magazine referred). Rohling's book was republished in an Italian edition during the racial campaign (Augusto Rohling, *L'ebreo talmudista*, Edizioni de "L'Idea di Roma," [no location, no date]).

24. On this subject, see *The Ritual Murder Libel and the Jew: The Report by Cardinal Lorenzo Ganganelli (Pope Clement XIV)*, Cecil Roth, ed. (London: Woburn Press, 1934); Furio Jesi, *L'accusa del sangue. Mitologie dell'antisemitismo* (Brescia: Morcelliana, 1993); R. Po-chia Hsia, *The Myth of Ritual Murder* (New Haven, CT: Yale University Press, 1988); and *The Blood Libel Legend: A Casebook in Anti-Semitic Folklore*, Alan Dundes, ed. (Madison, University of Wisconsin Press, 1991). It is interesting to note that neither Ganganelli nor Manzini and the contemporary authors, here quoted for their works on the ritual murder libel, cite the one who is probably the first modern author to write in defense of the Jews against this accusation: the Roman rabbi, Tranquillo Vita (Hezekiah Manoah Hayyim) Corcos (1660–1730), who, on the occasion of one accusation aroused in Viterbo (State of the Church) in 1705, wrote two very learned documents: a *Memoriale* (Alla Sagra Consulta Illustriss. e Reverendiss. Monsig. Ghezzi Ponente Per L'Università degl'Hebrei di Roma. Memoriale. In Roma, Nella Stamperia della Rev. Camera Apostolica 1705) and a *Summarium* (Sacra Consulta Sivè Illustriss. & Reverendiss. D. Ghezzio Ponente Viterbien. Calumnie super praetensa Attentata Iugulazione. Pro Gioiello de Core, & Iosepho Samen Hebreis. Summarium. Romae, Typis Rev. Cam. Apost. 1706.).

25. The doctrine of transubstantiation promulgated by the Fourth Lateran Council in 1215 and the introduction of the feast day of Corpus Christi in 1264 probably constitute the basis for the origin of these legends.

26. See Po-chia Hsia, *The Myth of Ritual Murder*, 11.

27. In the Catholic Church, which holds that, "At the heart of the Eucharistic celebration are the bread and wine that, by the words of Christ and the invocation of the Holy Spirit, become Christ's Body and Blood" [*Catechism of the Catholic Church* (Città del Vaticano: Libreria Editrice Vaticana, 1992), 1332], an ordinary believer participates in the rite of the Eucharist only by consuming the consecrated Host (the bread), since the wine is only for the priest (communion under both species). In the early Church, communion took place with both bread and wine, and the present-day custom (communion

under one kind) was not decreed until the Council of Constance (1414) and ratified by the Council of Trent (1545) [*Dictionnaire Historique des Cultes Religieux* (Paris: Vincent, 1775), under the entry "Communion"].

28. But the accusations continued, especially in Eastern Europe, right up to the turn of the 1940s: the last trial for ritual murder took place in Kiev in 1913 against Mendel Beilis. Concerning the Beilis case, see A. S. Lindemann, *The Jew Accused: Three Anti-Semitic Affairs (Dreyfus, Beilis, Frank) 1894–1915* (Cambridge: Cambridge University Press, 1991). Concerning a number of cases of blood libel that triggered anti-Jewish pogroms in postwar Poland, see Anna Cichopek, "The Cracow Pogrom of August 1945," in *Contested Memories, Poles and Jews during the Holocaust and its Aftermath*, Joshua D. Zimmerman, ed. (New Brunswick, NJ: Rutgers University Press, 2003), and Bozena Szaynok, "The pogrom of Jews in Kielce, July 4, 1946," *Yad Vashem Studies* 22 (1992), 199–235.

29. As late as 1883 an Italian translation, with the *imprimatur* of the Ecclesiastical Curia of Prato, was published of a classic anti-Judaic pamphlet, *Il sangue cristiano nei riti ebraici della moderna sinagoga, rivelazioni di Neofito ex Rabbino, monaco greco* (Prato: Tipografia Giachetti, Figlio e C., 1883). The second part of the book contained an anthology of anti-Semitic articles that had already been published in *La Civiltà Cattolica*, the well-known Jesuit magazine.

30. Let us remember the role played by the concept of *limpieza de sangre* in Spanish history, or the Nazi law of 1935 that was titled "Gesetz zum Schutze des deutschen Blutes und der deutschen Ehre" (Law for the Protection of German Blood and Honor).

31. Guido Landra, "La razza e le differenze razziali," *La Difesa della Razza*, I, 1, August 5, 1938, 14–15.

32. Giuseppe Lucidi, "Sangue e razza," *La Difesa della Razza*, I, 3, September 5, 1938, 22–3.

33. For the supposed uses of Christian blood and for the conspiracy theory, see Manzini, *La superstizione omicida* and *Il sangue cristiano . . . Rivelazioni*.

34. The woodcut appeared in Hartmann Schedel's *Weltchronik* (Nuremberg: Koberger, 1493).

35. "Prozess gegen die Juden von Trient," Manuscript record, Yeshiva University Library, New York. See in this respect, R. Po-chia Hsia, *Trent 147: Stories of a Ritual Murder Trial* (New Haven, CT: Yale University Press, 1992).

36. Here we are repeating and supporting an observation made by R. Po-chia Hsia (*Trent 1475, Stories of a Ritual Murder Trial*, 60), but restricting it to Renaissance iconography of Baby Jesus. For we cannot agree with that author's statement concerning a supposed Renaissance iconography of Jesus crucified naked. To the best of our knowledge, there is one example of a naked crucified Jesus: a work by Sansovino (Jacopo Tatti, Florence 1486 – Venice 1570) in Santa Maria Maggiore, the oldest church in Florence. The peculiarity of the nakedness, extremely rare if not the one and only, has aroused great perplexity among art historians.

37. Sigmund Freud, *Der Mann Moses und die monoteistiche Religion: drei Abhandlungen*, in *Gesammelte Werke* XVI [Italian: *L'uomo Mosè e la religione monoteistica: tre saggi*, in *Opere* (Turin: Boringhieri, 1974), vol. 11] [English: *Moses and Monotheism*].

38. Otto Fenichel, "Elements of a psychoanalytic theory of anti-Semitism," in *Anti-Semitism: A Social Disease*, E. Simmel, ed. (New York: International Universities Press, 1946).

39. C. G. Schoenfeld, "Psychoanalysis and anti-Semitism," *Psychoanalytic Review*, 53 (1966), 24–37.

40. Henry Loeblowitz-Lennard, "The Jew as symbol," *Psychoanalytic Quarterly*, 16 (1947), 123–34.

41. See in this respect, Henry Loeblowitz-Lennard, "A psychoanalytic contribution to the problem of anti-Semitism," *Psychoanalytic Review*, 32 (1945), 359–61.

42. According to Manzini, *La superstizione omicida*, 88–9, the first such accusation took place in 1330; according to Anna Foà, in her *Ebrei in Europa dalla peste nera all'emancipazione* (Bari: Laterza, 1992), 13, in the year 1348.

43. *La Difesa della Razza*, III, 14, May 20, 1940, 35–9.

44. *La Difesa della Razza*, I, 3, September 5, 1938, 24–5. Apparently nobody realized that the proposed model for the Italian (Aryan) mother was, in fact, the portrait of a young Jewish woman.

45. Prior to the Italian conquest of Ethiopia, it was fairly common for officials and functionaries of the Italian colonies (Libya, Eritrea) to engage in what was known as "madamismo," that is, cohabitation with native women. This situation had not been particularly worrisome to the regime, given the limited dimension of the phenomenon, but the conquest of Ethiopia had posed the problem in stark new terms. "But the conquest of the Empire has brought to the forefront the problems that are generally described as racial. Ignoring those problems has led to dramatic and bloody repercussions upon which we need not focus in any detail today. Other peoples have sent to the lands of their empires a few, highly select officials; we shall send to Libya and to AOI (Africa Orientale Italiana, or Italian East Africa), with the passage of time and out of absolute vital necessity, millions of men. Now, to prevent the catastrophic blight of crossbreeding, i.e., the creation of a bastard race, neither European nor African, which would only foment disarray and revolution, the strict laws promulgated and applied by Fascism are not sufficient" (*Informazione Diplomatica no. 18*, August 5, 1938). For the connections between Fascist racial legislation and colonial problem in Africa, see Luigi Preti, *Impero fascista, africani ed ebrei* (Milan: Mursia, 1968).

46. *La Difesa della Razza*, III, 10, March 20, 1940, 31.

47. *La Difesa della Razza*, III, 8, February 20, 1940.

48. *La Difesa della Razza* almost never indicated the sources of its illustrations: in this case the cartoon was originally published in the French satirical magazine *Caran D'Ache*; see Eduard Fuchs, *Die Juden in der Karikatur* (Munich: Verlag Albert Lange, 1921).

49. *La Difesa della Razza*, II, 9, March 5, 1939, 21–3.

50. *La Difesa della Razza*, I, 3, September 5, 1938, 33–4.

51. *La Difesa della Razza*, II, 8, February 20, 1939.

52. *La Difesa della Razza*, I, 6, October 20, 1938, 52–3.

53. *La Difesa della Razza*, V, 7, February 5, 1942, 40.

54. See Giovanni Preziosi, *Come il giudaismo ha preparato la guerra* (Rome: Tumminelli, 1940); *Gli ebrei hanno voluto la guerra* (Rome, 1942). The latter book

contains the transcripts of a series of five radio talks beginning on October 15, 1941, expressly devoted to racial topics. Alberto Luchini organized the program, which was broadcast weekly by EIAR, the Italian state radio network (Ente Italiano Audizioni Radiofoniche); Also see *Chi è che volle la guerra* (Edizioni di "Antibolscevismo": Rome, 1941) which, after an anonymous introduction, presents the Italian translation of two articles published by the French anti-Semite Georges Batault in the *Revue Hebdomadaire* from the year 1935.

55. *La Difesa della Razza*, IV, 18, July 20, 1941, 16–17.

56. *La Difesa della Razza*, II, 17, July 5, 1939, 20.

57. See Roberto Finzi, *L'università italiana e le leggi antiebraiche* (Rome: Editori Riuniti, 1997).

58. *La Difesa della Razza*, I, 3, September 5, 1938, 32.

59. Julius Evola, *Imperialismo pagano. Il fascismo dinnanzi al pericolo euro-cristiano* (Todi and Rome: Atanor, 1928).

60. Julius Evola, *Rivolta contro il mondo moderno* (Milan: Hoepli, 1934).

61. Julius Evola, *Tre aspetti del problema ebraico* (Rome: Edizioni Mediterranee, 1936).

62. See "Il virus Evola e il nazi-pragmatismo," *Il Sole-24 Ore*, July 29, 2001.

63. *La Difesa della Razza*, III, 8, February 20, 1940, 24–5.

64. *La Difesa della Razza*, II, 17, July 5, 1939, 16–19.

65. Here mention is made to the architect Gino Levi Montalcini (1902–74), an Italian Jew. The other reference is probably to Eugenio Faludi, a Hungarian architect active in Italy in the 1930s. Faludi was likely not Jewish just as the iron industrialist Falk, quoted by the author, was misidentified as a Jew. The attribution of Jewishness to non-Jewish people was very common in *La Difesa della Razza*.

66. *La Difesa della Razza*, II, 10, March 20, 1939, 34–5.

67. *La Difesa della Razza*, IV, 6, January 20, 1941, 27.

68. *La Difesa della Razza*, II, 11, April 5, 1939.

69. *Additions to the Book of Daniel*, chapter 13. These additions form part of the Catholic Bible Canon but not the Jewish one.

70. In particular, this cover, given the poses and positions of the protagonists and the depiction of Susannah, seems to have taken inspiration directly from the painting by Sisto Badalocchio (1585–1619).

71. Léon Poliakov, *Storia dell'antisemitismo* (Florence: La Nuova Italia, 1976), 3:375. [Original edition: *Histoire de l'antisémitisme de Voltaire à Wagner* (Paris: Calmann-Lévy, 1968)].

72. For evidence of this theme, see Fuchs, *Die Juden in der Karikatur*.

73. On this point, see Gordon W. Allport, *La natura del pregiudizio* (Florence: La Nuova Italia, 1973), 514 [Original English: *The Nature of Prejudice* (Cambridge, MA: Addison-Wesley, 1954)]. For a comparative analysis of anti-Semitic and anti-black prejudices, see B. Bettelheim and M. Janowitz, *Dynamics of Prejudice: A Psychological and Sociological Study of Veterans* (New York: Harper & Brothers, 1950).

74. *La Difesa della Razza*, III, 3, December 5, 1939, 40.

75. Michele Sarfatti describes this as the intention of Fascism in his recent excellent book, *Gli ebrei nell'Italia fascista* (Turin: Einaudi, 2000), 176, as well as in his essay in this book, which continues this line of argument.

76. When Evola, in his 1936 book, *Three Aspects of the Jewish Question*, wrote the following, he was clearly onto something: "But in order to achieve something serious, we cannot simply give the term 'Aryan' a vague racist foundation, or else a merely negative and polemical content, comprising all that which is, generically, 'non-Jewish.' Instead we should try to define 'Aryan-ness' as a positive and universal idea, to be opposed, in terms of the divine, religious worship and feeling, and world vision, against all that which refers to Semitic civilizations and, then, especially against the Jews." See Julius Evola, *Tre aspetti del problema ebraico* (Rome: Edizioni Mediterraee, 1936), 14.

77. Let us mention only what Mussolini told the German Jewish author, Emil Ludwig: "Naturally, there is no such thing anymore as a pure race, not even the Jewish race.... Race: that is a sentiment, not a reality. It's 95% sentiment. I don't believe that there is any way to prove biologically that a race is more or less pure." [*Colloqui con Mussolini* (Milan: Mondadori, 1932), 73], or what Mussolini stated on September 6, 1934, in a speech delivered in Bari: "Thirty centuries of history allow us to gaze with Olympian pity certain doctrines practiced north of the Alps, supported by the offspring of people who did not know how to write, how to hand down the documents of their own lives, when Rome could boast Caesar, Vergil, and Augustus."

78. Extrapolating a psychoanalytic approach to a social and historical dimension, we can say that the Jew represents for the anti-Semite the father, with whom he identifies and from whom he must free himself, allowing him to divide the paternal image into two parts, one of which (the fatherland, the Regime) is entirely good, the other (Jews) completely bad. The fatherland, the Duce, and the party are exclusively the good father, to whom blind obedience and all good feelings are due; the Jews must be eradicated from the face of the earth. See Bela Grunberger, "The anti-Semite and the Oedipal conflict," *International Journal of Psychoanalysis*, 45 (1964), 380–5.

79. Let us consider, for instance, what an anti-Fascist Jew wrote "in the heat of the moment," in his heartfelt book, published in February 1946: "[The Fascist anti-Semitic persecution] was imposed by Germany and applied only through a sort of conformism or blending in that served to show just how low our country had fallen during the Fascist period." [Eucardio Momigliano, *Storia tragica e grottesca del razzismo fascista* (Milan: Mondadori, 1946), 9].

80. See De Felice, *Storia degli ebrei italiani*, 188–90.

81. For instance, Daniel J. Levinson's Anti-Semitism Scale (A-S), which is presented in his "Lo studio dell'ideologia anti-semitica," in *La personalità autoritaria*, Adorno, Frenkel-Brunswik, Levinson, Sanford, eds. (Milan: Edizioni di Comunità, 1973), 89–149 [English: *The Authoritarian Personality* (The American Jewish Committee, 1950)].

82. We say this without any disrespect for the courage of the minority – and a minority it was – which, for religious or political reasons or simply at the dictates of conscience (or for that typically Italian spirit – and here, truly praiseworthy – whereby laws are made to be broken), stood up against anti-Semitic violence, at times at the risk of life and limb.

8 The Impact of Anti-Jewish Legislation on Everyday Life and the Response of Italian Jews, 1938–1943

Iael Nidam-Orvieto

This chapter will focus on one aspect of the wider issue of Fascist anti-Semitic policy in Italy in the years 1938–43: the impact of the laws on individual Jews and Jewish identity and the varied responses of Jews.[1] I have chosen, therefore, to concentrate on Jews as subjects of the events rather than as objects, thereby enabling us to gain a wider understanding of the period. In collective memory, Fascist Italy has often been considered a safe haven whereby Jews could find a secure place to reside without being persecuted.[2] This stereotype is even reinforced by some latent problems laying within the collective memory of Italian Jewry. We find in interviews and in memoirs an often apologetic tone in Italian survivors' descriptions of everyday life under the anti-Semitic legislation, such as "that was, of course, nothing compared to Auschwitz," or "we didn't really suffer."[3] Memory of the German occupation from 1943 to 1945 (which includes both the memory of the extermination of Jews and the help received by many from the non-Jews) clouds the memory of the previous period, therefore obscuring the real extent of the impact of Italy's own anti-Semitic legislation. This problem can be specially found in memoirs and in oral testimonies. Thus, we need other personal materials from the period itself, such as diaries, letters, and official documents, that can help to rectify these problems because they often dictate and describe Jewish life under Italy's anti-Semitic legislation.

Another issue lies in what we may call *collective guilt feelings*. Italian Jews are still ashamed to admit that many of them believed in Fascism. As discussed in other chapters in this volume, the allegiance of Italian Jews to Fascism and belief in Mussolini were natural outcomes of their total integration into early twentieth century Italian society. However, after World War II, these allegiances were considered sins that needed to be covered up and even denied.

I will first briefly describe the influence of the laws on some aspects of everyday life (labor, education, social life, and so on). In the second part I will analyze some of the major reactions and responses of individual Jews, concentrating mainly on a remarkable set of more than 1,000 letters written between 1938 and 1941 by Jews to the authorities. These letters represent an important window into the self-understanding and identity of the individuals who wrote them.[4]

Historical Background

Italian Jewry between the two world wars belonged mainly to the middle and upper-middle classes, as an urban community whose educational level was above average in the country. They were also integrated into the economic, cultural, and political life of Italy. Their attitudes toward social and political issues were similar to the rest of the population in general and to their parallel social class in particular.[5]

Italian Jews reacted in the same way as the Italian population as a whole to the establishment of Fascist rule, particularly in the first fourteen years when there was a lack of official anti-Semitism. Similar to the rest of the population (especially to the same sociodemographic group), most Jews came to accept Mussolini's leadership and his totalitarian regime. Nevertheless, statistically, the number of Jews who opposed Fascism from the beginning was greater than the rest of Italian population.[6]

From the second half of 1936, anti-Semitism became more and more frequent in the local Italian press. This brought the issue of the "Jewish problem" to the forefront, which until 1935, Mussolini had alleged to be nonexistent in Italy. Until the summer of 1938, when the official anti-Jewish policy began, Italian Jews had considered themselves – and were considered by the general society – equal citizens who loved their country and were completely loyal to it. Mussolini, however, decided to adopt anti-Semitic laws similar to those of the Nazi model. In September 1938, the first of these laws was promulgated. By the following year, Jews were deprived of most of their civil rights, including the right to own property, to work, to study, or to have relations with non-Jews. Even so, Jews were still legally Italian citizens, albeit at an inferior level.[7]

In October 1938, Mussolini introduced a new concept into the Italian anti-Semitic legislation: the so-called *Discriminazione* (literally, "discrimination"). Under this concept, Jews who had particular merits and prerogatives (such as having been awarded a medal during military service in World War I, membership in the Fascist party from its beginning, or extraordinary service to the country) could receive exemptions from some of the restrictions. A *discriminato* (an exempted Jew) could for example hire a non-Jewish maid or own unlimited property. Many Jews believed that Mussolini wanted to ensure that those who had been good citizens would not be afflicted by the anti-Semitic legislation. They thought that most Italian Jews would be considered *discriminati* and, thus, only Jews not loyal to the regime would suffer.[8]

It is interesting to note the way the Italian population in general and Jews in particular understood the relationship between Nazi Germany and Fascist Italy. The common belief was that Mussolini was forced into the Axis. Despite the fact that Mussolini had decided, on his own initiative, to persecute the Jews without any pressure from the Germans, Italians generally felt that the Duce liked and even admired his loyal Jewish citizens and never wished to undermine their status. Rather, he was forced to do so by his German ally against his will.[9]

This understanding of the regime's intentions was caused by several reasons. The first is the fact that until 1938 Mussolini deliberately denied any anti-Semitic position found within the Fascist party. Moreover, on several occasions he presented an extremely positive attitude to the Jews and even to the Zionist movement. These statements did not reflect Mussolini's real opinion of the Jews but were only an outcome of a political strategy that created a common belief that the Duce was in favor of the Jews. His attacks against Nazi racist anti-Semitism in particular and against Nazi Germany in general during the years 1933–5 only reinforced this belief.[10]

The second reason is the fact that when the anti-Semitic policy started, Mussolini tried to confuse and hide his real intentions in order to avoid opposition to the new legislation. His confusing and contradictory statements continued after the promulgation of the anti-Jewish legislation.[11]

In meetings with Jewish representatives, high government officials often repeated reassuring statements. One of these was that Mussolini was forced to establish anti-Jewish legislation because of unfortunate political reasons stemming from Italian foreign policy. A second was that Mussolini wanted to help the Jews despite the legislation because he knew that the Jews were in actuality loyal citizens. The officials also related to the representatives that this was only a temporary crisis and would be over in a short time.[12]

The Impact of the Racial Laws on Everyday Life

Despite Mussolini's declaration – "Discrimination does not mean persecution" – Fascist anti-Jewish legislation had a profound impact on the life of Jews as can be seen in various aspects of everyday life: in the workplace, the school, in Jewish–Catholic relations, in the family sphere, and in mixed families.

One of the most severe damaging effects of the laws was in the sphere of employment. Within a few months after September 1938, thousands of Jews in education, public service, banking, commerce, the military, and the professions were fired from their jobs. Between 1938 and 1942 Jews were banned from many professions and in others they suffered from severe restrictions, for example in medicine, law, and commerce.[13] Since men, in most cases, were the main breadwinners of their Jewish families, they were the direct victims of these laws and were the main group that searched for new employment. Women who were discharged from their work tended more to stay home or to find some occupation within the family or home environment. Thus, we find fewer unemployed women than men.[14] Finding an alternative job was very difficult as most sectors had been already closed to Jews. The new means of income were usually at a much lower pay scale than the former and, therefore, it was often necessary to work at more than one job. Some Jews found work in the area of commerce, doing simple jobs for private companies or within the local Jewish community. Many, however, remained unemployed. Consequently, most families suffered and many of them fell into poverty.[15]

A harsh blow came in 1941 when even Jewish peddlers, who were on the lowest rungs of the economic ladder, lost their licenses. In most cases, these peddlers were the sole breadwinners of large families that often consisted of five to nine children in addition to their elderly parents or in-laws. Losing their sales licenses was for them a complete disaster, leading to even deeper poverty. A group of fifteen peddlers from Rome sent petitions, in October 1941, to the Ministry of the Interior, in the hopes of having their licenses returned or reactivated. As one of the peddlers wrote,

> At present, I am without work and my family is suffering enormously, especially the children who are being deprived of the most basic necessities. I have a disabled child who needs special care. . . . Since this is a very sad case of an extremely poor family, I beg you, Your Excellency, to show some interest [in our case]. Otherwise, during the winter, we will have to sleep on the street because of the lack of money for rent.[16]

Losing one's job was also a terrible psychological shock for most men since it was one of the main components of male self-identity. In her wartime

diary, Sylvia Lombroso wrote about the pain her husband was experiencing in a
September 1938 entry:

> Eight o'clock. Time to get up, to be on the move, time to go. But
> where? To do what? [...] He went to his work table and opened
> a registered letter. It was his last piece, due to be serialized. The
> editor returns it herewith; a few embarrassed words, no longer
> able to proceed with publication, most regretful, etc. He opened
> the next letter. The president of the Academy of Science wishes
> to advise that, following instructions received to that effect, he is
> removing his name from the membership list. [...] The fearful
> sense of emptiness invaded him again, sweeping over his heart.
> He saw, suddenly and for the first time how his one true reason
> for living had been torn from him. He stared at the spectacle
> of his shattered life. Then slowly he got to his feet, and stood
> motionless in the middle of his study. Everything around him
> was as it had been yesterday – everything the same – with the
> sameness that was to endure forever.[17]

Another sector that was hurt by the anti-Semitic laws was the educational
sphere. In contrast to Nazi Germany, where the Jews were banned from schools
several years after the beginning of anti-Semitic legislation, in Italy Jews were
banned from schools and universities at the very beginning of the discriminatory
policy (September 1938). Children and youth were, therefore, among the first
sectors of the Jewish population to be persecuted because the school system was
considered the place where the new Fascist generation was about to be formed.[18]
Most of the Jewish university, secondary, and primary school students clearly
remember, even today, the moment they realized that they had been banned
from school and the deep emotional pain they felt as a result of this shocking
discriminatory action. One Italian Jewish mother painfully recorded the following
in her diary on the first day of the school year following the legal ban on Jews in
Italian public schools:

> "Have you seen Lilly? Do go and see her, please. She's been shut
> in her room all morning. Won't eat anything.... It's the first day of
> school, you know.... Maybe she'll let go a little with you...." The
> first day of school – life beginning again for the world of children,
> but not for you, my little one. I went to her room with my heart
> in my throat. Young people's tears are so difficult to dry.... The
> room was quiet, looked empty. Then I saw her, stretched across
> the bed, asleep. Her cheeks were still wet and her hand still

clutched her handkerchief, and her "why" still echoed in the quiet room.[19]

In addition to the expulsion of Jewish pupils from Italian schools, 279 high school teachers and principals, more than 100 elementary school teachers and principals, hundreds of university professors, 114 authors of schoolbooks, and many school custodians and secretaries were deprived of their jobs.[20] In the weeks following the ratification of the anti-Semitic legislation, we detect a major effort on the part of parents, rabbis, and other Jewish leaders to organize Jewish schools. Within a short period of time, a Jewish school system was created.[21] What started as misfortune became a major source of Jewish educational and cultural activities, and the Jewish school became the main place where questions of identity could be raised and discussed. For the first time, many children had the opportunity to meet other Jewish children and to develop a Jewish identity and culture. Moreover, thanks to the autonomy given by the authorities, Jewish youth could openly deal with ideology and moral issues that were taboo in the Fascist regime, such as liberalism and democracy.[22] Nevertheless, many children, in cities with small Jewish communities, could not enjoy this type of solution. Due to the law of compulsory education, children ages six to eleven could continue their study in public schools but in segregated classes, at different times, in order to avoid any contact with the non-Jewish pupils. This separation accentuated even more their differences. Other pupils could only continue their studies by way of private lessons, isolated in their houses, away from their former friends. Universities were closed to Jewish high school graduates.

A third aspect in which the racial laws affected the Jews' daily lives was the impact on Jewish–Gentile relations. Many laws were intended to segregate the Jews from the non-Jewish population, such as in the school system and in the workplace. In fact, these laws separated Jews and non-Jews in every aspect of social life even though Jews were never confined to special Jewish neighborhoods (like ghettos) and were never required to wear yellow badges. Therefore, they continued living side by side with non-Jews, separated by invisible barriers. Jews were forbidden, among other things, to marry non-Jews, to be members in Italian social organizations and clubs, to use public libraries, or to publish books.

Once again, one notices a gender differentiation in the perception of the insult. Women suffered mainly from the attitudes of neighbors and acquaintances, from the prohibition on hiring non-Jewish housekeepers or of being members of voluntary social institutions. Walking around the streets became often a show. As Lombroso reflected in her diary entry of January 12, 1942:

> We live every day of our lives in the midst of people who think they know us and instead they know nothing about us at all... except for what we show on the surface which the passing of time, constant contact, and the agony of being misunderstood, has made very smooth indeed. This is the way it has to be, they say. You must be reasonable, must be calm and self-possessed, and keep quiet. This is most important. You must keep quiet... how hard it is, sometimes, to keep everything inside and to live in silence.[23]

As mentioned previously, men were mainly hurt in their identity as breadwinners, as Italian citizens, and many also as Fascists. For years Italian Jews had followed Mussolini and his ideology and several thousands joined the Fascist party. All of a sudden, as if overnight, this same regime abandoned them, leaving them with a deep sense of betrayal. When Italo Levi, who had proudly fought as a soldier for Italy during World War I and before, was forced to leave the organization of the veterans, he wrote the following to one of his comrades in November 1941:

> You see, today they forbid me the honor of wearing the blue string. This was the last symbolic tie with my comrades from the war of independence in which we won fighting against the eternal enemy. They denied me even this spiritual bond and the promise is broken. [...] This new blow that destroys this mystical tie with my comrades hurts me not only because of the aggravation in the damage caused to me in the last three years. It also hurts the Institute itself and its high and pure ideals. [...] Betraying Italian brothers who proved their loyalty cannot be a good sign for future victories. I had to write to you, dear Pellizzari, in order to relieve the pain of my broken soul.[24]

According to contemporary Jewish sources, relations between Jews and non-Jews changed drastically after September 1938. Most non-Jewish Italians began to ignore their Jewish acquaintances after the enactment of anti-Jewish laws. "Out of egoism, partly, superficiality and the selfish need for peace," Sylvia Lombroso wrote in her diary, "they [non-Jewish acquaintances] prefer not to see, not to know, and not to feel."[25]

In spite of the positive image of the Italian attitude to the Jews in the historical literature, hundreds of non-Jews denounced Jews for professional, ideological, or personal reasons.[24] Others showed hostility, attacked Jews in public, and denied them help and assistance. Nevertheless, we can find a clear tendency in Jewish sources to emphasize the positive attitude of many Italians and above all the "real friends," those who chose to ignore the risk of having contact with Jews and helped them in any possible way. Because of this help many Jews could continue secretly to keep their property or to work.[27] Similarly positive attitudes are often connected with people from the lowest socioeconomic class.[28] As a result, most Jews felt secure in Italy. Moreover, they were sure that in the near future the Italian people would raise their voices against the unjust persecution, a feeling of security that would later influence the decisions of many Jews facing life-threatening danger, after September 1943.

The tensions and problems caused by the laws directly influenced Jewish life in the domestic sphere. In some cases, the economic problems as well as the moral insult developed into anger, despair, and even clinical depression. Michele Sarfatti has evaluated more than thirty Jews, mainly men, who committed suicide during the years 1938–43.[29] In most cases, however, the average family succeeded in adjusting to the difficulties and found a new balance based on mutual help and cohesion. Family members learned how to cope with economic stress and with the sense of sadness and betrayal caused by the forced division from the rest of the society. One way to overcome the difficult situation as well as the isolation was by developing closer ties to the extended families as well as to the Jewish community.[30] Often we see that children took upon themselves new tasks and chores, including working, searching for more food, and taking care of the household.[31]

A very interesting aspect of the domestic sphere was the case of the families of mixed marriages. According to anti-Semitic Italian law, a child of mixed parents could be considered "Aryan" under certain conditions (for example, if the child was baptized before October 1938).[32] This was, of course, very different from the Nazi concept of *Mischlinge*. Out of 6,820 mixed families, the father was Jewish in the majority of the cases (4,000). Therefore, even in those cases in which the children were legally non-Jewish, mixed Jewish families suffered from immediate economic distress.[33] Although 3,500 out of 13,000 children in mixed marriage households declared themselves Jews, many more were defined as Jews under the racial principle. In many cases, households were split with some children being defined as non-Jewish while their siblings were considered racially Jewish. Needless to say, this placed even more stress on family life.[34] These families were exposed to many of the restrictions because of the Jewish members. Very often the law created an often absurd situation, as we can see in the case of the

C. family. Although the non-Jewish husband and son, who was recognized as "Aryan," fought in the Italian army, the Jewish mother and wife were affected by all the restrictions of the laws, creating terrible distress and despair.[35]

The case of mixed marriages caused strong opposition from the Vatican as well as from many sectors within the Fascist party that wished to find a more benevolent solution for families that included non-Jewish members. In fact, files from the minister of the interior reveal how he pondered different ways to find some solution.[36]

Even more complicated was the situation of foreign Jews (mostly men), many of whom had been naturalized after 1919 and who in some cases converted and married non-Jewish Italians. After 1938 they lost their citizenship but were sometimes allowed to remain in Italy. These families suffered from discrimination, humiliation, and even violence because of the foreign identity of the Jewish spouse. The lack of Italian citizenship drastically lowered the possibility of finding a job and support for the family. In many cases, despite the non-Jewish spouses, these Jews were forced to leave the country.[37]

It is nevertheless important to note that the family stayed united and did not abandon the Jewish member in most mixed marriages. The guilt feeling of the Jewish parent was consequently very strong due to the "innocents" who were being hurt. One Italian Jew appealed to Mussolini in the following manner: "Your Excellency [...] my children must quit their studies. I am destroyed. I feel like a father who is about to lose his children and to witness the total ruin of his family, and yet he has to live with the terrible guilt knowing that he is the cause of it all."[38]

In some cases the sense of guilt led to tragic decisions, as in the Foà family from Turin. After months of searching for new employment, Emilio Foá chose what he saw as the only way to help his family: he committed suicide. The letter he left read, "My dear wife, I leave you. This way I save the family. With the insurance money you will be able to have a regular income. [...] Now you are safe. [...] Please do not judge me. Love me and remember me."[39]

After Italy joined the war in June 1940, the anti-Jewish legislation became more severe. Regarded as enemies of the fatherland, Jews became more suspect by the authorities. Their radios were confiscated, many Jews were arrested, and many were subsequently taken as forced laborers. More than 400 Italian Jews were sent to internment camps or other locations, as were thousands of foreign Jews who were still residing in Italy. In 1942 close to 2,000 Jews were called up for forced labor, many of them far away from home. As a result, the Jewish family had to cope with new and even more severe hardships.

One example is the difficult decision Jews had to make on whether to remain or to leave their place of residence. Due to the intense Allied bombing of many cities, citizens were evacuated for safety reasons. Jews were often hesitant to leave due to the fact that such an evacuation created new problems for them. They were not allowed to reside in many localities that were considered of interest to tourists and Jewish children had to give up studying in Jewish schools; the economical hardships caused by the impoverishment of many Jews made everyday life extremely hard under the war conditions.

In coping with the anti-Semitic policy, every Jew searched for different solutions to his or her problems. The changing context, as well as the self-identity of every person, influenced one's understanding of the situation, the possibilities that each person had, and each person's consequent reactions and responses. A small minority of Jews, including anti-Fascists and Zionists, had from the very beginning a clearer perception of the reality and, therefore, could search immediately for solutions.[40] The majority of the Jews, however, had to go through a long and painful process of coping with reality in order to reach a better understanding of the real nature of the anti-Semitic legislation.

In summation, it was difficult to believe in the beginning that the Duce, the man that in the past attacked Nazi barbarism, would eventually fail to defend his loyal Jewish citizens. The contradictory statements of many officials, as well as the ambiguity of many laws, made it impossible during the first months to fully understand what was happening. Most Jews were convinced that this was simply a tactical and temporary step to appease the Germans and that the government would do everything possible to avoid any real damage against the Jews. This understanding was not merely a Jewish one, for the same pattern could be found among the general Italian population.[41] Jews were also convinced that any drastic reaction from their side could have been used as an excuse to strengthen the anti-Semitic policy.[42] They thus espoused obedience to the new laws and adjustment to their new social situation and longed for a change in their status. Only with time and by prolonged disappointment did their view slowly change into a growing awareness of the true nature of the anti-Semitic laws.

Italian Jews Respond to Racial Persecution: Contemporary Appeals to the Government

This process of growing awareness, as well as some of the responses to the laws, may be seen through the analysis of more than 1,000 letters that Jews wrote to Mussolini and King Victor Emmanuel III. The authors of these letters believed that direct appeals to their state leaders would bring about an amelioration of the conditions of the Jews. As one letter addressed to Mussolini put it, "You have always clearly stated that you are always willing to listen to anyone, even the most humble person."[43]

These letters reveal a variety of responses. Some of them sought a collective solution to the problems raised by the anti-Semitic legislation. Others sought a personal or a familial solution. Other responses demonstrated a clear rejection of Jewish identity, and some were an outcome of very strong Jewish identification with the Jewish community. Finally, the responses show different attitudes to Italy, Italians, and Fascism.

We can find three main categories of letters. The first includes several hundred petitions on various aspects of the legislation: many applied after being dismissed from their positions of employment. Some were approaching retirement and had no chance to find a new job, as in the following appeal: "Considering my past and the pure fascist faith of my family, I ask not to be chased like a thief, but to keep my place at least for the remaining 20 months. This is a moral satisfaction – an act of justice I ask from you, Duce."[44] They also emphasized the necessity of maintaining their employment position from both an economic and a civic point of view. We can see one example in the letter of a female teacher.

> Dismayed by the step taken against the Jewish teachers, which put me in an extremely painful situation, I dare address Your Excellency.... I always tried to give my pupils pure Italian love, a truthful fascist faith and endless love for their Duce; for You, Duce, who I have always admired and loved.... I am no longer young, and I don't have any other means of income. I have an old mother and a deaf and disabled father. What do I have left in life without my pupils to whom I have dedicated my life? Most of all, I am hurt and humiliated in my honest and real fascist faith.[45]

Others applied directly to Mussolini to receive the *discriminazione*. They believed they could convince the Duce of their loyalty. Commonly held by many was the misunderstanding that the laws would eventually abolish the citizenship, but the *discriminazione* would enable them to maintain it as a reward for being "good citizens."[46] Thus, we find Jews who applied merely for moral reasons – that is, to prove that there were many good Jews who served Italy with loyalty.[47]

Nevertheless, we can also find Jews who were entitled to receive the "discrimination" but did not apply for it. It seemed to them that by applying for a *discriminazione* they recognized the legitimization of the anti-Jewish legislation. They preferred, therefore, to remain on the side of the majority of the Jews who had to cope with all the hardships. This must not be seen as passivity but rather as an active statement of condemnation of the laws.[48]

In the first years of the racial legislation, approximately 6,000 Jews left the country each in search for a new life of work and freedom. Since the process of emigration was very long and complicated, Jews frequently appealed to the authorities in order to hasten receipt of a passport or other necessary documents. Most writers emphasized their grief at having to leave Italy, as did one Italian Jew writing to Mussolini: "I find myself obligated to find an arrangement abroad, fighting the immense grief of abandoning the fatherland my parents and ancestors have taught me to love and honor."[49] Many declared that they would continue keeping alive the memory of their country and represent Italy with honor.[50] These feelings are representative of many Jews who left Italy. Most of them saw their emigration as a temporary step, taken in order to overcome the difficulties of life under the racial restrictions.

> My career has recently been destroyed by the steps against Italian Citizens of Jewish descendent...I, therefore, must go abroad for some years...an exodus that I hope will be temporary. My strongest and dearest hope is that I will be able to come back and enjoy some years of calm, before my eternal rest, in what I see as my only and beloved fatherland.[51]

Another type of petition concerned people who asked to be considered "Aryan" by race. Between 1938 and 1942 close to 6,000 Jews abandoned their Jewish identity through conversion or detachment from the Jewish community.[52] Some of them hoped to spare their non-Jewish spouses or children the burden of Jewish identity, whereas others did it out of ideological reasons, wanting to show total loyalty to Fascism and contempt for Judaism. In most cases these requests were denied, leaving this category of people in a very difficult status: on one side they were accepted into the non-Jewish community, and on the other side they no longer belonged to the Jewish collective. The attitude to conversion was usually a negative one. In a letter to his mother, A. C. referred to a converted Jew as "derided by the Christians and scorned by the Jews."[53]

Vittorio Foa, an anti-Fascist activist who was imprisoned for many years for his activities, dealt with the issue of conversion in many of his letters to the family. In his opinion converted Jews were to be pitied, "but when I speak of pity I mean the pity you can feel toward lepers, as people that are doomed forever, condemned without hope. But we wouldn't give a leper any task of responsibility. [...] We would be scared and disgusted to shake his hand."[54]

Finally, we find petitions from Jewish parents requesting special dispensations that their children be allowed to attend Italian schools as well as to receive special permission to hire non-Jewish housekeepers, and so on.

The above-discussed letters provided a variety of justifications for petitioning the government. Some writers based their request on personal merits. They referred to their loyalty to Fascism and to Mussolini or to their service in the Italian military during World War I, and so on. They showed no general dissatisfaction with the essence of the racial legislation, but rather presented themselves as a specific case that required favoritism. A second group emphasized their non-Jewish identity, stating clearly that they had completely separated themselves from the Jewish community. They did not understand why they should be considered Jews and, thus, be subjected to the collective punishment. Again, in these cases, there was no complaint about the legislation, but rather a personal justification based on a misunderstanding of the intent of the laws. A third group raised what can be described as civil justification. Because they were citizens and because they loved Italy and considered it their fatherland, they deserved the same rights as the rest of the population. Here, one notices a more general argument concerning the unjust nature of racial laws. Finally, there are those letters that made appeals on humanitarian and moral grounds. Because of the suffering caused by the restrictions, the writers asked for help in alleviating the adversities. Here, too, we find an argument concerning the immorality of the laws. The main difference between this justification and the others is the fact that these requests depended only on the goodwill of Mussolini; thus, they were appeals to his perceived charity.

The style used by the writers depended on many factors, including the justification offered for the individual request. Applicants, who drew attention to their service to Italy and the Fascist party as well as enumerated their merits in a very official manner, expressed complete faith in a positive outcome to their requests. Letters from writers who no longer identified themselves as Jews included detailed evidence to show that they were not members of any Jewish community. Sometimes, they added an emotional acknowledgment of the justification for the racial legislation, attacking Jews for a lack of loyalty to Fascism and to Italy in order to magnify their distance from them. In letters with a civil justification, we frequently find superlatives as *italianissimi* (very Italian) in order to emphasize their deep feelings toward Italy.

The most emotional letters were those that appealed to moral and humanitarian values. They included pitiful descriptions of the adversities and the suffering of everyday life. Many were also sent to the royal family or to Mussolini's family in the hope of receiving greater sympathy, as we can see from a young Jewish mother:

> My Duce, it is a Jewish woman by religion, but Italian by blood and heart [that writes to you].... I beg you on behalf of my two children... and of many other children that now you reject, but who have always loved you tenderly. Your intelligent sight, your noble and gentle soul... opened my heart to the hope that you will not abandon children who can tomorrow become the honor and pride of this sacred Italian soil.... Why, my lord, your gentle hand doesn't want to accept tenderly these Jewish sons of Italy? May posterity remember you as the worthy successor of Julius Caesar and Caesar Augustus.[55]

Others were even written by children. A fascinating example is that of F. M. She wrote in September 1939 to Mussolini's son, Romano, asking him to convince his father to accept her request. With pathos and emotion, F. M. explained that her father had immigrated to Italy at the beginning of the century and had converted to Christianity. "Dear Romano," she wrote,

> I write to you because you are a child and I'm a child too. I hope you will understand me and, if possible, help me. Lately I noticed that my mother is sad and after insisting, she told me what happened. I didn't know anything and I didn't understand much of it, but what I understood is that my father is not like us.... Your dad can do anything and I'm sure he will help my dad because he is a veteran Fascist and he married my mother who is Italian and Christian and because he is very good with everybody, because he loves me so much and also because he is very sick now and the doctor asked him to stay calm or he will never get better.... Dear Romano, please ask your dad to consider my dad as an Italian and a Christian and you and all your family will have the gratitude and love of a little girl.[56]

A second category of letters, which we can describe as declarative, contains no personal requests but a general condemnation of the racial laws. Crying out against the injustice inflicted on Jews who had always proven their devotion and loyalty to the state, most of the writers were convinced that their arguments would lead to the abolition of discrimination. Moreover, many considered themselves good Fascists who could prove their loyalty to Italy and Mussolini. They spoke of their great suffering and humiliation, and the impossibility of remaining silent in the face of the tragedy of the Jewish community. They appealed to their beloved Duce, emphasizing the alien nature of the anti-Semitic legislation, which they believed was imposed by the Germans. As one anonymous Italian Jew wrote to Mussolini in June 1939:

> Everybody knows around the world that the racial laws were not programmed by the Duce, who has always admired Italian Jews.... But the racial laws were simply imposed by Germany. In Rome they blindly accepted everything that was prepared with infamy at Nuremberg. One day Italy and the leadership will finally open their eyes and will understand... that the racial issue was only an excuse to eliminate an uncomfortable enemy of Mister Hitler who wants a German invasion of Italian commerce and industry... We, Jews of Trieste,... we have faith in our fatherland... we are waiting for better times.... Time is a gentleman and the peaceful and righteous sun of Eternal Rome will shine again.[57]

In some cases Jews wrote to the royal house as one of the main authorities still operating in the country. The Jews felt a deep loyalty to the royal house, which in the nineteenth century had given them equal rights and recognized them as full citizens of the unified Kingdom of Italy. It was, therefore, a natural option to seek out help from the king, the highest authority for many Italians, as we can see in one example:

> In this moment, when one of the biggest injustices in history is being perpetuated, can Your Majesty remain indifferent to the cry of indignation and of suffering that comes spontaneously from the heart of each of your Jewish subjects?... Italy is our land, is our fatherland.... No human nor divine force can ever make [Italian Jews] stop loving or abandoning it.[58]

These writers did not isolate themselves from the rest of the Jewish community, as in some previously mentioned cases. On the contrary, they saw themselves as representatives of some particular subgroup (Jewish women, fathers, children, Jews from Trieste, Italian Jewry, etc.). They indicated specific difficulties in everyday life asking why they deserved to suffer. Opponents should be punished, they conceded, but not the entire community. They also reminded Mussolini that he had always emphasized the absence of a Jewish problem in Italy, contrary to his present actions. One example is that of the Jewish writer Luciano Morpurgo, who wrote the following letter to Mussolini on September 9, 1939, a year after the beginning of the racial legislation. "I cannot argue with your decision and I don't want to. I'm not capable of judging," Morpurgo wrote. He continued,

> Nevertheless, may I present a number of considerations, as an Italian, a man and a Jew. In your humanity and wisdom please take them into account.... If possible, I would like to defend the little nucleus of Italian Jews who loves Italy immensely and did so much for it. I cannot believe in their guilt.... The Jews afflicted by your laws do not raise their voice. Those who can leave the country and become not enemies but propagandists for Italy.... They leave in silence, carrying the flame of Italian sentiments.... They bow their heads astonished, they do not yet believe.... They consider the laws separating them from their Italian brothers, impossible.... If your mother hit you without reason, did you hit back? So do we. Italy hits us – she no longer considers us her sons, and although we feel proudly that we have no guilt, no shame, still we bow our heads and wait![59]

These declarative letters reflect and represent a very interesting process that occurred within the Jewish community. After decades of assimilation, when facing forced isolation from the rest of the society, most Jews reacted by finding their way back to the Jewish collective. The young generation was the first to feel this need and organized extracurricular activities. In many groups that came into existence around the country, people started with time to speak freely about anti-Fascism, Judaism, and even Zionism. The new hardships developed into new forces of Jewish solidarity, which enabled others also to enlarge the help offered to Jewish refugees and to the growing number of poor.[60]

The third and final category of letters contains more than 400 letters from Jews who wanted to join the Italian army. When World War II broke out, the Italian authorities believed that Jews were against the Axis and hoped for the victory of the Allies. Official documents of the Italian police reported clearly that the Jews did not formulate in public any opinion about the war that could prove their real tendency, and nevertheless, they were considered to be the enemy of Italy and Germany.[61] In fact, personal material proves that Italian Jews faced a very deep conflict: on the one hand they were devoted to their "homeland" which was involved in a war, and on the other they were opposed to Nazi Germany and the Axis and therefore against the war. Moreover, the bombings, the hunger, and the destruction enlarged the existing antagonism and developed into a more open hope for a victory of the Allies within the general Italian population and within the Jewish community as well. Still, for many it was very difficult to hope for the defeat of their country. It was not out of loyalty to Fascism but out of a deep feeling of belonging to Italy and its population.[62]

The racial laws had included a ban on Jews in the army. But when World War II began and later, when Italy joined the war in June 1940, many Jews felt compelled to volunteer in accordance to their civic responsibility and, therefore, wrote to Mussolini to offer their help. These particular letters were written to Mussolini mostly by Jewish men from all ages and every social class.

About half of the writers of this category of letters still emphasized their faith in the Duce and Fascism. A very interesting subgroup consists of young Jews in their twenties, who had grown up in Fascist schools and youth movements and absorbed the ideals and the atmosphere of the Fascist revolution. In their eyes, Mussolini was the one and only leader, a caring, strong, and merciful father, and they were convinced that he would accept their appeals. In these letters, we can see the suffering and hopes of one small group of young Jewish Fascists who, despite the anti-Jewish laws, still believed in Fascism and were not able to find an answer to their identity in the Jewish sphere. As one of these young men wrote on June 2, 1940,

> I was raised in the atmosphere of the [fascist youth movements –] Littorio.... I remember emotionally the day on which I received the honor to present you with the coat of arms.... Despite the fact that the racial laws have banned me from wearing the black shirt, they cannot erase my sentiments. I have always tried, even from the outside, to keep my fascist pledge and your motto: 'Believe – Obey – Fight'. Duce, I believed and still do, I obeyed and still do: Please let me fight.[63]

These examples demonstrate the importance of the youth movements in shaping the Fascist identity of many youngsters who grew up expecting to be loyal soldiers, ready to defend Italy and fight for the Fascist empire.

The second half of the requests to volunteer came from Jews who were patriotically motivated, but without the Fascist element. These Jews were willing to fight in the name of Italy, their beloved home, as their forefathers had done. They, too, emphasized the humiliation they suffered as a result of the racial laws. Nevertheless, they still considered themselves citizens who had to fulfill their obligations to the state, even though they had been deprived of many civil rights. These requests were meant to prove collective Jewish loyalty to Italy and to deny the false accusations of Jewish betrayal. The style of these letters is, therefore, less emotional and more official, as we can see in this short letter to Mussolini: "I submit a strong and respectful request to you that in case of need,

I will be allowed to receive the high honor to serve my fatherland like all the other citizens and like his brothers did during the Great War."[64] Some, like the following letter written shortly after World War II broke out, even contain an open protest against the discrimination:

> I am a Jewish Italian.... I worked as long as I was allowed to and then I retired without protest. Until now I believed that within the limits of your laws it was possible for me to live with honor. I've naturally taught my sons to love Italy. Due to the current situation I asked to join the army. But I've heard your words to the Tenth Legion. No, Duce, my sons are not trash and in their name I ask to let them have a chance to live with honor.[65]

Common to all these letters is the hope that the war would lead to a proper adjustment of the situation: fighting the "real enemy" would eventually result in the abolition of the racial laws. For the Jewish Fascists this was not merely a hope, but a certainty. As they tried to explain the legislation as merely an outcome of the Axis alliance, they felt certain that in the crucial hour, Mussolini would realize that the real enemy was not the Jew and that Italian Jews were loyal to him and to Italy. The negative responses that Jews usually received from the very ministers to whom they appealed and in particular to the letters of volunteering led to a more correct understanding of the unchangeability of their inferior status.[66]

Conclusion

An examination of Jewish responses to Fascist anti-Semitism challenges the predominantly positive evaluation of the Jewish experience in Fascist Italy. The racial laws inflicted much pain, distress, and suffering on the Jewish community in Italy. They ruined the civil status of the Jews, as well as the economic, social, and demographic one, as we have seen in several aspects of everyday life. There is no doubt that this process influenced the fate of Jews in the later period of 1943–5.

When analyzing the responses of the Jews, some points are worthy of emphasis. Most Italian Jews saw themselves as citizens with rights and duties. Their civil position was altered, and endangered, yet as long as they continued to identify themselves as part of Italian society they felt encouraged to ask for help and even to protest. Even among those who emigrated, one still notices the deep emotional bond they had to Italy.

Only a minority sought total detachment from the Jewish community. Rather, the majority identified themselves as Jews and saw no contradiction between their religious identity as Italians of the Mosaic Faith on the one hand and their feelings toward Italy on the other. In the letters to Mussolini and the royal family, we see that they proudly emphasized these two aspects of their self-identity. There were also Jews who, despite the racial laws, still clung to the Fascist ideals. This latter group had greater faith in a positive response to their requests, and, therefore, felt more hurt upon receiving a negative answer.

Even after the promulgation of the racial laws, Mussolini was perceived as a leader who listened to the common people and to whom they could appeal for help. Many remained convinced that he would not disappoint them. Jews did not remain passive when the restrictions and persecution ruined their world. They searched for solutions to their problems, according to their economic, political, and social status. Because the racial laws were perceived as an alien imposition, they were thought to be a temporary hardship. Therefore, many Jews thought it would be possible to convince the authorities to alleviate their personal or collective situation by bringing forward rational explanations and arguments.

The increase in anti-Semitic laws as well as the negative answers to the many petitions led to a sobering realization of the gravity of the situation for the Jews in Italy. With time, Italian Jews realized that although they had remained citizens, their civil rights had been severely violated. They were not allowed to work freely in their professions, to study, to hire non-Jewish household help, to continue to own large amounts of property, and above all, to serve their country in the military during time of danger. When the Jews realized they would not be allowed to defend Italy as they had proudly done since the *Risorgimento*, they finally understood that the racial laws were intended to be permanent and were stronger than their own sense of Italian or Fascist identity.

NOTES

1. For an interesting description of the differences on the impact of the anti-Semitic legislation between different age groups, see Guri Schwartz, "Un'identità da rifondare: note sul problema dei giovani tra persecuzione e dopoguerra (1938–1956)," *Zakhor* 3 (1999), 181–210; see also Luciana Brunelli, "Generazioni di ebrei nel 1938: il caso di Perugia," *Zakhor* 5 (June 2002), 109–135.

2. The perception of Italy as a safe haven for Jews can be especially found in testimonies of Jewish refugees in Italy. See, for example, Bronka Halperin, *A Ray of Light in the Darkness* (Hebrew) (Jerusalem: Reuven Mass, 1967).

3. See, for example, the testimony of Giulio Levi Casellini in Marco Coslovich, ed., *Racconti dal Lager* (Milan: Mursia, 1997), 10.

4. For an in-depth analysis of the letters, see Iael Orvieto, "Letters to Mussolini," in *Remembering for the Future: The Holocaust in an Age of Genocide*, Vol. 1, John K. Roth and Elisabeth Maxwell, eds. (New York: Palgrave, 2001), 466–80.

5. See Sergio Della Pergola, *Anatomia dell'ebraismo italiano* (Rome: Carucci, 1976); Sergio Della Pergola, "La popolazione ebraica in Italia nel contesto ebraico globale," *Gli ebrei in Italia. Storia d'Italia- annali 11* (Turin: Einaudi editore, 1997), vol. II, 897–936; Mario Toscano, "Ebrei ed ebraismo nell'Italia della grande Guerra," in *Israel-Un decennio 1974–1984*, Francesco Del Canuto, ed. (Rome: Carucci, 1984); Mario Toscano, ed., *Integrazione ed identità. L'esperienza ebraica in Germania ed in Italia dall'Illuminismo al fascismo* (Milan: Angeli, 1998); and Michele Sarfatti, *Gli ebrei nell'Italia fascista. Vicende, identità, persecuzione* (Turin: Einaudi, 2000).

6. Sarfatti, *Gli ebrei nell'Italia fascista*, 22–4.

7. For elaboration on the issue see ibid.; Renzo De Felice, *Storia degli ebrei italiani sotto il fascismo* (Turin: Einaudi, 1972); and Meir Michaelis, *Mussolini and the Jews* (Oxford: Oxford University Press, 1978).

8. This impression was also caused by the fact that many Fascist high officials clearly misled Jewish leaders as to the extent and the number of the "discriminations" that would be given. For an example of such deception, see the minutes of the meeting between Aldo Ascoli, vice president of the Union of Jewish Communities, and Antonio La Pera, director of the DEMORAZZA, the department responsible for the enforcement of the anti-Jewish legislation in the Ministry of Interior, on October 22, 1938, Archivio Unione Comunitá Israelitiche Italiane (UCII), b. 83/A, p. 3.

9. See Simona Colarizi, *L'opinione degli italiani sotto il regime, 1929–1943* (Bari: Laterza, 1991). This impression can be also found in many personal memoirs and diaries of the period. Meir Michaelis proves how wrong the impression is that Mussolini was forced into anti-Semitic legislation, stressing several reasons of internal and foreign policy that brought Mussolini to the anti-Semitic policy. See Michaelis, *Mussolini and the Jews*; See also De Felice, *Storia degli ebrei italiani sotto il fascismo*, and Michele Sarfatti, *Gli ebrei nell'Italia fascista*.

10. Regarding the contradictory statements see Michaelis, *Mussolini and the Jews*, chs. 2–3.

11. Michele Sarfatti, *Mussolini contro gli ebrei* (Turin: Silvio Zamorani, 1994); Michaelis, ch. 5; see also Iael Nidam-Orvieto, "Between Discrimination and Persecution: The Reaction of Italian Jewry to an Ever Increasing Crisis (1938-1945)" (Hebrew) (Ph.D. diss., The Hebrew University of Jerusalem, 2003) chs. 2–3.

12. For the minutes of some of these meetings, see UCII, b. 83/A. For an in-depth analysis see Nidam-Orvieto, "Between Discrimination and Persecution," 69–77.

13. De Felice, 328; Michele Sarfatti, "Scuola di razza," *Diario della Settimana 3*, no. 27 (July 1998), 18; Sarfatti, *Gli ebrei nell'Italia Fascista*, 187–99.

14. See "Lista delle occupazioni degli ebrei di Varese," Archivio Centrale dello Stato, Roma (ACS), Ministero dell'Interno (Min. Int.) Demorazza, 1938–1943, Pt. 1, b. 11, file Varese.

15. See, for example, the very interesting epistolary of the Canarutto family, Archivio Centro di Documentazione Ebraica Contemporanea (CDEC), Fondo Canarutto, b. 119.

16. A. S to the minister of interior, October 25, 1941, ACS, Ministero dell'Interno, Direzione Generale Demografia e Razza (Demorazza) 1938–1943, b. 9, file 9–39; See also M. S. to the ministry of Interior, October 24, 1941, ACS, Min. Int. Demorazza, 1938–1943, b. 9, file 9–39. In Rome alone there were more than 800 Jewish peddlers. Quoting from these letters I use the initials of the authors' names in order to maintain their privacy.

17. Sylvia Lombroso, *No Time for Silence* (New York: Roy, 1945), 10–12.

18. Giuseppe Bottai, "Primo: la scuola," *Critica Fascista*, September 15, 1938; For numerical data about students see De Felice, *Storia degli ebrei italiani*, 328; Michele Sarfatti, "La scuola, gli ebrei e l'arianizzazione attuata da Giusseppe Bottai," in *I licei G. Berchet e G. Carducci durante il fascismo e la resistenza*, D. Bonetti, R. Bottoni, and G. Gargia de Maio, eds. (Milan: Liceo classico statale G. Carducci 1996). As to the statistics of school students, Michele Sarfatti evaluates 2,500 elementary school students, 4,000 junior and senior high school students, and approximately 1,500 university students. Michele Sarfatti, *Gli ebrei nell'Italia fascista*, 196; see also Roberto Finzi, *L'università Italiane e le leggi antiebraiche* (Rome: Editori Riuniti, 1997), ch. 3; Ruggero Zangrandi, *Il lungo viaggio attraverso il fascismo-contributo alla storia di una generazione* (Milan: Feltrinelli, 1962), chs. 3–4.

19. Lombroso, *No Time for Silence*, 6–7; See also *Una Gioventú offesa. Ebrei genovesi ricordano* (Florence: Giuntina, 1995); Guido Lopez, "La scuola ebraica: Dall'emarginazione all'autocoscienza," in *Scuola e Resistenza*, Nicola Raponi ed. (Parma: 1978); and Daniel Carpi, *Walking on the Way* (Hebrew) (Tel Aviv: Hasifria Hatzionit, 1999).

20. Michele Sarfatti, "Scuola di Razza," *Diario della Settimana*, anno III, no. 27, July 1998, 18; Sarfatti, *Gli ebrei nell'Italia fascista*, 195–6; See also Maria Zevi, "Dati statistici," *Conseguenze Culturali delle leggi razziali in Italia-atti dei convegni LINCEI* (Roma: LINCEI, 1990), 56–62.

21. During the 1920s, a few Jewish elementary schools were established and operated in the major communities. After September 1938 we observe a drastic increase in the number of schools when twenty-three communities either created or enlarged (in the case of the major Jewish communities) elementary schools and fourteen communities founded high schools. See Daniel Fishman, "Una risposta ebraica alle leggi: l'organizzazione delle scuole," *La Rassegna mensile di Israel*, Vol. LIV, no. 1–2 (January–August 1988), 339–40.

22. See *In memoria del prof. Giacomo Tedesco, primo preside delle scuole medie Israelitiche di Turin*, December 17, 1941, Archivio Comunitá Israelitica di Venezia (ACEV), b. 91; See also, Comunitá ebraica di Livorno, *1938: La scuola ebraica di Livorno: un'alternativa alle leggi razziali* (Livorno: Fondazione Primo Levi, 1997); *La Scuola media ebraica di Trieste 1938–1943. Storia e memoria* (Trieste: Lint, 1999), 29–54; Daniel Fishman, Una risposta ebraica alle leggi; Bruno Maida ed., *I bambini ebrei e le leggi razziali in Italia* (Florence: Giuntina, 1999); Bice Migliau and Michela Procaccia, "La documentazione della scuola media ebraica di Roma del 1938," *Italia Judaica-Gli ebrei nell'Italia Unita 1870–1945*, Atti del IV convegno internazionale, Siena, Giugno 1989 (Rome: Ministero per i beni culturali e ambientali, 1993), 453–63; and Alberto Cavaglion, *La scuola ebraica a Torino, 1938–1943* (Turin and Florence: Pluriverso, 1993).

23. Lombroso, *No Time for Silence*, 35–7.

24. Italo Levi, to Pellizzari, November 3, 1941, CDEC, 5HB, b. 109, file Levi.

25. Lombroso, *No Time for Silence*, 17.

26. On the sensitive topic of denunciations, see Mimmo Franzinelli, *Delatori, Spie e confidenti anonimi. L'arma segreta del regime Fascista* (Milan: Mondadori, 2001), 138, 144, 152; Direzione Generale di Publica Sicurezza a Demorazza, October 16, 1939, ACS, Min. Int, Demorazza 1938–1943, b. 13; Emanuele Artom, *Diari. Gennaio 1940–febbraio 1944* (Milan: Centro di Documentazione Ebraica Contemporanea, 1966), 33; Massimo Della Pergola, *Storia della SISAL e del suo inventore* (Milan: Laser, 1997), 18.

27. See Mario Tucchi a Dot. Rantzer, 13.7.39, CDEC, 5HB, b. 111, file Rantzer; Enzo Levi, *Memorie di una vita* (Modena: S.T.E.M Mucchi, 1972), 104–5; Giulio L. Cantoni, *From Milan to New York by Way of Hell* (San Jose and New York: Writers Club Press, 2000), 68–70; Massimo Della Pergola, *Storia della SISAL*, 21; Luciano Morpurgo, *Caccia all'uomo* (Rome: Casa Editrice Dalmatia, 1946), 64–5.

28. See, for example, Vittorio Finzi, *Il mio rifugio in Val Borbera* (Genova: Le Mani, 2001); for the attitude of the people of Nonantola to the Jewish children of Villa Emma, see Iael Orvieto, "The Children of Villa Emma: A Case Study of Children Rescued during the Holocaust" (Hebrew) (MA Thesis, Hebrew University, Jerusalem, 1996); See also Lombroso, *No Time for Silence*, 19–20.

29. Sarfatti, *Gli ebrei nell'Italia fascista*, 210; See also the testimony of Lea Ottolenghi, CDEC, 5HB, b. 110, file Ottolenghi.

30. See, for example, the diaries of Mario Tagliacozzo, *Metà della vita* (Milan: Baldini & Castoldi, 1998); Guido Lopez, *I Verdi, i Viola e gli Arancioni* (Vicenza: Mondadori, 1972); Giancarlo Sacerdoti, *Ricordi di un ebreo bolognese. Illusioni e delusioni* (Rome: Bonacci, 1983); See also the amazing collection of letters by Vittorio Foa to his family, *Lettere della giovinezza* (Turin: Einaudi, 1998) as well the correspondence of the Momigliano family kept in CDEC, Archivio 5HB, file Momigliano.

31. See, for example, Guido Weiller, *Via Eupili 1938–1943*, CDEC, 5HB, b. 112, file T2; Guido Lopez, *I Verdi, i Viola e gli Arancioni*, 40; Bruno Portaleone, *Pru Urvu* (Florence: Portaleone, Giuntina, 2001), 59–61.

32. For more details on the law, see Sarfatti, *Gli ebrei nell'Italia fascista*, 155–9.

33. For the official figures on mixed Jewish families, see Direzione Generale Demografia e Razza, "Situazione degli ebrei" (October 1940), ACS, Min. Int., Demorazza, 1938–1943, b. 13, file 13–43.

34. For further discussion the problem of mixed marriages and race, see Sarfatti, *Gli ebrei nell'Italia fascista*, 155–9.

35. H. C. to Mussolini, February 1, 1941, ACS, Min. Int. Demorazza, 1938–1943, b. 13, file 13–43; T. D. to the ministry of interior, August 14, 1941, ACS, Min. Int., Demorazza parte 1, b. 6.

36. Promemoria, no date, ACS, Min. Int. Dir. Gen. Demorazza, 1938–43, Pt. I, b. 2 fasc. 2–9; Min. Int. Dir. Gen. Demorazza, "Situazione degli ebrei" (October 1940), ACS, Min. Int. Demorazza, 1938–1943, Pt. 1, B. 13, fasc. 13–43; Daniel Carpi, "The Catholic Church and the Italian Jewry under Fascists," *Yad Vashem Studies* IV (1960), 43–56; on mixed marriages see Giuliana, Marisa, Gabriella Cardosi, "La questione dei matrimoni misti durante la persecuzione razziale in Italia 1938–1945: Aspetti della legislazione razziale"

Libri e documenti 6 (1980), 6–21; and Giuliana, Marisa, Gabriella Cardosi, *Sul confine. La questione dei matrimoni misti durante la persecuzione antiebraica in Italia e in Europa (1935–1945)* (Turin: Zamorani, 1998).

37. See, for example, Adriana Municelli, *Even, Pietruzza della memoria* (Turin: Edizioni Gruppo Abele, 1994), 40–50. For an authoritative study of foreign Jews in Italy, see Klaus Voigt, *Il rifugio precario*, 2 vols. (Florence: La nuova Italia, 1993–6).

38. P. P. to Mussolini, September 16, 1938, ACS, Segreteria Particolare del Duce (SPD), Carteggio Riservato (CR) 1922–1943, 480/R, b. 144.

39. Cited in Fabio Levi, *Un'identità imposta. Un padre ebreo di fronte alle leggi razziali* (Turin: Zamorani, 1996), 144.

40. A fascinating example can be found in Vittorio Foa, *Lettere della giovinezza, dal carcere* (Turin: Einaudi, 1998). For the response of Zionists see Simonetta Della Seta and Daniel Carpi, "Il movimento Sionistico," *Storia d'Italia. Gli ebrei in Italia, Annali 11*, (Turin: Einaudi, 1997), 1324–68; Simonetta della Seta, "Italian Zionism Confronts Fascism and the Racial Laws," in *Fascist Antisemitism and the Italian Jews*, Robert Wistrich and Sergio della Pergola, ed. (Jerusalem: The Vidal Sassoon Center for the Study of Antisemitism, The Hebrew University of Jerusalem, 1995), 37–48.

41. See Simona Colarizi, *L'opinione degli italiani sotto il regime*.

42. See, Nidam-Oveito, "Between Discrimination and Persecution," 46–7, 59–60, 72–4.

43. C. and A. M. to Mussolini, May 25, 1940, ACS, Min. Int. Demorazza, 1938–1943, b. 5.

44. M. L. to Mussolini, September 5, 1938, ACS, SPD, CR 1922–1943, 480/R, b. 143.

45. V. G. to Mussolini, no date, ACS, SPD, CR. 480R, b. 145.

46. See for example, file 153, ACS, SPD, CR, 1922–1943, 480/R, b. 142, and other files in this box and box 143. Most of the letters were passed on to the "Demorazza," and in the files we can find the annotations concerning each case and the end response of the authorities. Sometimes we find a photostat of the original letter, but usually there is merely a full description of it; also see G. M. to Osvaldo Sebastiani, July 20, 1939, ACS, SPD, CR 1922–1943, 480/R, b. 143; file 315, ACS, SPD, CR 1922–1943, 480/R, b. 144.

47. See, for example, P. R. to Mussolini, October 1940, ACS, SPD, CR 480/R, b. 144; file 322, ACS, SPD, CR 1922–1943, 480/R, b. 144.

48. See, for example, the correspondence between Sabatino Lopez and his family, and especially the letters from October 15, 1938 and July 9, 1939, kept by his son, Guido Lopez, Milan; See also the letter of Italo Levi to a friend, June 6, 1940, CDEC, Historical Archive, 5HB, b. 109, file Italo Levi.

49. File 261, ACS, SPD, CR, 1922–1943, 480/R, b. 143.

50. G. M. to Osvaldo Sebastiani, The private secretary of Mussolini, December 15, 1938, ACS, SPD, CR 1922–1943, 480/R, b. 143; file 356, ACS, SPD, CR 1922–1943, 480/R, b. 145.

51. G. M. a Sebastiani, October 11, 1938, ACS, SPD, CR, 480/R, b. 143; See also Sylvia Lombroso, *Si puo' stampare. Diario di una madre-pagine vissute 1938–1945* (Rome: Dalmatia, 1946), 13, 30. (The Italian version of the diary contains the whole entries, including some that were omitted in the English version); Enzo Levi, *Memorie*

di una vita (Modena: S. T. E.M Mucchi, 1972), 101–6; Momigliano, *Elogio alla li̇* (Attraverso un semplice epistolario famigliare 1921–1945), CDEC, Archivio Storico, 5HB, file Momigliano, p. 75.

52. Minutes of the meeting of executive committee of the Union of Jewish Communities, October, 19–20, 1941, UCII, Libro dei Verbali, Giunta, V, p. 1.

53. A. C. to his mother, September 7, 1938, CDEC, Fondo Canarutto; See also some of the letters by Vittorio Foa, *Lettere della giovinezza. Dal carcere 1935–1943* (Turin: Einaudi, 1998), 436, 500, 523.

54. Vittorio Foa, *Lettere della giovinezza*, 523, 500.

55. V. T. B. to Mussolini, September 16, 1938, ACS, SPD, CR 480, b. 144.

56. F. M. to Romano Mussolini, September 6, 1939, file 222, ACS, SPD, CR 1922–1943, 480/R, b. 143.

57. Anon., June, 16, 1939, ACS, Min. Int. Dmorazza 1938–1943, b. 4.; See also Anon., 1938, ACS, SPD, CR 1922–1943, 480/R, b. 141; V. T. to Mussolini, September 16, 1938, ACS, SPD, CR 1922–1943, 480/R, b. 144.

58. R. A. to the King, August 21, 1938, ACS, Min. Int. Demorazza, 1938–1943, b. 4

59. Luciano Morpurgo, *Caccia all'uomo-pagine di Diario 1938–1944* (Rome: Dalmatia, 1946), 43–5.

60. See Nidam-Orvieto, "Between Discrimination and Persecution," chs. 6, 8.

61. See, for example, the dossiers kept in Archivio Centrale dello Stato, Ministero dell' Interno, Publica Sicurezza, Segreteria del Capo della Polizia, Senise, 1940–1943, b. 11, especially from February 1943.

62. See, for example, Emanuele Artom, *Diari-Gennaio 1940–Febbraio 1944* (Milano: Centro di Documentazione Ebraica Contemporanea, 1966), 73; Giovanni De Luna, "Dall'antifascismo alla resistenza," *La moralità armata-Studi su Emanuele Artom 1915–1944* Alberto Cavaglion, ed. (Milano: Franco Angeli, 1993), 62–4; Lombroso, *Si puó stampare*, 108–14; Angelo Diena, *Gli anni che lasciano il segno*, (Turin: Edizioni Gruppo Abele, 1997), 54; Guri Schwarz, "Un'identitá da rifondare: note sul problema dei giovani tra persecuzione e dopoguerra (1938–1956), *Zakhor*, III (1999), 189.

63. V. K. to Mussolini, June 2, 1940, ACS, Min. Int. Demorazza, 1938–1943, b. 5; See also M. E. to Mussolini, June 10, 1940, ACS, Min. Int. Demorazza, 1938–1943, b. 5; F. C. to Mussolini, June 12, 1940, ACS, Min. Int. Demorazza, 1938–1943, b. 5.

64. E. O. to Mussolini, November 10, 1939, min. Int, Demorazza 1938–1943, b. 5.

65. R. J., September 23, 1939, ACS, Min. Int. Demorazza, 1938–1943, b. 5; See also, for example, E. S. to Mussolini, ACS, Min. Int. Demorazza, 1938–1943, b. 5; I. S. R. to Mussolini, September 1939, ACS, Min. Int. Demorazza, 1938–1943, b. 5; F. C. to Mussolini, June 12, 1940, ACS, Min. Int. Demorazza, 1938–1943, b. 5.

66. For more information about these letters, see Iael Orvieto, "Letters to Mussolini."

9 The ... of Villa Emma at Nonantola

Klaus Voigt

At the beginning of the Second World War, Jews in Germany and in Austria, then annexed to the Third Reich, were almost totally deprived of their rights, impoverished, and excluded from society. Their condition became even more dramatic as most escape routes were cut off. Borders became frontlines, passenger ships no longer could cross the North Sea and the Baltic, and the powers at war with Germany denied admission to all persons living in territories under Nazi domination. The only remaining chances of escape were now remote destinations in North, Central, or South America or in Asia – which could be reached via neutral and nonbelligerent European countries that as a rule denied permanent residence – or illegal immigration to Palestine.

During the first two weeks of war, "enemy aliens" were interned in Germany, as they were in all other belligerent countries. This measure chiefly affected Polish citizens. At the end of 1938 there were 13,000 Jews with Polish citizenship still living in Germany, although their number had declined by the time the war began. On September 7, 1939, Gestapo headquarters in Berlin issued an order that all Jewish males over sixteen having Polish citizenship were to be taken into custody, while all women and children were to be registered. Jews were therefore arrested in their homes and taken to the concentration camps at Dachau, Sachsenhausen, and Buchenwald. If the purpose of the mass arrests during the pogrom of November 9, 1938, had been to frighten Jews into emigration, now the plan was to bring about their death by exhaustion due to forced labor or by outright murder.[1]

It is with the deportation of Polish Jews to the concentrations camps that the story of the children of Villa Emma begins. Out of the forty boys and girls who formed the first group to arrive at Nonantola in July 1942, twenty-four had been living in Germany (in Berlin, Frankfurt am Main, Leipzig, Hamburg, and Kiel) before their flight, thirteen in Austria (in Vienna and in Graz), two in Yugoslavia (in Zagreb), and one in a small town in southern Poland. Out of the twenty-four children from Germany, twenty-two belonged to families of Polish Jewish immigrants, one came from a family of Russian Jewish immigrants, and only one girl possessed German citizenship. They all declared German as their mother tongue. Of the thirteen children who had been living in Austria, eight were Austrian, three Polish, and two Hungarian citizens. The fathers of most of the twenty-five Polish Jewish children had been taken to a concentration camp in the autumn of 1939; many of them were already dead by the time the children arrived at Nonantola.[2]

The men's detention in the concentration camps usually left the women and children without income. In their dire need they found an advocate in Recha Freier, founder of the youth-aliyah, which until the start of the Second World War had enabled almost 5,000 boys and girls, mainly from Germany and Austria, to emigrate to Palestine. Recha Freier persuaded the relief organizations of the Jewish community in Berlin to aid the families with modest sums, which she herself would distribute. In July 1940, herself threatened with arrest, she fled with her youngest daughter to Zagreb via Vienna. Guided by smugglers along mountain paths, they crossed the border to Yugoslavia.[3]

In Zagreb, Recha Freier devised a plan to have as many children as possible join her in Zagreb, mainly from the families she had been assisting. From Yugoslavia there was still a chance to obtain for them immigration certificates to Palestine as part of the youth-aliyah. Freier's plan won the support of the Jewish community in Zagreb, of its relief committee for Jewish refugees, of the Palestine office, and of Zionist organizations. By that time, however, Jews no longer could obtain visas for Yugoslavia and were usually sent back, if they were caught within the area controlled by the border police. Therefore, one had to cross the border with the help of smugglers who were familiar with the terrain. The main escape organization set up by the smugglers was headed by a man in Graz, Josef Schleich, who worked in close association with the Gestapo, as the latter's goal at the time was for the Jews to leave the country. Schleich, in cooperation with the youth-aliyah Vienna office, managed to get most of the children belonging to Freier's group to their destination.[4] The first group, eleven boys from Berlin, arrived in Zagreb about the middle of October 1940. Fifteen girls left Berlin on January 29, 1941, but were caught a few days later near Maribor, because after crossing the border in freezing weather, they had been abandoned in the snow by their guides. A compassionate border police inspector, Uros Žun, ensured that they were not sent back, but were temporarily interned instead in an old castle at Krško, north of Zagreb. The last seven children, five of them from Vienna, managed to escape at the end of March. Altogether, approximately 140 boys and girls arrived in Zagreb without visas, but their presence there was tolerated as a result of the good offices of the Jewish community. The children were lodged with Jewish families and in Jewish hostels and would come together regularly on the premises of the Jewish community building to learn Hebrew and spend time with each other. After a long period of uncertainty, between March 25 and the April 1, 1941, – only a few days before the Germans occupied Zagreb – ninety children whose certificates had recently arrived finally left by train for Belgrade, from where they traveled on to Istanbul. Four weeks later they arrived exhausted in Palestine.[5]

Recha Freier had started for Palestine a little earlier. Before leaving Zagreb, she decided, together with the Jewish community and with the Zionist organization, to entrust the remaining children, whose number by then had increased to over fifty and who were meant to join the others in Palestine at a later date, to the care of Josef Indig. Indig was a member of the Yugoslav leadership of Hashomer Hazair (The Young Guard), an organization of leftist-socialist, secular, and antibourgeois orientation that attracted a great following among youngsters in the 1930s, especially in Eastern Europe.[6] Indig was barely twenty-four. He was the son of the cantor of the Osijek synagogue, came from a German-speaking family, and had trained as a motor mechanic. Besides studying intensively the history, topography, economy, and society of Palestine, he had also learned some Hebrew. He could envisage no future for himself other than living in a socialist kibbutz.[7]

After Germany and Italy jointly attacked Yugoslavia, and German troops entered Zagreb on April 10, 1941, where they were greeted enthusiastically by people lining the streets, it became impossible to travel to Palestine. The extremely nationalistic Independent State of Croatia, set up by the Ustashi movement under the protection of the occupation forces, zealously emulated the Nazi persecution of Jews. Within a few weeks, a racist legislation in line with the Nuremberg Laws caused Jews to be expelled from all public employment, ousted from political and cultural life, and largely excluded from economic activity. Starting from early May, they were forced, as in other territories under German occupation, to wear a yellow badge with a black Star of David and the letter Ž (for Židov [Jew]). In late June, deportations began from Zagreb to camps set up in various locations. The conditions there were appalling and cruelty and murder were common.[8]

Under the circumstances, Josef Indig made the only correct choice and decided to take the children as quickly as possible to the nearby southern part of Slovenia, which had been annexed by Italy, renamed Provincia di Lubiana (Province of Ljubljana), and placed under a high commissioner. Mussolini's Italy had enacted racist laws as well, in the autumn of 1938, imitating in many points the Nazis' Nuremberg Laws. Unlike in Germany and Croatia, however, Jewish lives were not threatened in Italy.[9]

In early June, Indig traveled by train from Zagreb to Ljubljana to make arrangements locally for the children's stay. He risked being arrested by the Ustashi police, as he was not wearing the obligatory yellow badge and had only an old Yugoslav travel document, but luck was on his side. In Ljubljana he met up with Eugenio Bolaffio, the local representative of Delasem (Delegazione per l'Assistenza agli Emigranti), the relief organization of Italian Jewry based in Genoa. Bolaffio and Indig opted for a hunting lodge standing practically empty at Lesno brdo, approximately eighteen kilometers southwest of Ljubljana, and reached an agreement with the owner about the rent.[10]

All depended now on the attitude of Italian authorities. Until the enactment of the racial laws, Fascist Italy had granted admission to Jewish refugees from territories under Nazi rule. Their situation then suffered a drastic setback with the decree of September 7, 1938, which threatened with expulsion the great majority of Jews who had entered Italy as immigrants or refugees after 1918 if they did not leave the country within six months. The expulsion, however, proved impracticable: by the time the deadline expired, approximately one half of the 9,000 Jews affected by the decree, 4,500 of whom were refugees from Germany and Austria, were as yet without visas to another country and therefore unable to leave Italy. Until August 1939, Jews could still enter Italy with a tourist visa, which enabled them to remain in the country up to six months. When authorities realized that 5,000 mostly destitute people had used this kind of visa only to flee Nazi persecution, it was suspended. After that, and until May 1940, entry into the country was allowed only on a transit visa in order to board a ship in an Italian harbor. When Italy entered the war in June 1940, the border was closed to Jews. After Yugoslavia's defeat, this ban was extended to include the territories annexed by Italy.[11]

To take the children from Zagreb to Slovenia, special permission had to be obtained from Emilio Grazioli, high commissioner for the Province of Ljubljana. This was granted, with the interior ministry's consent, the reason being probably that children were concerned and also because at the time there were as yet few Jewish refugees in the region. In any case, it remains to date the only known instance of Jews being granted permission to enter Italy during the war. As soon as the answer arrived, Indig returned to Zagreb and on July 4, 1942, in a train journey fraught with danger, he took the children over the border to Slovenia.[12]

The hunting lodge at Lesno brdo stood on a hill, surrounded by woods. The building, erected in the seventeenth century, was furnished in farmhouse style. It even had a grand piano, but not enough beds for almost fifty people, so that many had to sleep on straw mattresses. On the main floor were the day rooms and the kitchen with a stone oven to bake bread. This oven and a vast fireplace were the main sources of heating, and in winter the house, which was lit by candles and oil lamps, was freezing cold. After the well in the lodge's courtyard dried up, water had to be carried in buckets from a spring about half an hour's walk away. In the winter it was mainly obtained by melting the snow.[13]

Providing food out of the inevitably limited budget was the task of the group's treasurer, Marco Schoky, who is described as a man well versed in black market dealings. Schoky traveled frequently from Lesno brdo to Ljubljana with a pass, to look for whatever was required. He sent the older boys with backpacks to faraway farms, where they could buy coveted goods like butter, cheese, and eggs. All the same, the children were seldom able to eat their fill.

In Lesno brdo the children, after an interval of many months, were again able to attend regular school lessons. Besides the general curriculum, there were courses in Hebrew and Italian. Boris Jochvedson, a refugee music teacher from Berlin, taught some of the children to play the piano. The lessons were held in the afternoon, as the morning was taken up with chores about the house, like tidying up, cleaning, fetching water, and splitting wood.

One problem in educating the children for their future life in a kibbutz was the varied nature of the group. To begin with, there was a considerable difference in age. The youngest child was ten and the two oldest were twenty. Second, only a few of the children, despite their parents' Zionist views, had been in a Zionist youth organization. Some of the children from Vienna came from assimilated backgrounds. Education in the Hashomer Hazair was aimed at enhancing awareness of the tasks awaiting people in Palestine, building up self-reliance, and at the same time forging a strong community in which the common purpose would take precedence over individual needs. At Lesno brdo, too, morning roll calls, teamwork, and regular meetings to discuss the problems of living together were all designed to further this aim. On the Sabbath and on holidays there were performances of various kinds, such as piano playing, singing, poetry recitals, and conferences. On Zionist memorial days celebrations were held with speeches and music. Indig, in accordance with the policy of Hashomer Hazair, did not approve of religious education, such as was imparted in some Zionist organizations. Consequently Lesno brdo did not keep a kosher kitchen.

Life at Lesno brdo, however "romantic" in some ways, was overshadowed by the uncertainty of the fate of parents, brothers, and sisters. Some of the children had not heard from them since Zagreb. When the deportation from German towns to the ghettos in Łódź, Riga, Kovno, and Minsk began, in October 1941, a few of the children's mothers were still able to inform them of their "departure," as it was termed. Only occasional standardized postcards arrived then from the ghettos. Eventually all communication ceased. The separation from their families and in many cases their fathers' death in a concentration camp already weighed heavily on the children's minds. Their mothers', sisters', or brothers' silence was now all the harder to bear. The grown-ups tried to cheer them as best as they could, but the children were often overwhelmed by grief, especially on festive occasions. "I cannot begin to describe," wrote Indig after Rosh Hashannah, "the weeping that shook the walls of the castle. Everywhere, in every corner, children were standing or were stretched out on the floor, sobbing as if their heart would break. Twelve-year-old girls were loudly calling their dead mother and father."[14]

In the spring of 1942, Slovene partisan units began to operate in the woods around Lesno brdo. At night the partisans would demand to be admitted into the lodge, where they would nurse their wounded and had to be fed. During the day there would be Italian Carabinieri or military patrols, who also requested to be let in. For Indig and the children the situation became increasingly hazardous. While their sympathies lay with the partisans who were fighting for the liberation of their country, they had to maintain good relationships with Italian authorities and avoid giving rise to suspicion that they were close to the partisans. Considering the group to be in danger, Delasem, the relief organization, decided to move the children to Nonantola, near Modena, and to lodge them at Villa Emma. Shortly before the Italian army's summer offensive against the partisans, High Commissioner Grazioli approved the plan suggested by Delasem and asked for the interior ministry's consent, which was granted within two days. On July 16, the group left Lesno brdo and traveled by train, escorted by a few Carabinieri, from Ljubljana via Mestre and Bologna to Modena, where they arrived early the next morning and were assisted by the local Jewish community. In the afternoon they proceeded to Nonantola, a small town with a population of 10,000.[15]

When the children entered Villa Emma, a two-storied building standing free among fields on the outskirts of the town, they found the forty-six rooms allotted to them totally empty and had to sleep on the floor. After two months, camp beds, mattresses, pillows, kitchenware, and other household goods were brought to Nonantola from a summer camp for young Italian Jews. Sacks filled with straw were used in place of blankets. A cooker was installed only at the beginning of September; before that the children had their meals in some local trattorias. At first, water had to be pumped up from a well for three hours every day. In winter only six rooms could be heated. Electricity was installed after a while, and most rooms could be dimly lit by light bulbs. Gradually several repairs were carried out. Once the carpenter's workshop was in operation, it was used mainly to build furniture for the house.[16]

While at Villa Emma, the children and the adults in charge of them were not regarded as internees by authorities. In this their status differed from that of most foreign Jews in Italy, who, after the country had entered the war, had been either taken to internment camps or subjected to "free internment," that is, forced residence. The children could therefore have moved around freely. As the population of Nonantola had greeted them with great friendliness, however, Delasem thought it advisable to exercise some sort of self-control, so as not to annoy local Fascists. Children were therefore allowed to go into town only in groups and escorted by an adult. Otherwise they could leave the grounds only with the principal's permission.[17]

A young graduate in literary studies who worked with Delasem in Genoa, Umberto Jacchia, was appointed principal of Villa Emma. He was twenty-six, six months older than Indig. Jacchia ran the house like an ordinary Italian school. Until then, the relationship between the adults in charge of the group had been based chiefly on personal trust, and Indig, although madrich (group leader), had always considered himself as an equal among equals. Now the roles and duties of each were set down in writing. Indig became the principal's subordinate, acting as deputy in his absence, and was responsible with him for what was called "internal discipline."[18]

Particular stress, against Indig's wishes, was now laid on religious worship, which many children had missed at Lesno brdo. A prayer room with Torah scrolls was set up in one of the rooms of Villa Emma. The daily schedule set aside half an hour for prayers in the room each morning and evening. Attendance was voluntary. On the other hand, attendance to religious functions on the Sabbath and on holidays was compulsory. After a while the kitchen became strictly kosher.

Jacchia's way of running the house plunged Indig into a moral dilemma. He felt he was being pushed aside and would no longer be able to impart to the children the Zionist education he believed was necessary for their future life in Palestine. He therefore withdrew from his duties in late September as deputy principal and limited himself to teaching Hebrew.

Because of increased support from Delasem, the children were considerably better provided for at Villa Emma than they had been at Lesno brdo. Their meals were almost entirely vegetarian, because vegetables were amply available on the market and were not rationed. Potatoes, which were cheaper than bread, pasta, or rice, were the main staple. Secondhand clothes, shoes, and basic necessities were also supplied. School lessons, chores about the house, cultural activities, and above all Jochvedson's piano playing took up a great part of the day, as at Lesno brdo.

Villa Emma was surrounded by 7.5 hectares of farmland. In the contract with a real estate company in Milan it was agreed that the group should lease the land together with the building and farm it. Ernesto Leonardi, a farmer who lived close to the villa, was paid a monthly salary in order that the children might learn farming under his guidance, as this was of fundamental importance for settling in Palestine. The training began in November and at first involved only four boys. The number of boys and girls who helped with the harvest in the following summer was however considerably higher. In January a carpenter's workshop was set up under the guidance of Hersz Naftali Schuldenfrei, a carpenter who had been released from an internment camp. Eventually it was fitted out with seven joiner's benches, so that twelve boys could work in it at one time. Gradually the girls' sewing room became a proper tailoring workshop, with two sewing machines. Several of the older boys and girls worked in the Delasem's storeroom, which had been transferred to Villa Emma after the first air raids on Genoa and which took up the entire attic. Relief goods of all kinds were stored there, to be made into aid packages that were sent to internees all over Italy.

The forty-six rooms of Villa Emma could accommodate quite a larger number of children than the Lesno brdo group. After December 1942, therefore, a plan was conceived to take in another thirty-three children, who had fled from Bosnia and Croatia to Split, in the territory annexed by Italy. Twenty of these children were from Sarajevo. Twenty-four were orphans, four had lost one parent, and only five had been able to flee together with their parents. The children and the adults in charge of them arrived in Nonantola on April 14, 1943. These children, nineteen boys and fifteen girls, were younger on average than the group already at Villa Emma. They spoke Serbo-Croatian, so separate classes had to be set up for them.[19]

After the arrival of the children from Split, Villa Emma became quite crowded. There were now eighty-six people living in it: seventy-three children and thirteen adults, and more were to arrive later on. Meals had to be taken in shifts, as the kitchen could not cope with so many meals at once and there was not enough room in the dining room to seat everybody. The din in the house was such that Indig chose to hold his Hebrew lessons in a quiet corner of the Delasem storeroom in the attic. Jacchia complained that the discipline was getting increasingly lax, day after day, and that he no longer could keep the children from going into town. He was forced to admit that running such a large house with difficult children scarred by refugee life and coming from various countries and different social backgrounds would have required an experienced educator, which he was not. After some hesitation, therefore, and pending a decision as to his successor, Delasem replaced him with a board formed by Indig, Schoky, Jochvedson, and Armand Moreno.

Because the children could not go out freely, due to the limits imposed by Delasem, for a time they had contact only with people who had dealings of some kind with Villa Emma, such as the local doctor Giuseppe Moreali, an anti-Fascist and a liberal, the many workmen who came into the house, and the owners of the shops where Schoky and the older children did their buying for the group. Nevertheless, everybody in Nonantola knew them. The children were a constant topic of conversation, and most of the population sympathized with them from afar. Contacts became more frequent after some of the older boys and girls were issued work permits because of the labor shortage caused by the war. Some worked in a canning factory, others were employed in the workshop of a basket maker, and others helped farmers with the harvest. Friendly relations developed also with some young priests in the seminary adjoining the abbey church, especially with Don Arrigo Beccari, who, like Moreali, was averse to the Fascist dictatorship. After Mussolini's fall on July 25, 1943, the children increasingly ignored the prohibition of going out by themselves.

On the evening of September 8, 1943, when the armistice between the government headed by General Badoglio and the Allies was announced on the radio, the group understood at once that German occupation was imminent. By that time the group leaders were already aware of the Nazi extermination policy, from information they had received from Switzerland. They knew therefore that if the children stayed on at Villa Emma they would be defenseless against a roundup, and arrest would mean their death. Within half an hour from hearing the news of the armistice, the members of the board and some of the older boys went to see Giuseppe Moreali, the local doctor, and discussed with him where the children might hide. Moreali got in touch with Don Arrigo Beccari, who was able to persuade the rector of the seminary, Don Ottaviano Pelati, to shelter the children in the seminary itself, which at the time stood almost empty because of the summer holidays. The decision to leave Villa Emma was made on September 9, when German troops were already in Nonantola. That same evening Don Pelati received about thirty to forty boys and girls under sixteen into the seminary. After a few days the girls were moved to a nunnery. Farmers and workmen both in the immediate neighborhood and in the surrounding area took in the older boys and girls, hiding them in a room, a barn, or a cowshed. Several boys slept for some nights out in the open, until a shelter was found for them as well.[20]

Occasionally some children would venture into the street and even go back to Villa Emma, in order to retrieve food and other items from the house, take clothing from the Delasem storeroom, and bring them to a safe place. The food was taken to the seminary, where the nuns who worked in the kitchen would use it to prepare meals for the children. Sometimes one of the younger boys, whom it was almost impossible to tell from local boys, would bring the meals on a handcart to the hiding places strewn all over the town. Indig stayed in the seminary, but kept constantly in touch with all the children by means of messengers. Whenever the necessity arose, he would arrange to meet up with some of them, somewhere outside the seminary.[21]

In the territory of the Salò Republic, set up by Mussolini with Hitler's consent, the arrest and deportation of Jews by German police began on October 16, 1943, with the roundup in the former Roman ghetto overlooking the Tiber, where many Jews still lived. As a consequence of the roundup, 1,023 men, women, and children were deported to Auschwitz: only seventeen survived. There is no indication to date of earlier arrests of Jews by either the Nazi Security Police (Außenkommando der SIPO) or the SS Security Service. Units of the Waffen-SS carried out most captures and all the murders of Jews in this early phase. Only a few instances of arrests by ordinary Wehrmacht units are known.[22]

Under the circumstances one can practically rule out that the local command of the Nazi Security Police and SS closest to Nonantola, that is in Bologna, was planning a roundup during the barely six weeks the children spent in hiding and was therefore looking for them. The local Security Police was in all likelihood entirely unaware of their presence. It might have obtained information from the German military command in Bologna. It is documented that in several provinces the military command requested that the local provincial police headquarters (Questura) hand over lists of internees. However, since the children did not have internee status, it is unlikely that the Questura in Modena disclosed their names, unless the military command had asked for a list of all Jews living in the province, something which – as far as we know to date – happened in just one province. Another possible source of information would have been the town commandant. According to Indig, the commandant knew that the children were hiding and reportedly said that as long as he was in command nothing would happen to them, even if they returned to Villa Emma.[23]

The adults in charge of the children were well aware that in the long run these hiding places could not provide full protection from a roundup, which, it was feared, might take place any day. Moreover, the archbishop of Modena was insisting that the seminary be vacated, so that lessons might resume at the beginning of October as usual. At first Indig considered moving with the children to some locality farther south. However, when the Allies' advance toward the north came to a halt between Naples and Rome, he had to give up this plan.[24]

Fleeing to Switzerland now became the only possible alternative. Nevertheless, nine boys and one girl, almost all over eighteen, decided to travel south and left either alone or in small groups. Indig gave his consent to the plan and provided them with some money and with the addresses of Jewish communities and Delasem representatives along their route. Three of the boys actually managed to cross the front line south of Naples and to reach Allied territory. Four boys and the girl made it only as far as Rome and remained hidden there for over two months. A nineteen-year-old from Frankfurt and a slightly older man who had been among the adults in charge of the group joined the partisans, fought alongside them, and were liberated by the Allies in the summer of 1944.[25]

At the border between Switzerland and Italy, at the time, only children under sixteen were let through. No adults were admitted into Switzerland, apart from mothers with small children, pregnant women, and people in jeopardy because of their political engagement. To ascertain the situation at the Swiss border, Indig and Goffredo Pacifici, an employee of Delasem, traveled to Ponte Tresa, where they found a smuggler who agreed to guide the children against payment.[26]

After Indig returned from Ponte Tresa to Nonantola, two groups of six to eight children and adults were sent to the Swiss border to begin with. Out of the first group, two boys and a girl who were over sixteen were sent back by the Swiss border police and returned to Nonantola. The second group turned back shortly before reaching the border. Besides these two groups, four older boys and girls and two adults started on their own and with unbelievable good luck managed to cross the border in the mountains north of Ponte Chiasso without being seen, boarded a train in Lugano, and reached Zurich.[27]

After the failed attempt by the first two groups, Indig and Pacifici traveled again to the Swiss border, this time to Ponte Chiasso. Here Indig approached a Swiss haulier and gave him a message for Nathan Schwalb, the director of the Zionist youth organization Hehaluts in Geneva. As soon as he received the message, Schwalb contacted the Bern legation of the Yugoslav government-in-exile, which gave a guarantee to Swiss authorities that maintenance would be provided throughout the children's stay in Switzerland and that they would leave after the war. The Federal Department of Justice and Police then consented to the children's entry. Indig learned of this the next day, when the Swiss haulier returned to Ponte Chiasso.[28]

After his return to Nonantola, Indig arranged for the children's departure the very next day. In the early afternoon of October 6, Indig, together with thirty-three children, seven adults belonging to the group, and three Libyan Jews who had lived as internees in a separate wing of Villa Emma, boarded the train to Modena. On the train to Milan they had to go through a check by the German military police (Feldgendarmerie). However, no objections were raised to the identity cards issued by the municipality of Nonantola. At the railway station in Milan they were met by Pacifici. Some of the children traveled on with him to Varese, twenty kilometers south of the Swiss border. The rest spent the night in Milan, probably in the station's bathrooms. The next day, at nightfall, they all crossed the border near Ponte Tresa. A second group of twenty-one children and five adults followed on October 10 at the same point. A third group of one adult and four children crossed the border a little farther to the west, in the night from October 15 to 16.[29]

Crossing the border was fraught with danger. On September 16, German military authorities declared the closure of the border. From that day on a unit of the German border police (Zollgrenzschutz) was stationed in barracks at Ponte Tresa and arrested anybody who came near the border. If the children had been captured, they would have been taken to the jail in Varese, from where they would have been sent to the local command of the Security Police and SS Security Service in Como, to be deported to Auschwitz.[30] To reach Switzerland, the river Tresa, which marked the border, had to be forded at a shallow point after nightfall. A chain was formed, with older children and grown-ups taking the smaller children between them. Anyone who stumbled risked being swept away by the strong current. On the far side of the stream, which they all reached safely, the Swiss border guards were already waiting for them. Two anxious days passed before the first group, led by Indig, knew for sure that it had been admitted to Switzerland. The border authorities had found out that several of the children were over sixteen and that most of them were not Yugoslav citizens at all, contrary to what they had been told. They therefore referred the matter to the police headquarters in Bern. Luckily the deputy chief of police called Richard Lichtheim, the Zionist delegate to the League of Nations in Geneva, and requested that he vouch also for the maintenance of the children without

Yugoslav citizenship and for their leaving after the war. A short while later, in a second telephone call, this assurance was given. Only then were all the children and the adults in charge of them allowed to remain in Switzerland.[31]

The last group to reach Switzerland was made up of the five young people who had been hiding in Rome. When they heard that the others were in Switzerland, they returned to Modena, from where Pacifici led them together with other Jews to the Swiss border near Tirano. They too were admitted into the country.[32]

All the children who were in Nonantola on September 8 were saved. Only a boy from Sarajevo, who had been sent to a sanatorium in the Apennines because he was ill with tuberculosis, could not be taken to Switzerland with the others. His name appears for the last time on a list of deportees from the camp of Fossoli near Carpi to Auschwitz, in April 1944. Goffredo Pacifici was also murdered at Auschwitz, after being arrested near Ponte Tresa by the Italian police.[33]

In Switzerland the children were sent to various quarantine camps near the border and then to internment camps. They were separated and scattered in several places. Indig and the Zionist organizations in Switzerland therefore undertook to reunite the group in a home where they might continue their schooling and their training in farming and manual work. In October, Hehaluts and the Swiss Zionist Organization bought a vast building surrounded by farmland at Bex in the Rhône valley. The first children from Villa Emma arrived there late in December 1943. In the course of the following months other children came to Bex from internment camps and internment "homes," as they were called. Almost one-third of the children of Villa Emma did not join the group at Bex, preferring to remain instead in internment homes or to attend vocational schools.

On May 29, 1945, a first group of forty-two children and young people from Villa Emma together with Indig, Schuldenfrei, and other adults in charge of them traveled by train from Geneva to Barcelona, where they boarded the Plus Ultra for Palestine. Some children and young people followed later to Haifa or returned to relatives in Yugoslavia. Others emigrated to Great Britain or to the United States; three stayed on in Switzerland.[34]

Shortly after their arrival in Switzerland, Indig wrote to Richard Lichtheim in Geneva. "All I can say is that the group arrived at the very last moment, and it is hard to imagine the fate of all these young people, if they had stayed on in N."[35] These words convey his awareness that only in Switzerland were the children safe at last. And in fact their rescue was chiefly due to the determination and the courage of Indig, Pacifici, and other adults in charge of the children who had organized their flight at the risk of their own lives.

A role of almost equal importance in the successful outcome of the flight was played by the population of Nonantola and the shelter they gave to the group. By hiding, the children reduced the risk of being arrested, and at the same time, by scattering within a fairly limited area, they remained within reach of the adults in charge of them. Had they dispersed – and the departure for Southern Italy of a few of the older children signalled that such a development could not be ruled out – they would no longer have been able to flee as a group. Sooner or later some of them would most likely have been victims. The priests, the nuns, and the approximately thirty families who so generously assisted the children in Nonantola, giving them shelter, braved a danger that it is hard to assess. Such spontaneous help, which involved so many people, as witnessed in Nonantola, remains unique even in Italy, where Jewish refugees generally met with compassion and friendliness.

One important element that led the people of Nonantola to offer shelter was that the children had been living there for over a year. The population knew them well and no longer regarded them as strangers. Practically everybody knew, and had been shocked to learn, that most of the children's fathers had been murdered in a concentration camp and that their mothers and siblings had been deported to Eastern Europe and that nothing more had been heard of them. The Fascist propaganda that accompanied the racial laws had been unable to engender a widespread feeling that the Jews were enemies and to suppress spontaneous stirrings of humanity among the population. When the children were in deadly danger, after the arrival of German troops in town, many people sympathized with their fears and for this reason, if for no other, were ready to come to their rescue. Their action was not prompted mainly by political motives, although Giuseppe Moreali and Don Arrigo Beccari were openly opposed to Fascism and even more, of course, to Nazism. They were the ones who arranged for the children to be taken into the seminary and who searched for other suitable hiding places. They would appeal to people and were often instrumental in persuading them to take the children into their homes. Both were later honored by the Yad Vashem Memorial in Jerusalem, and a tree was planted for each of them in the Avenue of the Righteous among the Nations.

The children of Nonantola were chiefly assisted by Jews and Jewish organizations: the relief committees in Zagreb, Delasem, and the Zionist organizations in Switzerland. One has only to think of what Recha Freier did for them, when she decided entirely on her own to have them brought across the border to Zagreb with the aid of smugglers. However, they also met repeatedly with people who were not Jewish and yet helped them. This was by no means a matter of course and was therefore all the more remarkable. Let us remember first of all the border police inspector in Maribor, who made sure that the girls from Berlin were not sent back, or the unknown Swiss haulier, who gave Nathan Schwalb Indig's message, announcing the imminent flight. Because of this, Schwalb, by calling in the Yugoslav embassy, was able to negotiate the children's admission into Switzerland and thus to ensure their survival.

Translated from the German by Loredana M. Melissari

NOTES

This paper is based on a book I recently published both in German and in Italian: Klaus Voigt, *Villa Emma. Jüdische Kinder auf der Flucht. 1940–1943* (Solidarität und Hilfe für Juden während der NS-Zeit 6) (Berlin: Metropol Verlag, 2002); *Villa Emma. Ragazzi ebrei in fuga. 1940–1945* (Milan: La Nuova Italia, 2002). Reference will be made to the book, in its Italian edition, only where numerical data on the children or specific interpretations and conclusions are borrowed from it. For bibliographical references, see Klaus Voigt, "I ragazzi di Villa Emma a Nonantola," in *Le Comunità ebraiche a Modena e a Carpi. Dal medioevo all'età contemporanea*, Francesco Bonilauri and Vincenza Maugeri, ed. (Florence: Giuntina, 1999), 241–69 (242). Also see the photographic documents in the bilingual catalog of the exhibition: *I ragazzi ebrei di Villa Emma a Nonantola – The Jewish Children of Villa Emma at Nonantola*, ed. Ombretta Piccinini and Klaus Voigt (Nonantola: Comune di Nonantola, 2003).

1. Yfaat Weiss, *Deutsche und polnische Juden vor dem Holocaust. Jüdische Identität zwischen Staatsbürgerschaft und Ethnizität 1939–1940* (Schriftenreihe der Vierteljahreshefte für Zeitgeschichte 81) (Munich: Oldenbourg, 2000); Ze'ev Rebhun, ed., *Autumn 1939 – Yamim Noraim. Memorial Book for East European Jews Who Lived in Germany* (Jerusalem: Erez, 1999).

2. Voigt, *Villa Emma*, 15–29.

3. Recha Freier, *Let the Children Come: The Early History of Youth Aliyah* (London: Weidenfeld & Nicolson, 1961), 64–8. On Recha Freier cf. Gudrun Maierhof, *Selbstbehauptung im Chaos. Frauen in der jüdischen Selbsthilfe. 1939–1945* (Frankfurt and New York: Campus Verlag, 2002), 227–34.

4. Yad Vashem Archives, Jerusalem, M 20/14/2 Korrespondenz Recha Freier – Abraham Silberschein; Freier, 68–72. On Schleich cf. Walter Brunner, "Der Steirer Josef Schleich (1902–1949) – Judenschlepper oder Fluchthelfer im Dritten Reich?" *Zeitschrift des Historischen Vereins für Steiermark. Festschrift* (2000/01), 598–8.

5. Freier, 68–71; Josef Ithai, *Yaldei Villa Emma* (Tel-Aviv: Sifriat-Moreshet, 1982), 16–21, 23–7, 32–9. An Italian edition of Josef Ithai's (Josef Indig's) memoirs was recently published: Josef Indig Ithai, *Anni di Fuga. I ragazzi di Villa Emma a Nonantola*, Klaus Voigt and Loredana Melissari, eds. (Florence: Giuntina, 2004). For a summary of the memoirs with some additions, see Josef Ithai, "The Children of Villa Emma: Rescue of the Last Youth Aliyah before the Second World War," in *The Italian Refuge: Rescue of Jews*

during the Holocaust, Ivo Herzer, ed. (Washington DC: Catholic University of America Press, 1989), 178–202.

6. Freier, 71–2. On Hashomer Hazair cf. Yehuda Reinharz, "Hashomer Hazair in Germany (I), 1928–1933," *Leo Baeck Institute, Yearbook* 31 (1986), 173–208; and "Hashomer Hazair in Germany (II). Under the Shadow of the Swastika, 1933–1938," *Leo Baeck Institute, Yearbook* 33 (1987), 183–223.

7. Author's interviews with Josef Ithai, Kibbutz Gat, 12.1.1995 and 6.7.1996.

8. Dragutin Rosenberg, "Bericht über die Lage der Juden in Jugoslawien," in Zdenko Levental, *Auf glühendem Boden. Ein jüdisches Lebensschicksal in Jugoslawien*, Erhard Roy Wien and Jacques Picard, eds. (Konstanz: Hartung-Gorre Verlag, 1994), 215–54. Also see Rosenberg's report in Yehuda Bauer, *American Jewry and the Holocaust: The American Jewish Joint Distribution Committee, 1939–1945* (Detroit: Wayne State University Press, 1981), 277–84.

9. Michele Sarfatti, *Gli ebrei nell'Italia fascista. Vicende, identità, persecuzione* (Turin: Einaudi, 2000), 103–230.

10. Ithai, *Yaldei Villa Emma*, 68–74.

11. Klaus Voigt, *Il rifugio precario. Gli esuli in Italia dal 1933 al 1945*, Vol. 1 (Florence: La Nuova Italia, 1993), 11–29, 291–349; and Ibid., Vol. 2 (Florence: La Nuova Italia, 1996), 245–6, 255–9. On Jewish refugees in Italy cf. also the articles in *The Italian Refuge*, ed. Herzer, *Uncertain Refuge: Italy and the Jews during the Holocaust*, Nicola Caracciolo, ed. (Urbana and Chicago: University of Illinois Press, 1995) and Klaus Voigt, "Refuge and Persecution in Italy, 1933–1945," *Simon Wiesenthal Center Annual* 4 (1987), 3–64.

12. Ithai, *Yaldei Villa Emma*, 77–82; Voigt, *Villa Emma*, 80–1.

13. For a description of the hunting lodge, see Ithai, *Yaldei Villa Emma*, 91–3. The main sources on the stay in Lesno brdo as depicted in this and the following paragraphs are, besides Ithai's memoirs, his correspondence with Richard Lichtheim in Geneva, in Central Zionist Archives, Jerusalem, L 22, 338, 1412, and with Nathan Schwalb in Geneva, in Archivion ha-Histadruth, Tel Aviv, Nathan Dror (Schwalb) Hechaluz Collection; also see the autobiographical notes by Robert Weiss, *Joshko's Children*, Robert Weiss Collection, Boynton Beach, Florida; the memoirs of Leo Koffler, "Die Entstehung unserer Jugendgemeinschaft und ihr Leben bis zum Zusammenbruch Italiens," in Central Zionist Archives, A 256 – 4/1 Recha Freier, and Bericht zum einjährigen Bestehen des Kinderheims Lesno brdo, in Central Zionist Archives, L 22, 338.

14. Ithai, *Yaldei Villa Emma*, 125–8, 140, 155–7.

15. Ibid., 181–2, 208–26; Koffler, 9–10.

16. The main documents on the children's stay in Nonantola up to the beginning of German occupation, on which this paragraph and the following are based, are – besides the sources listed in note 13 – the correspondence between the principal of Villa Emma and Delasem, and the memos of the Delasem representative in Modena, Jewish Community Archives in Modena, Busta 380, 479, 537, 574.

17. Relazione dell'avvocato Gino Friedmann su Villa Emma a Nonantola, 3–4, Jewish Community Archives in Modena, Busta 537.

18. Fundamental sources are Regolamento di disciplina, August 20, 1942, and Norme per i componenti della direzione e del collegio scolastico, August 20, 1942, Jewish Community Archives in Modena, Busta 537.

19. Voigt, *Villa Emma*, 174.

20. Ithai, *Yaldei Villa Emma*, 271–5; Koffler, 17–18; replies to a circular by Ombretta Piccinini and Klaus Voigt, Nonantola 3.2.1998, with queries on the time spent in hiding in Nonantola; interviews with Giambattista Moreali, Nonantola 6.27.1996, 6.30.1997, 5.15.1998, 6.9.2000, and with Don Arrigo Beccari, Nonantola, 4.11.1996 and 6.9.2000.

21. Ithai, *Yaldei Villa Emma*, 275–8; Koffler, 18; replies to the circular.

22. Liliana Picciotto Fargion, *Il libro della memoria. Gli ebrei deportati dall'Italia (1943–1945)* (1991; reprint Milan: Mursia, 2002), 868, 877–944; Voigt, *Villa Emma*, 202.

23. Voigt, *Villa Emma*, 198–203.

24. Ithai, *Yaldei Villa Emma*, 277, 280.

25. Ithai, *Yaldei Villa Emma*, 278, 280–1; Koffler, 19; account by Hans Silbermann in *Kantor Salomon Sulzer und seine Zeit. Eine Dokumentation*, Hanoch Avenary, ed. (Sigmaringen: Thorbeke Verlag, 1985), 278–9; account by Joseph Ben-Zion on his flight to the Allies, Joseph Ben-Zion Collection, Quiryat Ono; interviews with Zvi Schneider, Tel-Aviv, 6.3.1996 and 5.4.2000, and with Max Federmann, Frankfurt 6.1.1998 (Federmann fought alongside the partisans in the Marche region).

26. Ithai, *Yaldei Villa Emma*, 278, 282–91.

27. Interviews with Robert Stein, Jerusalem, 6.3.1996 and 4.28.2000. Information on the flight to Switzerland is provided mainly by the statements taken down by the police, in the personal files of the refugees in the Schweizerisches Bundesarchiv, Bestand E 4264 1985/196.

28. Ithai, *Yaldei Villa Emma*, 282–3; Mieczeslaw Kahany, Aktennotiz betr. Interventionen bei der jugoslawischen Gesandtschaft, Central Zionist Archives, L 22, 338.

29. Ithai, *Yaldei Villa Emma*, 286–7. The names of the people forming the various groups and the date of their crossing the border are in the statements now in the Schweizerisches Bundesarchiv, Bestand E 4264 1985/196.

30. Voigt, *Villa Emma*, 212.

31. Ithai, *Yaldei Villa Emma*, 290–1; interviews with Robert Stein; Kahany, Aktennotiz.

32. Personal files in Schweizerisches Bundesarchiv, Bestand E 4264 1985/196; interviews with Hans Silbermann, 4.27.1997 and 10.27.1999.

33. Picciotto, 488; Voigt, "I ragazzi ebrei di Villa Emma a Nonantola," 57.

34. Voigt, *Villa Emma*, 233–271. Sources on the children's stay in Switzerland, which lasted a year and a half, are mainly in Schweizerisches Bundesarchiv, Bestand 4264 1985/196 und J.II.55(-) 1970/95 Schweizer Hilfswerk für Emigrantenkinder, also in Central Zionist Archives, L 17, 161; L 22, 46, L 22, 338.

35. Central Zionist Archives, L 22, 338, Indig to Lichtheim, October 16, 1943.

10 Anti-Jewish Persecution and Italian Society

Fabio Levi

Italian Jews have a rich historic past.[1] We know they were in Rome in ancient times. We possess much of the cultural heritage the different communities left throughout the peninsula during the Renaissance. We are aware of the strong influence the vicinity of the Papacy exerted on subsequent events and of the long and painful period of the ghettos. Less reflection, however, is paid to the particular factors that were at play in the process of emancipation.[2] I am referring here to the clean break with the Church required by the liberal state during and after unification in 1861.[3] This separation did much to ease the processes of Jewish integration and acculturation set in motion by the French at the end of the eighteenth century and which extended, through shifting events, to and beyond the definitive granting of equality between 1848 and 1870.

Without a doubt, we could go as far as to say that Italy was one of the countries in nineteenth-century Europe with the fewest difficulties in minority–majority relations. By the same token, secularization, which affected vast sections of the Jewish community, helped to amplify the different ways Jews experienced their relationship with their tradition. All this helped to minimize the tangibility and, to a greater extent, the visibility of a group that, on its own, was very keen to take full part in the social and political life of the nation.[4] In an attempt to tackle the title theme of this essay, I will focus on how the Jewish presence in Italy was perceived in the country as a whole before, during, and after the period of anti-Jewish persecution.

The tendencies mentioned above, which also resulted in powerful drives toward assimilation, did not cease to exist after Mussolini's rise to power.[5] Besides everything else, in those years, the media, which was imbued with nationalism and strongly centered in the hands of the government, further contributed to

199

erasing the Jews from any image the population might have of itself (apart from the very marginal influence exerted by some explicitly anti-Semitic news sheets). At the same time, laws passed in 1930–1[6], invoked to achieve stiffer state control of the Jewish community and enacted during a time in which the gap between the Fascist regime and the Church was narrowing, delegitimized even further any public presence of the Jews as such.

In this light, it is not inaccurate to characterize the 1930s campaign that raged in the major Italian newspapers against an allegedly Jewish anti-Fascist and anti-Italian leaning as a sort of discovery (or – if you like – rediscovery) of Jews in a country that had seemed to have filed away their existence. This press campaign had been set in motion following the arrest, in 1934, of a group of anti-Fascists, some of whom were of Jewish origin. On that occasion, Mussolini decided, for the first time, to add a theme to his propaganda arsenal that had heretofore been little employed in Italy, except for some restricted circles of a nationalist bent that had gradually become sensitive to the anti-Semitic ideas emanating from Germany.

Equally new, in the early 1930s, was the idea of identifying the figure of the Jew with the organizations of international Zionism and using them as pawns of Fascist foreign policy in the Mediterranean. On another front, but in the same period, the regime, which was now heading in a clearly totalitarian direction, began to perceive the small universe formed by the Italian community as a place where relatively autonomous decisions – on the home front, on help to refugees from other countries – were taken and subsequently as an anomaly that sooner or later would have to be standardized.

The rediscovery of the Jews by the Italian Fascist regime continued on various fronts. First and foremost, this took place in the political arena. For it was essentially political factors – racism in a colonial mold, totalitarian impulses, and the alliance with Hitler – that firmly placed Mussolini on the road to anti-Semitic persecution. The discovery of the Jews as a group with social features only came later, and by that time the racist campaign was already under way. The census of August 1938 had provided the Italian government, which was previously totally devoid of any precise knowledge of the Jewish question, with a more detailed view of the number of Italians it had decided to strike at and marginalize. To give an example, from that survey, data began to clearly emerge regarding the presumed economic power of Italian Jews, which was a good deal less significant than had been believed; quite the opposite, the regime was running the risk of being misled by overestimations in its own propaganda. At the same time, more accurate information was to help better direct the persecution to places where the presence of Jews was greater, such as public administrations and education, the freelance professions, trade, and real estate.[7]

By the late 1930s, the focus of attention was no longer individuals or small groups held worthy of notice for whatever reason, or local and national leading bodies in the community, but was rather Italian Jewry as a whole. It was the intrinsic logic of the persecution policy that led the regime to this perspective, not vice versa. Just like another act of general policy, the decision to go to war at Hitler's side resulted in the Fascist apparatus reflecting on a further aspect of Italian Jewry. This was the possible defeatist reaction to a government strongly committed to anti-Semitism at home and abroad. Such an idea implied a person had to defend him or herself from Jews not because they had been previously judged as a threat to the nation, but because the politics of war (which Mussolini had just decided on) placed them in a condition to become so.

In any case, a closer watch on Jews was now necessary through the organizations of public order. Proof of this new policy of monitoring the country's Jewish citizens is seen in regular reports from the local police stations to the national chief of police. This was a police surveillance that constituted the compulsory inclusion of the practice of social marginalization carried out first by the institutions of the state and based, in turn, on the systematic record filing of every individual. Furthermore, the Provisions for the Defense of the Race (*Provvedimenti per la difesa della razza*) of November 17, 1938 had established that it was the persecuted themselves that were to report to the authorities so the latter could deprive them of any right and hold them up to public scorn.[8] The uttermost visibility of the Jews in the eyes of the government should lead to their definitive invisibility in the eyes of society.

A society that was widely lacking information about a minority group small in numbers that was devoid of any precise public identity also made its first discovery of the Jews through the efforts of Fascist propaganda first in 1934 but mainly in 1938 after the publication of the *Manifesto of Racist scientists*. With a great expenditure of energy, the negative and despicable image of the Jew was suddenly imposed on the country.[9] All Italians were urged to suspect their neighbors, their doctor, their business partner, and the shopkeeper downstairs, although without ever conveying the idea that individuals of Jewish "race" constituted a real threat. What was to be feared, rather, was the regime, ready to strike at anyone who did not contribute immediately to identifying and marginalizing the Jews.

The thrust of racism, which, from the echelons of public administration, gradually penetrated the different levels of administration, was aimed at convincing ordinary citizens to mobilize against a background of widespread nationalism fueled with a certain degree of success by governmental propaganda. Following the introduction of anti-Jewish laws, the places suddenly left empty by the Jews who had been sacked, dismissed from school, or taken away for other reasons in a wide range of occupations became the supporting evidence that the racist laws were being applied seriously. At the same time, those empty spaces helped to give credence to the unpredictable and disquieting presence of the Jew. Against this presence the woeful reality of actual, living Jews seemed powerless, as they were forced to hide in the crevices of society and, until 1940 and then again until September 8, 1943, to contend, apart from a few exceptions, with the widespread indifference of other Italians. For most Italian Jews, the campaign of 1938 constituted a combination of wholly new and painful discoveries. Many, who had for years or even decades severed their links with the culture and the world of their origins, found themselves having to sustain an identity – Jews by race – that conflicted with the feelings, behavior, and relations they had long been used to enjoying outside environments of the community. It was as if, by taking an unexpected look in the mirror, they had difficulty in recognizing themselves behind this other, alien, and imposed image.[10] Moreover, the power of that image was to be found in its will to restore a purported collective identity and bonds that, on the contrary, had been severed and that were now being imposed to imprison individuals often proud of having won for themselves an incoercible independence.

The imposition from without of this new identity for most Italian Jews was another reason the awareness of being bound to an increasingly harsh and irreversible persecution was so slow to take hold. Certainly support for Fascism, which was very widespread among the Jews as it was with other Italians, played its part and brought about the ensuing incredulity in the face of the Duce's and sovereign's apparent betrayal. But what played an even greater part was the difficulty of incorporating the plausibility of a prospect they judged, as far as they were concerned, completely unpredictable and nonsensical. And though there was no lack of those who succeeded immediately in grasping the meaning of what was happening, as they had, for some time, no doubts as to the true nature of Fascism,[11] there were also those who saw in Mussolini's anti-Semitic policy an opportunity to rediscover the old adage, according to which the salvation of the Jews had to be entrusted exclusively to a full pledge of loyalty to the Powers. The main example of this response was the group La Nostra Bandiera,[12] which, between 1934 and 1938, believed that there was no other solution but that of appealing to the Duce despite being well aware of the risks it was running.

With the coming of state-sponsored anti-Semitism, similar positions clashed with Mussolini's inflexible determination to strike indiscriminately at all Jews, even those closer to the regime, by applying the persecution law in increasingly grave and repercussive forms. Thus the turning point marked by the armistice of September 8, 1943, was reached when, in the regions throughout Italy that came under German occupation, salvation of the racially persecuted depended exclusively on the possible chance of escape or going into hiding. At that point discovery meant immediate arrest and deportation to the death camps. In the search for Jews, the armed forces and the police of the Italian Social Republic had an advantage over the Germans, because they knew the territory and could easily count on a network of informers. And in fact, Mussolini's Republic carried out most of the arrests. It was up to the Nazis to capture the others and to deport them all to the death camps.[13]

There was also another way of becoming aware of the Jews in the period from September 8 to the liberation of northern Italy. I am referring here to those non-Jews who, with the collapse of the institutions following the fall of Fascism, found a way to rediscover their own dignity by offering help to those who were in extreme danger.[14] All this took place primarily on a personal basis: even when help came from within the sphere of institutions linked to the Church, it was, to a large extent, individual solidarity that prevailed. In those mostly chance and unexpected encounters, there was no clouding of the other's image and each instance of aid was carried out with immediate naturalness. Even relationships that had formed prior to these events – between employers and housemaids, employers and employees, or colleagues, neighbors, and simple acquaintances – found a way to act in unusual and new ways. Often it was the socially weaker member who discovered that the other, who previously had been the stronger, was in need of help. In each instance, however, there had to be in the people who aided Jews a willingness to evade control by the Fascists or by the occupying forces and to translate into an unaccustomed form their deeply rooted mistrust of all official authority and their habit of bending the rules imposed by it.

In this way many thousands of Jews succeeded in escaping the same fate of almost 8,000 deportees from Italy and were able to return to a life once the war was over. It was nonetheless a difficult return after seven years of darkness and fear.[15] The loss of loved ones, the difficult economic situation of the moment, and the discovery, in hindsight, of how bottomless the abyss just experienced had been, all weighed heavily. They were obliged to reestablish steady relations with those who, after 1938, had been even worse than indifferent to the persecutions or with a great deal of non-Jews who had continued their schooling or had advanced their career despite the war. What prevailed at that juncture, for them and for the country as a whole, was the compelling will to modestly start afresh without exposing (especially in the public sphere) one's Jewish origins. Even the community institutions maintained a low profile for many years after the war, avoiding opening any cases about the past other than mild, meek requests for reintegration.

The surrounding climate was anything but favorable in the postwar years. Having survived the worst period and – immediately after liberation – a brief moment of collective warmth, even the tightest bonds of neighborhood and solidarity had lost a great deal of their capacity to operate. Italian Jews tried to get home as quickly as possible. In a back-to-normal life all of them turned their thoughts to themselves and their nearest and dearest; concrete help was almost exclusively found within the family or, at most, among fellow believers and was never in any way proportionate to the extent of the suffering that had been sustained.

There were also those who had aided the Jews, almost all of whom were united by a similar attitude. For these rescuers, the fact that it was Jews whom they helped was not particularly relevant. For obvious reasons of caution, the least importance possible was attached to the event. Discussing their rescue activities after the war was an equally low priority, as those who boasted about their noble actions were almost always those who had something to be forgiven for. Thus, if Jews who survived thanks to Gentile helpers retreated into the shadows, then those who had helped them never came out of them.

The prevailing prescription of public authorities and institutions after the war was similarly one of distraction and silence. No longer enforced, the anti-Jewish laws were abrogated very, very slowly.[16] Everything possible was done to avoid acknowledging the Jews their rights as a persecuted people. One explanation for this was the tightly knitted continuity between the public apparatus of Fascism and that of the postwar Italian Republic.[17] Another reason was the largely pervasive nature of the Fascist–anti-Fascist dichotomy, which had taken root in the public debate during the immediate postwar years. Experiences such as racial persecution could not be made to fit these circumstances. The subject of the Jews was left on the sidelines to such an extent that, at times, it almost seemed as if the victims of the anti-Jewish laws were being reprimanded for not having been able to transform their persecution into an open struggle against Fascism.

Thus the world of politics and institutions also required that the Jews go back into the shadows. Recollections of the drama that had just been enacted had to be silenced. It was almost as if Mussolini's real responsibility was not that he had personally initiated state-sponsored anti-Semitism and then took part in Hitler's campaign to annihilate European Jewry, thus releasing the worst forces within the institutions and Italian society. Rather, his real crime was having improvidently restored visibility to an issue such as that of the Jews, notoriously pregnant with obscure threats. Until the 1930s, this aspect of Italian history had been successfully filed away. It thus followed that it would be better to remove the problem of the Jews from sight once more and as quickly as possible.

So, once again, the Jews disappeared from the national horizon and as little as possible was said of the persecutions and extermination, and of the survivors even less. That way, it was easier to credit the Italians – all the Italians – with an innate aptitude for solidarity[18] and to give further room, in the postwar years, to universalistic visions that were largely ill disposed to acknowledging the legitimacy of the peculiarities of any minority group. In a different way, a similar attitude united both the Roman Catholic world and a broad spectrum of the Socialist and Communist left. For everyone alike, the period of racial persecution and extermination had been ineffectual in making them sensitive to diversity. To the contrary, it was as if the reaffirmation of the idea of a single and undifferentiated humanity had become more urgent than ever.

NOTES

1. For general histories of the Jews in Italy, see C. Vivanti, *Gli ebrei in Italia, Storia d'Italia, Annali 11*, 2 vols. (Turin: Einaudi, 1996–7), and A. Milano, *Storia degli ebrei in Italia* (Turin: Einaudi, 1992).

2. M. Toscano, *Integrazione e identità. L'esperienza ebraica in Germania e Italia dall'illuminismo al fascismo* (Milan: Angeli, 1998); and G. Luzzatto Voghera, *Il prezzo dell'eguaglianza* (Milan: Angeli, 1998).

3. G. Miccoli, "Santa sede, questione ebraica e antisemitismo fra Otto e Novecento," in *Gli ebrei in Italia, Storia d'Italia, Annali 11*, C. Vivanti, ed. (Turin: Einaudi, 1997), Vol. 2.

4. Toscano, *Integrazione e identità.*

5. R. De Felice, *Storia degli ebrei italiani sotto il fascismo* (Turin: Einaudi, 1988); and M. Sarfatti, *Gli ebrei nell'Italia fascista* (Turin: Einaudi, 2000).

6. G. Fubini, *La condizione giuridica dell'ebraismo italiano* (Turin: Rosenberg & Sellier, 1998).

7. F. Levi, "Il censimento antiebraico del 1938," in *L'ebreo in oggetto. L'applicazione della normativa antiebraica a Torino*, F. Levi, ed. (Turin: Silvio Zamorani editore, 1991).

8. M. Sarfatti, "1938 Le leggi contro gli ebrei," *La Rassegna mensile di Israel*, no. 1–2 (1988).

9. For the fundamental traits of anti-Semitic propaganda through images, see Centro Furio Jesi, *La menzogna della razza* (Bologna: Grafis, 1994).

10. F. Levi, *L'identità imposta. Un padre ebreo di fronte alle leggi razziali di Mussolini* (Turin: Silvio Zamorani editore, 1991).

11. V. Foa, *Lettere dalla giovinezza* (Turin: Einaudi, 1998).

12. L. Ventura, *Ebrei con il duce. "La nostra bandiera" (1934–1938)* (Turin: Silvio Zamorani editore, 2002).

13. L. Picciotto, *Il libro della memoria* (Milan: Mursia, 2002).

14. S. Zuccotti, *L'olocausto in Italia* (Milan: Mondadori, 1987).

15. Fondazione Centro di Documentazione Ebraica Contemporanea, *Il ritorno alla vita. Vicende e diritti degli ebrei in Italia dopo la seconda guerra mondiale*, Michele Sarfatti, ed. (Florence: Giuntina, 1998).

16. M. Toscano, *L'abrogazione delle leggi razziali in Italia (1943–1987)* (Rome: Senato della Repubblica, 1988).

17. C. Pavone, *Una guerra civile. Saggio sulla moralità nella Resistenza* (Turin: Bollati Boringhieri, 1991).

18. D. Bidussa, *Il mito del bravo italiano* (Milan: il Saggiatore, 1994).

PART THREE

CATASTROPHE –
THE GERMAN
OCCUPATION,
1943–1945

11 The Shoah in Italy: Its History and Characteristics

Liliana Picciotto

After the coup of July 25, 1943, which temporarily ousted Mussolini from power, there were 39,907 Jews in Italy.[1] In the dramatic events that followed, including Germany's rescue of Mussolini, the armistice with the Allies, and Italy's change of status – from being a country allied with Germany to being a country occupied by it – the Italian territory was dismembered. In southern Italy the Allied armies were laboriously advancing toward the north, liberating in the process more and more territory and internment camps for anti-Fascist Italian Jews and foreign Jews, whereas central and northern Italy remained for several months firmly in the clutches of the German occupying forces. In the north, Italians were totally subordinate to the Germans in military matters and subjected to massive restrictions in political affairs. They nonetheless remained largely independent as far as bureaucratic-administrative matters and domestic order were concerned.

In the central and northern regions the Repubblica Sociale Italiana (RSI) was formed, a new Fascist (and this time republican) Italian state. Its capital was Salò on Lake Garda, and Mussolini was once again at the head of its government, with Rudolf Rahn, the Third Reich's plenipotentiary, looking over his shoulder.[2]

At the beginning of September 1943, the Jews, both Italians and foreign refugees,[3] were trapped in the territory of the RSI. The 32,307 Jews who remained in central and northern Italy were at the mercy both of the Nazi extermination policy, which was extended to Italy at the end of September 1943, and of the RSI's anti-Jewish policy, which was launched a month and a half later.[4] Italy and Germany, as we shall see, entered a sort of competition as to who should have the right to round up, imprison, and intern Jews. This gave rise to a situation that for Jews was fraught with deadly danger. An estimated 23,778 were saved because of the good relationships they had with their non-Jewish neighbors and to the generosity of people who sheltered and fed them, many of them belonging to the clergy.

During the next twenty months, the rabidly anti-Semitic regime of the RSI and the Nazis, which lasted nine months in Rome and ten months in Florence, arrested approximately 8,529 Jews.[5] Whereas in the other occupied countries the Germans waited for several months before putting into effect their anti-Jewish policy, in Italy they dispensed completely with the preliminary stage, first because of the rush of events (it was already September 1943), but mainly because they did not consider it necessary: in Italy the bureaucratic stage of persecution had already been accomplished. Prior to the German occupation, the Italian Fascist regime had worked to instill anti-Judaism in public opinion, had already passed anti-Jewish laws, had kept its records on Jews constantly up to date, and had already set up a special department in the interior ministry, named the Department for Demography and Race (Direzione Generale per la Demografia e la Razza), in charge of managing and implementing anti-Jewish policies.[6] One cannot fail to notice how perfectly the policy of the Fascist regime before the occupation coincides with the actions undertaken elsewhere by the Nazi regime after occupation.

I do not mean to argue here that Italy had followed a deliberate course of action aimed at extermination. As a matter of fact, if the occupation had not occurred, Mussolini's anti-Semitism would most likely have remained limited to discrimination and would not have shifted toward genocide. For Auschwitz is *not* the inescapable albeit extreme outcome of any form of anti-Semitism. Having said this, however, one cannot but emphasize once more that in Italy the first building blocks of the edifice of anti-Semitism where put in place by Fascism at the time of the monarchy and not by Nazism, thus paving the way for the extermination planned by the latter.

Nazi Jewish Policy in Occupied Northern Italy

On September 23, 1943, the Nazi Central Office for the Security of the Reich (RSHA) sent a directive to all its local branches ruling that Jews possessing Italian citizenship who were abroad would no longer be exempted from deportation. This is the first document providing evidence that the Nazi extermination policy implemented in Western Europe since the spring of 1942 was now extended to Italian Jews as well.[7] In fact, the issue of how to deal with Jews in Italy coincided with German plans for invading Italy back in May 1943. It was about that time that Adolf Eichmann, chief of the Anti-Jewish Office in the Gestapo Headquarters in Berlin, which was in itself a branch of the RSHA, asked his legal advisor, Friedrich Bosshammer, to submit informative reports and to communicate with the German ministry of foreign affairs on this issue.[8]

As elsewhere in Nazi-occupied countries, the local branches of the RSHA were put in charge of the anti-Jewish repression.[9] Karl Wolff, a man of great consequence within the organization of the German state, took office at Gardone as supreme commander of the SS and of police (Höchster SS- und Polizei-Führer, Hst.SSPF). Wilhelm Harster was installed at Verona as chief of the security police, or Sipo-SD, the most important branch of the German police (Befehlshaber der Sipo-SD, BdS), and would later, at the beginning of October 1943, set up the network of local security police branches in Italy.[10] Besides losing its southern regions, which were liberated by the Allies, Italy also forfeited part of its northeastern regions to its German occupant/ally. These territories were now renamed *Alpenvorland* and *Adriatisches Küstenland*: two governors who had previously been in charge of Austrian Gaus were installed, a separate branch of the RSHA was set up, and Odilo Globocnik, recently arrived from Poland where he had "successfully" completed the *Aktion Reinhard*, was appointed superior commander of the SS and of police (Höherer SS- und Polizeiführer, HSSPF).[11]

Even before they had finished setting up their complex repressive police organization in the first month of occupation, the Germans carried out massacres and roundups. These, however, cannot be considered as part of the classic extermination policy. Rather, these actions were linked to the course of war and to the way the disarming of the Italian army by the German Wermacht was progressing. In the first phase, German massacres and roundups included the following: the slaughter of 54 refugees in hotels and private homes on Lake Maggiore (September 15–23, 1943);[12] the rounding up of 328 foreign Jews who from St. Martin-de-Vesubie in France had crossed the Alps on foot and had reached the valleys around Cuneo (September 18, 1943);[13] the arrest ten days later of 24 Jewish residents of Cuneo who were later released; the rounding up in September of Jews interned in the central Italian region of Marche (in the provinces of Ascoli Piceno, Macerata, and Chieti);[14] and the request by various German military commands that the prefects hand over the lists of Jewish residents.[15] Even the arrests of Jews on September 15, 1943, in Merano, in a northern and separate region as the Alpenvorland then was, were due to reasons unrelated to formally organized anti-Jewish persecution.[16] This organized persecution began later, in October 1943, first with a flying unit sent from Berlin especially for this purpose and then with a permanent office located in the headquarters of the Central Command of the Sipo-SD in Italy, at Verona.

The flying unit was in operation from the beginning of October until Christmas Eve of 1943. It was formed by approximately ten men led by Eichmann's trustee, SS Captain Dannecker, whose task it was to plan and carry out roundups of Jews in all main Italian towns, starting from the south and proceeding north. This arrangement was decided on by the RSHA as it was not considered advisable for the moment to involve the permanent structure of the German police, which was still fragile and busy organizing its own activity. The German units acting specifically to apprehend Jews had to work in a territory that was not at all easy, as the political situation in Italy was far from clear and the terms and limits of the autonomy enjoyed by the government of the Third Reich and the new Fascist government in regard to each other were still under discussion.[17]

The most dreadful raid was carried out unexpectedly in Rome on October 16, 1943, when a thousand innocent victims were rounded up in little over half a day. Until recently, it was believed that this raid was to some extent linked to Rome's importance as the country's capital – a sort of exemplary action that would serve as a warning and a threatening gesture toward Italian rulers. The recent discovery of a document in the National Archives and Records Administration in Washington suggests an entirely different interpretation. The document, dated October 6, 1943, and sent by Kappler, chief of German police in Rome, to his boss Wolff, reads thus: "The RSHA has sent captain Dannecker to capture all Jews in a lightning operation and to dispatch them all to Germany. Due to the general mood in the town and to the unpredictable situation, this operation cannot be carried out in Naples. The arrangements made by this office for the operation in Rome have now been concluded."[18] This document reveals two new facts: (1) that Roman Jews were destined for Germany and not for Poland, and (2) that Naples, and not Rome, was the intended setting for the first anti-Jewish operation.

Let me make these points clear. As we all know, the destination for Western European Jews in September 1943 was, apart from a few exceptional diplomatic cases, one and one only – the camp of Auschwitz-Birkenau. That the Jews of Rome were originally to be deported to Germany, instead, can mean one thing only: that they were not destined for extermination but only to a concentration camp with a harsh regime. In fact a later document, dated October 9, addressed by the foreign ministry to Eitel Friedrich Möllhausen, the German consul in Rome, mentions Mauthausen.[19] The latter document confirms that the original destination of the Roman Jews was most likely Mauthausen. The choice of a concentration, as opposed to an extermination, camp was probably made out of consideration for the place where the roundup itself had taken place: Rome, the Jewish quarter, almost next to the Vatican. Only later, seeing that there was no reaction at all from the Vatican, the transport – which left from Stazione Tiburtina, a minor railway station in Rome, on October 18 – instead left for Auschwitz and extermination.

With regard to the intended starting point for German anti-Jewish repressions, we can now affirm with certainty that the Germans had indeed meant to begin their roundups of Italian Jews from Naples, but that their plan was thwarted by the hasty German retreat on October 1, 1943, due to a popular uprising.[20]

The roundup in Rome, which was carefully arranged, followed a blueprint that had already been carried out in Paris in July 1942 during the "rafle du Velodrome d'Hiver," where Dannecker had also been in charge: the town divided into sectors according to the location of Jewish homes, the house to house searches, the lorries waiting along the streets, the mass of people detained for dozens of hours in some enclosed area, the immediate departure for Auschwitz.[21]

The train with the Jews from Rome arrived at Auschwitz-Birkenau on the night of October 22 and was left sealed until early the next morning. The deportees, after a journey made more distressing by the presence among them of dozens of children of all ages, tortured by fatigue, hunger, thirst, dirt, and the stench of bodies confined to a cramped space for five days and five nights, were subjected to selection on October 23. The percentage of those destined to the gas chambers was unusually high: 89 percent, possibly because a typhoid epidemic was raging in Auschwitz at the time. Of the 1,020 who arrived from Rome, only 149 men and 47 women passed the selection and were admitted to the camp.[22]

Having accomplished the roundup in Rome and organized the transport for deportation, Dannecker's flying unit moved north to carry out similar surprise raids in all major towns of the country. These included Genoa on November 3, Montecatini and Siena on November 5, Florence on November 6 and 26, and Bologna on November 7 and on the following days.[23]

To achieve all these roundups, Dannecker's men scattered all over Tuscany and the Emilia and Liguria regions. But as they were few, they resorted to the help of the local Italian police and relied largely on their collaboration. The result of these terrible roundups was one more transport of deportees that left Florence on November 9, 1943.[24]

Thanks to an important testimony, we have only recently been able to confirm that the November 6 roundup in Florence followed the very same pattern already seen in Rome. There were surprise raids around town, in the buildings of the community, and in all places that sheltered Jewish refugees who had just arrived from Southern France. The people were then gathered in an empty barracks facing the Arno River and loaded on a train leaving for Auschwitz after three days. Because Dannecker had fallen ill after the roundup in Rome, it was his deputy, Alvin Eisenkolb, who was put in charge of the operation.[25] The transport of Jews from Florence stopped at Bologna to load more prisoners and arrived at Auschwitz on November 14. After the selection of the transport, thirteen men and ninety-four women were admitted to the camp.[26] Despite many years of research, I have not been able to ascertain most of the names of these deportees, as the majority were illegal refugees and have left no trace of their presence.

After more roundups in Milan, in all of northern Italy, and along the Swiss–Italian border, the Germans were able to arrange one more transport leaving from the jail of San Vittore in Milan.[27] The train left on December 6, 1943, and arrived in Auschwitz on January 12.[28] At the end of December 1943, Dannecker's task was regarded as completed. He was transferred to Hungary while his men, after their Christmas holidays, were sent back to Italy to work with his replacement who was now given a permanent post.[29]

Mussolini's Republic of Salò and the Nazi Final Solution

On September 27, 1943, even before moving his government north in compliance with Hitler's wishes, who no longer wanted Rome to be the capital, Mussolini convened a meeting of the new cabinet. There were serious and urgent matters that needed to be discussed. The relationship with the German occupant/ally had to be more clearly defined and the cabinet had to take into account the new reality that part of the Italian territory had been annexed by the Third Reich and that the Italian army was totally disbanded and thousands of Italian soldiers were already imprisoned far from their country in German internment camps. There was also the requisition of the Italian workforce, the hefty share of the cost of occupation that Italy had to pay. Besides the problems with the Germans, there were also specifically domestic and no less serious ones: the setting up of and the control over the armed forces and the police, the appointment of new politically and ideologically reliable prefects (chief officers of the counties), and replacements in the civil service.

For a time the treatment of Jews remained a secondary issue while the new government was busy grappling with other problems. Dannecker's arrival in Italy at the beginning of October was not due to any Italian–German talks or negotiations on Jewish matters. The German captain acted on orders from his superiors without regard for diplomatic relations between the two countries. Mussolini could hardly be pleased that Italian citizens, even if Jewish, were now being rounded up on his territory without prior notice or negotiations with his government. By sending Dannecker, the RSHA was plainly exploiting for its own ends the power vacuum and the weakness of the Italian administrative machinery.

On November 14, 1943, a general assembly of the Partito Fascista Repubblicano was convened with delegates arriving from all Italian towns. On that occasion the general policy of the new state and the new regime was outlined. The program was expounded in eighteen points that had been worked out with the perhaps not entirely welcome assistance of Rudolf Rahn, the plenipotentiary of the Third Reich. The so-called Jewish question was set down in point 7: "Persons belonging to the Jewish race are aliens, and during this war belong to an enemy nationality." When this statement was approved by acclamation by the Fascists assembled at Verona, two trains with deportees had already left for Auschwitz and the great majority of the Jews thus deported had already been murdered.

The measures to execute what had been proclaimed were not long in coming. On November 30, the interior minister issued Police Order no. 5, which ruled that all Jews, both Italian and foreign, were to be arrested and interned and that their property should be seized.[30] Jews were eventually to be interned in a large national camp that had not yet been selected. Meanwhile, after their arrest by Italian police, Jews were to be gathered in small local camps exclusively for Jews that for the time would be opened in the various provinces.

To date, research has revealed the location of and information on thirty camps. Detainees were guarded by Italian police and were later dispatched to the jail of San Vittore in Milan. On January 30, 1944, German police loaded at least 605 Jews onto an overcrowded transport headed for Auschwitz. After selection, 128 of them were admitted to the camp and the rest were immediately murdered in the gas chambers.[31]

The infamous Order no. 5 meant that from December 1, 1943, each and every Jew was liable to being arrested by Italian authorities. And in fact, during the following months, captures were directly carried out by the *Questure*, the provincial police detachments of the RSI, after meticulous house-to-house searches. This marked the start of a new and terrible stage, surely worse than the previous one, because Italian police officers knew everyone's address from the census and the checks carried out by the former Fascist regime under the monarchy. In addition, it was much easier for the Italian police to hunt down Jews who were hiding. The Italian government of the RSI put the full weight of its apparatus in the service of the anti-Jewish persecution. Several ministries were involved at various levels, such as the Ministry of Interior Affairs both through its Direzione Generale per la Demografia e la Razza and through its entire hierarchical structure: prefects (highest provincial government officials), *Questori* (provincial police chiefs), and the Commissariati di Pubblica Sicurezza (district police stations). Also involved were the Ministry of Finance, the Ministry of Justice, the Ministry of National Education, the Ministry of Popular Culture, and the district headquarters of the Carabinieri (so-called lieutenancy), which were usually in charge of minor urban centers.

The victims were nonetheless not all treated equally. Less severe treatment was granted to Jews who were over seventy, to the seriously ill, and to children of mixed marriages if converted before October 1, 1938. But while Italian law exempted certain categories, German law knew no such exception. On the other hand, the Italian decrees from November 30 and December 10 created a certain ambiguity and discrepancy in contrast to the German decrees regarding the treatment of the Jews. Conflicts thus arose between the police forces of the two countries in the following cases: (1) Jews over seventy years old, (2) severely ill Jews, (3) children of mixed marriages baptized prior to October 1938, (4) unbaptized children of mixed marriages, and (5) and Jews married to non-Jews. According to the Italians, cases 1, 2, and 3 were not to be arrested, case 4 was to be arrested, and there was not a clear understanding on case 5.

According to the Germans, however, case 5 could remain at large while cases 1 and 2 were to be arrested. As for cases 3 and 4, there was some discrepancy between the two administrations derived from the different principles according to which Italians and Germans determined race. According to German law, a Jew was to be considered Jewish if he or she had three Jewish grandparents. A mixed Jew who had only two Jewish grandparents was to be considered a Jew under the following conditions: (1) if he or she was registered in the Jewish community before the Nuremberg laws, or entered later; (2) was married to a Jew at the time of the laws or after; (3) was born from a marriage between an Aryan and a Jew, a marriage that would have been illegal under the Nuremberg Laws; and (4) was born from an extramarital affair with a Jew out of wedlock after July 31, 1936.

According to the Italian law, a Jew was to be considered Jewish if he or she was born from Jewish parents. If just one parent was Jewish, a person was to be considered a Jew under the following circumstances: (1) a person was born from one Jewish parent and a foreign parent; (2) was born from a Jewish mother and an unknown father or; (3) had decided to practice Judaism, was registered in the Jewish community, and had not been baptized before October 1, 1938. This discrepancy created a chaotic situation: those who were indeed safe under Italian law were in danger under the German one and vice versa. Many people no longer knew whether they should remain in their homes or go into hiding like all other Jews. In some agonizing cases people were arrested, released, and then rearrested.

The reasons behind the Italian authorities' order of November 30 lies in the subtle interplay between the occupier and the occupied – a formerly allied country – in which each country tried to assert its sovereignty. The anti-Jewish question seemed the perfect issue for the new Fascist rulers to assert an authority they were unable to uphold on other matters. Arrogating to themselves the handling of the Jewish question – where they could look back on a tradition established since 1938 – and declaring legal the arrest of Jews was a decision which no doubt was aimed at competing with the Germans.

Whatever the reason, the Italian government machinery immediately set to work. We have found hundreds of arrest warrants issued by provincial chiefs of police (Questori) of the RSI. Everywhere the police received orders to arrest any Jews they could lay their hands on, be they children or adults. On December 5–6, 1943, the chief of police in Venice staged a roundup akin to those carried out by the Germans in Rome, Florence, and Genoa.[32] In Mantua the arrests started on December 1: people were imprisoned in the local Jewish home for the aged, which had been converted into a provincial concentration camp.[33] In Milan the jail of San Vittore was put to the same use, and hundreds of Jews, some from Milan and some also captured elsewhere in northern Italy, were detained there. After the order of November 30, 1943, the former camp for prisoners of war at Fossoli di Carpi (near Modena) was chosen to become the large and definitive camp for the internment of all Jews arrested within the RSI. Fossoli already had suitable barracks and moreover was conveniently situated near a railway junction connecting the north and the south. The camp was opened on December 5, 1943, although the renovation work had only just begun.[34]

With the setting up of the provincial camps and then Fossoli, Italy entered a new phase and became directly involved in the physical persecution of the Jews. Until Order no. 5 of November 30, 1943, it had been Dannecker who set into motion the roundups, with the Italian police simply being called on for assistance. Now the Italians acted on their own: arrests, internment, and the seizure of property were all the result of a specific Fascist government policy.

At the very same time when the interior ministry was setting up the internment camp for all Italian Jews, the German government in Berlin was examining the new Italian anti-Jewish policies. On December 4, there was a top-level conference between officials of the German foreign ministry and those of the RSHA who were involved in Italian matters: Eberhard von Thadden was present for the former and Dannecker and Bosshammer, both of whom came from Eichmann's office, represented the latter. Minutes of this meeting reveal German plans with regard to the treatment of Jews and also their frame of mind toward the Italian leadership.[35] The participants expressed dissatisfaction with the "disappointing" results the roundups had yielded. The preliminary operations, they maintained, had taken too long, thus enabling Italian Jews to go into hiding. Furthermore, the paucity of German forces available had not permitted them to comb through every village and every town, whether large or small. Now, however, the Italian government had ruled that all Jews of Italy were to be transferred to an internment camp and the plenipotentiary Rudolf Rahn had been instructed to convey to the Fascist government Germany's satisfaction with that order. The government of the Third Reich would put Dannecker's men at the disposal of the Fascist government as counselors. The German foreign ministry was instructed not to upset Italian internment operations: they should appear as being the goal and not as just preparatory measures in view of the "evacuation to Eastern Europe."

More documents on the December 4, 1943, meeting between the German foreign ministry and the RSHA regarding the Jews of Italy, both dated December 14, complete the information available to us. Let us examine some aspects that emerge from this entire documentation that deserve our attention. According to the Germans, Italian authorities had decided on their own, and deserved praise, to be conveyed through the plenipotentiary. Because the Jews had by then gone into hiding, the Germans determined that their own police forces were not enough to carry on the persecution. It was impossible to comb through every small town in the country and was thus best to let Italians do the job.

Before we can ascertain the degree of Italian complicity in the Nazi Final Solution, it is necessary to assess what the Italian authorities knew of the extermination taking place in the east and of the German plan to include Italian Jews in their genocidal policies with the assistance of the Italian government. First let me state that, since the fall of 1942, it is clear that both Mussolini and his government circles were fully cognizant of the German extermination policy.[36]

The answer to the second and more sensitive issue is implied by the fact that there existed between the Italian and the German police an operational understanding to share tasks. The Italians searched, arrested, and interned Jews while the Germans organized deportation. Although no explicit document has been found to date to prove this understanding, there are a great many rather unequivocal references to it in several documents scattered in various places. Even more unequivocal are the preparations for the deportation from Milan on January 30,

1944. This transport was made up mostly of Jews who had been arrested by the Italian police and detained in the provincial camps that had dotted Italy. The German police then collected local Jewish camp inmates and transferred them all to Milan. Such accurate organization could have been achieved only on the basis of some kind of agreement.

In fact, we find the same task sharing after the opening of the camp at Fossoli, where deportations began on February 22, 1944. During the period of the deportation actions from Fossoli, a small German contingent had already appeared on February 20, as Primo Levi wrote and as Laura Geiringer confirmed in her diary.[37] Another prisoner, Franco Schönheit, recalled that he immediately saw the Germans as soon as he arrived at the camp on February 26.[38]

Within a few days the Germans had ousted the Italian guards who were under the authority of the chief of police in Modena and installed a German garrison. A few days later Friedrich Bosshammer arrived in Verona.[39] Eichmann had sent him with orders to organize a permanent office within the Gestapo in Italy that would keep a watch on the arrests of Jews and organize their deportation with the help of the men who had formerly been on Dannecker's staff. Nine more transports were arranged from the camp at Fossoli, which was evacuated on August 1, 1944, fearing the Allied armies advancing from the south.[40] A new internment camp was set up farther north, near Bolzano in the Alpenvorland. Three more transports left from there.[41]

While the events I have recounted here were taking place, the anti-Jewish persecution followed a similar course in the territories directly administered by the Third Reich under the name of Adriatisches Küstenland. First, the Italian political authority there was virtually nonexistent. The arrests were made directly by German police without any Italian involvement. The first roundups in the autumn of 1943 were carried out by the special anti-Jewish branch of the Gestapo in Trieste. From December on they were carried out instead by a special unit formed by men who had worked with Globocnik in the Aktion Reinhard in Poland and whom he had had transferred to Trieste. The Jews arrested in Fiume, Trieste, and Padua, as well as some of those arrested in Venice were detained before their deportation in the Risiera di San Sabba, the camp tragically known also for having been a place of torture and death for many anti-Fascists and partisans. Altogether, the anti-Jewish persecution in the Küstenland involved more than a thousand victims.[42]

In the whole of Italy there were 8,529 victims of the Shoah: 6,806 were deported, 322 died in Italy during detention while trying to escape or through suicide, and 950 were missing after the war.

Conclusion

There have been only small numbers of Jews in Italy ever since ancient times, never more than 30,000–40,000. Under Fascism, this held true: never more than 0.1 percent of the Italian population. Following emancipation and the process of assimilation, which extended from the middle until the end of the nineteenth century, Jews had become virtually invisible in Italian society. The Fascist government alone conferred actual visibility on the Jews, singling them out as the culprits behind the worst problems afflicting the nation and introducing anti-Semitism into popular culture. In fact, the political use of anti-Semitism was a new development engineered by the Fascists, considering that the history of the Italian state from its foundation (1861) was free of anti-Semitism. Fascism borrowed the themes of anti-Hebraic hostility that formed part of Catholic theology and practice, joined them to the nationalistic themes of anti-Jewish hostility – singled out as internal enemies against whom to direct a permanent psychological mobilization – and draped the whole assembly in a racist garb. The anti-Semitic policies of the Fascists, decided upon in 1936 and implemented beginning in the summer of 1938, were meant to isolate the Jews from society and national life to the point of physically expelling them from Italy. With the German occupation and the establishment of the Italian Social Republic in September 1943 under German influence the objective changed. The policy of the so-called Final Solution was extended to include the approximately 32,000 Jews still trapped in the territory of the Italian Social Republic: house searches, police sweeps, arrests, internments, and deportations to the death camp of Auschwitz.

As long as the bureaucracy and administration of the new Fascist state, after the capital and all the ministries had been moved from Rome to the north, were still in an unsettled state, the arrests were carried out directly by the German police. When the new state felt sufficiently powerful in November 1943 to reclaim from the occupying ally its margins of political and administrative autonomy, it developed an anti-Semitic protocol for action. Beginning at the end of November 1943, the neo-Fascist government issued laws calling for all the Jews in Italy to be arrested and interned and their possessions confiscated. The Italian police took over from the German police for the first phase of the "dirty work," while the German police took on the task of organizing the deportations. This clearly appears to have been the way things were arranged, even if, from the sources we currently possess, no formal agreement between the two governments has yet been found. The Jews in Italy who fell victim to the Shoah constituted 26.24 percent of the total Jewish population, based on the total population just before the German occupation in September 1943 (8,529 victims of the Shoah, dead or in any case deported, out of the total of 32,000–33,000 Jews then living in Italy).[43] This percentage, by no means a small number if compared with other occupied countries in Western Europe, is at least comparable with the situation in France (21–23 percent of the total) and Belgium (43–44 percent of the total).[44]

In Italy, 73.76 percent of the Jews survived, first and foremost as a result of their ability to organize their own rescue. The relatively high survival rate was also due to the Jews' relationships as good neighbors with the non-Jewish population, to the generosity of much of the civil society, to the ideological anti-Fascism that drove some Italians, and to the sense of Christian charity that drove many of the men and women of the Church. The subject of hidden Jews and their protectors in Italy still awaits examination.

Translated from the Italian by Loredana M. Melissari

NOTES

1. Liliana Picciotto, *Il libro della memoria. Gli ebrei deportati dall'Italia 1943–1945* (Milan: Mursia, 2002), 856. I arrived at this figure through a complex calculation that takes into account both the shifts in population after the outbreak of the war and the border changes.

2. Frederick W. Deakin, *La brutale amicizia. Mussolini, Hitler e la caduta del fascismo italiano* (Turin: Einaudi, 1990) [original: *The Brutal Frienship: Mussolini, Hitler and the Fall of Italian Fascism* (London: Weidenfeld and Nicolson, 1962)]; Lutz Klinkhammer, *L'occupazione tedesca in Italia 1943–1945* (Turin: Bollati Boringhieri, 1996) [German: *Zwischen Buendnis und Besatzung. Das nationalsozialistische Deutschland und die Republik von Salò 1943 bis 45* (Tuebingen: Max Niemeyer GmbH & Co.KG)].

3. On foreign Jews in Italy, see Klaus Voigt, *Il rifugio precario. Gli esuli in Italia dal 1933 al 1945*, 2 vols. (Florence: La Nuova Italia, 1993–6) [original: *Zuflucht auf Widerruf. Exil in Italien 1933–1945* (Stuttgart: Klett-Cotta, 1989 and 1993)].

4. Picciotto, *Il libro*, 857.

5. Ibid., 28.

6. On the general history of Jews in Italy under the Fascist regime, see Renzo De Felice, *Storia degli ebrei in Italia sotto il fascismo* (Turin: Einaudi, 1988) [English: *The Jews in Fascist Italy: A History* (New York: Enigma Books, 2001)]; Meir Michaelis, *Mussolini e la questione ebraica* (Milan: Comunità, 1982) (original: *Mussolini and the Jews: German-Italian Relations and the Jewish Question in Italy 1922–1945* (Oxford: Clarendon Press, 1978)]; Michele Sarfatti, *Gli ebrei nell'Italia fascista* (Turin: Einaudi, 2000).

7. Nuremberg, doc. NG-2652 H: *From von Thadden to missions abroad*, September 12, 1943, enclosed circular letter of RSHA, September 23, 1943.

8. Picciotto, *Il libro*, 857.

9. Raul Hilberg, *La distruzione degli ebrei d'Europa* (Turin: Einaudi, 1999) [Original: *The Destruction of the European Jews* (New York and London: Holmes & Meier, 1985)].

10. Enzo Collotti, "Dati sulle forze di polizia fasciste e tedesche nell'Italia settentrionale nell'aprile 1945," *Il Movimento di Liberazione in Italia* 31 (April–June 1963), 3–24; Liliana Picciotto, "Polizia tedesca ed ebrei nell'Italia occupata," *Rivista di storia contemporanea* 12, no. 3 (1984), 456–73; Picciotto, *Il libro*, 858–66.

11. Karl Stuhlpfarrer, *Le zone di operazione Prealpi e Litorale Adriatico 1943–1945* (Gorizia: Adamo, 1975).

12. Marco Nozza, *Hotel Meina. La prima strage di ebrei in Italia* (Milan: Mondadori, 1993).

13. Alberto Cavaglion, *Nella notte straniera. Gli ebrei di Saint Martin de Vesubie e il campo di Borgo San Dalmazzo. (8 settembre–21 novembre 1943)* (Cuneo: L'Arciere, 1991).

14. Costantino Di Sante, *L'internamento civile nell'ascolano e il campo di concentramento di Servigliano (1940–1944)* (Istituto provinciale per la Storia del Movimento di Liberazione nelle Marche, Ascoli Piceno, 1998).

15. There were requests of this kind at least in Venice, Florence, Lucca, Bergamo, and Varese, as far as we know. See Klaus Voigt, *Il rifugio*, vol. 2, 409.

16. Cinzia Villani, *Ebrei fra leggi razziali e deportazioni nelle province di Bolzano, Trento e Belluno* (Trento: Società di Studi Trentini di Scienze Storiche, 1996).

17. Picciotto, *Il libro*, 877–84.

18. NARA, Washington, OSS, Record Group 236, Entry 122, box 1: *From Rome (Kappler) to Berlin*, October 6, 1943; Liliana Picciotto, *Il libro*, cit., p. 878.

19. Nuremberg, doc.NG-5027: *From von Sonnleithner to Foreign Ministry*, October 9, 1943; *From von Thadden to Moellhausen*, October 9, 1943.

20. The newly discovered document cited above in fact only confirms a previous one dated September 24, 1943 whose interpretation had escaped us until recently.

21. Michael Tagliacozzo, "La comunità ebraica di Roma sotto l'incubo della svastica. La grande razzia del 16 ottobre 1943," in Guido Valabrega, ed., *Gli ebrei in Italia sotto il fascismo* (Milan: Quaderni del CDEC, 1963), vol. 3, 8–37; Robert Katz, *Sabato nero* (Milan: Rizzoli, 1973) [(original: *Black Shabbath: A Journey through a Crime against Humanity* (London: Barker, 1969)] ; Liliana Picciotto, *L'occupazione tedesca e gli ebrei di Roma* (Rome: Carucci, 1979).

22. Danuta Czech, *Auschwitz Chronicle 1939–1945* (New York: Henry Holt, 1990), 512.

23. Picciotto, *Il libro*, 884–9.

24. On the subject of the November raids carried out by Dannecker's men, Liliana Picciotto, "Le retate del novembre 1943 a Firenze," in "Saggi sull'ebraismo italiano in memoria di Yehudà Nello Pavoncello," eds. Angelo Piattelli and Myriam Silvera, *La Rassegna mensile di Israel* 67, nos. 1–2 (January–August 2001), 243–64.

25. Louis Goldman, *Amici per la vita* (Florence: Coppini, 1999), 41–3.

26. Czech, *Auschwitz*, 526.

27. Liliana Picciotto, *Gli ebrei in provincia di Milano, 1943–1945* (Milan: Provincia di Milano-CDEC, 1992).

28. Czech, *Auschwitz*, 545.

29. Claudia Steur, *Theodor Danneker. Ein Funktionaer der "Endloesung"* (Essen: Klartext, 1997).

30. Picciotto, *Il libro*, 891–2.

31. Czech, *Auschwitz*, 581.

32. Picciotto, *Il libro*, 899–900.

33. Ibid., 901.

34. Ibid., 903–4.

35. Ibid., 909–10.

36. Ibid., 906–9.

37. Primo Levi, *Se questo è un uomo* (Turin: Einaudi, 1986), 19; Marco Coslovich and Tristano Matta, eds., "Memorie coeve e memorie postume: i 'diari' di Angelo Vivante e di Laura Geiringer," *Qualestoria* 1 (June 2000), 101–36.

38. Franco Schönheit, personal interview with author, October 6, 1985. Center for Contemporary Jewish Documentation Milan (CDEC) Fondo DRED, Milan.

39. Picciotto, *Il libro*, 911.

40. Ibid., *Table of the convoys*, 58–65.

41. Ibid., 929–32.

42. Ibid., 932–9.

43. The percentage of the victims of the Shoah is quite difficult to establish and depends on the initial population considered, a number that, clearly, varies depending on the period studied. The percentage of victims also depends on the method used to count them, by addition or by subtraction. If, for instance, we take the number of Jews present in Italy in 1938, the time of the great Fascist classification undertaken by the government, we will see that there were 46,656 individuals professing the Jewish faith and that in 1945 in Italy there were 26,938 Jews (including those liberated in the South, excluding refugees in Switzerland waiting to return to Italy, and excluding the deportees awaiting repatriation). According to this calculation, therefore, the anti-Jewish policy caused a decline in the Jewish population of 57.73 percent, as a result of emigration, flight, murder, and deportation. It is our belief that the number of victims of the Shoah should be considered strictly as a result of the Nazi policy of extermination, not as a result of the policy of anti-Jewish intimidation undertaken by the various Fascist governments of the period.

44. Calculations of the victims of the Shoah in the various countries, with the limitations explained in the previous footnote, are taken from three different studies that differ one from another and to which I have applied a mathematical average. They are as follows: Yehuda Bauer and Robert Rozett, "Estimated Jewish Losses in the Holocaust," *Encyclopaedia of the Holocaust*, Israel Gutman, ed. (New York: MacMillan, 1990), 1797–1802 ; Wolfgang Benz, ed., *Dimension des Völkermords. Die Zahl der jüdischer Opfer des Nationalsozialismus* (Munich: R. Oldenbourg Verlag, 1991); and Raul Hilberg, *La distruzione degli ebrei d'Europa* (Turin: Einaudi, 1995), 1303–20. (The Italian edition is the most recent one, and it takes into account the English edition of 1985, the French edition of 1988, and the German edition of 1994).

12 The Möllhausen Telegram, the Kappler Decodes, and the Deportation of the Jews of Rome: The New CIA-OSS Documents, 2000–2002

Robert Katz

In 1997 the Central Intelligence Agency (CIA), with barely concealed reluctance, turned over an unusually large number of long-classified documents to the National Archives (NARA). The bulk of these papers had been accumulated in the last three years of World War II by the CIA's precursor organization, the OSS (Office of Strategic Services), America's first spy agency. A promiscuous band of castaway career officers, freelance adventurers, and a few idealists led by a larger-than-life American hero called Wild Bill (General William J. Donovan) had compiled a record of high-minded derring-do but one that was far from unblemished. Such an assessment had already emerged from the main body of the agency's files declassified between 1975 and 1996, but not before the 1997 documents had been pulled from their folders for continued concealment from public scrutiny. Invoking a 1947 act of Congress shielding "sources and methods" of intelligence operations from disclosure, the heirs of the OSS had found a way to rebury anything that might reasonably claim the sources-and–methods exemption. There they would have moldered for an eternity had it not been for the passage of the anti-cover-up Nazi War Crimes Disclosure Act in 1998.

Pried loose from what one mainstream daily called the "white-knuckled grip" of the CIA,[1] the secrets considered most precious seemed certain to cast new light on the wartime agency, but not luster. The sheer quantity of these withdrawn documents held out a promise of surprises. At the time of the transfer, only the overall volume was known – 617 cubic feet (c. 175 cubic meters) – a not-very-edifying number. Yet if the same cubic footage were arranged in a column of standard-size $8\frac{1}{2}$- by 11-inch paper it would stand as high as the Eiffel Tower. Expressed in total number of pages, it would come to some 2.75 to 3 million wartime records waiting sublimely for more than half a century to emerge like spy-story sleepers.

The declassification process proceeded over the next three years, much of it spent wrangling with the CIA, and was far from completion when in mid-2000 the first batch of 400,000 pages was released, accompanied by a report by NARA historians Richard Breitman and Timothy Naftali on the value of the material.[2] Their examples of some previously unknown documents signed by high-profile names touched on the war's most singular phenomenon – the industrialized genocide we call the Holocaust – and no amount of sober and cautious presentation could dampen the excitement they stirred worldwide, as a flock of front-line journalists descended on leafy College Park, Maryland, home of NARA's Archives-II and the new documents.

The documents highlighted by Breitman and Naftali span the tumultuous summer and fall of 1943 from the overthrow of Mussolini to Italy's surrender to the Allies and the German occupation of most of the peninsula. Declassified, they revealed a body of decoded intercepts of wireless traffic between Reichsführer Himmler's representative in Rome, SS officer Herbert Kappler, and the Central Office for the Security of the German Reich (RSHA) in Berlin – communications whose existence could only be surmised until now.[3] As for content, they preserved much detail, most of it new, about the early German decisions to deport Italian Jews to Auschwitz. "In fact," Breitman and Naftali wrote, "we now have a much better picture of how the Holocaust in Italy began."[4]

Moreover, their very presence in the OSS files, underscored by the smoking-gun nature of real-time interception, pinpoints what the Allies knew about this particular extermination-in-progress – which in the decodes cited culminates in the October 16, 1943, roundup and deportation of more than a thousand Roman Jews ("[on train] numbered X70469 . . . travelling by way of Vienna and Prague to Auschwitz") – and raises the question, the NARA historians observed, "what might have been done with the information they possessed."[5]

Despite the string of zeros, the 400,000 pages of that summer of 2000 did not, in fact, an Eiffel Tower make, constituting less than 15 percent of the original estimate. Since the 2000 release, in fact, ongoing NARA inventories have more than validated the Breitman–Naftali hint of new things to come. We are thus in the vanguard position now to examine what the new documents contribute to our understanding of the fate of the Jews of Rome.

*

One of World War II's most extraordinary anti-Nazi conspiracies was the sustained effort by some Nazis themselves in high positions of the occupation to spare the Jews of Rome from the Holocaust. From day one of the German takeover, all

Italian Jews, though hounded ceaselessly since Mussolini's 1938 discriminatory legislation, had suddenly lost their immunity to German-style persecution, the deadliest scourge wrought by human design. This immense advantage had been begrudgingly granted by Berlin in recognition of Fascist Italy as a sovereign member-state of the Axis powers. Clashing with the intent expressed in the Wannsee Conference on the Final Solution, the problem had been particularly vexing to Adolf Eichmann, who was committed to an eleven million benchmark figure of the number of Jews to be "relocated." Eichmann, as the Reich's chief "relocater," needed every one of the quota of 58,000 Italian Jews – an erroneous figure he himself had established (it was about 20 percent higher than the actual number) and now that Himmler had made the roundup and deportation of the Jews of Rome the first order of business in the punishment schemes in store of the treasonous ally, Eichmann would brook no further shenanigans.

Shenanigans, however, were what he would get from his fellow Germans running the occupation in Rome. The principal players in this covert attempt in favor of the Roman Jews brought together six men from three distinctly different branches of Hitler's regime. Four were high-ranking diplomats – two accredited to Fascist Italy and two from Berlin's mission to the Holy See – another, coming from the military, was the Stadtkommandant of Rome, and finally, and most improbably, the loose association included the RSHA's Kappler. Kappler had served in Rome for years as a lone police attaché in the German embassy, but the recent events had catapulted him into the role of de facto Gestapo head of the occupied city. This opposition group – calling them, at least in this case, Hitler's unwilling executioners seems fairer than the rigged term "'good' Germans" – would later make no claim to have acted out of humanitarian considerations alone, nor would they deny being motivated by practical concerns consonant with their branch of service and their sense of duty to their country. Until now, all accounts of their efforts to save Rome's Jews came from their own lips, with some evidentiary and witness corroboration, though often challenged by others. The CIA release, however, provides a small but significant array of indisputable material independent of what was said by and about those involved. The episode as a whole, already well parsed, now seems destined to reexamination by more powerful instruments of scholarship.

The new documents relate directly to only two of the German oppositionists – Kappler, the least-believed of them all, and at the other extreme, the most convincing, then acting head of the German embassy in Rome, Consul Eitel Friedrich Möllhausen – but since they affect the credibility of all involved, the entire incident merits review.[6]

The consensus version of what was said and done has long been well established.[7] The German opposition to a major assault on the Roman Jews akin to the mass arrests and deportations that had already occurred in other occupied cities of Western Europe, most recently in Paris, arose more or less simultaneously with a dispatch from Himmler's Berlin headquarters calling for "a final solution to the Jewish question" in newly occupied Italy, beginning immediately with Rome. The message, received on September 25, 1943, was addressed specifically to Kappler, whose prestige had soared in recent days. For outstanding services to the Reich, the thirty-six-year-old SS major had just been promoted to lieutenant colonel and awarded the Iron Cross, with personal best wishes from Himmler himself.[8] Now, the Reichsführer was relying on him once again. He was to ensure, his orders read, that all Jews, regardless of age, sex, and health, were to be deported "for liquidation."[9] The success of such an operation, the dispatch went on, required that the victims be taken by surprise and therefore, while preparing the roundup, it was "absolutely necessary to suspend the application of any anti-Jewish measures of an individual nature in order not to arouse any suspicions among the population of an imminent action."[10]

Although Kappler's message bore a higher-than-usual classification – more than simply secret (*Geheim*) it was termed a *state* secret (*Geheime Reichssache*) – and was marked for his eyes only, by the time it was handed to him, it had already been read by General Stahel and Consul Möllhausen. It had arrived in the code room of the embassy, where all three men had offices. As Stadtkommandant, literally, the commander of the city, Stahel had exercised his authority to satisfy his curiosity. According to Möllhausen's 1948 memoir and my 1968 interview,[11] Stahel came to him with the message still in his hands and voiced immediate opposition, saying he would never have anything to do with such *Schweinerei*. An air force captain in World War I, Stahel had risen in the ranks of the Luftwaffe and was well removed from the day-to-day workings of the Holocaust, but few men invested with significant powers of the Nazi state could have been further from the culture of genocidal anti-Semitism than thirty-year-old Möllhausen. Only a day earlier, he had been placed in charge of the embassy, acting for the ambassador, Rudolf Rahn, who had been in a serious car accident and would be incapacitated indefinitely.

A rare nonmember of the Nazi party, with a record of repeated refusals to join, Möllhausen could have no career aspirations in the Foreign Office. As the son of a French woman and a half-German father of considerable wealth, he had spent only brief periods in the *Vaterland*. Born in Turkey, raised in Trieste, he had spoken Italian before German and was fluent in Greek and French. His language skills had landed him a post as a translator in the foreign service. Tours of duty in North Africa and the Middle East from the outbreak of the war until being posted in Italy in 1943 continued to keep him isolated from the murderous Nazi ethic. Meanwhile, taken under the wing of Ambassador Rahn, he rose along with him in spite of his maverick reputation.

By his own admission, Möllhausen had had few thoughts about Nazi designs on Europe's Jews. He knew they were continually hunted down and shipped off to remote places of no return, but he had never until now seen the word *liquidation* used in official documents, and so unequivocally associated as the end result of arrest and deportation. Thus he agreed to add his own as yet informal disapproval to Stahel's and on the following day, certain that Kappler's message had in the meantime been expertly resealed and properly delivered, he went to see the Gestapo chief hoping to enlist him in an alternative plan.[12]

Kappler has told his side of the story in great detail, once at his 1948 war crimes trial in Rome and again, while serving a life sentence in Italy,[13] in a long deposition taken in 1961 for the Eichmann trial in Jerusalem. Kappler's representation of his contacts with Möllhausen and Stahel is consistent with Möllhausen's, though, as the recipient of Himmler's orders, he cast himself as the one attempting to gain *their* support in opposing the roundup.

Earlier that week, Kappler had been officially relieved of his embassy post as police attaché and moved into the role of chief of security of occupied Rome. Apart from his promotion, this entailed a major shift in his responsibilities. Unlike Möllhausen, he had pursued a conventional career, beginning as an ordinary policeman in the pre-Hitler regular police force, the *Ordnungspolizei*, had joined the SS early and had landed a dream job in being sent to Rome in early 1939 as a consultant. His one-man office, in which he was his own typist, driver, and errand boy, never expanded beyond the early addition of a one-man staff (police lieutenant Erich Priebke, of future notoriety), but in the coming days he would be in command of a dozen officers, seventy-five SS men in all, and move into a refitted two-winged building, offices on one side, prison facility on the other – the Rome headquarters of Gestapo – in a street to be remembered in infamy: the Via Tasso.

In his postwar testimony, Kappler portrayed himself as being out of the Holocaust loop. The demand for a "final solution to the Jewish question" in Italy – a phrase he would insist he had never heard before[14] – was, he said, typical Berlin babble by people who did not understand local conditions. Italy was not Germany, where the Jews had grown rich "off the backs of the people," he would say later. Most Italian Jews, at least in Rome, were poor, orderly, and docile. True, their leaders had contacts with the "international Jewish conspiracy," he believed, but that was a matter that could be exploited for intelligence purposes. Finally, there were more pressing matters demanding his time in this period of rapidly expanding Gestapo operations in the occupied city. Rome as a strategic staging ground for the southern front had vast security implications that required his expertise and immediate attention. According to Möllhausen, Kappler said, "My problem is not the Jews, but the anti-Fascists."[15] Rounding up Jewish riffraff, he felt, was simply "one more gross political stupidity" (*"eine neue grosse politische Dummheit"*), and he would later maintain that he had used that very expression in protesting to his superiors.[16]

Finding Kappler amenable, Möllhausen recounted a similar situation during his service in North Africa. The Tunisian Jews had been faced with deportation, but Ambassador Rahn had intervened to remove them from the Gestapo's jurisdiction. Those Jews were organized in labor service building fortifications for the Wehrmacht. Rahn could be of no help now, but Kappler suggested they go to Field Marshal Kesselring, supreme commander of the southern front, which included Rome. If Kesselring were to agree to a Tunisian-like solution, Kappler would regard his orders from Berlin as having been countermanded. Within an hour, both men were seated before the field marshal, who on hearing Kappler's estimate that the roundup, in addition to his own men, would need reinforcement by at least one motorized battalion, Kesselring declared the matter settled. He could not spare a single man, let alone a battalion. He further approved the idea of using Jewish labor for defense construction around Rome.[17]

Although there remains some confusion as to the exact date of the meeting with Kesselring, what Kappler did that Sunday evening is well recorded. Through an intermediary, he had on his own initiative summoned the two ranking leaders of Roman Jewry: the president of the Rome community, Ugo Foà, and the president of the national organization of Jewish communities, Dante Almansi. Sometime after 6:00 p.m., Kappler received them in his embassy office. Friendly enough at first, before long he hardened and delivered an ultimatum. The two presidents had thirty-six hours to hand over fifty kilograms of gold. That was the amount required, he said, to ransom "200 of your Jews" from deportation to Germany. Kappler later confirmed both Foà's and Almansi's nearly identical accounts,[18] with the exception of the threat to deport two hundred Jews. He was more severe; if the gold were not paid, he said, there would be a general roundup and deportation of Rome's Jews.[19] Adding a villainous note to what was tantamount to his debut performance as a Gestapo chief, he sent Foà and Almansi away with a frightful lie. "Mind you," he said, "I have already carried out several operations of this type and they have always ended well. Only once did I fail, but that time a few hundred of your brothers paid with their lives."[20]

Kappler would later call this perplexing exercise in extortion "my last attempt at trying to avoid the roundup."[21] He had heard that the SS intelligence services were seriously short on funds, and here was an opportunity for them to draw directly from what he believed to be a link to the bottomless well of the phantasmagoric Jewish financial world. In the real world of occupied Rome, the Jewish leaders turned to the ghetto poor to finance the ransom; over the next two days they queued outside the main synagogue surrendering whatever gold they possessed, mostly items of personal jewelry weighing under one gram. A promise by the Vatican of a loan to make up any shortfall was gratefully received but unneeded. The ransom was paid, the unauthorized threat left in a limbo, and the gold was shipped off without delay to Berlin. It was addressed to the chief of the entire Reich security apparatus, the RSHA, the man second only to Himmler, General Ernst Kaltenbrunner. Kappler had never met Kaltenbrunner, but had chosen him, he said later, for his reputed interest in the intelligence services and because he had had nothing to do with "all the discussions that had been going on about the advisability of executing a roundup in Rome."[22] Kappler brought Kaltenbrunner up to date in a letter, explaining why the deportation of the Jews of Rome would be counterproductive. The SS, he said, would lose the chance to tap into, for intelligence purposes, known Jewish contacts with the Allies and with Jewish financial groups abroad.[23]

Until now, the only known reaction from Kaltenbrunner was a gesture of total indifference: at war's end Kappler's crate of Jewish gold was found by the Allies in a corner of Kaltenbrunner's office never even opened.[24] It seemed clear enough that Kappler's opposition had been given short shrift and that he undoubtedly caught on and fell into line. Although Kappler would continually declare in postwar legal proceedings that he had resisted the deportation order, his unauthorized and rather nonsensical extortion deflated his overall credibility to zero. The scheme has usually been treated as a crude deception tactic designed to lead the Roman Jews into the trap of a false sense of security. As will be seen, however, the decodes, which in fact contain Kaltenbrunner's unambiguous response, may induce some writers to revise that finding.[25]

Certainly, Möllhausen could not fathom why Kappler had, it seemed, complicated the understanding they had reached with Kesselring about using the Roman Jews for their labor. Möllhausen had learned of the extortion from von Kessel, who in turn had heard it from his Vatican contacts. Now that Kappler had himself threatened deportation, Möllhausen moved to unite with his more natural allies, Weizsäcker and Kessel.

The two diplomats to the Holy See had been working since the first days of the occupation on a very specific project to forestall what would almost certainly provoke a major crisis in Vatican–German relations. At this stage in the war, both men were secretly abetting Pius XII's peace strategy: a general rapprochement between the western Allies and Germany to contain, if not roll back, the fearsome advance of godless Communism. The pope, hoping to mediate such an accord, had worked assiduously to maintain a neutral position. How neutral that was in practice need not be argued here, but neutrality as a tenet to uphold was what lay behind his already foundering and controversial policy of silence in the face of the Holocaust. Now, in occupied Rome, the most crucial test of that silence was at hand. He had not protested the distant slaughter of Europe's Jews, but Weizsäcker and Kessel were concerned about what he might do should the perpetrators stage the clamorous spectacle of Rome's Jews being torn from streets of his own diocese; indeed, both men concurred that such an affront to the Holy Father was inevitable, and they saw their task, as Kessel has said, as an effort to spare the German nation "a loss of dignity," protect the pope from a situation in which he might have to break his neutrality policy of silence and protest, and finally to save the Jews.[26] Möllhausen was in full agreement.[27]

With Kappler left to his own machinations, Möllhausen turned to the remaining nondiplomat, General Stahel, seeking his support for the Weizsäcker–Kessel approach – the need to prevent a breach in Vatican–German relations. Stahel quickly agreed that he would not permit the roundup to take place without the express approval of the Foreign Office.

This was precisely what Möllhausen wanted and with the encouragement of Kessel and Weizsäcker, but without consulting Rahn, he composed and dispatched what is undoubtedly one of the most cited documents of the millions generated by the day-to-day transactions of the Holocaust. The Möllhausen telegram to Berlin, dated October 6, 1943, made history when received, made history when revealed, and now – returned from the time capsule of secrets withdrawn by the CIA and bearing extraordinary value added – seems certain to make history once more.

Arriving in the Reich Foreign Ministry office on Wilhelmstrasse in Berlin early that afternoon, the consul's message was unusual even at first glance, bearing a nonexistent and as such slightly hysterical "very very urgent!" classification (the highest being "very urgent") with the vaguely presumptuous demand that it be delivered to Foreign Minister von Ribbentrop "personally." What followed were three breathless sentences, reporting, first, that Kappler had been ordered to seize the 8,000 Jews of Rome, ship them off to northern Italy, "where they are to be liquidated [*wo sie liquidiert werden sollen*]"; second, that Stadtkommandant Stahel would not permit this to take place without Reichsminister von Ribbentrop's express approval, and finally, the Tunisian alternative of putting the Jews to work in a labor service, which he said both Kappler and he would propose to Kesselring.[28]

When queried many years later, not even Möllhausen himself could explain why he advanced his September 26 meeting with Kesselring and Kappler by ten days.[29] Moreover, the 8,000 figure and the destination of the deportees were both mistaken, but he certainly was correct about their one-word destiny, which was all that mattered, of course. The next morning, without waiting for a reply to his sign-off request for advice, he dispatched another very-very-urgent telegram, reporting his visit with Kappler to Kesselring but making it sound fresher. Kesselring had asked Kappler, he wrote, "to postpone the planned action against the Jews" and voiced his preference for the plan "to utilize the able-bodied Roman Jews in fortification work near here."[30]

With these two cables, Möllhausen said later, he believed that he was "giving good news." Weizsäcker and Kessel had from the start been kept abreast by the consul, and they in turn informed the Vatican.[31] It was good news for everyone in that camp, to be sure, but from that day on the highest authorities in the Church, including the Holy Father, could have no doubt what the SS was at least planning for the Jews of Rome.

The telegrams, however, continued down an unpaved road of history, gaining significance and leaving their milestones behind them. In Berlin, Ribbentrop, confronted with the "good news," was furious. What irked him most was not the substance of the message but that this was the first time that someone in the Reich Foreign Ministry – from the capital to its missions and outposts ringing the globe – had used the word *liquidate* when speaking of Europe's Jews in an official document. Worse, the unmentionable verb and its unmistakable connotation had made its appearance in a telegram addressed to him *personally*. Ambassador Rahn, convalescing in Salò, was called at once forced to admit his ignorance of the entire affair, and promised a prompt explanation. Rahn, hoping no doubt for the best – a coding glitch would do fine – called his protégé in Rome, who could do no more than confirm the worst. "I expressly included in the telegram," he said later, "the word contained in the orders imparted to Kappler, precisely because it was this word that had upset me and compelled me to intervene decisively."[32]

In the meantime, Himmler, told of the meddling in Rome, accused Ribbentrop of overstepping his authority. Ribbentrop was embarrassed. Kesselring was embarrassed. Rahn was embarrassed. Möllhausen was recalled and ordered to provide a full accounting of his behavior. Before departing, however, he finally received the advice requested. In two "very urgent" dispatches from the Foreign Office, dated October 9, 1943, and addressed to Möllhausen personally, the consul was told that on the basis of the Führer's instructions, the Roman Jews were indeed going to be deported and that Ribbentrop "requests you not to interfere in any way." The second telegram was rather sharper, the Reichsminister no longer requesting but insisting, "Keep out of all questions concerning Jews."[33] Möllhausen understood. Weizsäcker, informed by Möllhausen, understood. The Vatican, informed by Weizsäcker, understood.[34] It would take a greater effort still to save the Jews of Rome.

✳

At this point the new documents fall silent for seven days, until the appearance of Ultra's decode of the October 16 midnight dispatch from Kappler's office to Berlin, which begins, "Action against Jews started and finished today."[35] There is nothing in the new material that suggests that anyone other than the perpetrators knew the precise date and time the arrests began.[36] Similarly, the prompt intervention of the German diplomats in Rome on hearing that the roundup was in progress, the roles played by Weizsäcker, Kessel, and the final member of the opposition, Legation Secretary Gumpert (filling in for Möllhausen, who was out of Rome still explaining his telegrams), require no alterations. What the CIA release does appear to change – though as already noted, only Kappler and Möllhausen are directly affected – is the perspective from which we view the known events.

Let us consider Kappler first. One of the reasons his credibility in declaring his opposition to the roundup seems to self-destruct is an apparent incoherence in his behavior. Even his nakedly intimidating demand for fifty kilograms of Jewish gold, which left his colleagues scratching their heads, is often seen as an act of deception in some master plan, when in fact it clearly flouts the Himmler categorical order against adopting anti-Jewish measures "of an individual nature" as an act of *deception.*

Kappler – the only German tried specifically for any of the monstrous crimes against the Jews of Rome, the relatively innocuous gold extortion – has from the start been seen as the primary culprit in the roundup and deportation. His opposition is viewed as self-serving, and lesser attention is given to Eichmann and his "Jewish expert," the formidable SS Captain Theodor Dannecker.[37] The

Kappler decodes, however, provide an indisputable record that lends support not only to his story but to an overall estimation of his character, that with Kappler, though anything but benign, what you see is what you get.

Kappler's change in job description – from an advisory role to broad executive powers – first appears in a September 18, 1943, decode from the head of the SS in Italy, General Karl Wolff to Himmler – less than ten days into the occupation – informing Himmler that he has immediately transferred 100 SS police to Kappler's command, augmenting his preoccupation staff of one.[38]

Security had always been Kappler's specialty and now it became his primary concern. The 100 men were yet to arrive and in fact never reached more than 75. Moreover, with regard to the overriding desire in Berlin to round up the Jews, Kappler was aware that his reinforcements were as completely inexperienced in such operations as he was. Thus, in his first expression of opposition preserved in the decodes, he notes the arrival of Dannecker "with orders to seize all Jews in lightning actions and to forward them to Germany," but warns Berlin of what happened in Naples. "Because of the attitude in the town and uncertain conditions, action could not be carried through."[39] By "attitude" and "uncertain conditions," we learn from other decodes that another of his major concerns was that the non-Jewish population of Rome could be expected to be hostile in the event of a raid on the Jews, and the possibility of passive, even armed resistance on the part of the Romans was very high.

In the same first-opposition decode, dated incidentally the same day as the first Möllhausen telegram, Kappler, like the consul, suggested the Tunisian alternative, that of the Jews being used "for employment on defensive works." An even "more expedient" solution, he said, would be to assign the task of rounding up the Jews to the local Fascist authorities, thus deflecting popular hostility away from the Germans.

As for the gold extortion, the decodes are consistent with, though they do not confirm, Kappler's explanation. Why the Gestapo chief needed one or another "last attempt" to avoid the roundup leaps unmistakably from at least three decodes. When the Germans occupied Rome they emptied the gold reserves of the Bank of Italy in the amount of 110 metric tons, so Kappler, whose participation in that operation is revealed in a decode dated October 5, knew that milking another measly fifty kilograms from the Roman Jews would add little to the wealth of his nation.[40] The poor financial situation of the SS intelligence services was unlikely to receive high priority, however, and, as the court found in Kappler's 1948 trial, his awareness of Kaltenbrunner's interest in developing those services was a way to curry favor from his new boss.[41]

Kessel has termed whatever it was Kappler had in mind "complete nonsense"[42] and Möllhausen simply switched to the diplomats. But there was apparently more to it than previously known. The decodes are rich here, revealing not only that Kappler was the originator of quite another kind of roundup and deportation about to take place at that time, but the extent of his determination to see it through.

On the night of October 6, the Fascist-led colonial police (Polizia Africana Italiana), carrying out a plan initiated by Kappler and authorized by Kesselring, surrounded the barracks and armories of the carabinieri in Rome and began arresting as many as they could. Traditionally loyal to the king, the carabinieri had been targeted by Kappler early in the occupation as a security risk.[43] By some unspecified experiment, Kappler had convinced himself of their continued unreliability and had proposed that they "be disarmed at one fell swoop because of their participation in plots, etc. and that they be removed to Germany as workers."[44] More than 1,500 of the local force of 6,500 men and officers were captured in their quarters or in flight. They were carried off in trucks, herded into a train of boxcars, and deported to the Reich. The fate of the Rome carabinieri and how a large number of those who escaped the raid, most with their weapons, joined and distinguished themselves in the resistance has long been known,[45] but not Kappler's role and its connection to the Jews of Rome. Neutralizing the carabinieri – and in a related operation arresting all Italian officers who failed to shift their allegiance to the Mussolini puppet regime at Salò – had become Kappler's pet project and the decodes bear witness to his pride in having proposed the idea to Kesselring and gained his approval.[46] As reflected in the decodes, a great part of Kappler's invariably negative attitude toward the Jewish roundup was his concern that as a logistical rival, it might interfere with the carabinieri operations.

That the various forms of Kappler's opposition had become something more than a nuisance in Berlin is another long-known facet of the affair. Eichmann, for example, who was accustomed to occasional resistance from German officials on the scene – usually on the grounds that it placed an additional burden on limited resources and manpower engaged in the war – had grown convinced that the opposition stemming from Kappler and the diplomats required special treatment. He sent his ace troubleshooter, Dannecker.[47] The CIA papers, however, show Kappler's own agenda to have been more than a garden variety pest in Eichmann's killing field. One of the most sensational documents to come from the Ultra listening post on the Rome–Berlin radio is the missing link between Kappler courting Kaltenbrunner and what seems to be Kaltenbrunner's extravagant spurning gesture of never even opening the crate of Jewish gold. Existing in no other form but the Ultra intercept, the October 11 decode reads as follows:

> To KAPPLER. It is precisely the immediate and thorough erad-
> ication of the Jews in Italy which is in the special interest of the
> present internal political situation and the general security in
> Italy. To postpone the expulsion of the Jews until the carabinieri
> and the Italian army officers have been removed can no more
> be considered than the idea mentioned of calling up the Jews in
> Italy for what would probably be very improductive [*sic*] labour
> under responsible direction by Italian authorities. The longer the
> delay, the more the Jews who are doubtless reckoning on evac-
> uation measures have an opportunity by moving to the houses
> of pro-Jewish Italians of disappearing completely. [Undecoded]
> has been instructed in executing the RFSS [Himmler's] orders
> to proceed with the evacuation of the Jews without further delay.
>   KALTENBRUNNER[48]

The undecoded item in Kaltenbrunner's final sentence is almost certainly a reference to Dannecker, who by then was already in Rome, secretly at work on his methodical little envelopes, each of which was to be stuffed with the names and address of one Jewish family to be wrenched from its home on that day. Kappler, receiving Dannecker on his arrival, would always be proud of the shortness with which he treated him, but in the end, as was his style, he would yield to the doctrines of his oath – in this instance, agree to act as Dannecker's go-between to Stadtkommandant Stahel to resolve the crucial manpower issue.

The decodes continue on through October, but only those of October 16 and 17 need citing here. The Ultra intercept of Kappler's report some hours after the roundup would be virtually unintelligible if the original had not survived. Only partially received, it is riddled with square-bracketed question marks and indications of "corrupt" or "missing" letters, words, and whole passages. Nevertheless it has its own intrinsic merit, indicating what was known at the time by the Allies.[49] Moreover, taken with the earlier Kappler Ultra material, with his emphasis on the hostility of the Romans, it adds to the consistency of his opposition to the deportations. As in the original, about half the message is his analysis of the reaction of the city's population in general. Their attitude was "unequivocally one of passive resistance," and at times "developed into active assistance." His complaint in the original about the total absence "of the anti-Semitic part of the population" is missing from the decode, but his own I-told-you-so attitude is underscored by the tone of the decodes – culminating in the new, postroundup "survey of morale," sent on October 17.

Intercepted again only partially, this document observed that although sympathy for the victims was "artificially heightened by whisper propaganda," the Romans are "excited and angry after the action against the Jews. Sympathy is the uppermost feeling among the lower classes, especially because women and children were taken." There was, he noted, "growing indignation, especially against the German police." Even the Fascists were unhappy, said Kappler, but only because "the Jewish question has not been solved by Fascism."[50]

Unlike the Kappler decodes, which were part of British intelligence at Ultra's Bletchley Park, fifty miles north of London, and given away like spy candy to the Americans, the Möllhausen telegram was a full-fledged American espionage triumph that put the British to shame. At about the same time in that summer of 1943 that Kappler installed his shortwave radio to open a direct line to Berlin (and to the wizards of Bletchley Park), a mild-mannered German official in Ribbentrop's Foreign Office crossed into Switzerland and, declaring his anti-Nazi sentiments to the British, offered his services as a spy. Despite his goodwill offering of a packet of stolen documents taped to his body, he was taken for an obvious plant and rudely dismissed. Undeterred, he turned to the Americans, to the person who headed the Berne office of the OSS, the future director of the CIA, Alan Dulles. Dulles, against the advice and then ridicule of his counterparts in British intelligence's MI6, apparently knew how to detect the right stuff, and a perfect spy, code-named George Wood, was born. His real name was Fritz Kolbe, whose job in the Foreign Office was to screen and reroute top-secret messages to and from the Nazi hierarchy around the world. By war's end, he had rerouted more than 1,600 duplicates of such documents – known in OSS parlance as Kappa cables – piling one coup upon another, and among them was the cable received in the Wilhelmstrasse ten days before the roundup of the Jews of Rome "to be liquidated," the Möllhausen telegram.[51]

Now in the hands of the Americans, its import escaped no one, least of all Kolbe. In passing it to his OSS handlers, he wrote: "It is our wish, for reasons which will be perfectly clear, that you receive this message in its original form. For this reason, we are resorting to a described way of transmitting it."[52] Underlining the hot-button nature of this advance information, was an OSS notation appended to Kolbe's: "Note from Message Center: For security reasons method of circulation will not be circulated."[53] The special if not unique treatment given to this one document can still be felt in the research room of Archives-II as one pores over the OSS files, seeing copies – many bearing postreceipt markings – turn up in box after box otherwise unrelated, and with some guidance is led to box number 440 to find the copy hand-delivered to the White House, to the Oval Office, landing on the desk of Franklin Roosevelt.[54]

That journey from the Wilhelmstrasse to Pennsylvania Avenue remains a dimly lit pathway but surely worthy of further research. An aspect of such a study would, no doubt, be an attempt to delve into a final curiosity in the new material. As noted above, the Foreign Office's final word to its sentimental young consul in Rome was a categorical order not to interfere in the roundup and deportation of the Roman Jews; it was to go forward "on the basis of the Führer's instructions." This is a direct quote from the telegram and until recently had seemed nothing more than a synonym for the highest level of command, since no other document linked Hitler directly to deportation orders of Roman Jews for the express purpose of liquidation. The new CIA material, however, contains a Kappa message in which it is pointed out that the Möllhausen October 6 telegram was marked "For the Führer and the Reichs Minister personally."[55] Since the microfilmed original from the German Foreign Ministry reads "For Herrn Reichsminister personally," the message suggests that the marking was added in Berlin after receipt from Rome.[56]

*

By the time the Möllhausen telegram reached the American president, it was more than two months too late for the Jews caught in the roundup, almost all of whom were dead. Nevertheless the full extent of the threat to the Jews was clear from the Kappler decodes. The transmission to and from Berlin were intercepted in real time, quickly deciphered and translated by Ultra, and made available immediately. Thus Washington and London, aside from advance knowledge of the roundup, were aware of the number of arrests, where the prisoners were being held, the date and time of their departure, the train markings and its route, and the inadequate size of the escort.

Could the Allies have alerted the Roman Jews, without revealing their vital capability for interception? Would the Jews have believed them? The researcher is unlikely to find those answers in the CIA papers. What has emerged, however, is that a much larger number of people than previously known were in on the precious state secret meant for Kappler's eyes only. The expansion of that pool of cognoscenti matters; it is a measure of the moral pressure applied or applicable on those most suited to act and instead remained inert.[57] In Rome and the

Vatican – and now we know, in London and Washington as well – countless individuals in a position to lift their voice or alternatively, as Kappler put it, engage in "whisper propaganda" either in warning or in protest, waited in silence for the proverbial other shoe to fall, one might say, but in the harsh reality were mute witnesses to a preannounced journey to a gas chamber.

NOTES

1. *Boston Globe*, March 11, 2001, A1.

2. Breitman and Naftali, "Report to the IWG on Previously Classified OSS Records," June 2000, at *www.archives.gov/iwg*. IWG refers to the Interagency Working Group, which administers the provisions of the Nazi War Crimes Disclosure Act.

3. The Kappler decodes are located in NARA (Archives-II) RG 226, CIA, Box 4, cited herein as "Decode doc. xxxx." That they were also decoded was news in itself. In his 1998 book on Ultra, the system set up by British intelligence to intercept and decode the high-level German war communications sent by the Enigma encryption machine, Breitman reported that the Ultra cryptanalysts, in a rare failure, had never broken the code used by the Gestapo, which would have had information about the deportations (Richard Breitman, *Official Secrets* [New York: Hill and Wang], 90). Now, however, Breitman and Naftali were able to write that Rome–Berlin traffic, in this instance, was deciphered in late August 1943 and the newly declassified material contained these decodes through October (Breitman-Naftali, "Report to the IWG on Previously Classified OSS Records").

4. Breitman and Naftali, "Report to the IWG on Previously Classified OSS Records."

5. Ibid. The previously unknown train number and the first specific mention of Auschwitz as the destination (with the Vienna–Prague route given more precisely as "via Arnoldstein") come from decode doc. 7732, Rome to Berlin, 1100 GMT, October 20, 1943, signed by SS General Wilhelm Harster. These are incidentals of the main message that the detachment of *Ordnungspolizei* that departed with the victims is "urgently required" back in Rome. Harster is requesting Vienna and Prague to relieve the Rome contingent and provide a fresh police escort.

6. The remaining four who acted concretely to prevent the deportation are Ambassador to the Holy See Ernst von Weizsäcker, his principal aide, Albrecht von Kessel, Legation Secretary Gerhard Gumpert, temporarily second in command of Möllhausen's embassy, and Stadtkommandant General Rainer Stahel.

7. For an early account that has changed little since, see Raul Hilberg, *The Destruction of the European Jews* (Chicago: Quadrangle Books, 1961), 427–30; see also my full-length treatment of the subject in *Black Sabbath: A Journey through a Crime against Humanity* (New York: Macmillan, 1969), and most recently, Susan Zuccotti, *Under His Very Windows* (New Haven: Yale University Press, 2000), 150–70. For the Vatican's version, see "Les Juifs dans l'Italie Occupée" section in the introduction of the editors-historians to *Actes et Documents du Saint Siege Relatifs à la Seconde Guerre Mondiale*, IX, 50–61.

8. On a secret mission for Himmler, Kappler had performed brilliantly as the sleuth tracking down the mobile prison in which Mussolini was being held since his arrest. This

had been the key to the Duce's rescue from an Apennine peak by a commando team on orders from Hitler.

9. Text in Michael Tagliacozzo, "La persecuzione degli ebrei a Roma," in *L'occupazione tedesca e gli ebrei di Roma: Documenti e fatti*, L. Piccioto Fargion, ed. (Rome: Carucci, 1979), 152.

10. Ibid.

11. E. F. Möllhausen, *La carta perdente* (Rome: Sestante, 1948), 111; I interviewed Möllhausen several times and corresponded with him, contacts that lasted into the 1980s.

12. Ibid., 112–14.

13. He had been sentenced to life for his role in a war crime, the Ardeatine Caves massacre in Rome. In mid-August 1977, he escaped from a prison hospital in Rome and died in his homeland in February 1978.

14. He also claimed he had never heard the name Eichmann until after the war. See the transcript of Kappler's testimony in the Eichmann trial (cited hereafter as *KT*), 2, 6. The witness was examined by the Israeli court at the military prison in Gaeta, June 27, 1961, under the auspices of the Court of Appeal of Rome, Department of Preliminary Investigations. I have used the original documents filed in Rome, but an English tranlation is available at *www.nizkor.org*.

15. Möllhausen, *La carta perdente*, 114.

16. *KT*, 3.

17. Möllhausen, *La carta perdente*, 115; cf. *KT*, 3.

18. Foà wrote two accounts on the Nazi persecution during the occupation, the first dated November 15, 1943 and June 20, 1944, and the second dealing specifically with the steps taken to protect the religious artifacts in the Rome synagogue from Nazi pillage, dated November 27, 1950. Almansi's account, addressed to the postliberation Italian government and dated August 15, 1944, was substantially the same as Foà's first report. The manuscripts of both accounts are located in the Title C collection of the Centro di Documentazione Ebraica Contemporanea (CDEC), Milan.

19. Transcript of the final verdict in the trial of Herbert Kappler et al., handed down January 10, 1954, by the Military Tribunal of Rome after several appeals. Text in *Le Fosse Ardeatine*, 6th ed. (Rome: Edizioni ANFIM, 2001), 121–82. (Cited hereafter as *Kappler sentenza*.)

20. Quoted in Foà–Almansi reports.

21. *KT*, 9. See also Katz, *Black Sabbath*, 62–8.

22. *KT*, 9.

23. Letter from Kappler to Kaltenbrunner, quoted in *Kappler sentenza*, 146.

24. Ibid. Postwar requests by Rome's Jewish community for restitution were finally satisfied in 1961. The crate of gold had long since vanished but in an indemnification agreement between Italy and West Germany, the community agreed to a one-time payment of $625,000 to settle all claims on the gold and other items seized by the Nazis. See Katz, *Black Sabbath*, 313.

25. On the other hand, Breitman's reading of the new material led him to agree with Zuccotti, *Under His Very Windows*, 153, et al. – all of whom took their position prior to the

CIA release – that deception was Kappler's game. See Richard Breitman, "New Sources on the Holocaust in Italy," *Holocaust and Genocide Studies,* 14 (Winter 2002), 402–14. For another view, see, for example, Meir Michaelis, *Mussolini and the Jews: German-Italian Relations and the Jewish Question in Italy 1922–1945* (Oxford: Clarendon Press, 1978), 352.

26. Kessel claimed in a 1967 interview with me that in agreement with Weizsäcker he turned to a credible third party to warn influential people in the "Jewish colony" of Rome of the likelihood of catastrophe and the immediate need to go into hiding. The warning was passed on but met with disbelief. The new documents do not touch on this matter, but for some independent corroboration see Katz, *Black Sabbath,* 44–45.

27. Ibid., 139.

28. NARA, *Inland II Geheim,* Documents of the German Foreign Ministry, 1920–45, Microcopy T-120, Roll 4353, doc. E421525.

29. Letter from Möllhausen to me, dated January 16, 1968, cited in Katz, *Black Sabbath,* 136.

30. NARA, *Inland II Geheim,* Documents of the German Foreign Ministry, 1920–45, Microcopy T-120, Roll 4353, doc. E421524.

31. Interview with Möllhausen for *Black Sabbath,* which he reconfirmed after publication.

32. Möllhausen, *La carta perdente,* 117.

33. Telegrams from Thadden to Möllhausen, October 9, 1943, NARA, *Inland II Geheim,* Documents of the German Foreign Ministry, 1920–45, Microcopy T-120, Roll 4353, doc. E421521.

34. Katz, *Black Sabbath,* 139; see also Zuccotti, *Under His Very Windows,* 366, note 30, regarding the pope's early warning of the impending deportation of Rome's Jews; and Michael Phayer, *The Catholic Church and the Holocaust, 1930–1965* (Bloomington: Indiana University Press, 2000), 98.

35. Decode doc. 7668.

36. This, however, places one of the oppositionists in the perpetrators' camp as well. Eating his words about *Schweinerei,* General Stahel on the eve of the roundup provided three companies of troops to bring the operational task force to the required one-battalion size. (Stahel war diary in NARA Microcopy T-501, Roll 331.)

37. An early and influential assessment of Kappler's motives along these lines was made by Michael Tagliacozzo, "La comunità di Roma sotto l'incubo della svastica," in *Quaderni del Centro di Documentazione Ebraica Contemporanea* (November 1963), 8–15. See also note 31.

38. Decode doc. 6253.

39. Decode doc. 7244, Rome to Berlin, October 6, 1943.

40. Decode doc. 7185, Rome to Berlin, October 5, 1943.

41. *Kappler sentenza,* 180.

42. Kessel interview in Katz, *Black Sabbath,* 100.

43. It was in fact a task force of fifty carabinieri, hiding in the gardens of the king's residence in Rome, who had physically arrested Mussolini and his entourage on July 25,

1943. Kappler, who had predicted the coup, had been drawn further into the loyalties of the carabinieri's in the cat-and-mouse game to deceive the Germans as to the whereabouts of the Duce after the arrest.

44. Decode doc. 7184, Kappler to Berlin, October 5, 1943.

45. See especially F. Caruso, *L'Arma dei carabinieri in Roma durante l'occupazione tedesca* (Rome: Instituto Poli-Grafico dello Stato, 1949).

46. "The disarming of the Carabinieri in ROME as proposed by me," Kappler wrote in one decode, "will be carried out tonight... on a plan authorized by Feldm. KESSEL-RING." Unnumbered doc., following 7244, Rome to Berlin, October 6, 1943. The same sentiment appears in the next doc., it too, unnumbered, this time with regard to the deportation of the army officers who failed to join Mussolini's new regime in the north.

47. See Katz, *Black Sabbath*, 105–9.

48. Decode doc. 7459, Kaltenbrunner to Kappler, October 11, 1943.

49. This included the essential facts: the number of arrests, where the prisoners were being held, the date and time of their departure, and the inadequate size of their escort.

50. Decode doc. 7672, Rome to Berlin, October 17, 1943. The intercept breaks off before the signature, but is uniquely attributable to Kappler.

51. For an up-to-date, authoritative telling of the Kolbe story, see the ongoing series of articles by Greg Bradsher, in NARA's quarterly online publication, *Prologue:* "A Time to Act: The Beginning of the Fritz Kolbe Story, 1900–1943" at *www.archives.gov/iwg.*

52. Kappa message 1494–95, RG 226, Entry 210, Box 534.

53. Ibid.

54. RG 226, Entry 210, Box 440. The president's copy was Report no. 9, of the so-called Boston Series, top-secret intelligence summaries prepared from the Kappa material by the OSS.

55. RG 226, Entry 210, Box 534, Kappa message 1494–5.

56. Whether Hitler knew of the extermination of Jews unfortunately is still being asked. See the FAQ's *www.nizkor.org*, which specializes in combating Holocaust denial.

57. Coincidentally or not, two days after the Möllhausen telegram and the Kappler decode revealing Dannecker's arrival and mission in Rome, Churchill proposed to his war cabinet issuing a denunciation of Nazi atrocities as a deterrent to future crimes. He was opposed by Foreign Minister Anthony Eden on the grounds that "breathing fire and slaughter against war criminals" could not be sustained over time. Churchill backed off. See Martin Gilbert, *Auschwitz and the Allies* (New York: Holt, 1990), 158–9.

13 The Persecution of Jews in Two Regions of German-Occupied Northern Italy, 1943–1945: Operationszone Alpenvorland and Operationszone Adriatisches Küstenland

Cinzia Villani

In January 1944, the Löwy family was captured in a small mountain village in Northern Italy, because they were Jews. Here are some excerpts from the letters Riccardo Löwy wrote to his friends, pleading for help:[1]

> The four of us have now been detained here for five weeks; our women are kept separate from us.... we urgently need food, of whatever kind. Please be so good and kind as to send us something to eat.... I appeal to our friendship and to your kind heart. We are utterly destitute without any fault of ours. We do not ask for much, even bread would be enough. Take pity on us, but please, please hurry![2]

And then again:

> If you could send us a tomato to put on the bread we would be grateful. We protect ourselves from the cold by exercising. Please ... could you lend me underpants and a shirt and a towel, all old ones, so that we can wash our things, although to tell the truth I don't know how we can do the laundry. Our miserable life is all centred on eating, and in this manner we somehow forget our future which perhaps will be even more distressing.... I don't know why God is punishing us so hard![3]

We do not know if Löwy's plea was answered in time. A month later the entire family was deported and perished in Auschwitz.[4]

The Löwys had been captured in the province of Trento, in Northern Italy. From 1943 to 1945 the sovereignty of the Republic of Salò over this and eight additional Italian provinces was de facto cancelled. It was a vast area that comprised a continuous stretch of territory along the northern and northeastern borders of Italy. Although there was no formal act of annexation, this large part of the country was governed by the Third Reich's regional authorities, thus in practice suspending Italian sovereignty. Within this area German occupation authorities ran the military administration and – with the help of collaborationist local authorities – the civil administration as well. Elsewhere in Italy the Germans were in charge of military matters, but the civil service remained the responsibility of Mussolini's new Fascist government.[5]

On September 8, 1943, when the armistice signed between Italy and the Allies was made public, German armed forces immediately began their occupation of the country. On September 10, Hitler decreed that Italy was to be split up into so-called "occupied territory" and "operation zones." The operation zones thus created consisted of the Operationszone Alpenvorland comprising the provinces of Bolzano, Trento, and Belluno, and the Operationszone Adriatisches Küstenland consisting of the provinces of Udine, Trieste, Gorizia, Pola (Pula), Fiume (Rijeka), and Lubiana (Ljubljana). Lubiana had been annexed to the Kingdom of Italy in 1941, following the occupation of Yugoslavia.[6]

These were predominantly mixed-language areas. They included a German-language group in the province of Bolzano and both a Slovene and a Croatian population in the Eastern areas. Ethnic strife had considerably intensified due to the harshly repressive policy pursued by the Fascist government toward these minorities.[7]

The supreme political authority in both zones was invested in the local governors (*Gauleiter*) of the two adjoining regions of the Third Reich. Franz Hofer, the local governor of Tyrol and Vorarlberg, was named supreme commissioner (*Oberster Kommissar*) of the Alpenvorland. The Adriatisches Küstenland was placed under the authority of Friedrich Rainer, the governor of Carinthia. Both supreme commissioners were political authorities, independent both of the military command and of the government of Mussolini's Italian Social Republic (RSI). They were appointed by Hitler, were accountable to him directly,[8] and were "hierarchically subordinate to the Reichs's centre of political power."[9]

Rainer and Hofer arrogated to themselves full authority in all matters concerning Jewish life and property. Orders issued by the RSI government were ignored in both operation zones, apart from a very few exceptions. Police Order no. 5, issued on November 30, 1943, by the interior minister, which ruled that Jews in all of Italy were to be taken into custody and detained in concentration camps, was never put into effect. Neither was the Duce's edict of January 4, 1944, no. 2, *New Directives Concerning the Property Owned by Citizens of the Jewish Race,* which decreed the confiscation – that is to say the definitive seizure in favor of the Italian state – of all personal and real property of Jews.[10]

Elsewhere in Italy, Germans and Italians alike captured Jews from 1943 to 1945. In the two operation zones, on the other hand, German occupation forces alone decided and organized the arrests and the spoliation of Jewish property; they could, however, rely also on the help of local collaborators. The persecution, although equally tragic, followed therefore in these territories a different pattern as to timing and manner of execution.[11]

The Jews in the Operationszone Alpenvorland

The Jewish presence in this part of Italy had a history and traits of its own. In the Alpenvorland the largest group of Jews was to be found in South Tyrol (i.e., the province of Bolzano) and especially in Merano, not far from Bolzano itself. Merano was and is a town famous all over Europe as a health and tourist resort, which had – and still has – a Jewish community. The first Jews had settled in Merano fairly recently, in about the middle of the nineteenth century. About the turn of the century it had witnessed a presence of Jewish tourists, mainly from central and eastern Europe. After 1933, many refugees from Hitler's Third Reich chose this town for their exile: they were attracted both by the presence of people of their own faith and by a linguistic affinity with the local population, which spoke mostly German. In August 1938 a special census, aimed exclusively at Jews, had been carried out in all of Italy: at that time over 900 Jews, most of them foreigners, had been counted in Merano alone. The anti-Jewish laws passed from 1938 on, however, had caused the number of Jews present in the entire province to drop sharply.[12]

The first arrests of Jews in South Tyrol occurred on September 9, 1943: they were the very first ever to take place in Italy. These arrests were, however, few and limited to the province's capital, Bolzano, and to one nearby village: the order concerning the capture of all so-called "pure Jews" (*Volljuden*) – applicable only to this province – was issued a little later, on September 12. Four days later, twenty-two Jews, mostly old or sick persons, were rounded up in Merano. They were detained for hours in a building where they received neither food nor water and were deported that same evening to the transit camp at Reichenau, in Austrian territory. Some died in that camp; those who survived were deported to Auschwitz some months later, probably in March 1944.

In Merano the capture of Jews was carried out largely by local people belonging to a special police unit called the Security and Order Service (Sicherheits-und

Ordnungsdienst), which operated in the entire province. This unit had been assembled even before the Alpenvorland had come into existence and was later placed under the command of the Ordnungspolizei in Bolzano. To a large extent, the local population was actively involved in the arrest of Jews everywhere in the province. Until the end of the First World War, South Tyrol had been part of the Hapsburg empire: hostility toward Jews and fear of "others" were a long and well-established tradition in this land. The usual stereotypes, baseless accusations, and anti-Jewish prejudice had been nurtured for centuries by traditional Roman Catholic anti-Judaism and more recently by modern political anti-Semitism. At the beginning of the 1930s, a clandestine Nazi organization had been set up in South Tyrol: it had won ample support among the population and contributed greatly to the spreading of Nazi ideology.[13]

Forty-two Jews were deported from South Tyrol between 1943 and 1945. In the other two provinces of the Alpenvorland the captures began in October–November 1943 with over fifty victims. Riccardo Löwy, quoted at the beginning of this chapter, was among them. All the people thus arrested were presumably detained in the national concentration camp at Fossoli near Modena, which was used for this purpose from December 1943 to August 1944. From Fossoli the Jews arrested in the Alpenvorland were then deported to Auschwitz.[14]

Gino Tedeschi from Verona was sixty-nine when he was arrested on May 2, 1944, in a small town in the province of Trento. The following month he was interned at the Fossoli concentration camp. A few days before being deported to Auschwitz, from where he would never return,[15] he wrote the following to his family: "After being here for three weeks we have now been informed that on Monday we leave for Germany. I am well, and am full of courage and hope of seeing again all my dear friends. The Lord be with us."[16]

The Transit Camp in Bolzano

Beginning in July 1944, a police transit camp functioned in the outskirts of Bolzano (Pol.[izeiliches] Durchgangslager Bozen). Presumably, it had already been used as a place of detention in the past. Partisan actions and the withdrawal of the front had made the camp at Fossoli less secure and the departure of transports for the camps of the Third Reich increasingly uncertain. Wilhelm Harster, chief of the Sicherheitspolizei-Sicherheitsdienst in Verona, decided therefore to move the camp to a safer location. The camp at Bolzano was a continuation of the one at Fossoli; the commandant, SS-Untersturmführer Karl Titho, his deputy, SS-Hauptsturmführer Hans Haage, and almost all the guards were the same in both camps.

The persons imprisoned in the camp at Bolzano included members of the Resistance, Jews, soldiers, deserters, and hostages. Prison life was grim: the precarious sanitary conditions, the harsh winter climate, the scarcity of food, and the constant fear made daily life an ordeal; the use of violence, moreover, was extremely frequent. Fourteen Jews died in the camp. Giulia Fano, a woman over seventy, was subjected to an ice-cold shower and then locked up without food or water in the camp's jail, where she died.

In Fossoli, Jewish prisoners were allowed to keep their personal clothes; in Bolzano all the prisoners had to wear uniforms with different badges marking the various groups: Jews wore a yellow triangle. Within the camp Jewish women and children were lodged together with other women prisoners, whereas the men were locked up in a separate hut. Almost all the prisoners were coerced into working: with the exception of internees who were ill or considered dangerous and therefore held in the camp's jail, all prisoners were subjected to various types of forced labor, both inside and outside the camp. Internees working outside the camp were grouped into gangs under strict surveillance and sent into town to clear the streets from rubble, repair railway tracks damaged by bombings, set off unexploded mines, pick apples, and so on. Women were employed instead to clean barracks, hospitals, or living quarters or in the kitchen. Several internees worked in a ball-bearing factory.

Bolzano was the only camp in Italy to have satellite camps, all located within the province.[17] It was an internment and transit camp: almost all prisoners spent some time there waiting for deportation. As the relevant documents have been mostly destroyed, one can no longer ascertain exactly how many prisoners passed through the Bolzano camp: 11,116 at the very least, but the number was certainly higher. Over 200 Jews left Bolzano for the concentration and extermination camps of the Third Reich: their final destination would be Auschwitz, Ravensbrück, or Flossenbürg; they had all been arrested in Northern Italy.

The remaining prisoners were liberated and were able to leave the camp between the end of April and the beginning of May 1945.[18]

The Jews in the Operationszone Adriatisches Küstenland

The number of Jews living in the Adriatisches Küstenland varied greatly from one province to the other. In some towns it was decidedly large even in proportion to the prevalently Roman Catholic society. In October 1938, the first partial results of the census of Jews taken in Italy in August were made public: according to the returns, the province of Trieste, where 6,085 Jews had been counted, had the third highest number of Jews; the province of Fiume, with 1,782, was ninth.[19]

Trieste had one of the most important Jewish communities in Italy. Jews had begun to settle in Trieste in large numbers in the eighteenth century, when they were attracted by the economic and social prospects offered by a rapidly expanding center of trade. The Jews' contribution to the economic, political, and cultural advancement of the town had been substantial. Decidedly middle class, the Jews of Trieste were well integrated in the local society and had been hit particularly hard by the anti-Jewish laws. The 1940s had seen from the very onset a marked increase in anti-Semitism. There had been threats and physical attacks against people, anti-Semitic graffiti, and shops belonging to Jews had been damaged, plundered, and in some cases destroyed; in July 1942 the town's synagogue had been pillaged.[20]

In Trieste and in Fiume, as in other towns of the Küstenland, there had been a sizeable presence of foreign Jews; their number, however, had declined sharply after 1938.[21] From 1943 to 1945, Jews in this operation zone were systematically hunted down. There were arrests on a massive scale. In all of German-occupied Italy, Trieste was second only to Rome in the number of deportees and Fiume the eighth. In all, the Germans deported 554 Jews from Trieste and 225 from Fiume.[22]

In Trieste the first great roundup took place on October 9, 1943, the day of Yom Kippur. By the end of January 1944 the town could already claim to be basically *judenfrei*. The arrests of patients in hospitals and in homes for the aged were carried out in a particularly brutal manner. On a freezing January evening in 1944, for instance, the approximately sixty-five inmates of a home for the elderly and invalid, the Pia Casa Gentilomo, were driven out of the building with rifle-butts, to be imprisoned in the camp in the Risiera di San Sabba and then deported to Auschwitz.[23]

The bishop of Trieste, Antonio Santin, wrote to the deputy *Gauleiter* Ferdinand Wolsegger and to the prefect of Trieste, Bruno Coceani, protesting against the treatment meted out to Jews. He expressed, among other things, the outrage and distress felt by the entire population at the fate of the Jews.[24] During Mass in Trieste's basilica, St. Giusto, Bishop Santin once publicly pleaded for humanity and mercy "in the name of Christ, also for the sons and daughters of the people out of whose womb He was born a man, and among whom He lived and died."[25]

Jews were captured also in the other provinces of the Adriatisches Küstenland: thirty-nine Jews were arrested in Udine, thirty-four in Gorizia, and seven in Pola.

The arrests were carried out at different times. In Gorizia they took place mostly in November 1943; in Udine they stretched from January to June of the following year; the few arrests in Pola took place between October 1943 and September 1944; while in Fiume they were mostly carried out between February and June 1944.[26]

The arrests were mostly the work of a special police unit called Abteilung R (Section R) or Aktion R. This operational unit was formed by three different sections stationed in various towns of the Adriatisches Küstenland: R I in Trieste, R II in Fiume, and R III in Udine, while one unit was also in action outside the operation zone, near Venice. The men of the Abteilung R had been previously employed in Poland in the Aktion Reinhardt, an operation aimed at exterminating Jews and plundering Jewish property in the territory that German authorities had renamed *Generalgouvernement*. Several men of the Abteilung R had also taken part in Nazi Germany's notorious euthanasia program.[27]

In the Küstenland, this police unit was headed by SS-Gruppenführer and Generalleutnant Odilo Globocnik. As Höherer SS- und Polizeiführer (higher police and SS-chief) he was the chief of all police forces in the area, with the exception of the Lubiana province. Globocnik, like Rainer, was a prominent Austrian member of the Nazi leadership. He had arrived in Trieste from Poland, where he had been in charge of the Aktion Reinhard and had established the extermination camps at Bełżec, Sobibor, and Treblinka. He had also set up the camp of Majdanek on the outskirts of Lublin for the exploitation of forced labor and the physical annihilation of prisoners. Globocnik and the ninety-two men of Aktion Reinhard moved to Trieste as early as September 1943. SS-Sturmbannführer Christian Wirth, formerly commandant in Bełżec and then inspector in all three camps of the Aktion Reinhard – Bełżec, Sobibor and Treblinka – was put in charge of the Abteilung R.[28] The men who carried out the arrests of Jews and robbed them of their property in this operation zone were therefore specialists: they could boast a solid experience in the extermination of Jews. The men of the Abteilung R were also employed in the repression of the partisan movement, which was particularly active in the area.[29]

The Camp of the Risiera di San Sabba in Trieste

The Jews arrested in the various towns and villages of the Küstenland were all taken to Trieste. Until January 1944 they were held in the local prison and subsequently in the police detention camp (*Polizeihaftlager*) of the Risiera di San Sabba. Located in a working-class neighborhood, on the immediate outskirts of the town, this "urban camp" served several purposes. First, it was a collection and transit camp for partisans and for Jews destined for deportation, while also functioning as a place of detention for opponents of Nazism. Second, the camp held hostages while functioning as a center for eliminating partisans and people involved in the Resistance. The Risiera was the only camp in all of Western Europe that had a crematorium. Although rudimental, it still served its purpose and had been designed by Erwin Lambert, the same person who had built the death installations at Treblinka. It was used to eliminate the bodies of prisoners and also of partisans killed outside the camp.[30]

Risiera's police detention camp was set up in the autumn of 1943 and was in use until the end of the war. It was run by the men of the Abteilung R and also served as a storeroom for personal property plundered from Jews.[31] The building complex, a former factory for the polishing of rice, was not very large; the prisoners were therefore in close and constant contact with its horrors: executions, tortures, acts of violence, questionings, and beatings.[32] As Giulia Belleli of Trieste, who was deported to Auschwitz in July 1944, testified, "In the Risiera I witnessed some horrid, very horrid things."[33]

The total number of people killed and cremated in the Risiera, only some of whom have been identified, remains uncertain. According to some sources, 2,000 died at the very least. However, some scholars suggest that the number may have been considerably higher.[34] They were mostly partisans and political opponents, but also Jews, hostages, and civilians caught during roundups. The methods of execution varied. Most victims were gassed with exhaust fumes or were hit on the back of the head with a blunt instrument; death by shooting was less frequent. Both individual and mass murders took place at night.[35] Marta Ascoli, a Jewish woman from Trieste who was taken to the Risiera in March 1944 and then deported to Auschwitz,[36] recalled how "at night we could hear screams and moans, but they were drowned by the dogs' barking and by loud music blasting from the loudspeakers."[37] The bodies were cremated in the oven while the ashes and remains were collected in bags and thrown into the sea.[38] Approximately thirty Jews were killed in this camp, some of whom came from San Clemente, Venice's psychiatric hospital. They were murdered because the journey to Auschwitz would have been too much for them.[39]

Jews at the Risiera camp were subject to particularly harsh treatment. They were deprived of all their belongings, locked in vast rooms in which the men were separated from the women, and forced to do various types of work while they awaited deportation, including cleaning, loading and unloading goods, as well as acting as porters, cooks, tailors, and cobblers. Women were employed for cleaning, doing the laundry, or arranging the property robbed from Jews. As in the *Durchgangslager* in Bolzano, prisoners who were skilled craftsmen or whose work was considered essential for the camp's functioning were exempted from deportation. In both camps, these privileged prisoners were lodged separately.[40]

Beginning in January 1944, Risiera served as a transit camp for Jews arrested in the Adriatisches Küstenland. Jews captured in some adjoining areas were also detained there. After the camp at Fossoli was closed down, for instance, several persons who had been arrested in Padua and Venice were taken to the Risiera. In all, 1,197 Jews were deported from the jail in Trieste and from the Risiera di San Sabba. The first transport left Trieste for Auschwitz on December 7, 1943 and the last one in February 1945 for Bergen Belsen. The town would be liberated a little over two months later.[41]

The Risiera prisoners who remained in the camp, among whom were some Jews, were liberated on the night of April 29–30, 1945, when the Nazis, who by now were in full flight, blew up the crematorium with dynamite.[42]

Plunder of Jewish Property

Anti-Jewish persecution always went hand in hand with the plundering of Jewish property. The Republic of Salò's main order concerning Jewish property was the Duce's edict of January 4, 1944. As previously discussed, it decreed the confiscation of all personal and real property belonging to Jews. Henceforth, Jews could no longer own houses, land, bank deposits, stocks, or bonds. They could not even own clothes, furniture, or things of daily use. The chiefs of provinces (who under the Republic of Salò had taken the place of prefects, the highest civil administrative officials of each province) had a central role in implementing these measures, as they were empowered to issue the single confiscation orders. There were also instances in various parts of Italy in which Jewish property was stolen, robbed, or looted.[43]

The orders issued by the Republic of Salò on the matter of Jewish property were not enforced, apart from a very few exceptions, in either operation zone. Rather, the spoliation was decided and conducted by German occupation authorities and offices belonging to the supreme commissariat – its Finanzabteilung (division for financial affairs), to be exact – took over the administration of Jewish property. For this activity as well, Germans could rely on the help of local collaborators.[44]

Along with the "official" despoliation, if one may call it so, went the unofficial purloining and misappropriation of Jewish property. A Jew from Merano deposited some valuables with a person he trusted, who then did not return them.[45] Commenting on the episode, he later wrote: "At that time, I entrusted my belongings to just an acquaintance. I had no kind of safeguard because of the racist persecution."[46]

According to Arianna Szorèny, who was arrested with her family in June 1944, the robberies began at the moment of capture or in the places of detention.[47] "At six in the morning," she wrote, "about thirty brutes of the SS ... pushed all nine of us onto a lorry ... after taking everything away from us at the SS headquarters in Udine. On the evening of the 16th of June 1944 they brought us to the Risiera in Trieste."[48] Jews captured in Merano were robbed of all valuables they carried with them within hours from their arrest.[49]

In the Küstenland the despoliation was mostly the work of the Abteilung R men, the very same unit that carried out the arrests. The authority in charge of operations was the Höherer SS- und Polizeiführer Globocnick. In Trieste the houses in which the Jews had lived were plundered and appropriated for various uses. Clearing out the apartments assumed such ample proportions as to be actually termed Operation Furniture (*Möbel Aktion*). The Germans either sold furnishings to civilians or used them themselves. Bank deposits were collected in an account opened in the name of Supreme Commissioner Rainer; strongboxes were forced open. The synagogue of Trieste was used as a storeroom for books plundered in various towns of the area. All valuables (jewels, gold, precious books, and paintings) looted in the Adriatisches Küstenland were taken across the border to Vienna and Carinthia.[50] In Merano, in the Alpenvorland, the local police that carried out the arrests, the Sicherheits- und Ordnungsdienst, also had a relevant role in the plundering and administration of Jewish propriety. Here, as elsewhere, the houses belonging to Jews were looted and all bank deposits were transferred to a bank account opened in the name of the supreme commissioner. Many items were rifled, sold to private citizens, or given to people whose property had been bombed.[51] As Giulio Bermann, a hotel owner in Merano, summed up the situation, "Being Jewish, there was nothing I could do to protect my property."[52]

It is impossible to give total figures for the property stolen from Jews and the losses they suffered. The damage was in any case huge: the spoliation was extensive, systematic, and meticulous. The Jewish communities themselves also saw their property ravaged and plundered. Ritual objects and furnishings were removed from the synagogue and from the premises of the community in Merano and most documents were lost. In the Adriatisches Küstenland the synagogue in Fiume was set on fire in January 1944 and the archives and the library perished in the conflagration. Local shopkeepers used the documents of the Jewish community of Gorizia, some of them ancient, to wrap their wares in.[53]

Reactions of the Republic of Salò to German Policies

How did the Republic of Salò's authorities react to the situation that had arisen in both operation zones? It did in fact protest, but only on the issue of Jewish property, which the Salò government considered as its own. Not being able to confiscate this property, wrote the finance minister in April 1944, would mean a considerable loss to the treasury. Starting on February 10, 1944, the Salò government's foreign ministry sent several notes to the German embassy, mainly on the subject of the despoliation carried out in the Adriatisches Küstenland. These notes basically requested that Fascist laws should be in force in the operation zones as well. The reply came after several months – on September 16, 1944 – and stressed that the supreme commissioner had "exclusive" (*ausschliesslich*) authority on legal matters. Italy then suggested an agreement on the implementation in the Küstenland of the decree concerning the confiscation of Jewish property. This suggestion met with only a vague reply. All steps taken by the Republic of Salò, in short, were of no avail. There was no reaction or protest, so far as we know, concerning the arrests of Jews in both operation zones.[54]

In the Aftermath of Liberation

For the Jews in those territories, as elsewhere, the end of the war meant a return to normal life, the end of persecution and fear, and the joy of being alive and free. At the same time it brought the grief for missing relatives and friends. One had to cope with trauma and with the need to rebuild one's life, as well as with dreams and hopes that would often prove hard to fulfill. Many had to face practical problems and financial losses. Emigration and deportation had considerably thinned the ranks of the Jewish communities.[55]

When Anna Szorèny was liberated in Bergen Belsen in April 1945, she was only twelve. On her return to Italy she was admitted to an orphanage.[56] This is her testimony:

> On the first floor there was a window looking out towards the mountains. I spent hours behind those glass panes, staring at the mountains, and heard my family marching. . . . I imagined them exhausted and freezing in the snow, but still they walked on. One day they would arrive.[57]

They never did. At Auschwitz she had lost her mother, her father, and five brothers.[58]

Translated from the Italian by Loredana M. Melissari

NOTES

1. Cinzia Villani, *Ebrei fra leggi razziste e deportazioni nelle province di Bolzano, Trento e Belluno* (Trento: Società di studi trentini di scienze storiche, 1996), 185–6, 206–7; Maria Luisa Crosina, *Le storie ritrovate. Ebrei nella provincia di Trento 1938–1945* (Trento: Collana di pubblicazioni del Museo storico in Trento, 1995), 150, 194–5, 196–8, 213–14, where a different date is given for the arrests. I wish to thank Liliana Picciotto, Michele Sarfatti, and Stefano Veneri for their invaluable help.

2. Villani, *Ebrei*, 186.

3. Private archives of Giorgio Jellici (Erlangen, Germany), letter written by Riccardo Löwy to Carlo Jellici, January 21, 1944.

4. Villani, *Ebrei*, 186, 206–7; Crosina, *Le stone ritrovate*, 151, 194–5, 196–8, 213–14.

5. Enzo Collotti, "La politica culturale e delle nazionalità del Terzo Reich nell'*Adriatisches Küstenland*," in *L'Europa nazista. Il progetto di un nuovo ordine europeo (1939–1945)*, E. Collotti, ed. (Florence: Giunti, 2002), 188–9; Collotti, "L'occupazione tedesca in Italia con particolare riguardo ai compiti delle forze di polizia," in *I campi di concentramenti in Italia. Dall'internamento alla deportazione (1940–1945)*, Costantino Di Sante, ed. (Turin: Angeli, 2001), 251–2; Umberto Corsini, "L'Alpenvorland, necessità militare o disegno politico?" in *Tedeschi, partigiani e popolazioni dell'Alpenvorland (1943–1945)*, Istituto veneto per la storia della resistenza – Annali 1982–83, ed. (Venice: Marsilio Editori, 1984), 23, 26; Michele Sarfatti, *Gli ebrei nell'Italia fascista. Vicende, identità, persecuzione* (Turin: Einaudi, 2000), 233–4.

6. Lutz Klinkhammer, *L'occupazione tedesca in Italia 1943–1945* (Turin: Bollati Boringhieri, 1993), 48, 51–4; Collotti, "L'occupazione tedesca in Italia," in *Dizionario della Resistenza. Storia e geografia della Liberazione*, Enzo Collotti, Renato Sandri, and Frediano Sessi, eds. (Turin: Einaudi, 2000), 1: 43; Collotti, "La politica culturale," 188.

7. Collotti, "Occupazione e guerra totale in Italia 1943–1945," in *Un percorso della memoria. Guida ai luoghi della violenza nazista e fascista in Italia*, Tristano Matta, ed. (Milan: Electa, 1996), 18; Collotti, "L'occupazione tedesca in Italia," 46–7; Collotti, "La politica culturale," 189–90.

8. Klinkhammer, *L'occupazione tedesca in Italia*, 53; Klinkhammer, "Zone d'operazione Prealpi e Litorale Adriatico (Operationszonen Alpenvorland e Adriatisches Küstenland)," in *Dizionario dei fascismi. Personaggi, partiti, culture e istituzioni in Europa dalla Grande Guerra a oggi*, Pierre Milza, Serge Bernstein, Nicola Tranfaglia, and Brunello Mantelli, eds. (Milan: Bompiani, 2002), 682; Corsini, "L'Alpenvorland," 26.

9. Corsini, "L'Alpenvorland," 26.

10. Presidenza del Consiglio dei Ministri, Commissione per la ricostruzione delle vicende che hanno caratterizzato in Italia le attività di acquisizione dei beni dei cittadini ebrei da parte di organismi pubblici e privati, *Rapporto generale* (Rome: Dipartimento per l'informazione e l'editoria, 2001), 90, 96–7, 112–13, 181, 211–12; Silva Bon, *La spoliazione dei beni ebraici. Processi economici di epurazione razziale nel Friuli Venezia Giulia 1938–1945* (Gorizia: Centro isontino di ricerca e documentazione storica e sociale "Leopoldo Gasparini" – Comune di Gradisca d'Isonzo, Assessorato alla cultura, 2001), 55; Villani, "Le spoliazioni dei beni ebraici nell'*Operationszone Alpenvorland*," *Geschichte*

und Region/Storia e regione, XI, no. 1 (2002), 177; Liliana Picciotto, *Il libro della memoria. Gli Ebrei deportati dall'Italia (1943–1945)* (1991; reprint, Milan: Mursia, 2002), 891–2, 941–3.

11. Presidenza del Consiglio, *Rapporto generale*, 90; Sarfatti, *Gli ebrei nell'Italia fascista*, 236; Villani, *Ebrei*, 168; Bon, *Gli ebrei a Trieste 1930–1945. Identità, persecuzione, risposte* (Gorizia: Istituto regionale per la storia del movimento di liberazione nel Friuli-Venezia Giulia – Libreria Editrice Goriziana, 2000), 317–18.

12. Villani, "Antisemitismo ed ebraismo in Alto Adige. La Comunità israelitica di Merano," *La Rassegna mensile di Israel*, vol. LV (1989), 112–13; Federico Steinhaus, "La Comunità ebraica di Merano: frammenti di storia," in *Contributi per una storia della Comunità israelitica di Merano – Beiträge zu einer Geschichte der jüdischen Kultusgemeinde von Meran*, Karl Heinz Burmeister and Federico Steinhaus, eds. (Merano: Centro culturale "Anna Frank," 1987), 9–11; Rosanna Pruccoli, *Merano 1899. Suggestioni* (Mantova: Corraini Editore – Biblioteca Civica di Merano, 1999), 43–4, 50–1. On Jews in South Tyrol in the 1930s and 1940s, see Villani, *Ebrei*; Steinhaus, *Ebrei/Juden. Gli ebrei dell'Alto Adige negli anni trenta e quaranta* (Florence: Giuntina, 1994).

13. Villani, *Ebrei*, 166–8, 170–6; Villani, "Antisemitismo," 106–8, 111–12; Veronika Mittermair, "Bruchlose Karrieren? Zum Werdegang der Südtiroler Politikerschicht bis zur 'Stunde Null,'" in *Südtirol – Stunde Null? Kriegsende 1945–1946*, Hans Heiss and Gustav Pfeifer, eds. (Innsbruck-Vienna-Munich: Veröffentlichungen des Südtiroler Landesarchivs 10, Studien Verlag, 2000) 175–92; Karl Stuhlpfarrer, *Le Zone d'Operazione Prealpi e Litorale Adriatico 1943–1945* (1969; Italian translation, Gorizia: Edizioni Libreria Adamo, 1970), 114.

14. Villani, *Ebrei*, 191, 200–13; Presidenza del Consiglio, *Rapporto generale*, 179, 179 n. 93, 190; Picciotto, *Il libro della memoria*, 903–4, 914, 928–9, 934–5.

15. Crosina, *Le storie ritrovate*, 87, 93, 218; Villani, *Ebrei*, 191, 204–5.

16. Crosina, *Le storie ritrovate*, 93, 246.

17. On the camp in Bolzano, see *Anche a volerlo raccontare è impossibile. Scritti e testimonianze sul Lager di Bolzano*, Giorgio Mezzalira and Cinzia Villani, eds. (Bolzano: Circolo culturale Associazione nazionale partigiani d'Italia di Bolzano, 1999); Luciano Happacher, *Il Lager di Bolzano* (Trento: Comitato provinciale per il 30° anniversario della Resistenza e della Liberazione 1979); Leopold Steurer, "La deportazione dall'Italia. Bolzano," in Collotti, et al., *Spostamenti di popolazione e deportazioni in Europa 1939–1945* (Bologna: Cappelli, 1987), 417–24; Dario Venegoni, *Uomini, donne e bambini nel lager di Bolzano. Una tragedia italiana in 7809 individuali* (Milan: Associazione culturale Mimesis, 2004); Picciotto, *Il libro della memoria*, 919, 929–32; Villani, "Ebrei, antisemitismoie lager." (forthcoming).

18. Picciotto, *Il libro della memoria*, 31, 60–1; Happacher, *Il Lager di Bolzano*, 47.

19. Renzo De Felice, *Storia degli ebrei italiani sotto il fascismo* (Turin: Einaudi, 1993), 10; Sarfatti, *Gli ebrei nell'Italia fascista*, 28–29; Sarfatti, *Le leggi antiebraiche spiegate agli italiani di oggi* (Turin: Einaudi, 2002), 11–12.

20. Tullia Catalan, *La comunità ebraica di Trieste (1781–1914). Politica, società e cultura* (Trieste: Lint, 2000), 59–62; Catalan, "Presenza sociale ed economica degli ebrei nella Trieste asburgica tra Settecento e primo Novecento," in *Storia economica e sociale*

di Trieste. La città dei gruppi 1719–1919, Roberto Finzi and Giovanni Panjek, eds. (Trieste: Lint, 2001), 487–90, 502–11; Angelo Ara, "Gli ebrei a Trieste, 1850–1918," *Rivista storica italiana*, no. 1 (1990), 58–9; Anna Millo, *Storia di una borghesia. La famiglia Vivante a Trieste dall'emporio alla guerra mondiale* (Gorizia: Istituto regionale per la storia del movimento di liberazione nel Friuli-Venezia Giulia – Libreria Editrice Goriziana, 1998), 21–4; Silva Bon, "La spoliazione dei beni ebraici negli anni delle leggi razziali. Il caso Nord-Est," *Clio*, no. 4 (2001), 752; Bon, "I 'diversi': la persecuzione antiebraica," in *Friuli e Venezia Giulia. Storia del '900*, Istituto regionale per la storia del movimento di liberazione nel Friuli-Venezia Giulia, ed. (Gorizia: Libreria Editrice Goriziana, 1997), 310, 312–14; Bon, *Gli ebrei*, 203–5, 214–19, 227–31, 271–9; Raoul Pupo, *Guerra e dopoguerra al confine orientale d'Italia (1938–1956)* (Udine: Del Bianco Editore, 1999), 22–3.

21. Bon, "La spoliazione," 14–15; Bon, "Le comunità ebraiche dell'ex provincia del Carnaro 1938–1945, dai documenti dell'Archivio di Stato di Fiume," *La Rassegna mensile di Israel*, vol. LXVII, no. 3 (2001), 39–40; Adonella Cedarmas, *La Comunità israelitica di Gorizia (1900–1945)* (Udine: Istituto friulano per il movimento di liberazione, 1999), 133–4.

22. Picciotto, *Il libro della memoria*, 30.

23. Bon, *Gli ebrei*, 321–4, 328; Picciotto, *Il libro della memoria*, 938–939; Susan Zuccotti, *Il Vaticano e l'Olocausto in Italia* (2000; Italian translation, Milan: Bruno Mondadori, 2001), 314–15.

24. Zuccotti, *Il Vaticano*, 318–19, 322–3; Picciotto, *Il libro della memoria*, 938; Bon, *Gli ebrei*, 322–3.

25. Zuccotti, *Il Vaticano*, 318–19. The quotation is on p. 319. During the German occupation, Carlo Morpurgo, the secretary of the Jewish Community in Trieste, entrusted to Bishop Santin the most ancient and important documents of the Community; Morpurgo was arrested on January 20, 1944, and deported to Auschwitz, where he died; Bon, *Gli ebrei*, 326; Picciotto, *Il libro della memoria*, 455.

26. The data have been derived from the often mentioned work by Liliana Picciotto; one should note that in several instances the date of arrest is unknown. As for the province of Gorizia, see Cedarmas, *La Comunità israelitica*, 212–13; for the total number of Jews captured in the various provinces of the Adriatisches Küstenland, see Picciotto, *Il libro della memoria*, 30.

27. Picciotto, *Il libro della memoria*, 861–2, 932–3; Galliano Fogar, "L'occupazione nazista del Litorale Adriatico e lo sterminio della Risiera," in *San Sabba. Istruttoria e processo per il Lager della Risiera*, Adolfo Scalpelli, ed. (1988; reprint, Trieste: Associazione nazionale ex deportati politici nei campi di sterminio nazisti – Lint, 1995), 1: 7–30; August Walzl, *Gli ebrei sotto la dominazione nazista. Carinzia Slovenia Friuli-Venezia Giulia* (1987; Italian translation, Udine: Istituto friulano per la storia del movimento di liberazione, 1991), 250–1.

28. Picciotto, *Il libro della memoria*, 861–2, 933; Fogar, "L'occupazione nazista," 7–8; Raul Hilberg, *La distruzione degli ebrei d'Europa* (1961; Italian translation, Turin: Einaudi, 1995), 967–8, 970; *Topografia del Terrore. Gestapo, SS e Reichssicherheitshauptamt sull'area "Prinz Albrecht" a Berlino*, Reinhard Rürup, ed. (1987; Italian translation,

Berlino: Arenhövel, 1994), 166; Collotti, *Il Litorale Adriatico nel nuovo Ordine Europeo 1943–1945* (Milan: Vangelista editore, 1974), 142.

29. Matta, "La Risiera di San Sabba," in *Un percorso*, Matta, ed., 130; Collotti, *Il Litorale*, 51–2; Pupo, *Guerra e dopoguerra*, 46–7.

30. Picciotto, *Il libro della memoria*, 56, 933–7; Matta, "La Risiera," 126–7; Fogar, "L'occupazione nazistan," 15–16, 66; Giuseppe Mayda, *Storia della deportazione dall'Italia 1943–1945. Militari, ebrei e politici nei lager del Terzo Reich* (Turin: Bollati Boringhieri, 2002), 81–2; Fogar, "La Risiera di San Sabba a Trieste," in Collotti and others, *Spostamenti*, 456.

31. Matta, "La Risiera," 126, 128; Picciotto, *Il libro della memoria*, 933; Fogar, "L'occupazione nazista," 83.

32. Fogar, "L'occupazione nazista," 67–8; Fogar, "La Risiera," 453.

33. Marco Coslovich, *I percorsi della sopravvivenza. Storia e memoria della deportazione dall'Adriatisches Küstenland* (Milan: Mursia, 1994), 332; Picciotto, *Il libro della memoria*, 140.

34. In 1976 a trial was held against some members of the Abteilung R who were charged with multiple and continuing wilfull murder attended by aggravating circumstances for their crimes in the Risiera. In the end Joseph Oberhauser, last commandant of the camp and the only accused to be still alive, was sentenced in absentia to lifelong imprisonment. Giovanni Heimi Wachsberger, arrested in Fiume on April 15, 1944, together with his mother, had remained in the Risiera until the camp was closed. According to his testimony, the victims in the Risiera numbered "at least 2,000 persons," and this figure is quoted also in the verdict. See Fogar, "La Risiera," 460, 469; Fogar, "L'occupazione nazista," 84. The verdict, delivered on April 29, 1976, is printed in full in Scalpelli, *San Sabba*, 2: 271–324; the quotation from the verdict is on p. 309. The judgment delivered at the end of the instruction phase, on the other hand, mentions a total of 2,000 non-Jewish dead; this judgement is printed in full in Scalpelli, *San Sabba*, 2: 140–235. The part quoted here is on p. 165. According to a merely theoretical estimate by writer Ferruccio Fölkel, himself from Trieste, the prisoners cremated in the camp may have numbered 5,000; some Yugoslav sources also uphold an estimate of 4,000–5,000 cremated prisoners. The historian Tristano Matta writes of 3,000–4,000 persons killed and cremated. See Picciotto, *Il libro della memoria*, 937; Fogar, "L'occupazione nazista," 84; Matta, "La Risiera," 127.

35. Fogar, "L'occupazione nazista," 70; Fogar, "La Risiera," 455–6; Matta, "La Risiera," 128.

36. Marta Ascoli, *Auschwitz è di tutti* (1999; reprint, Trieste: Lint, 1998), 10–11; Picciotto, *Il libro della memoria*, 119.

37. Ascoli, *Auschwitz è di tutti*, 14.

38. Picciotto, *Il libro della memoria*, 936–7; Matta, "La Risiera," 128.

39. Picciotto, *Il libro della memoria*, 824. See also Angelo Lallo and Lorenzo Toresini, *Psichiatria e Nazismo. La deportazione ebraica dagli ospedali psichiatrici di Venezia nell'ottobre 1944* (Portogruaro (Venice): Nuova dimensione, 2001).

40. Scalpelli, *San Sabba*, 2: 7, 68–69; Ascoli, *Auschwitz è di tutti*, 12; Bon, *Gli ebrei*, 320; Picciotto, *Il libro della memoria*, 936; Mezzalira and Villani, *Anche a volerio raccontare*, 14.

41. Picciotto, *Il libro della memoria*, 56, 62–5; 937–8; Fogar, *Trieste in guerra 1940–1945. Società e Resistenza* (Trieste: Istituto regionale per la storia del movimento di liberazione nel Friuli-Venezia Giulia, 1999) 237, 241–4.

42. Fogar, "La Risiera," 466–7; Fogar, "L'occupazione nazista," 90–2.

43. Sarfatti, *Gli ebrei nell'Italia fascista*, 248–50; Presidenza del Consiglio, *Rapporto generale*, 96–7, 115–42; Claudio Pavone, "Prefazione," in Dianella Gagliani, *Brigate nere. Mussolini e la militarizzazione del Partito fascista repubblicano* (Turin: Bollati Boringhieri, 1999), XII–XIII; Gagliani, *Brigate nere*, 32.

44. Villani, "Le spoliazioni," 177–8; Bon, *Gli ebrei*, 334, 340; Bon, *La spoliazione*, 55, 66–7; Fogar, "L'occupazione nazista," 34, 44–5; Presidenza del Consiglio, *Rapporto generale*, 181, 211–12; Cedarmas, *La Comunita israelitica*, 228–9.

45. Presidenza del Consiglio, *Rapporto generale*, 196.

46. Presidenza del Consiglio, *Rapporto generale*, 196; Archivio di Stato di Bolzano (ASBz), *Intendenza di finanza, Servizio danni di guerra*, b. 245, fasc. "B.G. c.c.5779," s.fasc. "c.c. 5779/9000 Mobili di abitazione," request for war damages compensation submitted on September 10, 1945, and communication dated July 23, 1945.

47. Picciotto, *Il libro della memoria*, 503, 613–14; Luigi Raimondi Cominesi, "'Dossier Szörényi.' Olocausto di una famiglia," *Storia contemporanea in Friuli 19* (1988), 153–5.

48. Presidenza del Consiglio, *Rapporto generale*, 140.

49. Archivio della Comunità ebraica di Merano (ACEM), Appunti circa gli ebrei di Merano in relazione alla occupazione tedesca, undated, printed almost in full in Steinhaus, *Ebrei/Juden*, 92–99.

50. Bundesarchiv Berlin, *R 83 Adriatisches Küstenland*, Bd. 1, Report sent to Franz Zojer, director of the Supreme Commissioner's Finanabteilung, February 26, 1945; Presidenza del Consiglio, *Rapporto generale*, 108–11, 213, 219, 224, 228; Bon, *Gli ebrei*, 333–6.

51. Presidenza del Consiglio, *Rapporto generale*, 182, 186–7, 195; ACEM, Appunti circa gli ebrei di Merano in relazione all'occupazione tedesca, undated.

52. ASBz, *Intendenza di finanza, Servizio danni di guerra*, b. 245, fasc. "B.G. c.c.5779," s.fasc. "c.c.5779/9000 Mobili di abitazione," request for war damages compensation submitted on September 10, 1945, and communication dated July 23, 1945.

53. Steinhaus, *Ebrei/Juden*, 115; Presidenza del Consiglio, *Rapporto generale*, 162, 183; Pier Cesare Ioly Zorattini, "Prefazione," in Cedarmas, *La Comunità israelitica*, 10; Sarfatti *Gli ebrei nell'Italia fascista*, 270; Sarfatti, "Gli Archivi e le Biblioteche delle Comunità Ebraiche Italiane durante la persecuzione antiebraica fascista e nazista," paper delivered at the Vilnius International Forum on Holocaust Era Looted Cultural Assets (October 3–5, 2000), *La Rassegna mensile di Israel*, vol. LXVI, no. 2 (2000), 163; "La relazione del Presidente della Comunità Israelitica di Fiume, Arminio Klein, alla 'Commissione Circondariale per la contestazione dei delitti dell'occupatore e dei suoi complici' in data 10 dicembre 1945," in *Il tributo fiumano all'Olocausto*, texts by Amleto Ballarini, archival research by Neri Drenig and others (Rome: Società di Studi fiumani e Associazione per la cultura fiumana, istriana e dalmata nel Lazio, 1999), 71; Ester Capuzzo, "La fine della Comunità ebraica di Fiume," *Clio*, no. 3 (2000), 595.

54. Presidenza del Consiglio, *Rapporto generale*, 113–14; Sarfatti, *Gli ebrei nell'Italia fascista*, 261; Cominesi, "'Dossier Szörényi'," 176; Picciotto, *Il libro della memoria*, 503, 613–14.

55. Steinhaus, *Ebrei/Juden*, 115–16; ACEM, Appunti circa gli ebrei di Merano in relazione all'occupazione tedesca, undated; Bon, *Gli ebrei*, 328, 353.

56. Picciotto, *Il libro della memoria*, 613, 503; Cominesi, 175–6.

57. Cominesi, "'Dossier Szörényi'," 176.

58. Cominesi, "'Dossier Szörényi'," 176; Picciotto, *Il libro della memoria*, 503, 613–14.

MAP 3. Italy and the two German-controlled Operationszonen.

MAP 4. The two Operationszonen in detail with provincial capitals.

PART FOUR

THE VATICAN AND

THE HOLOCAUST

IN ITALY

14 The Papal Response to Nazi and Fascist Anti-Semitism: From Pius XI to Pius XII

Frank J. Coppa

> It is the task and duty of the Church, the dignity and responsibility of the Chief Shepherd and of his brother Shepherds whom the Holy Ghost has placed to rule the Church of God, that they should point out to mankind the true course to be followed, the eternal divine order in the changing circumstances of the times.[1]

Some two decades ago, when I was commissioned to write a paper on the responses of popes Pius XI (Achille Ratti) and Pius XII (Eugenio Pacelli) to the Nazi and Fascist dictatorships (1922–45), I believed that the two followed similar policies.[2] Ratti and Pacelli adhered to Benedict XV's (1914–22) dictum that it was a Christian's duty to submit to those in authority.[3] At the same time, both favored the conclusion of concordats to ensure Vatican interests and the institutional Church, and neither hesitated to come to terms with authoritarian regimes. Between them they concluded more than fifty such agreements with democracies and dictatorships.[4] The fact that neither proved able to reach an accommodation with the Soviet Union contributed to their overriding opposition to Communism. In the words of one author, Ratti and Pacelli were "of one mind in their hatred and fear of Bolshevism."[5] The two had worked closely for a decade with Pius XI calling upon Eugenio Pacelli, who later assumed the name Pius XII, to serve as his secretary of state in 1930. Five years later he appointed "his favorite Cardinal"[6] as chamberlain of the Church, enlisting him as chief collaborator on German affairs. Pacelli's brother played a key role in negotiating the Lateran Accords (1929) with Mussolini's Italy,[7] and Eugenio had been instrumental in the conclusion of the Reich Concordat of 1933 with Hitler's Germany. Supposedly, Pius XI was grooming Pacelli as his successor.[8] Pius reportedly predicted that Pacelli would make "a splendid Pope."[9] In my earlier article, I concluded that Pius XI had set the stage for the policy of accommodation with the Fascist regimes, which his successor pursued with unfortunate consequences.[10]

Pius XI and Pius XII shared a similar mindset on the Jewish question, which included a suspicious, sometimes arrogant attitude toward the older faith.[11] They both belonged to a pre-Vatican II Church culture that had long pursued an anti-Judaic (though not an anti-Semitic, or racial) course, opposing Jews on a theological rather than a racial basis. To be sure, the distinction was more fluid than many acknowledge, and to a degree the two merged into a broader anti-Jewish movement as clerical anti-Judaism from time to time had recourse to racial-like slurs promoted by anti-Semitism.[12] Still, there were differences between the two. The first was motivated by desire for conversion to achieve religious unity, while the latter aimed for elimination to achieve racial purity. Nonetheless, there is evidence that the Church and its leadership from time to time had recourse not only to negative religious images of the Jews, but also to hostile assessments of Jewish social, cultural, and political life closely identified with anti-Semitism – the term concocted by Wilhelm Marr following German unification. Such broad condemnations were found in the official *Osservatore Romano* and the Jesuit *Civiltà Cattolica*, which had close links to the Vatican. Not surprisingly, an examination of the dispatches of Ratti and Pacelli, when they served as nuncios respectively to Poland and Bavaria, betray the prevailing clerical attitude on Jewish issues.[13]

Despite the widespread anti-Judaism in the Church, which continued well into the twentieth century, the best available evidence[14] indicates that in the 1930s both figures regarded the Nazi mistreatment of the Jews with suspicion and antipathy.[15] Ratti and Pacelli understood that Catholicism could not, and officially did not, condemn Jews on the basis of biology, for that would violate the Church's universal ministry.[16] However, their reactions to anti-Semitism differed, as did their personalities. Ratti was "impulsive and irascible," swift to respond to provocations in strong and direct language.[17] Pacelli, on the other hand, was the consummate diplomat who weighed his words carefully and considered the ramifications of every sentence. This chapter focuses on the different reactions of Pius XI and Pius XII to Fascist and Nazi anti-Semitism.

Pius XI, who did not mince his words, denounced racism and refused to equate it with the anti-Judaism in the Church. In September 1922, he emphasized that "Christian charity extends to all men whatsoever without distinction of race."[18] In 1926, Pius XI did not hesitate to condemn Charles Maurras's allegedly Catholic, royalist, racist, and anti-Semitic *Action Francaise*.[19] Two years later, in

1928, the pope condemned anti-Semitism, when the Holy Office, with his approval, suppressed the Friends of Israel.[20] This organization, which called upon priests to pray for the conversion of Jews and proved sympathetic to Zionism, was formally founded in February 1926 by two friars (Anton van Asseldonck and Laetus Himmelreich) and a Jewish anarchist (Sophie van Leer) who converted to Catholicism. Precisely why it was suppressed is still debated.[21] It is true that in 1929 Pius XI concluded an agreement with Mussolini's Italy,[22] but at the time anti-Semitism was not a feature of the regime.[23] The pope was delighted that God had been restored to Italy and Italy returned to God.[24] However, relations between Mussolini's Italy and the Vatican were often strained.[25] The pope was especially sensitive to Fascist infringement on Catholic Action groups. This led to his encyclical *Non abbiamo bisogno* of June 1931, denouncing Fascist attempts to dominate all citizen organizations, youth groups, and private meetings. Pius XI was not prepared to forfeit either the bodies or the souls of the younger generation to the regime.[26] Subsequently, six bishops of the Cologne church province in March 1931 deemed the errors of National Socialism similar to those of the *Action Francaise* condemned by Pius XI.[27] Ecclesiastical circles in Rome received the news of Hitler's appointment on January 30, 1933 cautiously, avoiding any public statement.[28] In mid-March 1933, the Vatican simply took note of the fact that the Fuehrer had assumed police powers following his electoral victory.[29] The Nazis, hoping to bind the Church to the Reich, assumed the initiative in proposing an agreement between Church and state.[30] In the spring of 1933, Vice-Chancellor Franz von Papen visited Rome and suggested an accord.[31] Initially, Pius XI was not enthusiastic, but reconsidered his position following Nazi harassment of the organizational church.[32] Scandalized by the regime's dismantling of Catholic unions, *Civiltà Cattolica* branded the Nazi system "totalitarianism in action."[33] Determined to preserve Catholic youth organizations in Germany and to safeguard religious and educational freedom, Pius XI sanctioned negotiations.[34] Some charged that the Vatican, lured by the prospect of guarantees for its schools and other institutions, ignored the unfortunate features of the regime including its anti-Semitism. This is still debated.

We know that Vatican ratification of the concordat in September 1933 did not imply sympathy with Hitler's Reich.[35] Father Enrico Rosa, of the Society of Jesus and the editorial board of *Civiltà Cattolica*, denied that the accord legitimized or approved of the Nazi government.[36] On the contrary, the papal secretary of state confessed to the English chargé d'affaires that the Holy See deplored the anti-Semitism of the German government, its violations of human rights, and its reign of terror. He confided that the Vatican signed the accord because it appeared the sole means of preventing the destruction of the Catholic Church and its lay organizations in Germany.[37] Vatican expectations proved illusory as the Nazi government soon showed it would not adhere to the letter or even the spirit of the agreement.

Troubled by Reich developments, Pius XI rejected the Nazi contention that the Jewish question was an internal racial issue rather than a religious one.[38] Like John La Farge, the American Jesuit who had established himself as an authority on race, the pope deemed racism immoral and sinful.[39] He recognized that the glorification of racism presented a frontal challenge to Church teaching and authority. Antagonized by the neo-paganism of the regime, Pius promised a group of visiting German students that he would do all within his means to defend the faith.[40] His motto "Christ's Peace in Christ's Kingdom" revealed his conviction that the Church should be involved in the world, rather than isolated from it. Among other things, Pius XI deplored the Nazi's sterilization law, which directly opposed the doctrines expressed in his 1930 encyclical on Christian marriage.[41] Whether motivated primarily by moral principles or the practical consideration of preserving papal authority, contemporaries were convinced that the Church of Pius XI was the sole institution effectively championing human rights while resisting the Nazification of Germany.[42]

The persecution of the Church in Germany continued throughout most of 1934, and in October the pope again expressed his dissatisfaction to the German ambassador, Diego von Bergen. Bergen warned his government that without some moderating influence, the prospect increased that "the Pope will take disastrous decisions."[43] His analysis proved accurate. Pius XI, who had misgivings about concluding the concordat with Nazi Germany,[44] considered renouncing it, but was restrained by his secretary of state, Pacelli, who feared this would aggravate the position of millions of German Catholics. However, when the Fuehrer commissioned Alfred Rosenberg, author of the anti-Christian and racist *Myth of the Twentieth Century*, to provide philosophical instruction for party members, the Vatican responded by placing his book on the Index of prohibited books. The inclusion of Ernst Bergmann's *German National Church*, which sought to detach Christianity from its Jewish roots, on the Index, revealed that Rome sought to denounce all racist religious thought.[45] Between 1933 and 1936, Pius XI drafted over thirty notes protesting Nazi action toward the Church and its doctrines.

Pius XI's opposition to the doctrine of blood and race was reflected in the critical articles that appeared in *Osservatore Romano* and *Civiltà Cattolica*. One of these articles claimed that the Church had always opposed Jewish persecution.[46] Although it was far from accurate, it reflected the papal desire to disassociate past clerical anti-Judaism with the present pagan anti-Semitism. Meanwhile, *L'Osservatore* warned that a new *Kulturkampf* was a reality.[47] This sentiment was echoed by the German bishops who issued a pastoral reaffirming the Church's hostility to neo-paganism and sterilization.[48] Father Rosa charged that while Hitler condemned Stalin's Russia, Nazism elaborated a theory of racism in conflict with the faith. Rosa complained that by developing this immoral racist ideology, Nazism was in fundamental conflict with the doctrines of the Church.[49]

The triumph of Nazism and the elaboration of its anticlerical and anti-Semitic policies led Pius XI to reconsider his attitude toward *Anschluss* between Germany and Austria, which he had earlier favored.[50] Rome changed its position when it witnessed the policies pursued by Hitler's Germany. As early as June 1933, *Civiltà Cattolica* warned that the Vienna government had to protect itself not only from the onslaught of Bolshevism, but from the subversion of the Austrian Nazis, supported by their brethren in the Reich. *Civiltà Cattolica* praised those in the truncated Habsburg state who wished to preserve an Austria that has as its symbol the Cross of God and no other. In June 1933, Rome concluded a concordat with the Austrian state.[51] Pius was scandalized by the abortive Nazi coup of 1934 in Austria, and his outrage was reflected in a series of articles in the Vatican journal that condemned the Nazis' savage methods. The daily of the Holy See suggested that National Socialism might better be dubbed national terrorism and praised Mussolini for preserving Austrian independence in the face of Nazi aggression.[52]

Pius XI believed the dignity of the Holy See required a denunciation of German outrages, confident that the Church would survive the persecution.[53] Father Rosa, S. J., reflecting papal thought, acknowledged the danger of international communism, but insisted that the Nazi reaction was no less destructive of Christian values.[54] While Nazi strategy differed from the Bolshevist one, the Italian Jesuit wrote, its neo-pagan opposition to Catholic civilization was as insidious as atheistic Communism.[55] Nazism represented the German Socialist reaction against Soviet internationalism and it shared Communism's hatred of Christianity and the Catholic Church, declared another article in the Jesuit journal.[56] The pope concurred with Rosa's assessment.[57] By 1937–8, Pius XI was perceived as one of the few world leaders defending human rights against both Fascism and Nazism.[58]

Pius XI resented Nazi actions and laws that violated church teachings and basic human rights, complaining to the German ambassador that he was "deeply grieved and gravely displeased." Diego Von Bergen reported that Pacelli was upset by the pope's outburst and sought to pacify the German government, but was not prepared to contradict his chief.[59] Following the remilitarization of the

Rhineland, Pius XI confided to the French ambassador, "If you [French] had called forward 200,000 men you would have done an immense service to the entire world."[60] The continued attacks on the Church and its doctrines led Pius XI to speak out despite his secretary of state's restraining influence. In March 1937, he issued the encyclical *Mit brennender Sorge*, which was read from Catholic pulpits in Germany.[61] "With deep anxiety and increasing dismay," Pius wrote, he had witnessed the "progressive oppression of the faithful."[62] Denouncing the racism of the regime, the pope cataloged the articles of faith trampled upon by the Nazis. He concluded by urging the clergy to unmask and refute Nazism's errors whatever their form or disguise.[63] His action earned him respect in the western capitals, but condemnation in Berlin.[64] In June 1937, *Civiltà Cattolica*, which occasionally issued anti-Jewish pronouncements, proclaimed that the Church condemned all forms of anti-Semitism.[65] Its editors refused to recognize any similarity or relationship between clerical anti-Judaism and Nazi anti-Semitism. By the end of the year, Pius deplored anti-Christian developments in Germany no less than those in the Soviet Union.[66]

Relations between the Vatican and the Reich deteriorated during the course of 1938, as Pius condemned Nazi Germany's racist nationalism.[67] The private correspondence between Secretary of State Pacelli and the Nazi government reveals that things were far worse than either the Vatican or Berlin acknowledged.[68] In April 1938, the Sacred Congregation of Seminaries, presided over by Pius XI, condemned the pernicious racism championed by Nazi Germany.[69] The Catholic press deemed it a virtual encyclical against racism![70] In July, Pius XI stressed the absolute incompatibility between this nationalism and Catholicism, charging that the former opposed the spirit of the creed and violated the teachings of the faith.[71] In his view anti-Judaism, which flowed from the Faith for centuries, did not violate Church principles. Pius deplored the extension of anti-Semitism to Austria following the *Anschluss* of 1938, which saddened him both as Pontiff and as an Italian.[72] Not surprisingly, Pius XI repudiated Austrian Cardinal Innitzer and his fellow bishops who rejoiced at the union of Germany and Austria, obviously seeking an accommodation with the Nazis.[73] In April, *Osservatore Romano* made it clear that the bishop's statement did not have the Vatican's support, while Gustav Gundlach on Vatican Radio – Pius was the first pope to use the radio as a means of pastoral communication – denounced their pro-Nazi pastoral letter as inspired by a false political Catholicism. Meanwhile, Cardinal Innitzer was summoned to Rome and lectured by an angry pope.[74]

The pope's public denunciation of racialism worried Pacelli, who sought to prevent a break with the Fascist regimes.[75] Nonetheless, Pius XI was uncomfortable with the racism of the Berlin government. However Pacelli found it difficult if not impossible to silence the pope, who feared that Nazi racism would be adopted by Fascist Italy.[76] The Vatican journal reflected papal sentiments. Confronted by German agitation in Czechoslovakia, *Osservatore Romano* reported that the racial intolerance there could not be compared to the anti-Semitic policies pursued in "some other states." During the May 1938 visit of the Fuehrer to Rome, Pius left for Castel Gandolfo, closed the Vatican Museum that Hitler had hoped to visit, and did not allow any member of the German official party into Vatican City. Discounting Pacelli's call for conciliation, Pius XI lamented that it was out of place to hoist in Rome the emblem of a cross not of Christ.[77]

For reasons one can surmise, but of which one cannot be certain, Pius XI planned to issue an encyclical condemning racism and anti-Semitism without involving his secretary of state. We do know that Pacelli was not included in the pope's discussion with La Farge when he commissioned the encyclical, even though he had been with Pius XI moments before.[78] Indeed, at his accession Pius XII indicated he knew nothing about it.[79] In light of the fact that this encyclical would not only have led to a deterioration in the Vatican's relations with the Axis powers, and probably would have torpedoed the concordats, it was extraordinary that the pope did not inform his secretary of state.

Perhaps the pope feared that Pacelli would oppose the project and try to scuttle it. He had good reason to suppose so, considering his secretary of state's attempts to prevent a diplomatic rupture with the Fascist regimes. On the other hand, Pius XI might not have wanted to implicate his likely successor in a project that might not succeed? If Pacelli participated in the breach, it would tie his hands in seeking a rapprochement with them. Finallly, the pope may have recognized that the issuance of the encyclical would have seriously jeopardized Pacelli's prospect to succeed him, for his secretary of state favored conciliation rather than confrontation with Nazi Germany. Whatever the reason, Pacelli was excluded from this important encounter that resulted in Pius XI commissioning La Farge to draft the antiracist encyclical and was kept in the dark during its composition.

The chronology of events is telling. On May 2, 1938, Hitler began an official seven-day visit to Rome, marking a decisive turn in Fascist Italy's policy on the race issue to the consternation of Pius XI. Shortly thereafter, Mussolini appointed the anti-Semitic Roberto Farinacci as minister of state, and he immediately met with Dr. Walter Gross, head of the racial policy office of the Nazi party.[80] The Vatican feared that the latter provided both inspiration and instruction to the Italians on racial matters. In June 1938, the pope asked to see John La Farge, the author of numerous books and articles denouncing racism. Pacelli left the papal chamber just as the Jesuit arrived and was not briefed on the scope of the meeting.[81]

Once Pacelli left, the pope made it clear that he had read and liked La Farge's *Interracial Justice*, which had been published in 1937.[82] In this work, La Farge denounced the notion of "pure race" as a myth that could not serve as a practical basis for human relationships and an idea the Church could not tolerate. La Farge reminded his readers that the teachings of Christ proclaimed the moral unity of the human race and the Church offered all of mankind salvation. Furthermore, the doctrine of human rights was based upon the spiritual nature of man and therefore could not be taken away by law, social custom, or mores. He added that Christian social philosophy looked upon the deliberate fostering of racial prejudices as a sin. Consequently, it could not be ignored by the faith. La Farge posited that the universal Church, which represented a living union of all mankind, had to combat race prejudice that destroyed the creator's intended relationship of the individual to the rest of humanity.[83] Pius XI approved of La Farge's ideas, which reflected his own thought.[84]

To La Farge's surprise, Pius XI asked him to draft an encyclical for delivery to the universal Church that would demonstrate the incompatibility of Catholicism and racism. The pope, who deemed the enterprise of the utmost importance, swore La Farge to secrecy.[85] Perhaps he was belatedly responding to the earlier plea made to him by Edith Stein, a Jewish convert to Catholicism, later known as Sister Teresa Benedicta of the Cross, who urged the Pontiff to issue an encyclical on Nazi anti-Semitism and the Jewish question.[86] At any rate, the pope was determined to continue his condemnation of racism and by extension those regimes that flaunted it. Like La Farge, the pope saw the need for a spiritual defense of human rights.[87] Pius XI knew what he wanted to say, outlining the topic and its method of treatment, while discussing its underlying principles with La Farge.[88] "Simply say what you would say to the entire world if you were pope," Pius confided to La Farge.[89]

On July 3, 1938, La Farge dispatched a memorandum to Father Joseph Murphy, assistant to the New York provincial, describing his meeting of June 22, 1938, with Pius. He noted that the pope had enjoined him to write the text of the encyclical on what he considered "the most burning issue of the day." According to La Farge's memo, Pius XI told him that God had sent him, for he had been looking for someone to write on the topic.[90] When he informed father Vladimir Ledochowski, the Polish general of the Jesuits, of the pope's desire to have the encyclical quickly, the latter suggested that he collaborate with two other

Jesuits: the Frenchman Gustave Desbuquois and the German Gustav Gundlach. They worked throughout the summer of 1938 to prepare a draft, and in late September, following the Order's protocol, placed this encyclical titled *Humani Generis Unitas* (The Unity of the Human Race) in the hands of Ledochowski for transmission to the pope.

While its authors had met the papal deadline for the issuance of a condemnation of racism, delay ensued once the document left their hands. Ledochowski, apparently acting on his own initiative or following the advice of those who wished to avoid a confrontation with the dictatorial regimes, did not transmit it to the pope, but to a fellow Jesuit, Enrico Rosa, who scrutinized it slowly. Grundlach warned La Farge in mid-October 1938 that his loyalty and obedience to Ledochowski had been misplaced.[91] "An outsider might well see in all this an attempt to sabotage...for tactical and diplomatic reasons the mission entrusted to you by [the Pope]," Gundlach wrote La Farge, who had returned to the United States.[92] He was not far from the mark, for Father Heinrich Bacht, who translated it into Latin, reported that Ledochowski found La Farge's draft "too strong and provoking." The general agreed with Pacelli that it would be unwise to have a head-on confrontation with Rome, which had adopted Berlin's racism, and commissioned Rosa to tone down the encyclical.[93]

The long encyclical condemned anti-Semitism as reprehensible and "did not permit the Catholic to remain silent in the presence of racism."[94] Before the horror of the "final solution," the encyclical written for Pius XI noted that the struggle for racial purity "ends by being uniquely the struggle against the Jews."[95] Fully aware that Pius XI deplored anti-Semitism in both Italy and Germany, the authors reported that the Holy See had censured such persecution in the past. "As a result...millions of persons are deprived of the most elementary rights and privileges of citizens in the very land of their birth," the encyclical continued.[96] Indeed, the authors warned that this anti-Semitism served as an excuse for attacking the sacred Person of the Savior Himself, degenerating into a war against Christianity.[97] It stated, "The Redemption opened the doors of salvation to the entire human race." "It established a universal Kingdom, in which there would be no distinction of Jew or Gentile, Greek or barbarian."[98] Perhaps most disconcerting to those like Pacelli, who counseled moderation, the encyclical called for ecclesiastical action against racism. "It is the task and duty of the Church, the dignity and responsibility of the Chief Shepherd and of his brother Shepherds whom the Holy Ghost has placed to rule the Church of God, that they should point out to mankind the true course to be followed, the eternal divine order in the changing circumstances of the times."[99]

Pius XI, who was enraged by the racist and anti-Semitic policies that Fascist Italy adopted as it moved closer to Nazi Germany, shared this sentiment. The pope branded Fascist Italy's *Manifesto of Racist Scientists* of July 14, 1938, a "true form of apostasy," urging Catholic groups to combat it and initiating a chorus of opposition to the racism of the totalitarian regimes.[100] Speaking to a group of missionary Sisters, Pius XI denounced the racism of this exaggerated nationalism and made reference to the encyclical he was having prepared on this issue.[101] While Pius XI condemned this racism as contrary to the universality of the faith, Cardinal Ildefonso Schuster denounced it as a global danger.[102] At the end of July, during an audience to the students of the Propaganda Fide, the pope praised their universal mission at a time when there was so much talk of racism and separatist nationalism. In the mind of Pius, the two were interrelated.[103] He harped on the universality of the Catholic Church, denouncing racism while reminding the students that humanity consisted of one great, universal family, precisely the theme of his unreleased encyclical. He regretted that Italy had felt the need to imitate the German example by espousing a form of racism contrary to the teachings of the Church.[104] Count Galeazzo Ciano, Mussolini's son-in-law and foreign minister, described the pope's speech as violently antiracist.[105]

Although the Italian Foreign Office denied the papal charge that Italian racism was copied from Germany, the pope persisted in this belief while firmly rejecting the Fascist insinuation that the Italian regime's anti-Semitism was inspired by clerical anti-Judaism.[106] In fact, the encyclical that was being written against racism and anti-Semitism reflected the traditional anti-Judaism of the Church. It condemned the Jews' obstinate refusal to recognize Christ as well as their "spiritual blindness."[107] It argued that the only basis of the social separation of the Jews from Christians was religious, not racial, stressing the need of the Church to guard against "spiritual contagion."[108] Thus, the pope and the Jesuit authors of the encyclical did not see the contradiction of adhering to anti-Judaism while condemning racism and anti-Semitism. Pius complained that the Italian press censured his attack on racism and had his nuncio to Italy, Monsignor Borgongini Duca, denounce Italy's racist legislation.[109] Pius XI preferred to speak of peoples rather than races. Human dignity, he repeated, rested in a unified humanity.[110] Such papal statements guided the authors of the projected encyclical, and similar statements found their way into *Humani Generis Unitas*.[111]

In August 1938, when Pius XI visited the College of the Propaganda Fide, he warned the students to shun "exaggerated nationalism," which he branded a real curse.[112] It was a stance similar to the one enunciated in the projected encyclical.[113] These talks and their publication in *Osservatore Romano*[114] provoked criticism in Italy and Germany, whose respective presses accused the pope of polemicizing and going beyond the realm of religion in discussing the relations between the races. There were those in the Vatican who feared that Pius XI would break with Fascist Italy and Nazi Germany, with disastrous consequences for the Church, and called for a more diplomatic course.[115] This current hoped for the election of a more conciliatory successor to Pius XI and was responsible for the conclusion of an agreement with Fascist Italy on the racial issue. According to Father Angelo Martini, who was granted access to these Vatican documents, the pact of August 16, 1938 provided that in return for Fascist consideration of papal sensibilities on Catholic Action organizations in Italy, the papacy was to leave the Jewish question entirely to the regime.[116] It seems inconceivable that the pope would adhere to a pact that violated his convictions – and he did not.

The pope responded in early September that he could not remain silent in the face of grave errors and the violation of human rights.[117] Italy's racist legislation represented an attack on the Church's teachings.[118] "No, it's not possible for we Christians to participate in antisemitism," the pope told a group of visiting Belgians on September 6, 1938. "Spiritually, we are Semites."[119] While Pius XI did not personally denounce the barbarism of *Kristallnacht* in November 1938, a number of high Church figures did, including the cardinal archbishop of Milan, the cardinal archbishop of Paris, the primate of Belgium, and the patriarch of Lisbon, repeating Pius XI's rejection of the doctrine of blood as contrary to Catholic dogma. On November 10, 1938, Mussolini published a decree forbidding marriage between Italian Aryans with persons of "another race." Pius responded by writing both the king and Mussolini that this was a violation of the Concordat of the Lateran Accords.[120] He made public his displeasure in his Christmas allocution.[121] In light of the Vatican's campaign of increased opposition to totalitarian racism, the path was paved for issuing La Farge's encyclical, which echoed the pope's sentiments, but no word arrived of its release.[122]

There was little opportunity to explore the lack of response to their draft with the ailing eighty-one-year-old pope, whose schedule was severely curtailed, especially after his two heart attacks on Thursday, November 25, 1938.[123] Even public audiences with diplomats were now limited to five minutes because of his grave condition. Nonetheless, word leaked out that Pius XI remained incensed at the Nazis and was determined to continue to combat their pernicious doctrines. At the end of December when he met with British Minister D'Arcy Godolphin Osborne he made it clear to him "that Nazi Germany has taken the place of Communism as the Church's most dangerous enemy." In Paris, Eduard Herriot, president of the chamber, praised the pope's spiritual gallantry as protector of outraged weakness.[124] Unfortunately, the authors of the encyclical did not have ready access to the pope's person. Given the hierarchical structure of the Church and the quasi-military discipline of its order, an appeal to the pope over the heads of a superior was no trivial matter. Nonetheless, Father Gundlach convinced La Farge to write directly to Pius XI, who had charged him with the assignment of writing the encyclical. Only then did Ledochowski transmit the La Farge draft to Pius XI.[125]

Father Walter Abbot reports that the Vatican received the document on January 21, 1939, but is not certain if the pope saw or read it before his death on February 9–10.[126] Most likely he did not, even though the ailing Pius XI was working on the draft of a speech to be presented to the bishops cataloging Fascist abuses. He died on February 10, 1939, before he could deliver it.[127] The draft of La Farge's encyclical with an attached note from Monsignor Domenico Tardini, indicating that Pius XI wanted it without delay,[128] together with the address Pius XI planned to present to the Italian bishops on the tenth anniversary of the Lateran Accords, were found on the desk of the deceased pope.[129] His secretary of state, Eugenio Pacelli, who became Pope Pius XII on March 2, 1939, decided to shelve both. These documents reflected Pius XI's confrontational course toward the Fascist regimes, whereas Pius XII from the first opted for a conciliatory one.

The new pope's major concern was the preservation of the peace, and he urged the calling of an international congress to resolve outstanding issues. The German ambassador immediately perceived the difference between the old pope and the new and informed his government that Pius XII[130] favored a public truce.[131] His analysis proved accurate. Notably, Pacelli retained Cesare Orsengio, who was well-disposed toward the Nazi government, as nuncio in Berlin. Furthermore, as Nazi Germany menaced the peace of Europe, Pius announced papal neutrality in a radio message of August 24, 1939.[132] Even after the outbreak of war in September 1939, a truce of sorts was established between the Vatican and the Nazis, with the Holy See's protestations of violations of the concordat ceasing.[133] Both the volume and the intensity of Vatican criticism of the regime decreased during the pontificate of Pius XII in comparison to that of Pius XI, even though Nazi actions became increasingly brutal, anti-Semitic, and anti-Christian. Determined to preserve papal neutrality, Pius failed to raise his voice against the German invasion of Poland.[134]

It is true that Pius XII rejected the claims of absolute state authority in his first encyclical, but from the first he did not abandon his conciliatory, diplomatic course. His circuitous denunciation of totalitarianism remained general.

After the German invasion of Poland, in his Christmas message, he lamented the "calculated act of aggression against a small, industrious, and peaceful nation."[135] However, when German Foreign Minister von Ribbentrop visited the pope in March 1940, Pius confessed that the small nation he had referred to was Finland, the victim of Soviet aggression.[136] When the Vatican received reports of the euthanasia program in Germany at the end of 1940, no formal protest was lodged.[137] Domenico Tardini drafted a papal letter dated May 13, 1940 condemning the German invasion of Belgium, Holland, and Luxemburg, but Pius XII chose not to release it. He chose instead to dispatch messages of regret to their rulers.[138] A number of voices, including some cardinals close to the Holy See, urged Pius to follow the example of Pius XI and publicly denounce the Nazi persecution in Germany. Silence, they insisted, caused confusion and consternation among the faithful.[139] His conciliatory course and hazy language represented a departure from the strong-willed, often headstrong leadership of Pius XI.[140] "I am afraid history will reproach the Holy See for following the policy of convenience for itself, and not much more," lamented Cardinal Eugene Tisserant. He added that this was "extremely sad, above all for those who lived under Pius XI."[141] The French ambassador to the Vatican, Francois Charles-Roux, shared Tisserant's disappointment with Pius XII's failure to pursue the more courageous actions of his predecessor.[142] The pope refused to change course.

Pius XI and Pius XII also differed in their attitude toward the racist right in France. In 1926, Pius XI bluntly condemned the anti-Semitic *Action Francaise*, forbidding French Catholics to adhere to the movement or read its newspaper. Pius XII, on the other hand, did not assume a hostile or critical attitude toward the racist policies pursued by the Vichy regime established in July 1940. Supposedly Leon Berard, its ambassador to the Vatican, received assurances that the Vatican would not contest Vichy's discrimination against Jewish employment or property confiscation, while that government did not interfere with mixed marriages. A number of Church officials, including the Nuncio Valerio Valeri, however, claimed that the ambassador's report did not reflect the Vatican's real concern about anti-Semitism in Vichy France.[143] Unfortunately, this "concern" was not translated into a diplomatic or public protest.

Pius XII followed a cautious, diplomatic policy vis-à-vis the Nazis, issuing no clear condemnation of their blatant aggression, expressing no public outrage against their mass extermination, and failing to appeal to the conscience of mankind to suppress their madness. To the consternation of Catholics and non-Catholics alike, he refused to address the issue of who was responsible for the war. Clearly, Pius XII recognized that in the struggle between good and evil, neutrality or impartiality was morally indefensible. However, some apologists argue that the pope had to confront one evil versus another – Hitler's Germany versus Stalin's Russia. Anxious first to avoid war, and then seeking to mediate a peace, Pius XII did not clearly denounce their racism that violated Christian principles. During the war Pius XII pursued a policy of conciliation toward Germany in contrast to his predecessor's policy of confrontation. Had Pius XII seen fit to issue rather than shelve his predecessor's encyclical, which stressed the unity of the human race and the incompatibility of racism and Christianity,[144] might some of the millions exterminated have been spared?[145] We shall never know.

We do know that while both popes had collaborated in the conclusion of the concordats with the dictatorial regimes, they were divided in their estimation of how much the Church could endure to preserve them. One cannot explain their varied approaches simply on the basis of the times and circumstances, which were admittedly different during the two pontificates. Orientation and temperament also played a role. The two popes differed in style as well as substance, in tone as well as content. Pius XI did not hesitate to publicly condemn Fascist and Nazi racism and planned to denounce their anti-Semitism as well. During the course of the last two years of his pontificate, Pius XI had publicly characterized racism as a religious apostasy or heresy and a totalitarian tendency in violation of natural law as well as the Christian creed.[146] While Pius XI was prepared to negotiate with the devil himself on behalf of the Church, he did not shy from assuming the offensive on its behalf.

Pius XII, on the other hand, while also offended by Fascist and Nazi anti-Semitism and racism, apparently did not assign it the priority of his predecessor. Clearly, Pius XI's encyclical created potential diplomatic problems that Pacelli sought to avoid. If it weakened Fascist Italy and Nazi Germany, it aided Soviet Russia. Furthermore, Pius agonized over the consequences of a public condemnation, fearing it might make worse the plight of the people it sought to rescue. Monsignor Charles Radonski, who had been forced from his dioceses in Warthegau and who, as early as 1942, complained that the situation had deteriorated while the Vatican kept silent, denounced this explanation. Silence indicated consent, he charged.[147] The pope, who recognized the threat to his own person, did not concur. After 1943, Pius worried that the Nazis would capture him and apparently feared he could not resist their pressure. According to Monsignor Charles Burns, former archivist of the Vatican Archives, there is evidence therein to suggest that Pius XII left instructions that if the Nazis seized him, "the College of Cardinals was to consider him resigned and elect a new pope."[148] Perhaps this was yet another reason to avoid a confrontation with the Nazis.

Consequently, Pacelli's refusal to issue Pius XI's encyclical was consistent with his modus operandi. Pius XII considered it unwise to denounce the Axis regimes' racist policies publicly, providing them with the pretext to dismantle the concordats endangering the institutional Church. Furthermore, if issued as written, the encyclical would have antagonized not only Italy and Germany, but the United States, whose racial and segregationist policies were likewise morally indefensible. "The theory and practice of [racism,] which makes a distinction between the higher and lower races, ignores the bond of unity," the 1938 document warned. Indeed it added, "It is incredible that in view of these facts there are still people who maintain that the doctrine and practice of racism have nothing to do with Catholic teaching as to faith and morals and nothing to do with philosophy, but are a purely political affair."[149] These passages would have troubled American as well as Italian and German Catholics, as well as angered and aroused the United States government, whose military forces and many of its institutions remained legally segregated.

Unquestionably, Pius XII, who increasingly looked to the United States to balance the dictatorial regimes of Europe, did not wish to offend the Americans as well as the Germans and Italians by issuing Pius XI's encyclical. Perhaps this explains why *Summi Pontificatus*, his first encyclical that stressed the unity of mankind, abandoned its condemnations of racism and antisemitism.[150] While Pius XI had recourse to public opinion and based his arguments on religious convictions, Pius XII gave a priority to his diplomatic goals. As Gundlach predicted, the "ethical" course pursued by Pius XI was abandoned in favor of the more "expedient" one of Pius XII.[151] In many ways, Papa Ratti followed the path of the outspoken Pope Pius IX (1846–78), whereas Papa Pacelli pursued policies more similar to those of Pius IX's astute secretary of state, Giacomo Antonelli, who was a cardinal though not a priest.[152] The denunciations and condemnations of Pius XI, if continued, might have threatened the future of the institutional Church. However, the accommodating strategy, diplomatic finesse, and "silence" of Pius XII, which may have saved many lives, compromised the moral stature of the Holy See.

NOTES

1. Galleys of La Farge's copy of the draft encyclical *Humani Generis Unitas* authorized by Pius XI, but not issued by Pius XII. It was to be published in the *Catholic Mind* of 1973, but never appeared. The galleys were sent to me by Professor Robert A. Hecht, author of a biography of John La Farge. Quote comes from p. 38b of galleys, paragraph 154.

2. Frank J. Coppa, "The Vatican and the Dictators between Diplomacy and Morality," in *Catholics, the State, and the European Radical Right, 1919–1945,* Richard J. Wolff and Jorg K. Hoensch, eds. (New York: Columbia University Press, 1987), 199–223.

3. Letter to Cardinal Bello, December 18, 1919, in Harry C. Koenig, ed., *Principles for Peace: Selections from Papal Documents from Leo XIII to Pius XII* (Washington, DC: National Catholic Welfare Conference, 1943), 280.

4. John S. Conway, "The Vatican, Germany, and the Holocaust," in Peter C. Kent and John F. Pollard, eds., *Papal Diplomacy in the Modern Age* (Westport, CT: Praeger, 1994), 118, n. 5,

5. John Cornwell, *Hitler's Pope: The Secret History of Pius XII* (New York: Viking, 1999), 99.

6. Ibid., 111.

7. Francesco Pacelli, *Diario della Conciliazione* (Vatican City: Libreria Editrice Vaticana, 1959).

8. *Records and Documents of the Holy See Relating to the Second World War: The Holy See and the War in Europe, March 1939–August 1940* (Washington, DC: Corpus Books, 1968), I, 5–6.

9. Cardinal Domenico Tardini, *Memories of Pius XII,* Rosemary Goldie, trans. (Westminster, MD: Newman Press, 1961), 109.

10. Coppa, "The Vatican and the Dictators," 218.

11. Susan Zuccotti, *The Italians and the Holocaust: Persecution, Rescue, and Survival* (New York: Basic Books, 1987), 51.

12. David I. Kertzer, *The Popes against the Jews: The Vatican's Role in the Rise of Modern Antisemitism* (New York: Knopf, 2001), 5–6.

13. In this regard see Stanislaus Wilk, ed., *Achille Ratti (1918–1921). Acta Nunciaturae Polonae.* vv. 1–5 (Rome: Institutum Historicum Polonicum Romae, 1995–99) and Emma Fattorini, *Germania e Santa Sede. Le Nunziature di Pacelli tra la Grande Guerra e la Repubblica di Weimar, Annali dell'Istituto storico italo-germanico* (Bologna: Il Mulino, 1992).

14. The Vatican Archives remain closed for the Pontificates of Pius XI and Pius XII, although some of these documents have been published in Pierre Blet et al., eds., *Actes et documents du Saint Siege relatifs à la seconde guerre mondiale* (Vatican City: Libreria Editrice Vaticana, 1965–81; in 12 vols.). In 2001 the Vatican announced it would soon partially open the papers of these two popes for scholarly scrutiny.

15. Conway, "The Vatican, Germany, and the Holocaust," p. 106.

16. Gene Bernardini, "The Origins and Development of Racial Antisemitism in Fascist Italy," *Journal of Modern History,* vol. 49, n. 3 (1977), 434.

17. Jose M. Sanchez, "The Popes and Nazi Germany: The View from Madrid," *Journal of Church and State,* XXXVIII (Spring 1996), 367.

18. *Cum Tertio,* September 17, 1922, in *Principles for Peace: Selections from Papal Documents from Leo XIII to Pius XII,* p. 329.

19. Consistorial Allocution of December 20, 1926, *Discorsi di Pio XI,* ed. Domenico Bertetto (Turin: Società Editrice Internazionale, 1959), I, 647.

20. *Decretum De Conosciatione Vulgo, "Amici Israel" Abolenda,* March 25, 1928, *Acta Apostolicae Sedis,* XX, 103–4; Georges Passelecq and Bernard Suchecky, *The Hidden*

Encyclical of Pius XI (New York: Harcourt Brace, 1998), p. 144. This is a translation of *L'Encyclique cachee de Pie XI* (Paris: Editions La Decouverte, 1995).

21. The decree of suppression complained that the association had adopted a manner of acting and thinking that was contrary to the spirit of the Church, the Holy Fathers, and the Liturgy, but did not specify its alleged transgressions. For possible explanations, see J. Levie, S. J. "Decret de suppression de l'Association des Amis de Israel," in *Nouvelle Revue Theologique* (1928), 536–7.

22. The Lateran Accords included three parts: a conciliation treaty, which terminated the Roman Question and established Vatican City as an inviolable papal territory; a concordat, which regulated Church–State relations in Italy; and a financial convention to provide compensation for papal territory annexed during unification. The texts can be found in Nino Tripodi's *I Patti lateranensi e il fascismo* (Bologna: Cappelli, 1960), 267–79. For an analysis of the documents, see Ernesto Rossi, *Il Manganello e l'aspersorio* (Florence: Parenti, 1958), 227–36.

23. Bernardini, "The Origins and Development of Racial Antisemitism in Fascist Italy," 431–2.

24. *L'Osservatore Romano*, February 12, 1929; *Il Monitore Ecclesiastico*, March 1929.

25. Giuseppe Rossini, *Il Fascismo e la resistenza* (Rome: Cinque Lune, 1955), 48.

26. *The Papal Encyclicals in their Historical Context*, Anne Fremantle, ed. (New York: G. P. Putnam's Sons, 1956), 249.

27. Anthony Rhodes, *The Vatican in the Age of Dictators, 1922–1945* (New York: Holt, Rinehart, and Winston, 1973), 166; Guenter Lewy, *The Catholic Church and Nazi Germany* (New York: McGraw-Hill, 1964), 10–11.

28. *Anglo-Vatican Relations 1914–1939: Confidential Reports of the British Minister to the Holy See*, Thomas E. Hachey, ed. (Boston: G. K. Hall, 1972), 250.

29. "Cronaca Contemporanea," March 10–13, 1933, *Civiltà Cattolica*, anno 84 (1933), II, 205–6.

30. John Jay Hughes, "The Pope's Pact with Hitler: Betrayal or Self-Defense?" *Journal of Church and State*, XVII (Winter 1975), 64; Klaus Scholder, *The Churches and the Third Reich. II – The Year of Disillusionment: 1934 Barmen and Rome* (Philadelphia: Fortress Press, 1988), 1.

31. "Cronaca Contemporanea," April 7–20, 1933, *Civiltà Cattolica*, anno 84 (1933), II, 301.

32. *Anglo-Vatican Relations 1914–1939: Confidential Reports of the British Minister to the Holy See*, p. 250; "Concordat of the Holy See and Germany," *Catholic World*, August 1933, vol. 137.

33. "Cronaca Contemporanea," June 23–July 6, 1933, *Civiltà Cattolica*, anno 84 (1933), III, 203–5.

34. *Anglo-Vatican Relations 1914–1939: Confidential Reports of the British Minister to the Holy See*, p. 250.

35. *Concordato fra la Santa Sede ed il Reich Germanico*, July 20, 1933, *Acta Apostolicae Sedis*, XXV, 389–408.

36. E. Rosa, "Il Concordato della Santa Sede con la Germania," *Civiltà Cattolica*, anno 84 (1933), IV, 89; *L'Osservatore Romano*, July 27, 1933.

37. Mr. Kirkpatrick (the Vatican) to Sir R. Vansittart, August 19, 1933, *Documents on British Foreign Policy*, n. 342, pp. 524–5; *L'Osservatore Romano*, September 11–12, 1933; "Cronaca Contemporanea," September 7–26, 1933, *Civiltà Cattolica, anno* 84 (1933), IV, 89.

38. *Anglo-Vatican Relations 1914–1939: Confidential Reports of the British Minister to the Holy See*, pp. 253–4; Camille M. Cianfarra, *The War and the Vatican* (London: Oates and Washbourne, 1945), p. 96; *Documents on German Foreign Policy*, Series C, vol. IV, 793–4.

39. Robert A. Hecht, *An Unordinary Man: A life of Father John La Farge, S. J.* (Lanham, MD: Scarecrow Press, 1996), 103, 107.

40. Speeches of April 4, 1934 and April 29, 1934 in *Discorsi di Pio XI*, III, 90–3, 114–15.

41. *Casti Connubii*, December 31, 1930, *Papal Teachings: Matrimony*, Benedictine Monks of Solesmes, ed. (Boston: St. Paul Editions, 1963), 219–91; Waldemar Gurian, "Hitler's Undeclared War on the Catholic Church," *Foreign Affairs*, VI (January 1938), 262.

42. Nathaniel Micklem, *National Socialism and the Roman Catholic Church* (London: Oxford University Press, 1939), 157.

43. Lewy, *The Catholic Church and Nazi Germany*, p. 126.

44. *Mit brennender Sorge*, March 14, 1937, *Principles for Peace: Selections from Papal Documents from Leo XIII to Pius XII*, 498; Desmond O' Grady, "Pius XI – complex and imperious," *National Catholic Reporter*, December 15, 1972, p. 15.

45. Gurian, *Foreign Affairs*, VI, 261–2; Lewy, *The Catholic Church and Nazi Germany* 151–2; Scholder, *The Churches and the Third Reich* II, 104, 119.

46. "La questione giudaica," *La Civiltà Cattolica* (1936), anno 87, vol. IV, p. 45.

47. *Anglo-Vatican Relations 1914–1939: Confidential Reports of the British Minister to the Holy See*, p. 277.

48. Ibid., pp. 312–15.

49. E. Rosa, "Ricorsi di Barbarie nella civiltà contemporanea," *Civiltà Cattolica, anno* 87 (1936), III, 356.

50. *Principles for Peace: Selections from Papal Documents from Leo XIII to Pius XII*, pp. 304–6.

51. "Cronaca Contemporanea," June 9–22, 1933, *Civiltà Cattolica, anno* 84 (1933), II, 609; "Cronaca Contemporanea," May 25–June 8, 1933, *Civiltà Cattolica, anno* 84 (1933), II, 609; speech of July 29, 1934, in *Discorsi di Pio XI*, III, 183–5.

52. *Anglo-Vatican Relations 1914–1939: Confidential Reports of the British Minister to the Holy See*, pp. 274–9; Francois Charles-Roux, *Huit ans au Vatican* (Paris: Flammarion, 1947), 98.

53. "Ai giovani Cattolici di Germania," August 8, 1934, *Discorsi di Pio XI*, III, 188; Passelecq and Suchecky, *The Hidden Encyclical*, 93.

54. E. Rosa, "L'Internazionale della Barbarie nella sua lotta contro la civiltà," *Civiltà Cattolica, anno* 87 (1936), III, 447–8.

55. E. Rosa, "Gli estremi opposti nella crisis della civiltà," *Civiltà Cattolica, anno* 87 (1936), II, 91.

56. "Il pericolo russo e i progressi dell'invasione comunista," *Civiltà Cattolica, anno* 87 (1936), III, 266.

57. "Ai Giovani Cattolici Tedeschi," October 8, 1934, *Discorsi di Pio XI*, III, 218.

58. Owen Chadwick, *Britain and the Vatican during the Second World War* (Cambridge: Cambridge University Press, 1986), 16, 19.

59. *Documents on Germany Foreign Policy*, Series C, IV, n. 482; Rhodes, p. 199.

60. Charles-Roux, *Huit ans au Vatican*, 106.

61. For English versions of *Mit brennender Sorge* of March 14, 1937 see *The Papal Encyclicals, 1958–1981*, III, 525–535 and *Principles for Peace: Selections from Papal Documents from Leo XIII to Pius XII*, 498–510. The original version can be found in *Acta Apostolicae Sedis*, XXIX, 145–67, followed by an Italian version, 168ff.

62. Lettera enciclica sulla situazione della Chiesa Cattolica nel Reich Germanico, *Acta Apostolicae Sedis*, 1937, XXIX, 168.

63. Ibid., XXIX, 182, 185–6.

64. Chadwick, *Britain and the Vatican*, 20.

65. "La questione giudaica e l'apostolato cattolico," *Civiltà Cattolica*, June 23, 1937.

66. Allocution *Quod Iterum*, December 13, 1937, *Discorsi di Pio XI*, III, 671; Al Sacro Collegio e alla Prelatura Romana, ibid., III, 679.

67. *Principles for Peace: Selections from Papal Documents from Leo XIII to Pius XII*, p. 545.

68. Passelecq and Suchecky, *The Hidden Encyclical*, 109.

69. "Cronaca Contemporanea," *Civiltà Cattolica*, June 9–22, 1938.

70. Passelecq and Suchecky, *The Hidden Encyclical*, 157.

71. *Discorsi di Pio XI*, III, 770.

72. Charles-Roux, *Huit ans au Vatican*, 52.

73. *Anglo-Vatican Relations 1914–1939: Confidential Reports of the British Minister to the Holy See* , p. 387; *Tablet* (of London), March 26, 1938.

74. Charles-Roux, 122–3; Micklem, *National Socialism and the Roman Catholic Church*, 206–7; 96, 99; *Anglo-Vatican Relations 1914–1939: Confidential Reports of the British Minister to the Holy See*, p. 392.

75. William M. Harrigan, "Pius XII's Efforts to Effect a Detente in German-Vatican Relations, 1939," *Catholic Historical Review* XLIX (July 1963), 177.

76. Rhodes, *The Vatican in the Age of Dictators*, 229; Charles-Roux, *Huit ans au Vatican*, 155.

77. Cianfarra, *The War and the Vatican*, 122; *Anglo-Vatican Relations 1914–1939: Confidential Reports of the British Minister to the Holy See*, pp. 389–94.

78. John La Farge, *The Manner Is Ordinary* (New York: Harcourt Brace and Company, 1954), 272; Hecht, *An Unordinary Man*, 114.

79. Passelecq and Suchecky, *The Hidden Encyclical*, 124–6.

80. Michael R. Marrus, "The Vatican on Racism and Antisemitism, 1938–39: A New Look at a Might-Have-Been," *Holocaust and Genocide Studies* VII, n. 3 (Winter, 1997), 382.

81. La Farge had been sent by the editor of *America* to the International Eucharistic Congress at Budapest in April and on his way back stopped in Rome. La Farge, *The Manner is Ordinary*, 253–72.

82. Subsequently La Farge published *The Race Question and the Negro: A Study of the Catholic Doctrine on Interracial Justice* (1943) and *The Catholic Viewpoint on Race*

Relations (1956) among other volumes, as well as a series of articles in *America* and *Interracial Review*.

83. John La Farge, S. J., *Interracial Justice: A Study of the Catholic Doctrine of Race Relations* (New York: America Press, 1937), 12–15, 59–61, 75, 172–3.

84. La Farge, *The Manner Is Ordinary*, 272–3.

85. Hecht, *An Unordinary Man*, 114–15.

86. Lewy, *The Catholic Church and Nazi Germany*, 295; Johannes H. Nota, S. J., "Edith Stein unter der Entwurf für eine Enzyklika gegen Rassisumus und Antisemitismus," *Feiburger Rundbrief*, 1975, 35–41 quoted in Passelecq and Suchecky, *The Hidden Encyclical*, 55.

87. La Farge, *The Manner Is Ordinary*, 273.

88. "Jesuit says Pius XI asked for draft," *National Catholic Reporter*, December 22, 1972, p. 3.

89. Hecht, *An Uniordinary Man*, 115.

90. Castelli, *National Catholic Reporter*, December 15, 1972, p. 8.

91. Passelecq and Suchecky, *The Hidden Encyclical*, 110, 115.

92. Frederick Brown, "The Hidden Encyclical," *The New Republic*, April 15, 1996, p. 30.

93. "Jesuit Says Pius XI asked for draft," *National Catholic Reporter*, December 22, 1972, p. 4.

94. Galleys of La Farge's copy of the encyclical *Humani Generis Unitas*, which was to be published in *Catholic Mind*, are preserved in the offices of *America* and were uncovered by Professor Robert A. Hecht. The encyclical was supposed to appear in 1973 in *Catholic Mind* but was never published. In 1996, Georges Passelecq and Bernard Suchecky published a copy of the hidden encyclical in their volume called *L'Encyclique cachee de Pie XI*. My reference is to the galleys of the encyclical for the *Catholic Mind*, p. 31, paragraph 123.

95. Galleys of La Farge's copy of *Humani Generis Unitas*, p. 33, paragraph 131; Passelecq and Suchecky, *The Hidden Encyclical*, 283–4.

96. Galleys of La Farge's copy of the encyclical *Humani Generis Unitas*, p. 33, paragraph 132; Passelecq and Suchecky, *The Hidden Encyclical*, 284.

97. Galleys of La Farge's copy of the encyclical *Humani Generis Unitas*, p. 36b, paragraph 147; Passelecq and Suchecky, *The Hidden Encyclical*, 292–3.

98. Galleys of La Farge's copy of the encyclical *Humani Generis Unitas*, p. 34, paragraph 135; Passelecq and Suchecky, *The Hidden Encyclical*, 286.

99. Galleys of La Farge's copy of the encyclical *Humani Generis Unitas*, p. 38b, paragraph 154; Passelecq and Suchecky, *The Hidden Encyclical*, 296.

100. *Civiltà Cattolica*, July 29, 1938; Cianfarra, *The War and the Vatican*, 133–4

101. "Alle Suore di Nostra Signora del Cenaccolo," *Discorsi di Pio XI*, III, 766–72.

102. *The New York Times*, July 17, 1938; July 22, 1938; August 12, 1938; September 8, 1938.

103. La Farge, *The Manner Is Ordinary*, 273.

104. Agli Alunni del Collegio di "Propaganda Fide," July 28, 1938, *Discorsi di Pio XI*, III, 777–81.

105. Emile Poulat, "Preface" in Passelecq and Suchecky, *L'Encyclique cachee de Pie XI* (Paris: Editions La Decouverte, 1995), 13.

106. Bernardini, *Journal of Modern History* 49, No. 3 (1977), 434–5.

107. Galleys of La Farge's copy of the "encyclical" *Humani Generis Unitas*, preserved in the offices of *America*, pp. 34 and 34b, paragraphs 136–7.

108. Ibid. 35, 35b.

109. *The New York Times*, August 6, 1938; August 12, 1938, September 1, 1938.

110. *Discorsi di Pio XI*, III, 782–3.

111. In this regard see sections 111 on race and racism, 112 on denial of human unity, and 116 on denial of true religious and moral values in the galleys of La Farge's copy of the encyclical *Humani Generis Unitas* preserved in the offices of *America*, pp. 29b and 30 and in Passelecq and Suchecky, *The Hidden Encyclical*, 274–6.

112. Agli Alunni di "Propaganda Fide," August 21, 1938, *Discorsi di Pio XI*, III, 784–6.

113. This is apparent from reading sections 106 to 110 in the galleys of La Farge's copy of the encyclical *Humani Generis Unitas* preserved in the offices of *America*, pp. 28, 28b, 29 and in Passelecq and Suchecky, *The Hidden Encyclical*, 272–4.

114. *L'Osservatore Romano*, July 30, 1938, and August 22–23, 1938.

115. Giovanni Miccoli, "Santa Sede e Chiesa Italiana di Fronte alle Leggi Antiebraiche del 1938," *Studi Storici* 29, n. 4 (October–December 1988), 881.

116. Angelo Martini, "L'Ultima battaglia di Pio XI" in *Studi sulla questione romana e la conciliazione* (Rome: Cinque Lune, 1963), 186–7.

117. Ad Insegnanti di Azione Cattolica, September 6, 1938, *Discorsi di Pio XI*, III, 796.

118. *The New York Times*, September 8, 1938.

119. Passelecq and Suchecky, *The Hidden Encyclical*, p. 180.

120. *L'Osservatore Romano*, November 14–15, 1938.

121. Con grande, December 24, 1938, *Principles for Peace: Selections from Papal Documents from Leo XIII to Pius XII*, pp. 549–51; *Papal Pronouncements. A Guide: 1740–1978*, II, 114; *The New York Times*, December 25, 1938.

122. It was only after Pius XI's death that La Farge was informed that the encyclical had been delivered to the Pope and was among his papers. Ledochowski added that since the new Pope had not yet had time to go over the "sundry papers left on his desk," it was "premature" to ask Pius XII what he planned to do with the draft. Castelli, *National Catholic Reporter*, December 15, 1972, p. 8.

123. O' Grady, "Pius XI – complex and imperious," 15.

124. Chadwick, *Britain and the Vatican*, 25, 27.

125. Passelecq and Suchecky, *The Hidden Encyclical*, 116, 119, 138.

126. "Jesuit Says Pius XI asked for draft," *National Catholic Reporter*, December 22, 1972, p. 3.

127. *Acta Apostolicae Sedis*, LI (1959), 129–35; *Papal Pronouncements. A Guide: 1740–1978*, II,114.

128. "Jesuit Says Pius XI asked for draft," *National Catholic Reporter*, December 22, 1972, p. 4.

129. Jim Castelli, "Unpublished Encyclical attacked antisemitism," *National Catholic Reporter*, December 15, 1972, pp. 13–14.

130. He was the first Roman Pope since Innocent XIII in 1721.

131. Harrigan, "Fius XII's Efforts to Effect a Detente," 184.

132. Koenig, *Principles for Peace*, 584.

133. George O. Kent, "Pope Pius XII and Germany: Some Aspects of German-Vatican Relations, 1933–1943," *American Historical Review* LXX (October 1964), 66.

134. Charles-Roux, *Huit ans au Vatican* p. 343.

135. Koenig, *Principles for Peace*, 634.

136. Hansjakob Stehle, *Eastern Politics of the Vatican, 1917–1979*, trans Sandra Smith (Athens, Ohio: Ohio University Press, 1981), p. 197.

137. Kent, "Pope Pius XII and Germany," p. 67.

138. Carlo Felice Casula, *Domenico Tardini (1888–1961), L'Azione della Santa Sede nella crisi fra le due guerre* (Rome: Edizioni Studium, 1989), 163; Koenig, *Principles for Peace*, 668–9.

139. *Documents on German Foreign Policy*, Series C, I, n. 501.

140. Harrigan, "Pius XII's Efforts to Effect a Detente," 190; Peter C. Kent, *The Pope and the Duce* (New York: St. Martin's, 1981), 10

141. Stehle, *Eastern Politics of the Vatican*, p. 215.

142. *Records and Documents of the Holy See Relating to the Second World War: The Holy See and the War in Europe, March 1939–August 1940*, I, 169

143. Robert O. Paxton, "France: The Church, the Republic, and the Fascist Temptation, 1922–1945," in Wolff, *Catholics, the State, and the European Radical Right, 1919–1945*, p. 84.

144. Galleys of La Farge's copy of the encyclical *Humani Generis Unitas* pp. 20b, 21, paragraphs 73, 75; Passelecq and Suchecky, *The Hidden Encyclical*, 254–5.

145. "A lingering Question," *National Catholic Reporter*, December 15, 1972, p. 10.

146. Passelecq and Suchecky, *The Hidden Encyclical*, 197.

147. *Actes et documents du Saint Siege relatifs à la Seconde Guerre Mondiale.* 12 vol., Pierre Blet, Robert A. Graham, Angelo Martini and Burkhart Scheneider, eds. Volume III: *La Saint Seige et la Situation reliqieuse en Pologne et dans les pays Baltes, 1939–1945* (Vatican City: Libreria Editrice Vaticana, 1967), 635, 736–8.

148. John Thavis, "Talk of Pope's Resignation Is No Longer Taboo," *The Tablet* (Brooklyn) June 8, 2002, p. 11.

149. Galleys of La Farge's copy of the encyclical *Humani Generis Unitas*, p. 29b; Passelecq and Suchecky, *The Hidden Encyclical*, 275.

150. *Summi Pontificatus*, October 20, 1939, *Acta Apostolicae Sedis*, XXXI (1939), 413–53.

151. Passelecq and Suchecky, *The Hidden Encyclical*, 126, 129.

152. For my treatment of these figures see Frank J. Coppa, *Pope Pius IX: Crusader in a Secular Age* (Boston: Twayne, 1979) and idem. *Cardinal Giacomo Antonelli and Papal Politics in European Affairs* (New York: State University of New York Press, 1990).

15 Pius XII and the Rescue of Jews in Italy: Evidence of a Papal Directive[1]

Susan Zuccotti

Since the end of the Second World War, supporters of Pius XII have often claimed that he was instrumental in saving hundreds of thousands of Jews during the Holocaust.[2] Assistance from the Holy See allegedly included measures to facilitate Jewish emigration from Europe, as well as diplomatic interventions before and during the war. A third activity consisted of direct Vatican involvement in hiding, supplying, and guiding Jews who were trying to escape deportation. Some papal advocates maintain that Pius XII initiated these rescue efforts and ordered men and women of the Church to participate in them. More specifically, they assert that he issued directives to the heads of Church institutions to open their doors to Jews and other fugitives from the Nazis and local collaborators.[3]

Papal critics disagree with advocates on the extent and effectiveness of the pope's efforts in all three of these assistance options. They maintain that Vatican efforts to facilitate Jewish emigration were directed almost exclusively toward converts to Catholicism. They indicate, also, that most Vatican diplomatic interventions on behalf of Jews during the war were tentative, tardy, and ineffective. These positions have been examined elsewhere and are not described further here.[4] This chapter focuses exclusively on the third option, the issuance of a papal directive to save Jews. The analysis is limited to Italy, the country where Vatican officials, primarily Italian in origin, were most able to be helpful.

The conclusion that the pope did not issue a rescue order is based on several factors. First, there is no written evidence of a papal directive to save Jews. If a directive had ever been written and delivered, it is inconceivable that at least one copy would not have been preserved. By the time of the German occupation of Italy on September 8, 1943, many clergymen realized that the pope was being criticized for his failure to denounce publicly the ongoing destruction of

European Jews. They surely would have understood that written evidence of a papal order to rescue Jews would be important for the historical record after the war, and at least some of them would have saved such a document. Priests, monks, and nuns hid many documents and other personal belongings for those they assisted. They hid lists of names and addresses of their "guests" and of those who provided financial assistance for rescue efforts.[5] It would not have been difficult to hide a written papal directive. But no such document has been produced, either by those involved in Jewish rescue or in the *Actes et Documents du Saint Siège relatifs à la seconde guerre mondiale* (ADSS), the eleven volumes of Vatican wartime diplomatic documents published between 1965 and 1981.[6]

Of course, a papal directive to save Jews could have been issued orally. During the first eighteen years after the war, however, priests, nuns, and monks directly involved in Jewish rescue efforts in Italy did not testify that they had received or acted because of a papal order. Such testimony or claims of testimony, usually by individuals only indirectly involved in Jewish rescue, began to appear after the production in 1963 of Rolf Hochhuth's play *The Deputy*, which criticized Pius XII for failing to protest the Holocaust.[7] Many more testimonies and allegations have been forthcoming in response to the attention given to the subject by papal critics since 1999.[8] That evidence will be examined later in this chapter.

Careful scrutiny of the chronology of Jewish rescue in Italy also suggests the improbability of a papal directive. In Genoa, Turin, and Florence, where men and women of the Church protected large numbers of Jews, the rescue process began in mid-September 1943, at a time when Vatican officials in Rome were actually refusing to become involved. One refusal, for example, occurred on September 17, 1943, when a representative of the Roman Jewish community met with a highly placed Vatican official to ask if Jews could be hidden in Church institutions in the Eternal City. The answer, recorded in a document published in the ADSS, was an unambiguous negative.[9] This refusal was probably issued not because the pope and his advisors were anti-Semitic or pro-Nazi, but because they were determined to preserve Vatican neutrality and protect the Church. Whatever the reason, certainly no papal order to open Church institutions to fugitives was issued in mid-September. The pope would not have ordered men and women of the Church to do what he himself was refusing to do.

While the hiding of Jews in Church institutions in Genoa, Turin, and Florence began in mid-September, it occurred in Rome, for the most part, three or four weeks later, during or immediately after the roundup of 1,259 Jews on October 16, 1943.[10] That movement of Jewish fugitives into convents and monasteries was so fast and spontaneous that there would have been no time for a papal directive beforehand.

There is, in addition, considerable evidence of papal disapproval of the hiding of Jews and other fugitives in Vatican properties. In December 1943, for example, the rector of the Pontificio Seminario Romano Maggiore, near the Basilica of St. John the Lateran, wrote a letter to the pope in which he apologized profusely for troubling him by accepting too many fugitives.[11] The rector apparently had been reprimanded for excessive zeal. Also, after a raid by Italian Fascists and a few Nazis on the extraterritorial Basilica and Monastery of St. Paul outside the Walls in early February 1944, fugitives hiding in Vatican properties outside Vatican City itself were ordered to leave.[12] Officials felt that their continued presence in Vatican institutions had become, at least temporarily, too dangerous for both the Church and the fugitives themselves. The guests were not thrown out into the streets but were assisted in finding other refuges. Nevertheless, their removal from Church institutions is inconsistent with allegations of a papal order to accept Jews.

The presence within Vatican City of at least fifty fugitives, mostly non-Jews and converts but including some seven or eight who were Jewish in religion, was questioned in February 1944. The fugitives were living in a building called the Canonica, where they were guests in the private apartments of individual prelates. Monsignor Domenico Tardini, secretary of the Section for Extraordinary Ecclesiastical Affairs at the Vatican Secretariat of State and one of Secretary of State Luigi Cardinal Maglione's two closest aides, wrote at the time that, for security reasons, those hosts had been ordered to make their guests leave. "The matter caused an uproar," Tardini added.[13] After much discussion, the fugitives finally were allowed to remain, but it had been a close decision.

Evidence of high-ranking Italian prelates who did little for the Jews, or were even hostile to them, also challenges claims of a papal directive for rescue. One example was recorded by Don Leto Casini, a young priest recruited by Elia Cardinal Dalla Costa, archbishop of Florence, to hide Jews in his archdiocese. In his memoirs, Casini wrote of a dangerous train trip he took to Foligno on a frigid day in January 1944. His mission was to deliver funds to the bishop of Foligno, who was actively helping Jews. To reach Foligno, Casini had to change trains in Perugia, a transfer that involved a long delay. While waiting, he went to see the archbishop of Perugia, hoping, he later admitted, that he could leave the money with the archbishop, to be relayed to Foligno by someone else. But, as Casini wrote, "I had barely referred to the 'Jewish' problem ... he didn't let me finish the sentence before asking me to leave and showing me to the door."[14]

Stranded in Perugia again on his return from Foligno late that cold January night, the young priest was so intimidated that he did not even dare ask for shelter at the archbishop's residence. He preferred to spend the night, as he recorded, "sleeping out in the open, behind a gate." If the pope had issued an order to rescue Jews, why would he not have sent it to a prelate as important and as close to Rome as the archbishop of Perugia?[15]

Some scholars have argued for the existence of a papal directive based on the fact that the archbishops of Genoa, Turin, Florence, and Milan cooperated over a large geographical area to save Jews.[16] However, these coordinated efforts can be more correctly explained as the consequence of requests from local committees of an Italian Jewish assistance agency called Delasem. When each archbishop agreed to help, Delasem representatives turned over to him their funds and lists of local clients, along with information about other prelates who were engaged in the same activities. There is ample evidence of these Jewish–Catholic contacts.[17]

There is, finally, reason to doubt the existence of a papal directive to open Church institutions to Jews because such an order was usually not necessary or required. As the evidence shows, Jews were admitted spontaneously soon after the Germans arrived in Italy. At the parish level, priests had a certain leeway. They generally would have informed their bishops after the fact of any outside guests, and in Rome that bishop was the pope himself, who probably would not have objected, but they did not have to wait for a papal directive before acting. Nor was a papal directive required in most convents and monasteries, where the rules of the individual orders usually permitted outside guests in specified sections of the buildings. In fact, many such institutions operated hostels for traveling pilgrims. Others operated boarding schools with extra rooms. In most cases, Jewish and non-Jewish "guests" were separated by gender, with men and boys going to male institutions and women and girls to female ones. Only rarely and only in the most desperate cases did strict rules of cloister need to be lifted wholly or in part.[18] Under these circumstances, directors of religious houses often sought permission from the heads of their orders to take risks or dispense charity, but they were usually not required to inform the Vatican. From the pope's point of view, while he may have had the authority to issue a rescue directive, he would have refrained from interfering in most cases, especially when the substance of such an order was already being fulfilled.

An April 30, 1943, letter by Pius XII to his friend Bishop Konrad von Preysing in Berlin makes it clear that the pope was sensitive to the varying levels of risk in nations and locales throughout German-occupied Europe and preferred to give the clergy discretion in dealing with Jews and other fugitives from the Nazis. He wrote,

> Regarding pronouncements by the bishops [on the subject of Jews], We leave it to local senior clergymen to decide if, and to what degree, the danger of reprisals and oppression, as well as, perhaps, other circumstances caused by the length and psychological climate of the war, may make restraint advisable – despite the reasons for intervention – in order to avoid greater evils. This is one of the reasons why We limit ourselves in Our proclamations.[19]

Several years earlier, in 1935, while he was still Vatican Secretary of State Eugenio Cardinal Pacelli, the future pope had been similarly explicit in a conversation with Dietrich von Hildebrand, a German Catholic philosopher and outspoken anti-Nazi. Hildebrand asked Pacelli if he realized that possibly millions of German Protestants and Socialists would have flocked to the Catholic Church if all the German bishops in the country had opposed National Socialism from the beginning. According to Hildebrand's wife and biographer, Pacelli answered, "Indeed, but martyrdom is something that the Church cannot command. It must be freely chosen."[20]

✳

While all of these factors contribute to the conclusion that no papal directive was issued to save Jews in Italy, the absence of oral testimony by direct rescuers is the most convincing. Yet such testimony is the point upon which supporters of Pius XII recently have focused most strongly. Drawing on long-known statements in memoirs, newspaper articles, and secondary studies, as well as on some new material, supporters have, since about the year 2000, named two successor popes, several cardinals, and many other priests who allegedly claimed to have received a directive.[21] The remainder of this chapter focuses on these claims.[22]

The first pope, chronologically, whom many contemporary papal supporters invoke is the then Monsignor Angelo Roncalli, the future Pope John XXIII (1958–63), who was the apostolic delegate in Turkey and Greece during the war. According to papal supporter Ronald Rychlak, Roncalli once said, "In all these painful matters [meaning his efforts to save Jewish lives] I have referred to the Holy See and simply carried out the Pope's orders: first and foremost to save Jewish lives."[23] But the evidence for that statement is Pinchas Lapide, whose consistently erroneous *Three Popes and the Jews* (1967) is often cited by papal supporters. Lapide wrote that Roncalli made that statement to him personally in 1957 in Venice, when Roncalli was the patriarch of Venice and Lapide was the Israeli consul there.[24] No witnesses for this statement exist, so we have only Lapide's word. Moreover, Rychlak misquoted Lapide as having said "Jewish lives"; the phrase actually reads "human lives." Also, of course, Roncalli did not work in Italy during the war and was not referring to a papal order there.

The second pope who allegedly testified to a papal directive to save Jews was the then Monsignor Giovanni Battista Montini, the future Pope Paul VI (1963–78). As secretary of the Section for Ordinary Ecclesiastical Affairs at the Vatican Secretariat of State during the war, Montini was, along with Tardini, one of the two chief aides to Secretary of State Maglione. Rychlak wrote that in 1955 a delegation of Italian Jews asked Montini if "he would accept an award for his work on behalf of Jews during the war." Montini allegedly replied to the delegation, "All I did was my duty. And besides I only acted upon orders from the Holy Father. Nobody deserves a medal for that."[25] But the source for this incident is again Lapide, who provided no evidence for his claim.[26] Moreover, the statement itself is unconvincing, for two reasons. First, Montini allegedly said "All I did was my duty," but there is little evidence that he ever did much for the Jews. He was involved in some tentative diplomatic interventions, and he clearly knew that Jews were among those being hidden at the Seminario Romano, but he does not seem to have been actively involved in Jewish rescue. On the contrary, in the one solidly documented case published in the Vatican's *ADSS*, Montini actually refused a December 1943 request for assistance from an important Jewish convert to Catholicism, apparently without even referring that request to someone else.[27]

Montini's alleged statement implying a papal directive to rescue Jews is also inconsistent with his well-known letter of June 1963 to *The Tablet* in defense of Pius XII. That letter was prompted by Hochhuth's charges in *The Deputy*, which had recently opened in Berlin, that the pope had done nothing to help Jews during the Holocaust. In the letter, Montini wrote of Pius XII's goodness, sensibility, courage, and desire to be informed of everything. He declared that the pope "tried, so far as he could, fully and courageously to carry out the mission entrusted to him," and pointed out that "an attitude of protest and condemnation [of the Holocaust] would have been not only futile but harmful."[28] But Montini never claimed in his letter that Pius XII had issued a directive to save Jews or involved himself in any way in Jewish rescue – activities that, had they occurred, would have been most relevant to Hochhuth's accusations.

As in the cases of Roncalli and Montini, allegations regarding certain other clergymen and a papal directive to rescue Jews also seem to be without foundation. One of these concerns Father Pancrazio Pfeiffer, superior general of the Società del Divin Salvatore (the Salvatoriani), whose monastery in Rome is just north of the entrance to St. Peter's Square. Pfeiffer was Pius XII's personal liaison to the German military command in Rome. In a claim that is, like so many of the others, often repeated, papal supporter William Doino declared that Pfeiffer "swear[s] that [Pius XII] approved and urged [him], and all Catholics, to help Nazi victims."[29] Doino did not, it will be noted, specifically mention Jews. But Pfeiffer died in an automobile accident in mid-May 1945. No one was yet talking about Jewish rescue and the pope's involvement. Pius XII may have known about Pfeiffer's rescue activities, if indeed there were any, and he may not have disapproved. It is, however, unlikely that Pfeiffer ever claimed to have received a papal directive to help Jews. Doino provided no source. He may well have drawn his information from Lapide, who wrote that Pfeiffer saved at least eight Jews and many others, but who also provided no source.[30]

Another individual often cited for claiming to have received a directive is the Jesuit Father Paolo Dezza, rector of the Pontifical Gregorian University during the war and later a cardinal.[31] On June 28, 1964, during the controversy concerning Hochhuth's play, Dezza wrote in *L'Osservatore della Domenica* that when the Germans occupied Rome, the pope had told him "Father, avoid receiving the military, because since the Gregorian is a pontifical house and linked to the Holy See, we must keep away from that part. But [accept] the others very willingly: civilians, persecuted Jews." Dezza added, "In fact, we received several of them."[32] Given Dezza's stature and direct presence on the scene, this claim deserves careful attention. It is surprising, however, that in articles he wrote for *La Civiltà Cattolica* and other publications, Dezza did not repeat the statement. More significant, the Gregorian University was primarily a school for seminarians who lived elsewhere. For a short time during the first months of the German occupation, the school accepted some "false seminarians" disguised in clerical garb as day students, not as residents. But documents that have come to light identify these "false seminarians" as political fugitives, not Jews.[33] Also, in February 1944, after the Nazi-Fascist raid on the Basilica of St. Paul outside the Walls, Maglione instructed the abbot there "in the name of the Holy Father, not to permit disguises in other clothing: no one should wear religious habits if he is not a priest or a monk."[34] Without clerical garb, "false seminarians" could not attend the university. At around the same time, as noted, properties of the Holy See and many other Church institutions received instructions from the Vatican to remove all their clandestine guests.

Another alleged witness to a papal directive was Monsignor Giuseppe Maria Palatucci, the bishop of Campagna. About Palatucci, William Doino repeats a lengthy quote from an earlier writer, Fernande Leboucher, a French Catholic who worked during the war with rescuer Father Marie Benoît.[35] Leboucher's sentence reads, "The bishop of the Campagna, [Giuseppe Maria] Palatucci, who ... saved almost a thousand Jews from the Germans, was asked in 1953 why he had risked his life for the Jews. [He said he did so] 'because of Vatican orders, issued in 1942, to save lives by all possible means.'"[36] But as we shall see, it is clear that Leboucher simply had repeated, without attribution, information provided by Pinchas Lapide.

According to Lapide, who provided no source, "Monsignor Palatucci, bishop of Campagna, and two of his close relatives saved 961 in Fiume."[37] At first glance, it is difficult to see how anyone in Campagna, in the province of Salerno and roughly seventy-five kilometers from Naples, could have saved or even assisted Jews in Fiume, hundreds of miles away on Italy's extreme northeastern border. However, it appears that from May 1940 to September 1943 Bishop Palatucci may have worked with his nephew Giovanni Palatucci, a commissioner in the office for foreigners at police headquarters in Fiume. Commissioner Palatucci is best known for his assistance to Jews in Fiume after September 1943, when the Germans occupied the city and Jews for the first time were in danger of immediate deportation to Auschwitz. He withheld or destroyed municipal records of their residency, warned them of pending police raids, and helped them find hiding places. He may well have saved hundreds.[38]

Less well known are Commissioner Palatucci's activities between 1940 and 1943, when he apparently assisted in less dramatic ways foreign Jews in Fiume, especially recently arrived refugees from Yugoslavia. After Italy entered the war on the side of the Germans in June 1940, foreign Jews throughout the country were arrested and interned or placed in supervised residences, always within Italy. According to survivor testimonies, Commissioner Palatucci then provided many refugees in Fiume with false documents and helped them find safe and comfortable areas for supervised residence. He also seems to have arranged to send many foreign Jews in Fiume to an internment camp or supervised residence in Campagna, where his uncle, Bishop Giuseppe Palatucci, worked hard, and perfectly legally, to persuade local authorities and the civilian population to treat them humanely.[39] The maximum number of Jews interned in the main camp at Campagna was 272, in September 1940.[40] Around that time, the bishop made financial contributions from diocesan funds to supplement the small and inadequate government subsidies of 6.50 lire per person per day with which internees were to buy their own food and other supplies.[41] He even requested additional subsidies from the Holy See, receiving 3,000 lire in October 1940 and 10,000 lire in November 1940.[42] Thus, while Bishop Palatucci did not "save 961 in Fiume," as Lapide claimed, he did make life easier for many Jewish internees in Campagna.

Thirty-six-year-old police commissioner Giovanni Palatucci was arrested on September 13, 1944, and deported. He died at Dachau on February 10, 1945. Eight years later, in 1953, he was honored in Israel when a street in Ramath Gan was given his name.[43] Again according to Lapide and repeated by Leboucher, Bishop Giuseppe Palatucci and another uncle who was a Franciscan priest in the southern region of Apulia were interviewed at that time by the Israeli press and asked why they had decided to risk their lives for others. In answer to the question, Lapide wrote, "both referred to Vatican orders issued in 1942 'to save lives by all possible means'" – the phrase that Leboucher repeated.[44] But because Lapide provided no source or evidence for that statement, we cannot be certain that the two priests actually made such a claim. Also, without more information, it is difficult to know exactly what they had done to "risk their lives." In addition, their claim of having received "Vatican orders issued in 1942 to save lives by all possible means," insofar as it applied to Jews, is improbable because of the early date of the reputed statement. Jews in Italy were not threatened with deportation until the arrival of the Germans in September 1943.

Another alleged "witness" to a papal directive is the Capuchin Father Calliste Lopinot, who was sent in early July 1941 to minister to some 85 Jewish converts to Catholicism who were among the 1,144 foreign Jews then interned at Ferramonti di Tarsia near Cosenza, about 250 kilometers south of Naples.[45] While there, Lopinot made many conversions, but he also provided moral and physical support for many who remained Jewish. He wrote extensively about his service at Ferramonti di Tarsia. He noted, for example, that he received 3,500 lire from the Vatican in the early spring of 1942 to help the 494 Jewish survivors of the shipwrecked *Pentcho*.[46] The amount was small, but he wrote in another context that 3,000 lire were enough to provide a bowl of soup daily for thirty people for a month.[47] But Lopinot never claimed in his reports that he had received a papal directive to rescue Jews. Foreign Jews at Ferramonti di Tarsia were released a few days before the Italian armistice and the German occupation on September 8, 1943. They were obliged to hide from the otherwise engaged Germans for only a few days before the Allies reached them on September 14.

Father Marie Benoît, a French Capuchin priest known as Maria Benedetto in Rome, is also commonly cited, without evidence, as a witness to a papal directive.[48] The evidence suggests otherwise. After a direct personal request from Lionello Alatri, a friend and an important figure in Rome's Jewish community, and in constant cooperation with Settimio Sorani of Delasem, Benoît hid and supplied several thousand Italian and foreign Jews in Rome during the German occupation. Far from receiving an order or even encouragement from the Vatican, however, he met with disapproval. On November 20, 1943, for example, when the irrepressible young priest was already in trouble with Italian authorities for forging documents for his refugees, an exasperated Vatican official, Monsignor Angelo Dell'Acqua, wrote "I have repeatedly (and the last time very clearly) told Father Benoît, Capuchin, to use the maximum prudence in dealing with the Jews . . . : it can be seen, unfortunately, that he has not wished to listen to the humble advice given to him."[49] Then on December 29, in reference to reports of a joint Catholic–Jewish rescue group that could only have been the one headed by Benoît, Dell'Acqua wrote, "Several times . . . I have observed that persons employed at the Vatican or close to it interest themselves too much (in a manner that I dare to call almost exaggerated) with the Jews, favoring them . . . I have always believed . . . in using the maximum prudence in speaking with Jews, to whom it would be better to speak less."[50]

Despite the claims of some papal supporters, Father Benoît received no financial help from the Vatican for his highly successful rescue activities.[51] On the contrary, in March 1944 Vatican Secretary of State Maglione refused to become involved in the priest's proposal to convert dollars deposited in London by the American Jewish Joint Distribution Committee into lire with which to support Jews in hiding in Rome, although evidence suggests that he permitted similar transactions for British prisoners of war.[52] In reports after the war, Benoît, without mentioning the Vatican or the pope, made it clear that his funding had come entirely from Jewish sources.[53] But papal supporters continued to claim that Pius XII had provided substantial financial assistance.[54] Finally, in exasperation, Benoît wrote explicitly in an Israeli newspaper article that appeared on July 6, 1961, that he had received no financial help from the Vatican.[55]

The final two frequently cited "witnesses" are the most important, not because they provided credible evidence of a papal directive but because of another nuance in their testimony. The first, most important, and most directly involved in Jewish rescue is Father Pietro Palazzini. During the German occupation of Rome, the Seminario Romano sheltered from the Nazis and their Italian collaborators some 200 fugitives, about 55 of whom were Jews. According to papal supporter Rabbi David Dalin, then Cardinal Palazzini, during a 1985 speech accepting the designation of Righteous Among the Nations at Yad Vashem for his rescue of Jews at the seminary, stressed that "the merit is entirely Pius XII's, who ordered us to do whatever we could to save the Jews from persecution."[56] This statement is curious, for several reasons. First, Palazzini's file at Yad Vashem does not mention that he made such a claim. Second, as noted, in December 1943 Palazzini's immediate superior, the rector of the seminary, wrote the pope a letter of apology for displeasing him by accepting too many fugitives. Third, in February 1944, after the Nazi-Fascist attack on the Basilica of St. Paul outside the Walls, the Seminario Romano was among those institutions ordered to remove fugitives from the premises, at least temporarily. Finally, after Palazzini received his award at Yad Vashem and allegedly made his statement about a papal order, he wrote a book about his experiences at the seminary during the German occupation. The book was published in 1995.[57] In it, Palazzini made no reference to a papal order.

Palazzini's actual words on the issue, however, must be studied carefully. He wrote, "the guidelines provided by Pope Pius XII were to save human lives, on whatever side they may be."[58] That remark is significant, because Palazzini recorded that after liberation, Nazi and Fascist fugitives hid at the same seminary. He referred to them as "the persecutors of yesterday, now being scrutinized by the purge tribunals."[59] About the German occupation, Palazzini added, "Under the pressure of events, although so very tragic, men rediscovered the Christian message, that is, the sense of reciprocal charity, according to which it is a duty to charge oneself with the salvation of others. To rediscover it, one voice was often raised among the din of arms: it was the voice of Pius XII. The refuge offered to so many people would not have been possible without his moral support, which was much more than a tacit consent."[60] However, Palazzini's only concrete evidence of the "voice of Pius XII" was eight of his speeches. Three of the eight, at Christmas 1942 and on his name day, June 2, in 1943 and 1944, included brief references to the pope's compassion for those persecuted because of nationality and descent (*stirpe*), but did not directly mention Jews or ask Catholics to help them. The other five speeches simply stressed the need for charity to all victims of war.[61] Other than in the context of those papal speeches that were broadcast, Palazzini did not refer to Vatican Radio, which Rychlak, in particular, claimed sent out orders to help Jews.[62] Nor did Palazzini ever refer to any other more precise papal directives. In other words, this honest and courageous man never testified to a directive, but he did indicate that Pius XII provided "moral support" for efforts to hide fugitives. That perception was undoubtedly an important element in the story of rescue. The priests and nuns who hid Jews surely believed that they were acting in a manner consistent with the pope's will. But moral support is not the same as a papal directive.

Finally, there is the case of Father J. Patrick Carroll-Abbing, later a monsignor, who rescued and assisted escaped prisoners of war and destitute civilians during the war and founded Boys' Town of Italy after it. In an August–September 2001 article published in *Inside the Vatican*, William Doino claimed that Carroll-Abbing had told him in several telephone interviews the year before that "I spoke to Pope Pius XII many times during the war, in person, face to face, and he told me not once but many many [sic] times to assist the Jews."[63] Yet in his two books about his wartime activities, *A Chance to Live* (1952) and *But for the Grace of God* (1966), Carroll-Abbing rarely mentioned Jews at all.[64] He never wrote that he took personal initiatives to hide Jews, that the pope told him to hide Jews, or even that Jews were hidden in Vatican properties. Carroll-Abbing died in July 2001, before the publication of Doino's article.

Carroll-Abbing certainly did good and courageous things during the German occupation of Rome. Using vivid and dramatic examples, he described his work with Allied prisoners of war, political fugitives, partisans, civilian victims of bombing raids, the poor, and especially homeless children. But he mentioned helping Jews only once, writing vaguely that for a time after the October 16 roundup he was "in touch with many of the more than 150 religious institutions that were sheltering the Jews."[65] In *But for the Grace of God*, the only book that extended its description beyond his own personal activities, he also made many factual errors.[66] The one statement that Carroll-Abbing made about a papal directive should thus be viewed in this context. He wrote that after the German roundup of Jews in Rome on October 16, 1943, "word came from the Vatican that, because of the emergency, nuns *would be allowed* to give hospitality in their convents *to Jewish men* as well as their families" [emphasis mine].[67] He added that the permission was given specifically to the Sisters of Our Lady of Sion [Zion], who passed it along to other convents.

This statement makes perfect sense. The Sisters of Our Lady of Sion convent was in fact a large residence for nuns devoted to the conversion of the Jews. The house was across the Tiber from the former Jewish ghetto. When the Germans began their roundup in the ghetto on October 16, 1943, many Jews fled across the river and knocked on the gates of Our Lady of Sion. Because the house was not a cloistered convent, the nuns needed no special permission to admit outsiders temporarily, but they probably did need it to house men for any period of time. They may have sought permission from the head of their order, or they may have petitioned the Vatican. In any case, the men (and women) who had entered on October 16 remained. The Sisters of Our Lady of Sion was, in fact, one of the few female religious institutions that hid men as well as women. The Vatican may well have given explicit permission, as Carroll-Abbing said. But it took no initiative in rescuing Jews and issued no directive before or after the fact.

There is, however, much room for compromise and reconciliation between those who criticize Pius XII and those who defend him. Pius XII knew that Jews were hiding in Church institutions, although he probably knew few of the details. He and his closest advisors did not prevent that rescue effort, although some members of the Curia opposed it rather strongly and did try to interfere. However, some papal advisors, probably including Montini, approved of limited and cautious rescue efforts as long as they did not compromise the neutrality of the Holy See. Vatican documents reveal that, on a few occasions, papal advisors referred important political dissidents to Church institutions, and once or twice those referred may have been Jewish. As further documents become available, additional cases may become known. However, the documents also show that some Jewish supplicants were turned away without referrals.

It is possible that the pope and his advisors gave permission, on special request after the fact, to individual convents, such as the one Carroll-Abbing mentioned, to hide men on their premises. Vatican trucks continued to supply food to convents, schools, and other institutions sheltering Jews and many others. In late winter and spring of 1944, until the liberation of Rome on June 2, Vatican authorities also allowed thousands of Italian civilians fleeing from Allied bombing raids and the German Army's forced evacuations of the hill towns south of Rome to find shelter in the pope's nearby summer residence at Castel Gandolfo. Although it has never been proven, there may have been Jews among them.[68] In addition, the pope's public messages about his compassion for those persecuted because of their nationality or descent, along with two encyclicals that made reference to his love for all people regardless of race, and *L'Osservatore Romano*'s pleas for compassion in four additional articles, encouraged rescuers from among the clergy, like the young Palazzini, to believe that they were doing the pope's will.[69]

Clearly, papal involvement in Jewish rescue is not a black-or-white issue, but one of painfully nuanced shades of gray. Pius XII was a conscientious, deeply spiritual man, perhaps somewhat out of touch with reality and perhaps unable to comprehend fully the horrors of his age.[70] He struggled to do his job as he saw it, in the best way he could, given his training, experience, and temperament. He protected his institution while issuing general guidelines in favor of peace and charity to all who suffered. He permitted the establishment of the Vatican Information Service to enable thousands of refugees, including Jews, to communicate with their loved ones. Toward the end of the war, he encouraged the formation of a Vatican refugee assistance agency to provide hot meals and clothing for thousands of Romans. Jews may have been among the recipients. In a context that did not involve Jews, he also accepted certain risks. For example, he agreed to pass messages from anti-Hitler agents in the Third Reich to the British in late 1939 and early 1940, and he warned the Allies of German invasion plans throughout the spring of 1940.[71] Finally, he allowed men and women of the Church to make choices and to take far greater risks in acts of resistance and rescue. But there were limits to what the pope did, and those, too, should be recognized. Above all, he himself was not willing to take initiatives or become directly involved in the rescue of Jews in mortal danger of deportation and murder. Pius XII cannot take credit for the courageous acts of rescue taken by men and women of the Church in Italy and elsewhere in German-occupied Europe.

NOTES

1. Zuccotti, Susan, "Pius XII and the Rescue of Jews in Italy. Evidence of a Papal Directive," *Holocaust and Genocide Studies*, 18, no. 2 (Fall 2004). © Oxford University Press. Reprinted with permission of Oxford University Press.

2. See, for example, Pinchas E. Lapide, *The Last Three Popes and the Jews* (London: Souvenir, 1967), 133–5, 214–15, and 223; also published as *Three Popes and the Jews* (New York: Hawthorn Books, 1967). Lapide's claims were repeated most notably by the Holy See's Commission for Religious Relations with the Jews in "We Remember: A Reflection on the *Shoah*," included in *Catholics Remember the Holocaust* (Washington, D.C.: United States Catholic Conference, 1998), 47–56, 53.

3. A partial list of papal supporters published in English would include Pierre Blet, S. J., *Pius XII and the Second World War: According to the Archives of the Vatican*, trans. Lawrence J. Johnson (New York: Paulist Press, 1999); essays by Robert A. Graham, S. J., and Joseph L. Lichten in *Pius XII and the Holocaust: A Reader* (Milwaukee: Catholic League for Religious and Civil Rights, 1988 <1963>); Lapide, *Three Popes and the Jews*; Sister Margherita Marchione, *Yours Is a Precious Witness: Memoirs of Jews and Catholics in Wartime Italy* (New York: Paulist Press, 1997) and *Pope Pius XII: Architect for Peace* (New York: Paulist Press, 2000); Ralph McInerny, *The Defamation of Pius XII* (South Bend, IN: St. Augustine's Press, 2001); and Ronald Rychlak, *Hitler, the War and the Pope* (Columbus, MS: Genesis, 2000).

4. For more on Vatican diplomatic interventions on behalf of Jews, see especially John F. Morley, *Vatican Diplomacy and the Jews during the Holocaust, 1939–1943* (New York: KTAV, 1980) and Susan Zuccotti, *Under His Very Windows: The Vatican and the Holocaust in Italy* (New Haven: Yale University Press, 2000). On efforts to facilitate Jewish emigration, see Zuccotti, *Under His Very Windows*, 70–81.

5. Records of this type may be found in the archives of the Seminario Lombardo in Rome, the Archdiocese of Turin, and the Istituto Storico della Resistenza in Cuneo e Provincia, f. 5, Carte di Don Raimondo Viale.

6. These volumes, published in Vatican City by the Libreria Editrice Vaticana, consist of wartime diplomatic documents selected from the Vatican archives by an international team of Jesuit scholars, including Pierre Blet, Robert A. Graham, Angelo Martini, and Burkhart Schneider. Until 2003, other diplomatic documents written since 1922 had remained inassessible to scholars. Additional material from the papacies of Pius XI and Pius XII is now gradually becoming available.

7. Originally titled *Der Stellvertreter*, the play opened in Berlin in 1963. Translated in Britain as *The Representative*, it opened in London also in 1963. In the United States, it was translated as *The Deputy* and opened in New York in 1964. Grove Press published it under the latter title in New York in 1964. Most recently, director Costa-Gavras adapted the play for his film *Amen*, which opened in the United States in 2003.

8. Recent books critical of Pius XII's response to the Holocaust include James Carroll, *Constantine's Sword: The Church and the Jews: A History* (Boston: Houghton Mifflin, 2000); John Cornwell, *Hitler's Pope: The Secret History of Pius XII* (New York: Viking, 1999); Daniel Goldhagen, *A Moral Reckoning: The Role of the Catholic Church in the Holocaust and Its Unfulfilled Duty of Repair* (New York: Knopf, 2002); David Kertzer, *The Popes against the Jews: The Vatican's Role in the Rise of Modern Anti-Semitism* (New York: Knopf, 2001); Michael Phayer, *The Catholic Church and the Holocaust, 1930–1965* (Bloomington: Indiana University Press, 2000); Garry Wills, *Papal Sin: Structures of Deceit* (New York: Doubleday, 2000); and Zuccotti, *Under His Very Windows.*

9. *Actes et Documents du Saint Siège relatifs à la seconde guerre mondial (ADSS)*, IX, doc. 338, notes of the Secretariat of State, September 18, 1943, pp. 482–3. On p. 482, fn. 1 identifies the author of this document as Monsignor Di Meglio and declares that the Jewish lawyer was probably Ugo Foà, president of the Jewish community of Rome.

10. There were, of course, exceptions, and Pius XII was aware of some of them. For example, Monsignor Giovanni Battista Montini at the Vatican Secretariat of State noted on October 1 that an eighty-four-year-old man "of the Jewish religion" had asked for permission to stay at a particular Roman convent where the nuns were willing to accept his seventy-six-year-old wife, a niece, and an elderly female domestic servant. Special permission was necessary for the man because convents did not usually accept men. Montini added that the man had expressed a wish to make a gift in his will to a Catholic charity. That same day, with the note "Ex. Aud. SS.mi. 1.X.43," Montini indicated that he had mentioned the matter to the pope. He added, "We'll see if it is possible to help him." The pope, in other words, was not opposed. But the pope had taken no initiative and issued no directive. The following day, Montini wrote that he had spoken of the matter with Monsignor Luigi Traglia, assistant to the vicar, who "seemed to be favorable." No Vatican document indicates whether the man was actually accepted. See *ADSS*, IX, doc. 356, p. 496.

11. The letter is printed in Carlo Badala, "Il Coraggio di accogliere," *Sursum Corda*, anno LXXVII, n. 1, 1994, pp. 43–46, 43. It said, among other things, "It is with the greatest sorrow that I have learned that I also have added a displeasure to that mass of pain that

today weighs upon the paternal heart of Your Holiness.... I believed that it was in the heart of Your Holiness to welcome in your seminary, with the greatest possible reserve, caution and secrecy, some poor unhappy persons caught up in the current storm.... These grew in number: but I thought that it was not necessary to involve the highest responsibility of Your Holiness in individual cases."

12. See the Archivio del Seminario Lombardo (ASL), b.7.A.73, *Diario,* "Appendice," 17–18; Pietro Palazzini, *Il Clero e l'occupazione tedesca di Roma. Il ruolo del Seminario Romano Maggiore* (Rome: Apes, 1995), 42; and Ivanoe Bonomi, *Diario di un anno: 2 giugno 1943-10 giugno 1944* (Cernusco sul Naviglio: Garzanti, 1947), 146–7. I discuss this expulsion order in more detail in Zuccotti, *Under His Very Windows,* 222–32.

13. *ADSS,* X, note by Tardini attached to doc. 53, February 13, 1944, p. 129. Document 53 itself was written by Monsignor Guido Anichini, head of the Canonica di San Pietro, to the pope, informing him of the number of fugitives being sheltered in that building. Clearly, the pope did not know the full extent of these assistance efforts. For more on Jews sheltered within Vatican City, see Zuccotti, *Under His Very Windows,* 212–14 and 228–32.

14. Don Leto Casini, *Ricordi di un vecchio prete* (Florence: Giuntina, 1986), 61. After the war Casini received an award as Righteous Among the Nations at Yad Vashem in Israel.

15. Other examples of indifferent or hostile prelates include Patriarch of Venice Adeonato Piazza, who seems to have done little for the Jews (see Zuccotti, *Under His Very Windows,* 265–76); Archbishop Cesare Boccoleri of Modena, who insisted that classes in a seminary in Nonantola resume in early October 1943, as usual, and thus demanded that the roughly thirty to thirty-five Jewish orphans hiding there leave (Klaus Voigt, *Villa Emma: Ragazzi ebrei in fuga: 1940–1945* (Milan: La Nuova Italia, 2002), 207, 212, 217; the bishop of Mantua, known to the Allies as a Fascist sympathizer who refused to have anything to do with the incipient anti-Fascist Christian Democratic Party (Lamberto Mercuri, "La Situazione dei partiti italiani vista dal Foreign Office (dicembre 1943)," *Storia Contemporanea,* anno XI, (6), December 1980, pp. 1049–60, 1057); and a bishop in the Valle d'Aosta who expressed strong disapproval of the efforts of a priest in his diocese to hide a Jewish family (Centro di Documentazione Ebraica Contemporanea [CDEC], Milan, 9/1, f. Biella, statement of Davide Nissim, December 13, 1954). On the apparent indifference or hostility of Monsignors Antonio Riberi and Angelo Dell'Acqua at the Vatican Secretariat of State, and even of Secretary of State Maglione himself, to the rescue activities of Father Benoît, see below.

16. See, for example, Sergio Minerbi, *Raffaele Cantoni, un ebreo anticonformista* (Assisi: Beniamino Carucci, 1978), 118. Léon Poliakov did not make that claim specifically for Italy, but regarding all of occupied Europe he wrote that "We do not know what were the exact instructions sent by the Holy See to the churches in the different countries, but the coincidence of effort [by the Catholic clergy to help Jews] at the time of the deportations is proof that such steps were taken." See his *Harvest of Hate: The Nazi Program for the Destruction of the Jews of Europe* (New York: Holocaust Library, 1979 <1951>), 295.

17. For details and documentation, see my *Under His Very Windows,* 233–64. Delasem is an acronym for Delegazione Assistenza Emigranti Ebrei.

18. For example, Louis Goldman, in his memoirs *Amici per la vita* (Florence: SP 44 Editore, 1993), 57–64, described the convent of Spirito Santo in Varlungo, near Florence, where his mother, aunt, and about nine other Jewish women were sheltered and saved. This convent of strict cloister devoted entirely to contemplation and prayer did not operate a school or other public facility. According to Goldman, therefore, the mother superior had to obtain the permission of the cardinal archbishop of Florence before she could modify the rules of cloister. Even here, however, the Jewish women lived in separate quarters that were technically outside the cloistered area and did not have daily contact with the nuns. Also according to Goldman, the cardinal could grant permission, but he could not order the nuns to lift their rules of cloister.

19. *ADSS*, II, doc. 105, Pius XII to Preysing, April 30, 1943, p. 436.

20. Alice von Hildebrand, *The Soul of a Lion: Dietrich Von Hildebrand* (San Francisco: Ignatius Press, 2000), 285–6.

21. One of the first recent papal supporters to make such a claim was Ronald Rychlak, in a response to my oral presentation at a symposium at Trinity College, Hartford, CT, in February 2001. Written and revised versions of our presentations may be found in the *Journal of Modern Italian Studies* 7:2 (Summer 2002), 215–68. I questioned Rychlak's oral claims briefly in my published version, but this article discusses them in much more detail. Furthermore, in both his oral and his published versions, Rychlak referred to "forty-two witnesses, including five cardinals, [who] spoke directly of Pius XII's concern for and help given to Jewish people" in "sworn testimony, under oath" between 1967 and 1974. This reference is to testimony given in the Church's official proceedings for the beatification of Pius XII. Rychlak and some others have been authorized to examine that testimony. My written request to see it was refused by Father Peter Gumpel, relator for the cause of Pius XII, on the grounds that some scholars had abused the privilege.

22. Don Aldo Brunacci of Assisi's claim, made in 1982 and later raised not by papal supporters but by myself, is not repeated at length here because it was carefully examined in my *Under His Very Windows*, 262–4. Very briefly, Brunacci claimed that he saw a letter from Vatican officials in the hands of his bishop, Giuseppe Placido Nicolini. He did not read the letter, but his bishop told him that it contained instructions to hide Jews. This Brunacci certainly did. Apart from the question of why the bishop did not save the letter (he saved the personal papers of some of his guests), there is a problem of context here. Assistance activity for refugees from air raids began in Assisi in the summer of 1943, and clandestine efforts for Jews grew naturally from that. They were ongoing by September 1943, at a time when, as seen, Vatican officials were actually refusing shelter in Church institutions to Jews in Rome. For Brunacci's claim, see his "Giornata degli ebrei d'Italia: Ricordi di un protagonista," public lecture, Assisi, March 15, 1982, printed in full in Brunacci, *Ebrei in Assisi durante la guerra. Ricordi di un protagonista*, Assisi, January 27, 1985, pp. 7–15, 9.

23. Rychlak, *Hitler, the War and the Pope*, 242.

24. Lapide, *Three Popes and the Jews*, 181.

25. Rychlak, *Hitler, the War and the Pope*, 242.

26. Lapide, *Three Popes and the Jews*, 137.

27. *ADSS*, IX, doc. 453, Foligno to Maglione, December 2, 1943, and attached note of Montini, 589–90. The case involved a high-ranking Vatican lawyer named Foligno, who had been baptized a Catholic at birth and had a non-Jewish practicing Catholic wife and children. In early December, after Mussolini ordered his police to arrest all Jews in Italy, including converts, Foligno wrote to the Vatican Secretariat of State to ask if he and his family could be sheltered in Vatican City or in some extraterritorial building. If ever there was an appeal that should have evoked a response from Vatican officials, this was it. Other Jews, especially converts, were being sheltered in Vatican properties, and Montini knew it. On Foligno's letter, however, he wrote with terrible insensitivity and finality, "Unfortunately what he asks is not in our power. Respond accordingly." This was not the action of a prelate who had been ordered by the pope to rescue Jews.

28. G. B. Cardinal Montini, "Pius XII and the Jews," letter to *The Tablet*, received on June 21, 1963, and published on July 6; reprinted in *The Storm over "The Deputy,"* Eric Bentley, ed. (New York: Grove Press, 1964), 66–9; and in *Commonweal*, February 28, 1964, pp. 651–2.

29. William Doino, "A Distorted History of Pius XII," *Inside the Vatican*, February 2001, p. 55.

30. Lapide, *Three Popes and the Jews*, 134.

31. Dezza is cited by Doino, "A Distorted History," 55.

32. *L'Osservatore della Domenica*, 68–9. Doino gave an incorrect date (June 26, 1981). He also somewhat exaggerated Dezza's words, "Ma per gli altri ben volentieri: civili, ebrei perseguitati." He translated them as "for the others, help them willingly, *especially help the poor, persecuted Jews*" (emphasis added).

33. See the list of names and identification cards of "false students" at the Gregorian University in ASL, b. 7.A.77.

34. *ADSS*, XI, doc. 30, notes of Maglione, February 6, 1944, p. 126.

35. Doino, "A Distorted History," 55.

36. Doino cites Fernande Leboucher, *The Incredible Mission of Father Benoît* (London: William Kimber, 1970), 141. I verified the quotation in the American edition, titled *The Incredible Mission* (Garden City, NY: Doubleday, 1969), 121.

37. Lapide, *Three Popes and the Jews*, 134.

38. CDEC, Milan, 9/2, f. Benemeriti (medaglie d'oro), s.f. Palatucci Giovanni–Fiume.

39. Survivor testimonies may be found in Dipartimento della Pubblica Sicurezza, ed., *Giovanni Palatucci. Il poliziotto che salvò migliaia di ebrei* (Rome: Laurus Robuffo, 2002). See also Klaus Voigt, *Il Rifugio precario. Gli esuli in Italia dal 1933 al 1945*, vol. 2 (Florence: La Nuova Italia, 1996), 185.

40. Voigt, *Il Rifugio precario*, 91.

41. Bishop Palatucci referred to this contribution in a letter to Montini on April 16, 1941, reproduced in full in *Giovanni Palatucci*, 134. Government subsidies for male internees were later increased to 8 lire per day.

42. See letters to Bishop Palatucci from Vatican Secretary of State Maglione on October 2, 1940, and from Montini on November 29, 1940, reproduced in full in *Giovanni Palatucci*, 130–3. For a rough idea of the purchasing power of 13,000 lire, see below. Vatican officials later declined to send an additional 13,000 lire requested by Bishop Palatucci

for the same purpose. See the letter from Monsignor Francesco Borgonini Duca, the apostolic nuncio to Italy, to Bishop Palatucci, March 10, 1942, also in *Giovanni Palatucci*, 136.

43. Giovanni Palatucci was honored as Righteous Among the Nations at Yad Vashem in Israel in 1990. He was also proposed as a candidate for beatification in 2002.

44. Lapide, *Three Popes and the Jews*, 135.

45. Doino, "A Distorted History," 55.

46. Fr. Callistus a Geispolsheim (Lopinot), "De Apostolatu inter Hebraeos in publicae custodiae loco cui nomen v. 'Campo di Concentramento Ferramonti-Tarsia (Cosenza)," in *Analecta Ordinis Fratrum Minorum Capuccinorum* 60 (1944), 73. The *Pentcho* left Bratislava in May 1940, sailed down the Danube, and sank in the Aegean in October. Mussolini's government first interned the survivors in Rhodes, but transferred them to Ferramonti in February and March 1942.

47. Ibid., 74; and Lopinot, "Diario 1941–1944: Ferramonti-Tarsia," in *Ferramonti: Un lager nel Sud. Atti del convegno internazionale di studi*, Francesco Volpe, ed. (Cosenza: Orizzonti Meridionali, 1990), entry for March 31, 1943, p. 81.

48. Doino, "A Distorted History," 55.

49. *ADSS*, IX, doc. 433, attached note of Dell'Acqua, 569.

50. *ADSS*, IX, doc. 487, notes of the Vatican Secretariat of State, fn4, annotation by Dell'Acqua, 631–2.

51. See, for example, Leboucher, *Incredible Mission*, 141. Rychlak repeated the claim, citing Leboucher, in the *Journal of Modern Italian Studies*, 225.

52. *ADSS*, X, note of Maglione attached to doc. 103, March 16, 1944, p. 179. On Maglione's services on behalf of British prisoners of war, see Owen Chadwick, *Britain and the Vatican during the Second World War* (Cambridge: Cambridge University Press, 1986), 295.

53. See, for example, "Relazione sull'attività della DELASEM di Padre Benedetto," reprinted in full in Renzo De Felice, *Storia degli ebrei italiani sotto il fascismo* (Turin: Einaudi, 1988 <1961>), 633–4.

54. See especially Robert Leiber, S. J., "Pio XII e gli Ebrei di Roma 1943–1944," *La Civiltà Cattolica*, quad. 2657, February 25, 1961, 449–58, 451.

55. "Alcune precisazioni di Padre Benedetto," *Israel* 46 (36), 5.

56. Dalin, *The Weekly Standard*, February 26, 2001, p. 37. Doino, "A Distorted History," 55, also made this claim at about the same time.

57. *Il Clero e l'occupazione tedesca di Roma.*

58. Ibid., 35.

59. Ibid., 5.

60. Ibid., 17.

61. For the text of the messages evoking papal compassion for those persecuted because of their nationality or descent, see *L'Osservatore Romano*, December 25, 1942, pp. 1–3; June 3, 1943, p. 1; and June 3, 1944, p. 1. The other papal speeches mentioned by Palazzini, delivered on August 24 and December 24, 1939, June 2, 1940, December 24, 1941, and December 24, 1943, were also printed in *L'Osservatore Romano*.

62. For Rychlak's repeated claims about Vatican Radio, see *Hitler, the War and the Pope*, 144, 151; "Goldhagen v. Pius XII," *First Things*, June–July 2002, pp. 37–54, 39,

46–7; and his presentation in the *Journal of Modern Italian Studies*, 223. Since the original transcripts of wartime Vatican Radio broadcasts are not available, claims about their content cannot be confirmed. The sources for Rychlak's and other papal supporters' claims are usually allegations made during the war for propaganda purposes by the Allies, who were anxious to depict a Vatican partial to them. See Chadwick, *Britain and the Vatican during the Second World War*, 141–9.

63. William Doino, "The Pope Gave Me Direct Orders to Rescue Jews," *Inside the Vatican*, August–September 2001, special insert, p. x.

64. The first book was published in New York by Longmans, Green; the second, in London by Secker and Warburg.

65. Carroll-Abbing, *But for the Grace of God*, 56.

66. He was often mistaken with dates and statistics. For example, he wrote that Roncalli saved nearly the entire Jewish community of Bulgaria (p. 46); he made many errors in his description of Benoît's rescue activities of Jews in Rome (p. 56); and he was apparently a source for the false but often repeated claim that when the Nazis extorted gold from the Roman Jewish community in September 1943, the pope "made available 15 kilograms of gold by having some sacred vessels melted down" (p. 52). Even the pope's closest friends and supporters agree that this never happened and that the pope's offer of a loan at the time was never needed.

67. Carroll-Abbing, *But for the Grace of God*, 55–6.

68. In the *Journal of Modern Italian Studies*, 224, Rychlak claimed that "hundreds, perhaps thousands" of Jews were among those sheltered at Castel Gandolfo. However, his evidence from American archives is unconvincing because he did not show it to have ever precisely mentioned Jews. His citation of Marchione and Leboucher is faulty because those authors did not provide evidence. His final source is Emilio Bonomelli, whom he identified as the director of the papal villa at Castel Gandolfo. Rychlak stated that in his book *I Papi in campagna* (Rome: Gherardo Casini, 1953), 439, Bonomelli wrote, in Rychlak's words, "some of the people under his [the pope's] care were Jewish." However, Bonomelli actually wrote of "some families of Jews" who were present at a mass at Christmas 1943 given for a group of political refugees at the villa of the Congregation of the Propaganda Fide, next to the papal residence at Castel Gandolfo. Those families, in other words, were not numerous – certainly they were not "hundreds, perhaps thousands" – and they were converts. In his description of the thousands of local refugees who subsequently found shelter at Castel Gandolfo from Allied bombing raids in February 1944 and from German clearance of their villages later, Bonomelli did not ever mention Jews. I have, to date, found no personal testimony from Jews who were at Castel Gandolfo, while such testimony from Jews in Catholic convents, monasteries, hospitals, and schools is plentiful. The issue demands further investigation.

69. The pope's references to his love for all regardless of race occurred in *Summi pontificatus* on October 20, 1939, and, much more briefly, in *Mystici Corpus Christi* on June 29, 1943. They may be read in *The Papal Encyclicals*, vol. 4: 1939–1958, Claudia Carlen Ihm, ed. (Raleigh, N. C.: McGrath, 1981), 5–22, 37–63. Additional *L'Osservatore Romano* articles about the pope's position included two on October 25 and 29, 1943, p. 1, which in the wake of the Rome roundup spoke of his compassion for all regardless of

"nationality, descent or religion," and two on December 3 and 4, 1943, p. 1, protesting not the deportation and murder of Italian Jews by the Germans but a recent Italian measure ordering Italian police to arrest and intern Jews within their own country.

70. To suspect that Pius XII may not have been able to imagine the full horror of the war, however, is not to say that he was not well informed about the Holocaust. Even most papal supporters do not suggest that he was unaware that millions of Jews had been and were continuing to be murdered throughout the war. For more on what the pope knew, see Kevin Madigan, "What the Vatican Knew about the Holocaust, and When," *Commentary* 112:3 (October 2001), 43–52; and Zuccotti, *Under His Very Windows*, 93–112.

71. The German conspirators were seeking assurances that the British would not attack in the wake of a coup against Hitler. The pope seems to have issued his warnings of German invasion plans because he feared being accused of acting as a cover for a German attack. For details, see Harold C. Deutsch, *The Conspiracy against Hitler in the Twilight War* (Minneapolis: University of Minnesota Press, 1968), 111–46, 332–50.

PART FIVE

AFTERMATH: CONTEMPORARY ITALY AND HOLOCAUST MEMORY

16 The Rescued and the Rescuers in Private and Public Memories

Anna Bravo

Some time ago a friend and colleague, Anna Segre, requested that Yad Vashem in Jerusalem bestow the title of Righteous Among the Nations upon a medical doctor from Turin, Carlo Angela, for saving her parents, Renzo and Nella. This event is the starting point from which I will attempt to illustrate the relations between public and private memory and the "battle of memories" that was waged in Italy around the official ceremony in which the title was awarded.

In some ways this battle resembles the one witnessed in some European countries in the postwar period. The clash was especially marked in France where there was a tendency to assimilate all prisoners of concentration camps into the category of political deportees. This position was a natural one for those who had been politically active, or had been partisans, and also for those who had been politicized within the concentration camps. However, for many others, blurring the distinction between deportee and political prisoner tended to obscure the specific histories of individuals and groups. The camps also contained people taken as hostages, those captured in reprisals and punitive raids, people accused of black market trading, soldiers convicted of military offenses, and "free workers" taken to the camps as a punishment. On arrival at the camps, all these people were in fact classed as *red triangles*, that is, as political prisoners, not because they had been arrested for a political offense, but because they were categorized as saboteurs and enemies of the Third Reich. Yet, obviously, their histories were different and, by lumping them all together, their particular situations were obscured. This is clearly all the more true for the Jews.

The conceptual framework in which the most prominent theme is that of political deportees risks making the *Shoah* into merely a religious or ethnic subheading within the general framework of the repression of the Resistance and anti-Fascism. Thus the distinction between deportation and genocide tends to disappear, almost as if the latter were an extreme variety of the former.

This far-reaching and complex core marked the beginning of a public battle over the historical representations of the deportation, in which competing political, patriotic, and Jewish versions of memory have clashed.[1] In Italy the clash was less harsh and not so visible. The personal and associational links that many Jewish ex-deportees have had with political groups, especially on the Left (where many Jews have been activists or leaders) have been given their due weight here. The fact that some Italian political parties have been less sectarian than their equivalents in other European states has also been important. Then there was the decision to set up one single association for the survivors of the camps. In addition, it should be noted that a tacit agreement to keep disagreements within the family, as it were, without making them public, has prevailed. To a certain degree, however, this cautious attitude delayed a clarification of theoretical and historical issues concerning the relationship between deportation and Resistance, including that between Resistance and rescuers. The "battle of memories" around the awarding of the title of Righteous Among the Nations to Professor Carlo Angela reflects this complicated context. I have necessarily kept the profiles of professor Carlo Angela, as well as Renzo and Nella Segre, to an absolute essential.

In 1943, Carlo Angela ran the psychiatric clinic in a small town in the Turinese valleys, called San Maurizio Canavese. He had a wife and two children, Sandra and Piero, who were young adolescents. He was 70 years old and not in the best of health. He had been under surveillance as an anti-Fascist; the village had been sacked on many occasions, as Fascists and Germans would enter the clinic at their fancy. There was no lack of collaborationists among the staff. Carlo Angela's position embodied all the subjective and objective difficulties that would have advised against personal involvement in rescue activities. In many cases a single obstacle had been enough for people to decide against aiding Jews or anti-Fascists. Nevertheless, Carlo Angela acted. He opened the clinic doors to various Jewish families, to anti-Fascists, and to those who refused to be drafted into the neo-Fascist Republic of Salò Army. He wrote fake medical certificates, while facing Fascist inspections. He housed Renzo and Nella for eighteen months, passing Renzo off as a patient and Nella as an assistant, even going as far as facing up to the greatly feared Turin Fascist garrison to act as guarantee for their false identities. The paradox whereby the total institution of the psychiatric hospital is a rescuer from the total institution of the concentration camp was enacted.

Private Memories

In 1995, Anna published her father's wartime diary that he kept during the twenty months during which he and his wife were in hiding.[2] It had been a racking decision for a daughter so aware of the incumbent weight of the "candle of memories". If she had decided against it, today we would know very little about this event. It is almost always the rescued or their relatives who tell the story, and without them, the rescuers would remain in total obscurity. Many still remain so today and could remain so forever, as even family memories can fade.

This situation is not surprising. On the one hand, the Shoah has long been identified with the concentration camp whereas the ordeals suffered by those who managed to escape deportation have remained on the sidelines. On the other hand, a cultural tradition with its age-old roots perceived armed struggle as the noblest form of the citizen–state relationship and the epitome of active participation. Action implementing intangible resources such as moral courage and the skill to maneuver situations – the major resources of rescuers and of the civil Resistance[3] – is classified as secondary. Moreover, politics was identified with the undertakings of organized parties and not with the more often than not scattered action of individuals and small groups, tied by bonds of family, kinship, fellowship, friendship, and community, which were the major actors in aid and rescue operations throughout Europe. It goes without saying that this pattern provides a male and bellicose bias, whereby citizens who are unarmed and non-politicized, no matter the magnitude of their actions in rescuing the persecuted, are deemed second class. This conceptual framework was to be seen in the requirements that regulated formal recognition as a member of the Resistance and also in the field of historiography. And it was in place throughout Europe.

Yet there are specific Italian features. Unlike countries such as Denmark, in Italy the official institutions, professional associations, and leading cultural figures did not react in any way, neither at that time nor after the 1938 racial laws. Thus informal networks played an especially major role. Indeed, most rescue actions were undertaken by such informal networks or by single individuals. These included doctors, men and women from religious orders, some military chiefs and administrators in the zones occupied by the Italian army, and many so-called ordinary people. In this array, one category stands out – housemaids: frequently coming from the countryside, they used village networks to find shelter for "their" families. The networks were often very small, comprising one person with a small group of helpers. And almost always they were based on family and neighborly ties in which mutual trust enabled the creation of fluid routes that take the fugitives from one place to another following the ties of relationships. Entire communities were involved in rare cases. In Piedmont, in the Waldensian Valleys, some Jewish families lived in a small village called Rorà for two years using false names. Everybody knew but when the area was searched nobody said a word.

The reasons why these informal channels prevailed are compelling. On September 8, 1943, Italy was emerging from twenty years of Fascism under a regime that had shattered the opposition and had set off the "fascistization" of the social structures and the nationalization of the masses. Social cohesion was undermined and state institutions were seriously destabilized. Civic feelings – which were already historically weak – were crushed. Political parties and budding mass organizations lacked roots, cadres, and means. The family and private networks provided an entirely different situation. Traditionally strong, these informal networks continued to flourish, which was why they performed better.

The predominant feature of rescue operations, therefore, was that they were shaped above all through private relations and were carried out within the private sphere. The presence of women, by tradition very active and influential in informal networks, and who, according to a widespread stereotype of the time, were considered not cut out for politics, contributed to shaping this impression. The private register also prevailed in terms of motivation. Although in some cases political involvement was the motivator (and, in others, greed of gain), most were spurred by solidarity or mercy, moral sense, or maternal feelings.

However, it was a very particular private sphere. First of all, the boundaries separating the public and the private sphere (which had never been very stable) had been further blurred by the war. In actual fact, never before had the icons that represented the two different spheres appeared so inadequate. Nor had private action ever had such clear political consequences and meaning. Second, individuals motivated by solidarity or mercy must have previously rejected, more or less consciously, Fascist authority, acknowledging a new, though still budding and latent, sense of legitimacy. Otherwise, how could they have nurtured those feelings? And their advocacy was triggered by decisions that were not any less difficult and dangerous than those taken by the Resistance fighters.[4]

The historians' community did not grasp the novelty of this situation, and so the accounts of the rescued and the rescuers remained in the custody of family and private memories. In the initial memoirs and historical accounts that appeared, not one word is to be found of these stories, and deportation and genocide hardly get mentioned.[5]

An intricacy of factors – ranging from the primacy of armed action to political and party choices as well as the politicized bent of Italian contemporary history – has ensured the maintenance of this feature. Only in the 1990s, for reasons equally complicated, did attention turn to deportation and genocide, while the traditional meaning of Resistance was recognized as excluding many forms of opposition. And Resistance itself was gradually removed from its altar, all for the benefit of understanding.

Nevertheless research on the practices and episodes of protection is reluctant to take off. The only general work still remains that of the American historian, Susan Zuccotti, which appeared in 1987.[6] This would seem a paradox in a country that claims that such rescue operations are a founding aspect of its identity.

Another aspect of the story is the fact that some of the few large-scale rescuers, which have only recently been acknowledged in national memory, are a cause of some embarrassment. Giorgio Perlasca is a case in point.[7] Acting in Budapest in late 1944 and early 1945, he succeeded in rescuing about 3,000 Jews. Yet Perlasca was a former voluntary officer in the war in Ethiopia and in Spain, a Fascist who, though ceasing to be one, never declared his being an anti-Fascist, and who, for a short time after the war, was a leader of a right-wing group. His story would seem to be deliberately coined as a source of trouble for those who judge people by their political badge rather than their behavior.

On the other hand, a systematic study of rescue stories would dispel the idea that there was nothing to be done. It would show that very few people in Italy responded to anti-Jewish persecution, that help emerged only when it was clear that it was life or death for the Jews – that is, only after it was apparent that Germany was losing the war.[8] Behavioral patterns varied even among the Resistance groups, as had happened throughout Europe: in some areas major efforts were made to help Jewish families escape, while in others, partisans did not even seem to have been aware of the urgency of the situation.[9]

Italians have often attributed the lack of knowledge of the rescue operations to an alleged discrete and reserved attitude the protagonists were thought to have. Such a view, which cannot be proved, trivializes the whole situation, and oddly implies that the many underground anti-Fascist militants and partisans lacked discretion. The truth is that for decades no one asked the rescuers to tell their story because this would have questioned the historically and psychologically convenient stereotypes. When protectors asked the question, "Had you been in my shoes, what would you have done?" many people would have had to answer that in that situation they had failed to do anything at all. Rescuers carry a memory that causes pain, which is why many historians wish to normalize it, explaining their silence as a form of discretion, as keeping to themselves, rather than attributing it to the lack of interest for their endeavor, to the refusal to accept its meaning.

In recent years, after two television films have recounted the story of Perlasca and that of a police chief, Giovanni Palatucci, who was deported and then died in Dachau for having protected the Jews both from Fiume and those in transit to Palestine, a trickle of letters recounting episodes of rescue has begun to appear in the media generally by children and grandchildren of the protagonists. It would be unkind to deem them seekers of publicity. More often than not, these are events that have been passed on in small-range relations, stories that provide the possibility of accessing public memory.

Approaching Public Memory

Reviewed and presented on different occasions, Renzo's diary, *Twenty Months (Venti Mesi)*, reached Professor Angela's son and daughter, Piero and Sandra, whom Anna had not yet met. And so it transpired that the story was alive in the rich and accurate memories of two families, and in their baggage of letters, documents, photographs, and objects – the English gold coin Renzo had given to Carlo Angela in token of his affection and gratitude.

As the two memories came together, the characters of the protagonists emerged enriched. Sandra and Piero remembered Renzo and Nella and several events involving them, while others they learned from Anna. Anna discovered aspects of the story of her parents of which she was unaware. An intermittent relationship has sprouted between the children of the protagonists, affectionate and loaded with meaning. If it were not for Carlo Angela, Anna perhaps would never have been born. Without Anna, perhaps Carlo Angela would have remained an enlightening figure in the private family album.

On April 25, 2000, the remembrance day of wartime liberation, the ceremony in San Maurizio was simple and beautiful. A plaque was uncovered in Carlo Angela's memory, the first ever in Italy to bear the inscription, "civil Resistance." A few scholars and local government authorities recounted the events. The nuns who still run the clinic provided refreshments and the village band played tunes from the 1940s. The day was centered round Anna, Sandra, and Piero.

Things became more complicated in 2002, when the awarding of the title of Righteous Among the Nations placed the whole story in a much wider arena. To pay tribute to the roles of Carlo Angela's few assistants and his relationship with the village, Anna expressed her desire that the ceremony be held in San

Maurizio rather than at the Israeli Embassy in Rome or in Turin. She planned to invite speakers able to bring to light all the different facets of the story, including a meaningful representation from the Turin community, as well as Piedmontese Jewish music.[10] She also planned for a partially kosher buffet and offered to organize much of the event herself. What Anna had planned was substantially an out of the ordinary way to celebrate Liberation Day in Italy.

Nevertheless, amid prevarications and hesitations, there was no scholar of the history of the Shoah in the first program printed and posted. Actually there was no scholar at all. The official speech was to be given by the president of the Turin Partisan Association (Anpi). There was to be no Jewish music, nor any contribution by the Jewish community of Turin other than the role of the cultural attaché of the Israeli Embassy who was to award the title. The only religious ceremony was Catholic mass. Anna was not even provided with a place on the stand.

The story of Carlo Angela and Renzo and Nella Segre (alongside many other secret guests in the clinic) was to be incorporated in the April 25 celebrations, as if it could be entirely represented within the framework of the partisan struggle. A struggle ensued in order to redress the balance and to publicize it with a second invitation. Nevertheless only the Resistance prevailed in the official speech and several accounts. Anna was invited on the stand only through the request of the Angelas. There was absolutely no trace of kosher food in the buffet. The music included Gershwin's Rhapsody in Blue (because he was Jewish?) and had no relation to Piedmontese Jewish tradition.

There must have been many different factors in play in this story within a story. Some have pointed to the partialities of local historians and government actors as well as to the anti-Israeli tendencies widespread today throughout left-wing politics as major factors. The fact remains that the village was out to celebrate, and this deserves some more reflection.

What the events described above suggest is that there is no other channel but that of the Resistance to allow private memories to filter into the public domain (that is if we are not dealing with characters who cannot be incorporated, such as Perlasca). It is true that in research and the media a more respectful approach to the specific cases and the complexities of choices now prevails and in some cases the weight of anti-Fascism is overly played down. Yet in many small localities and limited environments, this channel is a dominating one, perhaps in reaction to the new current of opinions and studies. However, these are the environments in which most rescuers worked, in the most part independently and in ignorance of the official Resistance channels. Will anyone ever tell the story of Andrea Schivo, the prison guard from the Milan San Vittore Prison, who was deported and killed in Flossemburg for "having helped Jewish political detainees with their children (...) by offering eggs, jam, fruit and other useful goods?"[11]

Of course, Carlo Angela's case and its relationship with the Resistance must be underlined, because it is a success that his unarmed action has been whole-heartedly embraced within the Resistance. But these developments belong also to the history of wartime persecution and to over two millenia of European anti-Judaism. It is also an essential part of the process of working through and perceiving the concept of personal responsibility. While "promoting" events and stories, the Resistance model threatens to iconize them at the same time. In San Maurizio, for example, various oral and written accounts of Carlo Angela's life were given, yet any biographical aspect ended up appearing garnish when interpreted as an antecedent and precondition of the anti-Fascist commitment: as if only that choice could make sense, as if the richness of a life could be summed up in one single category.

In Italy there were thousands of anti-Fascist doctors and many of them must have received pleas for help. Yet we do not meet many Carlo Angelas, which confirms the fact that the phenomenon of rescue remains one of the most enigmatic.[12] Rescuers cannot be reduced to any one ideological orientation, nor to a social or human type; the altruistic character has turned out to be an abstraction. The direct encounter with the persecuted is the main spur to action, yet the same person can change his commitment from one situation to another.

Anti-Fascism, naturally, played an important role, but as a component of choices, not as an explanation. This is because what counts in these circumstances first and foremost is the individual. It is what we call subjectivity: a field that the historiography of the Resistance has quite rightly investigated for what concerns the partisans and that would be a pity to overlook in the case of the rescuers and the rescued. The Carlo Angela of 1943–5 was a result of political commitment, of exciting periods of work abroad, of the love for his young wife and children, and of a scientific background adverse to biological racism. I would underline his love for raw life, that life which gains no extra value from belonging to an alignment, faith, or group, as well as his subjective reaction to evil.

The same approach is suitable for the Segres. In September 1943, Renzo and Nella had already left the city, their network of relatives, and familiar places. They weighed up every glimmer of safety. They did not have much money at their disposal nor did they have politically or socially important connections. Nevertheless, they fled with their badly faked identity cards and their uncertain reference points. They met with refusals and fear and continued to seek salvation.

They were young, but they had immediately recognized that an exceptional situation required equally exceptional measures.

The same approach applies to the relationship between Carlo Angela and the Segres, which was of paternal concern and filial affection. The professor undertook to obtain news of Renzo's and Nella's relatives. He encouraged them, never mentioning the fact that there was definite suspicion as to their identities. Renzo and Nella allowed themselves to be guided as if by a father. He faked severe disorders and suffered the treatments necessary to keep up the fiction. Both of them kept a careful watch on every detail of their behavior to minimize any problems their presence there may cause. On both sides, there was respect, fondness, few words, and a modesty that could be defined as very *Piedmontese*. This is the story there is sense in telling.

Like nearly all rescuers, Carlo Angela left no records and spoke very little. At the April 25, 2002 ceremony, speakers spoke once again of a choice dictated by reserve and discretion. And, once again, nobody mentioned the fact that neither he nor any of his family had been asked for a record or to bear witness. I would not like it if we historians once again let the responsibility fall from us onto the protagonists as we justify the long period of oblivion. I have worked and work with subjects reputed to be unwilling to tell their stories: very old country women from the Piedmontese hills, deported Jews and political deportees, unarmed Resistance fighters, and so-called ordinary women who experienced World War II. The refusals I have obtained can be counted on the fingers of one hand.

In memory of my friend, Anna Segre

NOTES

1. See the important book by A. Wieviorka, *Déportation et génocide: entre la mémoire et l'oubli* (Paris: Plon, 1992). See also P. Vidal-Naquet, "L'uso perverso della storia," *Una città* 2 (1993).

2. R. Segre, *Venti mesi* (Palermo: Sellerio, 1995).

3. J. Sémelin, *Sans armes face à Hitler* (Paris: Payot, 1989).

4. A. Bravo and A. M. Bruzzone, *In guerra senza armi. Storie di donne 1940–1945* (Rome-Bari: Laterza, 2000).

5. See R. Battaglia, *La storia della Resistenza italiana* (Turin: Einaudi, 1953).

6. Susan Zuccotti, *The Italians and the Holocaust: Persecution, Rescue, Survival* (New York: Basic Books, 1987). In Italian: S. Zuccotti, *L'Olocausto in Italia* (Milan: Mondadori, 1988).

7. E. Deaglio, *La banalità del bene. Storia di Giorgio Perlasca* (Milan: Feltrinelli, 1991).

8. A. Bravo, "Der Umgang mit der Shoah in Italien," in *Der Umgang mit dem Holocaust. Europa-Usa-Israel*, R. Steininger, ed. (Cologne: Bohlau, 1994).

9. Thus, for example, the reports sent by Asti anti-Fascists on the repression in 1943–4 did not even mention the deportation of the town's Jews (M. Renosio, *Colline partigiane* [Milan: Franco Angeli, 1994], 55–6).

10. In Italy ritual and popular Jewish music has regional connotations. The aim of Yuval-Italia, the Milan Center for Jewish Music, is to collect regional Jewish music in Italy. It has recently published a CD under the auspices of the Santa Cecilia Music Academy and the Jerusalem Music Center.

11. S. Laudi, "Un giusto," *Ha Keillah* 3 (1998).

12. H. Arendt, *La banalità del male. Eichmann a Gerusalemme* (Milan: Feltrinelli, 1993). See also A. Zamperini, *Psicologia dell'inerzia e della solidarietà. Lo spettatore di fronte alle atrocità collettive* (Turin: Einaudi, 2001).

17 Return of the Repressed: Italian Film and Holocaust Memory

Millicent Marcus

As an observer of contemporary Italian culture, I have been struck by the recent outpouring of texts and films on the subject of the Shoah, evidence of what Fabio Girelli-Carasi sees as the belated emergence of a Jewish discourse in the Italy of today.[1] During my years as a student in the late 1960s and early 1970s, I was aware of a distinct reluctance on the part of writers and directors to confront this chapter in Italian history. Of course, there was Giorgio Bassani, but he was "ghettoized" by the intellectual Left for a perceived lack of ideological engagement – a failure to represent the possibility of an activist response to Fascism and the residual injustices of the postwar period. I was dimly aware of the achievements of Primo Levi, but that awareness was clouded by a kind of respectful reticence, almost a sense of embarrassment, about his writings on the part of the critical establishment. This discomfort took the form of taxonomic indecision – how to characterize this body of writing? Was it literature or history, autobiography or legal brief – in other words, how do we label and accommodate the text of witness? Such unease, of course, reflected a far deeper problem – the Italian hesitance to tell the Holocaust story at all, the reluctance to face what the eminent Italian director, Ettore Scola, would call "a passage little frequented, and hardly edifying, of our History."[2] In film, there was De Sica's magisterial adaptation of Bassani's *The Garden of the Finzi Continis* (1970), and Pontecorvo's somewhat Hollywood-ized *Kapo* (1960) as well as two works by Italian women, each of whom subordinated the Holocaust to her own authorial agenda. I'm referring to Lina Wertmuller's *Seven Beauties* (1976), in which Buchenwald becomes the pretext for yet another ironic inversion of the macho honor code personified by the actor Giancarlo Giannini throughout the director's 1970s works, and Liliana Cavani's *Night Porter* (1974) in which the filmmaker's obsession with sado-masochist sexuality finds fertile ground in a love affair begun in the Lager. To further deflect the Holocaust focus of these films, neither Wertmuller's protagonist Pasqualino nor Cavani's Lucia is Jewish – the former is a petty Neapolitan mafioso, who is declared criminally insane after killing his sister's pimp, is released into the Italian army, goes AWOL on the way to the Russian front, and is sent to the Lager, and the latter is interned because she is the daughter of a Socialist activist.

In a cinematic tradition known for its courage in confronting sociopolitical injustices past and present, the surprising reticence of Italian filmmakers with respect to the Fascist racial laws and the ensuing Holocaust has led to some critical comment. "In fifty years of Italian cinema," one Italian film critic notes, there has been "a decidedly limited production of works regarding this topic," a topic which constitutes "one of the most despicable and dramatic pages in our history, *never adequately reconsidered*" (emphases mine).[3] Fascist anti-Semitism and the fate of the Jews under the Nazi occupation of Italy is "a theme absolutely unpleasant to mass audiences" according to Paolo Finn, because "it would have raised *unresolved questions* about our embarrassing *recent past*"[4] (emphases mine). And yet, is this not precisely what the Italian *cinema d'impegno* (engaged cinema) was designed to do? Neorealist filmmakers Rossellini, De Sica, and Visconti in the 1940s and their successors in the realist tradition, the Tavianis, the early Bertolucci, and Pasolini, reveled in *temi sgradevoli* (unpleasant themes) – Fascist psychopathology, postwar unemployment, the social neglect of the elderly, worker exploitation, and the plight of the subproletariat. When treating historical subjects, they did so in order to make the *passato* (the past) indeed *prossimo* (recent) – linked to the present in causally significant ways, reading history, in Gramscian terms, as "current politics in germinal form."[5] Far from avoiding unresolved social issues, Italian cinema offered itself as the venue for raising them – the movie screen as collective sounding board for the acknowledgment, through representation, of the tensions and contradictions at the basis of the Italian national self.

Given the relative dearth of films on Italian Fascist anti-Semitism and the Holocaust to emerge from Italy during the postwar era, the interest on the part of directors in the last decade is all the more dramatic and noteworthy. This period has seen the release of Roberto Faenza's *Jonah Who Lived in the Whale* (*Jona che visse nella balena*, 1993), Benigni's *Life Is Beautiful* (*La vita è bella*, 1997), Francesco Rosi's adaptation of Primo Levi's *La tregua* (English: *The Reawakening*, 1997), Andrea and Antonio Frazzi's adaptation of Lorenza Mazzetti's *The Sky Is Falling* (*Il cielo cade*, 2000), Ricky Tognazzi's *Making Love*

(*Canone inverso*, 2000), Ettore Scola's *Unfair Competition* (*Concorrenza sleale*, 2001), and the made-for-television film *Perlasca* by Alberto Negrin (2002).

How should this surge of feature films on the Holocaust after so many years of relative silence be explained? The possibilities are many and varied, including first and foremost the passage of enough time to alleviate the mass guilt associated with acquiescence to Italian racial policy during the Fascist period. In addition, the respectability conferred on Fascism today by Gianfranco Fini's political party, Alleanza Nazionale (The National Alliance), the recent attempts to rehabilitate the memory of Mussolini, and the rise of right wing extremist groups have intensified the need to consider the past as an object lesson for the present. Adding to the urgency of this impulse toward historical retrospection is the influx of third world immigrants into the country, prompting Italians to reconsider their relationships to the "other in our midst" and acknowledge the extremes to which intolerance may lead. Apropos of the contemporary relevance of *Unfair Competition*, the recent film on the racial laws of 1938, Ettore Scola remarked on the injustice of discrimination based on difference in birth or race: "It happened in the past to Jews and blacks, it is happening today to immigrants and those outside the European Union."[6]

There remains one further explanation for why the 1990s should have been the time of a new openness toward the plight of the Jews in Italy under Fascist and Nazi rule. I am speaking of the hypothesis that links such a development to the end of the Cold War,[7] whose ideological polarization had prevented any serious engagement with Holocaust history, and to the consequent loosening of the monopolistic hold that the intellectual Left had on historiography. Because the identity of the postwar Left was based on the Resistance, its political legitimacy relied on a certain construction of World War II history. Call it hagiography, myth, or collective memory – this reading gained ascendancy over all others and conceded no space to alternative histories, especially those that could threaten the prestige and authority of the Resistance master narrative. With the fall of the Berlin wall in 1989, the collapse of the Soviet Union in 1991, and the subsequent demise of the Partito comunista italiano (Italian Communist Party), the Left's hold on World War II historiography relaxed and the other stories, or indeed the stories of "the other," could at last be told. In terms of the Shoah, it was as if the floodgates had finally been opened and the belated work of confronting this anguished episode in Italian national history could finally begin.

Perhaps the most dramatic proof of this thesis is the emergence into public notice of the story of Giorgio Perlasca – a kind of Italian Oskar Schindler who saved 5,000 Jews in Hungary by a series of daring diplomatic sleights of hand.[8] But Perlasca had been an ardent Fascist – a volunteer on the side of Franco in the Spanish Civil War and willing combatant in the Ethiopian campaign. Tainted by his background of right-wing militancy, Perlasca did not surface as a hero until the 1990s, when his official diary appeared in print and when journalist Enrico Deaglio published his excellent study, *La banalità del bene*, in 1991 (now in its twelfth edition).[9] Even more effective in bringing this story to public attention was the television film of Perlasca's biography, aired by RAI 2 in January 2002 on several consecutive evenings before a record-breaking audience of 11.5 million spectators.

In considering the urgent Italian need to represent the Holocaust cinematically at this particular historical juncture, I would like to analyze two recent films of note. These are Ricky Tognazzi's *Canone inverso* and Ettore Scola's *Concorrenza sleale* – films whose generic affiliations could not be more disparate – melodramatic, pan-European, and transhistorical in the one case and comedic, local, and quotidian in the other – and yet they share the commitment to confronting traditional Italian cinematic conventions with the challenge of Holocaust testimony.

Ricky Tognazzi's *Canone inverso*, based on the eponymous novel by Friulan writer Paolo Maurensig, unabashedly avails itself of the techniques of grand melodrama – sweeping romanticism, ambitious interweaving of sexual and artistic passions, all redolent of the grand nineteenth century narrative tradition – to tell the eventful story of a highly talented young violinist, Jeno Varga. The film traces Jeno's journey from his humble roots in a small village in pre–World War II Czechoslovakia, to Prague, where he falls in love with a concert pianist of Jewish descent, Sophie Levi, learns that he is the bastard brother of the aristocratic David Van Blau, his best friend and classmate at the Collegium Musicum, and his return to his hometown, where he dies a mysterious death in 1947.

Etymologically understood as a theater piece set to music, melodrama governs *Canone inverso* in a double sense, for music dominates the narrative content of the film, as well as providing its most spectacular formal element (thanks to Ennio Morricone's magisterial score). In keeping with the generic codes of melodrama, Tognazzi builds the narrative toward a climactic scene, which promises to fulfill all of the protagonist's unrealized desires and to resolve all of the interpersonal tensions of the preceding plot. This scene occurs, appropriately, in a concert hall, where Jeno will perform as soloist with Sophie at the piano as reward for graduating first in his class at the prestigious conservatory of Prague. Jeno's dream, ever since he had first heard a radio broadcast of Sophie in concert, had been to perform with her on stage. In the audience are a series of characters whose very presence marks the overcoming of narrative obstacles to happiness. His brother David is there in the balcony to signal his acceptance of the newly revealed fact that Jeno is his bastard sibling. Wolf, Jeno's stepfather and unstinting supporter of the young man's musical career, is there in the audience to claim his well-earned right to paternal pride in his stepson's accomplishments. Maestro Ischbaum, expelled from directorship of the conservatory because he is a Jew, appears in the audience to bask in the glory of his student's success.

But the satisfying grand finale that promised to resolve all the film's interpersonal relations, according to the grand nineteenth century literary formulae for closure, is not forthcoming. Macro-history takes over the narrative apparatus and blocks the conventional movement of the plot to resolution.

The scene begins with a shot of the drums, whose rolls set a rhythm of excitement and urgency to the ensuing action. The camera then rises to show a full orchestra and cuts to a series of disconnected shots: of Sophie's hands racing across the keys, of the balcony where Jeno's classmates gather, of the orchestra conductor, and back to Sophie's hands, before passing finally to Jeno and cutting to Maestro Ishbaum in the audience. Edited to the intense rhythms of Morricone's score, the camerawork shows that almost all the elements of the climactic finale are in place, for David will soon appear to complete the gallery of Jeno's listeners. But as Tognazzi crosscuts between the concert and David's frantic car ride toward the theater, we see that the melodramatic elements of the plot are soon to be obstructed by those of Holocaust history. David's car is overtaken by Nazi jeeps and when he arrives at the concert hall, the building is surrounded by German officers shouting orders and herding people to the sound of barking dogs. Morricone's orchestral score continues to dominate the soundtrack, but the Nazi cacophony is disturbingly evident. Back in the theater, Jeno's triumphant performance proceeds, visualized in cuts between his face in rapt concentration, Sophie's hands on the keys, her face in adoring and tearful appreciation, and the conductor's energetic movements to coordinate it all. David finally appears in the balcony to Jeno's grateful acknowledgment. Now the Nazis enter, prompting a series of quick shots of audience members' horrified reactions to the assault. In rapid succession, we see Sophie seized by two officers, Jeno dragged off stage, and David's balcony invaded by soldiers. The final shot in this wrenching montage shows an officer on stage, in place of the orchestra conductor, filmed from the perspective of the audience members as he "conducts" them according to the drumbeat of Nazi commands.

If the *Canone* is a contrapuntal form, then the counterpoint established in this scene is one between the forces of culture and those of authoritarian repression. This scene is edited contrapuntally – acoustically, through the opposition between Morricone's music and the din of the Nazi onslaught, visually through the crosscutting between events inside and outside the theater, between the orderly montage of the concert hall and the disorder of the military siege. Contrapuntal, too, is the relationship between the requirements of melodrama, which dictate a climactic scene of narrative closure, and the incursions of Holocaust history, which defy such generic satisfactions.

The ravages of European anti-Semitism wreak similar havoc on a very different generic tradition in Ettore Scola's *Concorrenza sleale*, the story of two shopkeepers, Umberto Melchiorri and Leone Della Rocca, whose competition becomes truly unfair when the racial laws of 1938 mandate that Leone, who is Jewish, forfeit his business. Scola's pivotal role in the evolution of the *commedia all'italiana* genre is well known: he has been credited with bringing Italian film comedy into alignment with the neorealist legacy of politically engaged art. Within the narrative of *Concorrenza sleale*, Scola marks the passage of the film from conventional comedy to one that subverts the complacency of its generic codes by extending its confines to include subjects that are disturbing and even taboo (as was homosexuality in the 1970s of *A Special Day*.) To this end, the first part of *Concorrenza sleale* presents a world of benign comedic events – a sitcom in period setting. It is the morning run of the trolley car, slow and quaint, which takes us into the space of the Via Ottaviano neighborhood in Rome, with its walls and gate, giving the impression of a closed, insulated world, a *hortus conclusus*, immune to the assaults of history. Within the confines of this set, daily life begins to stir, and Scola reconstructs those stirrings with a precision of detail that verges on the philological. This meticulous recreation of a bygone world is suffused with nostalgia for a past of security, innocence, and community, the *Italietta del ventennio* (the little Italy of the two decades of Fascism). True to the requirements of conventional comedy, there are gags, slapstick antics, quips – little accidents that really do not hurt, such as the piano teacher's regular fainting sessions, which end as soon as the pastry tray arrives. The competition between the two shopkeepers seems itself to be one extended gag – the adult version of the games played by Umberto's and Leone's sons. In fact, the rivalry between the fathers is reduced to a quarrel over publicity slogans (who has the right to use the advertising concept "tutti al mare" [everyone to the beach]). It is the younger generation, Pietruccio and Lele, who reveal the childishness of their fathers' behavior when they label the shopkeepers' war "battaglia dei mari" (battle of the seas) in a clever variation on the actual children's game that the boys will play later in the film: "battaglia navale." True to *commedia all'italiana* tradition, Scola casts in the leading roles two renowned film actors, Diego Abantantuono and Sergio Castellitto, making the *concorrenza* (rivalry) between Umberto and Leone a face-off between two *maschere* (established screen personae) whose familiarity will provide a ready source of comic pleasure for viewing audiences.

Thus everything seems to be preceeding according to the norms of conventional comedy and our expectations are set for a resolution to the commercial rivalry that will permit the fathers to put aside their childishness and to follow the example of maturity, wisdom, and solidarity of their eight-year-old sons. While this resolution will ultimately come about, it will do so against a historical background that will completely subvert the complacency and stability that we expect of the standard happy ending. The turning point, from routine comedy to something generically quite different, occurs when Umberto, in a quarrel with Leone, strikes below the proverbial belt of comic repartée. While exchanging insults permissible within the norms of their business rivalry, Umberto breaks frame by referring to the "razza" of Leone. "Un ebreo è sempre un ebreo," (a Jew is always a Jew) Umberto concludes, shattering not only the composure of his rival, but the comic hilarity of the film itself. It is as if this line had found its way into the wrong movie, hailing from an elsewhere completely foreign to the universe of *commedia all'italiana.*

With this racist slur, Holocaust history enters the protected confines of the neighborhood, and in fact, we discover that this day is indeed May 6, 1938: climax of the festivities accompanying the Hitler–Mussolini pact, with all its consequences for a future of genocide and war. To make this scene even more disruptive of our comic pleasure, Scola shows us the exchange of gazes between fathers and their sons – the latter, witnesses to the shame of the generation that accepted Fascism. Surrounding this turning point in the film, a number of previously quaint details recur, now as dire premonitions of the catastrophe to come. The windows of the trolley car which so innocently led us into the neighborhood at the beginning of *Concorrenza sleale*, are now festooned with Nazi flags, and the Fascist parade that filled the street with all its tackiness in the film's early moments now leaves the broken glass of Leone's shop window in its wake – a chilling, if highly localized, *kristallnacht all'italiana.*

The second half of the film requires us to reread the comedic codes of the first half from the critical distance afforded by historical hindsight. This doubling of perspectives, of course, is the prime ingredient of irony – a device made explicit in the rantings and ravings of the anti-Fascist high-school teacher Angelo, brother of

Umberto, as he grades a student paper brimming with pro-Mussolini sentiment. Assigning the student a grade of zero for the ideological content of the essay, Angelo fulminates "Dov'è finita l'ironia? . . . E' morta, l'ironia." (Where did irony go? Irony is dead.) Within the comedic structures of *Concorrenza sleale*, instead, irony is alive and well, thanks to the boys who see the absurdity of their fathers' behavior and who are aware that their own childhood games are, in fact, mere play, while their elders take seriously the silly antics of their rivalry. But a larger irony surrounds the entire comedic structure of *Concorrenza sleale*, when seen in the context of the macrohistory that threatens to swallow it up. The happy ending of the generational plot – fathers come to imitate the exemplary behavior of their sons – emerges as futile in the face of the larger historical forces at work. Comedic games, even when conducted on the various levels of awareness productive of irony, are nonetheless games whose outcomes hold only in the realm of play. At the level of Holocaust history, the rules are ironclad, the outcomes are horrific, and the line between imaginary and real is subject to systematic violation. In other words, the happy ending decreed by the canons of conventional comedy is not forthcoming in *Concorrenza sleale* because the year is 1938, the place is Italy, and Leone is Jewish. It is this thwarting of expectations, this clash of generic codes between comedy and historical realism, which constitutes Scola's way of bearing witness to Fascist anti-Semitism and the Holocaust history it portends.

Toward the end of the film, when Umberto pays a visit to the ailing Leone, their sons eavesdrop on the conversation. "Ridono, chiacchierano" (they're laughing, they're chatting), one boy reports. "Si vede che sono cresciuti" (It seems that they've grown up) concludes the other. The same could be said of Italian cinema itself, which has matured to the point of finally being able to confront what Primo Levi called "the central fact, the stain, of our century."[10] In so doing, contemporary Italian filmmakers have begun to remedy the strange reluctance of a cinematic tradition known for its unswerving social courage, to accept the formidable moral and representational challenge of Holocaust testimony.

NOTES

1. Fabio Girelli-Carasi, "Jewish Memoirists: The Role of Memory in the Discourse of Identity" (April 1999), 12 pp. Available at *http://academic.brooklyn.cuny.edu/modlang/carasi/articles/memorialistica2.html.*

2. "Un brano, poco frequentato e poco edificante, della nostra Storia." See the preface to the screenplay, *Concorrenza sleale: Un film di Ettore Scola* (Turin: Landau, 2001), 5.

3. "In cinquant'anni di cinema italiano [Finn notes] una produzione decisamente limitata di opere riguardanti questo argomento" [which constitutes] "una delle pagine più

spregevoli e drammatiche della nostra storia, *mai abbastanza* riproposte." These remarks appear in Paolo Finn's review of *Concorrenza sleale* in *Cinemasessanta* 4 (March–April 2001), 21–2.

4. "Un tema assolutamente sgradito alle grandi platee [because] avrebbe risollevato *questioni irrisolte* con il nostro imbarazzante *passato prossimo*." Ibid, 22.

5. Antonio Gramsci, *Il Risorgimento*, Maria Corti, ed. (Turin: Einaudi, 1952), 114.

6. "Scoprire di essere considerati 'diversi' per nascita e per razza. E' accaduto in passato a ebrei e neri, accade oggi a immigrati ed extracomunitari." See the preface to the published screenplay, *Concorrenza sleale*, 5.

7. A subtle explanation for this phenomenon can be found in Annette Wieviorka, *Deportation et Genocide: Entre la Mémoire et l'oubli*, (Paris: Plon, 1992), 20. I would like to thank Liliana Picciotto for calling my attention to Wieviorka's study.

8. I am indebted to Carla Ciseri Montemagno for bringing the case of Perlasca to my attention, and for her inestimable bibliographic help in researching this story.

9. For the diary, see Giorgio Perlasca, *L'impostore* (Bologna: Il Mulino, 1997), and for Enrico Deaglio's book, see *La banalità del bene: Storia di Giorgio Perlasca* (Milan: Feltrinelli, 2002).

10. "Il fatto centrale, la macchia, del nostro secolo." Primo Levi, *I sommersi e i salvati* (Turin: Einaudi, 1991), 10.

18 The Secret Histories of Roberto Benigni's *Life Is Beautiful*

Ruth Ben-Ghiat

"This is a simple story. But it's not easy to tell. Like a fable, there is sorrow, there is wonder and happiness." So begins Roberto Benigni's *Life Is Beautiful*, a comic's meditation on the tragedy of the Holocaust. Set in Fascist Italy, the movie recounts the story of the Italian Jew, Guido Orefice, who is deported to a Nazi concentration camp together with his son Joshua and his Christian wife Dora. Guido is an endearingly hapless buffoon whose world is shaped by a combination of happenstance, both felicitous and unfortunate, and by his belief in love's abilities to sustain and transform. Both these things mark his life in the camp, where he dedicates himself to shielding his son from all knowledge of the ghastly surrounding reality by telling him that they and the other prisoners are really competitors in an elaborate game. Although Guido is ultimately killed in the Lager, he saves the spirit as well as the life of his son, who, following the fiction his father has created, exalts that he has won the game when he is reunited with his mother at the end of the film.

Already known to international audiences for his manic performance in Jim Jarmusch's 1986 *Down by Law*, Benigni gambled in making his trademark bumbler the vehicle of a Holocaust narrative. Although a sardonic and dark humor is

I am grateful to the Mellon Foundation and the Library of Congress for funding my research on Italian prisoners of war and to Giorgio Rochat, Nicola Labanca, Claudio Sommaruga, and Angelo Bendotti for assistance in obtaining research materials. I thank Elliot Jurist for his helpful readings of this chapter and Julia Benghiat-Jurist for asking why and for reminding me of the joys of childhood play. This chapter is an expanded and updated version of my article by the same name that appeared in *The Yale Journal of Criticism*, Ben-Ghiat, Ruth. "The Secret Histories of Roberto Benigni's *Life Is Beautiful*." *Yale Journal of Criticism* 141 (2001), 253–66. © Yale University and the Johns Hopkins University Press. Reprinted with permission of The Johns Hopkins University Press.

present in some camp memoirs, such as Tadeusz Borowski's *This Way to the Gas, Ladies and Gentlemen*, Benigni's use of the comedic genre sparked a new round of debate about the parameters and possibilities of Holocaust representation.[1] Benigni also risked a more specific censure in his native country. Comedy has proved to be an acceptable way of publicly addressing the sensitive subject of Italy's participation and defeat in World War II, but the unmartial antiheroes of a long lineage of Italian postwar military spoofs – from Carlo Borghesio's 1947 *Come persi la guerra (How I Lost the War)* through Gabriele Salvadore's 1991 *Mediterraneo* – manage to sidestep the issue of Fascist aggression. Benigni's 1997 film draws on this tradition, but was made in a different political and cultural climate. In 1994, Italians became the first people since World War II to elect a party with its historical roots in Fascism to power when a center-right coalition led by Silvio Berlusconi won national elections. Although that government was short-lived, it facilitated the circulation of revisionist interpretations of Fascism and the war. Strengthened since then through official commemorations and a flood of memoirs and popular histories that intersect with a certain vein of academic writing, these revisionist views downplay Fascist violence and attempt to "correct" a supposed past overemphasis on the anti-Fascist Resistance by expanding the pantheon of national patriots and martyrs to include combatants for the Nazi-linked Republic of Salò.[2] Benigni's film counters such ideological operations and their implicit disavowals of Italian complicity in the Holocaust by reminding Italians of the place that Fascist racial persecution played in the overall implementation of the Shoah.

Other commentators have found the force of the film's moral thrust in its unsettling mix of comedy and tragedy. Through its serious humor, *Life Is Beautiful* disarms spectators, acting upon them to make them think and feel.[3] Through laughter, the movie opens a line of affective communication to the horror and pathos of the Holocaust. It is this emotional connection the film forges, I believe, rather than its sensitive subject matter, that accounts for the strong reactions spectators and critics have had to the movie. In this scheme, the riddles and games that maintain the film's childlike fantasy are integral to its gravity: they defend the realms of imagination and curiosity and play against a Nazi universe that mortified the spirit and abolished the right to ask that perennial child's question – why?[4]

The growing body of critical work on *Life Is Beautiful* has elucidated its structural and textual complexity and its strong ethical agenda. My essay on the film draws on this critical opinion but has a different focus: what *Life Is Beautiful* can tell us about the representation of Italian history in contemporary Italy. Although the film's putative subject is the Holocaust, I argue that its subtexts and paratexts engage other histories that still cannot be easily addressed in Italy because they feature Italians as the Nazis' allies rather than as their victims. My aim here is less to analyze the film itself than to explore the historical circumstances and critical traditions that contributed to the production of this Holocaust narrative. My contention is that although *Life Is Beautiful* forces Italian audiences to recall Italian anti-Semitism, it is also the indirect product of configurations of contemporary memory that function to obscure Italy's position as a German ally and anti-Semitic state during World War II. From this perspective, the story that "is not easy to tell," in the words of the opening voiceover, is not only that of a Jewish victim of the Holocaust, but also that of those Italians who fought alongside the Nazis before Italy surrendered to the Allies in September 1943.

Life Is Beautiful's status as a Holocaust narrative has concentrated critical attention on the slippage between reality and fiction in the film. A degree of historical accuracy was clearly important to Benigni and his co-screenwriter Vincenzo Cerami: they viewed documentaries, read memoirs and histories, hired a historical consultant from Milan's Center for Contemporary Jewish Documentation, and screened the film for Italian Jewish groups before its release.[5] Yet the filmmakers made clear that theirs would not be a realist representation. As Benigni stated in an interview, he made the movie not as a historian but as "a director . . . whose duty is to invent stories, so I invented this completely. It is a fable but invented from the truth."[6] Indeed, far from representing a failure of documentation, this blurred boundary between truth and fable is one of the points of the film. It finds articulation in the film's plot, narrative structure, aesthetic, and tone, and provides an interpretative frame for the film. The initial voiceover hints at the potential unreliability of the narrative to follow by announcing that it is "not easy to tell" and "like a fable." The Italian term used here, *favola*, can also be translated as fairy tale or folktale, emphasizing its fictive status, but the use of the simile also suggests that it is *not* a fable and therefore is perhaps possessed of some truth.[7] Indeed, if the opening voiceover's third-person narration implies and foregrounds an objective rendering of the historical drama, the closing voiceover reveals this narrative was in fact a retelling of childhood experience, a subjective blend of memory and imaginative recreation. This disclosure allows for an after-the-fact interpretation of the film's fairy-tale feel as reflective of a child's perspective, but its position at the close of the story means that it is the objective omniscient narrator who leads first-time viewers through the story. One would have to see the film a second time to receive it as an imaginative recreation by a now adult child.[8] Yet, as Millicent Marcus has argued, it is precisely through the "unreliable" quality of its narration that the film participates in a tradition of bearing witness to the Holocaust through testimonies whose documentary content is often mediated by the effects of trauma and the operations of emotional memory.[9]

The slippage between reality and fiction in *Life Is Beautiful* also serves the filmmakers to make a political point about the potential of fantasy to work both evil and good. Guido's motto "I am what I want to be," which he distills from his friend Ferruccio's own vulgarization of Schopenhauer, seems to be in character with his naïve and optimistic nature that is so outside of his history and his time.[10] Yet dreams of transformation also obsessed the Nazis and Fascists, and the destructive consequences of totalitarian utopian thinking are ubiquitous in the film. Visions of empire and racial superiority drive the Italian Fascists, who throw colonial-themed parties and reassure one another that they are Aryans and "the best of all races." But the director also finds a positive function for fantasy, as Guido repeatedly transforms ugly situations into opportunities for joyful conspiracy. In his hands, a school lesson on racial doctrine becomes an occasion to show the absurdity of all racism, and a horse that Fascist thugs have covered with anti-Semitic slogans becomes a means for him to whisk Dora away from her Fascist fiancé to begin their new life together. Once in the camp, he interprets rules, rituals, and symbols for his son under the rubric of the game, countering the Nazi will to power with a demonstration of the power of the will to make sense of the senseless and so interrupt the process of dehumanization.

The film's scenography, which juxtaposes careful period detail with over-the-top artifice, also emphasizes the film's deconstruction of the boundaries between reality and fantasy. Viewers familiar with the art and iconography of the Italian regime will recognize as authentic, for example, the individual images of the Duce displayed in the Fascist prefect's office Guido must visit: the futurist portrait with sunglasses, the monumental bust by Adolfo Wildt, and the photographic portrait of him as uniformed statesman were all produced (and often reproduced in the media) during the dictatorship. Grouped together, though, they create an absurdist aesthetic of semiotic excess that undercuts the scene's reality effect even as it stands for Fascism's rhetorical overkill. This surreal sensibility also permeates Benigni's reconstructions of the death camp, which have been criticized for their sanitized quality. Typical is his depiction of mass death: through dense fog, we glimpse a circular arrangement of skeletons whose theatrical arrangement calls to mind the rounds of Hell imagined by Benigni's literary hero Dante rather than the squalid results of genocidal rage.

Finally, the slippage between history and fantasy operates at a paratextual level as well. Benigni has stated that his sources of inspiration for the film's mix of humor and pathos were historical and contextual as well as cinematic and intertextual: along with Charlie Chaplin and a certain Italian comedic tradition, he drew on the stories about the war told to him from childhood onward by his father, Luigi, who spent two years in a German concentration camp. In interviews Benigni has recalled how his father sought to protect his family from knowledge of the horror by favoring humor and humanistic anecdotes as he related his experiences. The character of Guido, as well as the film's overall tone and approach to its subject, respect and reflect these paternal images and memories. Guido's unworldly and apolitical nature seems to mirror Benigni's perception of his father as an unfortunate innocent who comprehended little of the reality around him at the time of his deportation. "He didn't know why he was there," Benigni has said of his father's experience in the camp. "He didn't know why the German people were so mean to him; he couldn't understand." Joshua's film-homage to Guido is thus also Benigni's film-homage to his father the survivor, whose "story and face came to me each day during the making of the movie."[11]

One crucial fact complicates this narrative of filial love. Luigi Benigni was not an Italian Jew but a young member of the Italian Fascist army who had served as part of the occupation forces in Albania as part of the Axis alliance. Deported to Germany along with over 650,000 other Italian soldiers after Marshal Pietro Badoglio (who became head of state after Mussolini's July 1943 ouster from power) surrendered to the Allies in September 1943, Luigi Benigni formed part of a group of military captives who came to symbolize Fascism and Italian military defeat and whose experiences were until recently largely excluded from canons of national memory about the war.[12] There is no space here to fully address the story of these men, but I wish to make a few observations in this section of the chapter about this mass captivity and return because they are essential to understanding *Life Is Beautiful* as a text founded on the tension between family memory and public history. My first point is that the brutal treatment in the German Lagers by those who had been their former allies left many Italian ex-prisoners feeling victimized after the war. This worked against a recognition of the brutalities Italians committed as occupiers in the Balkans and elsewhere, especially since many of those soldiers and officers had also refused to collaborate with the Nazis while they were in the Lagers, and some had also obstructed the implementation of the Holocaust by refusing to hand over to the Germans the Jewish populations of Italian-occupied territories.[13] Knowledge among Italians of this latter course of action – which complemented the behaviors of the many Italians who hid and saved Italian Jews inside the country – together with the symbolic importance of the partisan Resistance in Italy, shaped postwar configurations of memory that minimized Italy's long alliance with the Nazis and its own anti-Semitic persecution. In many literary, cinematic, and journalistic accounts of the war, Germany served as the exclusive emblem of totalitarian evil and racial persecution, while Italians figure as a collective of "brava gente" (good people) who had remained largely unaffected by twenty years of Fascism.[14] These histories and perceptions have continued to shape contemporary Italian collective self-understandings of national behavior and morality during the war. They are relevant when considering the implications of the pretextual operations that saw the transformation of Benigni's soldier father into a Jewish bumbler. For *Life Is Beautiful* is a film that lays bare the limits of what can be told in Italy about painful subjects even after fifty years: not just the Holocaust, but also the saga of the millions of non-Jewish Italian soldiers who were trained by the regime to kill and command but became instead, as ex-prisoners, haunting reminders of a failed war and a discredited regime.

Rhetorics of victimhood had long been part of the landscape of Italian political discourse, but gained new meaning and popularity in the wake of World War II.[15] A series of debacles marked Italy's participation in the conflict (setbacks in Greece, Albania, Russia, and the loss of Italy's colonies), culminating in the unique humiliation of being invaded by the country's longstanding ally. The abrupt change of sides, which was a result of Badoglio's September 1943 armistice with the Allies, had grave consequences for those Italians who, like Luigi Benigni, were abroad fighting alongside the Nazis. Like the senior Benigni, most were then in their early to mid-twenties and had been raised amidst Fascist ideologies of victory at any cost. Their war diaries and memoirs convey their shock at their country's sudden *volte-face*, their shame at their forced disarmament by the Germans, and their incredulity at their former comrades' vindictiveness. A peer of Luigi Benigni's in Albania, Adolfo Bandiera, recorded that he awoke to find his camp surrounded by "Teutonic warriors" who "paralyzed the entire [Italian] headquarters in five minutes, officials included, without firing a single shot." As he and his unit were marched to a concentration camp, the first of many they would endure, he reflected on the shifting identities that accompanied the dramatic turn of events. Referring to the Albanian partisans who had often been executed for resisting Italian occupation of their country, he noted that "we have gone from being oppressors to being, like them, oppressed by the 'German steamroller,' and a sense of sympathy toward them is born."[16]

Judging from both published and unpublished sources, the grim routines of life in concentration camps such as Deblin Irina and Flossenbürg completed the sensitization to the experience of victimhood. To avenge their former allies' "treasonous" behavior, the Nazis treated Italians more brutally than their other Western European captives. Italians were classified as "military internees" rather than as prisoners of war (POWs), thus depriving them of protection under the Geneva Convention and Red Cross aid.[17] Although Italians of all ages shared fears about physical and mental disintegration, anger at their loss of freedom, and feelings of abandonment by family and country, feelings of humiliation were particularly acute among Luigi Benigni's cohort, which had imbibed twenty years of Fascist demands for military glory. Their diaries and memoirs air fears about the loss of their youth due to the rigors of confinement. As one nineteen-year-old soldier confided in his Lager diary, his generation of Italians had been "sentenced to a tragic fate that, in a very short time, has made us old in every part of our body and even more in our spirit. Hunger, cold, and nightmares are the three great monsters that have conspired against us."[18] Some soldiers – Luigi Benigni was not among them – escaped the camps by accepting offers to collaborate with the Germans, which for them meant being repatriated to serve in the armies of the Nazi-controlled Salò Republic or serving in the German Wehrmacht or the SS. The majority of soldiers and officers refused such offers, which meant an even harsher regime of forced labor and starvation rations. Overall, the death rate for Italian captives was one in ten. Those who survived returned home emaciated, tubercular, and traumatized; Roberto Benigni has reported that his father weighed eighty pounds upon release.

The second point I wish to make here is that the experience of repatriation, far from alleviating this trauma, often tended to exacerbate it by intensifying ex-prisoners' preexisting feelings of shame as defeated soldiers and abandoned members of a pariah nation. Alone among fighting nations, the Italian government had no coordinated repatriation plan, and the Allied powers were disinclined to offer men still associated with Fascism precious spots on transports going west. Captured Italian soldiers thus remained abroad long after their Allied counterparts; whereas 85 percent of French prisoners of war were home by July 1945, one-third of their Italian contemporaries did not repatriate until 1946 or 1947.[19] So dire was the situation of liberated Italian prisoners that the United Nations Relief and Rehabilitation Administration reluctantly agreed to classify them as Displaced Persons in August 1945, which improved these men's material conditions but further injured their pride. When they did reach Italy, many faced an indifferent reception and inadequate state aid that was only partially offset by the assistance programs of the Catholic Church. Interviewed decades after his return from Germany, one Italian spoke sarcastically of the "big celebration" that had awaited him in Bolzano, his point of arrival on national soil: "we got six cigarettes, a cup of broth, and an apple: all the Red Cross packages were long gone."[20]

While economic and political factors had their weight in creating this situation, psychological considerations are also relevant, namely the aversive responses POWs met with among Italians as particularly visible symbols of the regime *and* its defeat. With their haunted air and their often-mutilated bodies, they stood out even among Italy's landscape of devastation as disturbing reminders of the abyss between expectations and outcomes of World War II – between the past ideal of the Fascist conqueror and the present reality of national impotence.[21] No political party took on the advocacy of soldiers' issues, state aid remained spotty, and for many decades public commemorations of the war focused on the contributions of Resistance partisans who had come out on the winning side.

The publication history of ex-POWs' war diaries and memoirs provides a sense of their difficulty in gaining an audience for their testimonies in the public sphere. Of a total of 526 POW full-length diaries and memoirs that had appeared as of 1997, 35 were published in the years 1945–50.[22] Of course, this silence was also the result of self-censorship by ex-prisoners, who for reasons of trauma, guilt, and political prudence were often reluctant to publicly or even privately air their wartime experiences. It is safe to say that in the immediate postwar years returned Italian military captives had little of the political capital and none of the moral authority enjoyed to various degrees by other categories of German victims, namely anti-Fascist partisans, political deportees, and Jews. Only in the 1990s, when the fall of Communism and the rise of the center-right occasioned the emergence of new configurations of national memory, were these efforts to integrate these men's experiences into prevailing narratives about the war, for example through efforts to recognize their refusal to collaborate with the Nazis in the camps as part of a Resistance, better identified with the struggles of partisans inside Italy.

The perceived public dismissal of their experiences magnified the feelings of guilt and unworth felt by many Italian ex-prisoners, leading the majority to keep their sufferings to themselves. Traumatic states reinforced feelings of victimization among Italian camp survivors, leading many to a long-term silence about their sufferings that worked against their reintegration into social and civic life.[23] Thus, although many ex-prisoners had a burning desire to "tell, speak, and express all that inspires and torments us," relatively few of them found the open ears and arms they wished for after the war.[24]

My final point here is that the culture of shame and relatively public silence that surrounded the experiences of Italian military captives gave private and familial narratives such as Luigi Benigni's a special resonance. The failure of these men to find public forums in which to communicate their experiences meant that the transmission of testimony in private and familial settings took on an extraordinary weight and importance. The act of telling one's war stories to an attentive audience of sympathetic listeners assumed a special meaning at a time when Italian institutions and cultures were united in their desire to forget the Fascist past. At the same time, these stories were often transformed in their transmission from parent to child. Elisions and underdisclosures, born of trauma, shame, political caution, or a conscious desire to shield loved ones from pain, characterized many intergenerational communications by World War II veterans in Italy and elsewhere. These could take the form of verbal omissions or, as in the case of Luigi Benigni's accounts, of masking strategies such as the use of humor, understatement, or irony.[25]

Seen in the light of Roberto Benigni's position as the recipient of such testimony, *Life Is Beautiful* thus takes on a performative meaning as an act of bearing witness to his father's experiences and as a wish to "fill in the blanks" and understand the harsh realities of the Lager that were hidden from him as a child. Yet the director's reconstruction of history is founded on dissemblance. It reproduces, through the ruse and fiction of the game, the element of protective denial that marked his father's communications to his family. As he has stated, his father told him the story of his imprisonment "like in the movie, like a fable. He was afraid to make us fearful. He was protecting us like I am protecting the son in the movie."[26] Joshua's innocence at the end of the film about the raison d'etre of the camps mirrors Benigni's childhood innocence about the scope of the horror his father had faced. Yet Benigni's transfiguration of his father the Axis soldier into a casualty of both the Fascists and the Nazis is another kind of evasion of reality, one that respects the boundaries of a collective memory that affirms the portrait of Italians as casualties of the war rather than as its cobelligerents.[27] For the fulfillment of this particular fantasy, the choice of an Italian Jew as protagonist was all but overdetermined. The final section of the chapter briefly explores how this enduring culture of victimhood at the hands of the Germans has mediated the reception and representation of Fascist antisemitism and the Italian Holocaust in postwar Italy.

*

If Italians were reluctant to hear about the sufferings of ex-military internees in the years following 1945, many proved to be even more aversive to stories about Jewish suffering. Rather, multiple factors worked against a collective coming to terms among Italians with state-sponsored racism under Fascism and its links to the larger project of Jewish genocide. First, there is the meritorious behavior of many Italian Gentile military men and civilians who risked their lives to save and shelter their Jewish neighbors within Italy and foreign Jews in Italian-occupied territories such as Greece and Yugoslavia. An 83 percent survival rate, one of the highest in Europe, has ensured that the narrative of Italian–Jewish relations during the war has been dominated by tales of heroism on the part of Italian clergy, military, and civilians from every walk of life.[28] Second, there is also the pervasiveness of feelings of victimization among non-Jewish Italians, who had endured the effects of German occupation, Allied invasion, and a bloody civil war. The writer Corrado Alvaro's 1944 characterization of Italy as "a poor lamb, offered up in holocaust, who fights to defend itself the best it can" contained an implicit disavowal of Italians' identity as persecutors at a time when Jews were being deported to death camps from the Republic of Salò.[29] After the war, a combination of guilt, shame, subterranean persistence of anti-Jewish prejudices, a desire to focus on the present, and a feeling that Jews had already put their neighbors and saviours at great risk throughout the war fostered a climate of silence and resentment as well as of sympathy and stocktaking.[30]

These factors influenced the formation of paradigms of popular memory and critical inquiry regarding the fate of the Jews under Mussolini that remained predominant until recently and that inform *Life Is Beautiful*. These paradigms tended to produce accounts of the Salò Republic – the site and synecdoche of national complicity with Nazi genocide – that removed all Italian agency. Salò was bracketed off as a "German" episode and its ideology renamed and externalized as "Nazifascist."[31] They also dissuaded rigorous investigations into Fascism's racist ideology and culture, which was reduced to an imitation of Nazi anti-Semitism, or, as in Benigni's film, to something that can be subverted and caricatured. Recent research has revealed instead the scope and virulence of that culture and has clarified that the implementation of the Final Solution in Italy relied on bureaucracies and climates of opinion created by Mussolini's dictatorship.[32] Since 1938, censuses, concentration camps, and confiscation of Jewish assets had formed part of Italians' attempts to force Jews' conversion, expulsion, and ghettoization; during the war, these measures became essential links in a chain of persecution that culminated in the deportation and extermination of over 6,000 Italian Jews.[33]

Finally, these paradigms favored the memorialization of the valorous actions of the many Catholic laypeople and clergy who saved Jews at the expense of investigating the influence Catholic anti-Judaism had on the formulation and implementation of racist policies in Fascist Italy. In fact, Catholic voices such as the authoritative *L'Osservatore Romano* justified the racial laws as merely a return to centuries-old papal measures of segregation, expulsion, and coerced conversion; popular distrust of Jews was cultivated from provincial pulpits as well as from the Fascist press.[34] As I have argued elsewhere, the initial aims of Fascist racism were not to eradicate the Jews but to coerce changes in Jewish behavior so as to fulfill Italian and Catholic fantasies about a total Jewish assimilation.[35] Soon after he allied with Hitler, Mussolini gave a preview of this kind of thinking. "Antisemitism is inevitable wherever there is exaggerated Semitic visibility, interference, and arrogance," the Duce declared. "The excessive Jew gives rise to the anti-Jew (*il troppo ebreo fa nascere l'antiebreo*)." In the years to come, removing the "overly Jewish" from Italian life was pursued through policies that encouraged "Aryanization," baptism, and conversion to Catholicism and punished stubbornly "Jewish" Jews by segregating them from civil society. By 1941, Mussolini commented happily that the high rate of intermarriage meant that the "Jewish characteristics" of Italian Jews would be absorbed by the Aryan bloodline within a generation.[36] Such policies converged perfectly with preexisting Catholic desires for an integration of Jews that entailed the eclipse of their religious and cultural identities. This last critical and historiographical tradition, which still remains influential, speaks to the overwhelming strength of Catholic culture in Italy, where religious tropes and symbols have long saturated the rhetoric and imagery of secular and even anticlerical groups, including the Italian Communists.[37] Such has been the hegemony exerted by Catholic discourse – with its attendant repression of recent and remote episodes of Catholic intolerance – that a kindly non-Jewish Italian who was interviewed in the 1990s about her decision to hide Italian Jews during the war could state without a trace of irony that "it was enough to have been Christian, to have had a bit of humanity."[38] Her statement expresses a view of the obligations of true faith shared by many other "righteous Gentiles" who saved Jews, but also manifests a common blind spot among Italian Catholics about the Church's complicity in accepting and legitimating Fascist inhumanity.

Such rhetoric undoubtedly played on the assimilatory anxieties of a Jewish population saddled with the unique privilege and burden of cohabitation with the papacy. Indeed, among the legacies among Italian Jews of this assault on Jewish specificity from both Church and state was a protective tendency after 1945 to minimize difference from and conflict with the surrounding Christian population. In other ways as well, Italian Jews may have unwittingly facilitated the postwar repression of the memory of Italian anti-Semitism. As pioneering work by Carla Forti, Federica Barozzi, and other scholars has suggested, the effects of trauma, fears of continued victimization, survivors' guilt, and the desire for a pacific reintegration into their communities all may have contributed to weaken Jews' collective voice about the persecutions they suffered at the hands of Italian officials and communities after 1938.[39]

Of course, silence was also encouraged in Jewish survivors by the cultural and psychological climate of postwar Italy, in which competition for material resources and symbolic standing within the new republic discouraged any special recognition of Jews' persecuted status. Like returning military captives, Jewish survivors of the Lagers found that Resistance partisans occupied most of the available places in the pantheon of the Nazi-persecuted for the first decades after the war. Although partisans were far from universally popular in the immediate postwar years, they posed fewer moral anxieties than returned Fascist soldier prisoners or Jews, both of whom, for different reasons, evoked unwanted memories of Italy's former status as a Nazi ally. The resentment and aversion shown to Italian Jewish survivors had its most concrete manifestation in the difficulties Jews faced in recovering their former jobs, assets, and influence after the war.[40] Although more research needs to be done in this area, the example of the academy is enlightening. Starting in 1944, a series of laws provided for the reinstatement of Jewish scholars who had been forced out of their university posts six years earlier. The many restrictions and loopholes in these measures, however, ensured that relatively few got back their jobs without a long wait. Many who had survived exile, deportation, or a life in hiding never managed to reclaim their prewar positions. Instead, they saw prominent Fascist intellectuals remain in their jobs, undisturbed by state purges or informal peer censure.[41]

The unevenness of official responses to the Jewish community provides us with another window onto the question of the continuity of the state from the dictatorship to the republic.[42] Yet it also reveals a continuing ambivalence toward Jews that translated into an unwillingness to confirm their juridical status as victims of the regime. Postwar Italian governments long refused to place Jews in the category of the "politically persecuted," reserving this term for anti-Fascists and other Christian casualties of totalitarianism. This exclusion of anti-Semitism from the category of the political reinforced tendencies in academic and popular culture to remember racism (if it was remembered at all) as a marginal and extremist element of Fascism, rather than as a normalized component of later Fascist ideology.[43] Only in the late 1980s did a spate of new laws occasioned by the upcoming fiftieth anniversary of the start of racial persecution rid Italian institutions of the last residues of anti-Semitic legislation. This astonishing delay did not stop Italian politicians from upholding the myth of Italians' superior humanity and tolerance. "Racism never entered the collective consciousness of Italians," asserted Senator Giovanni Spadolini, a history professor and ex-prime minister of Italy who was the primary political backer of this juridical action. Spadolini's 1987 announcement that the new legislation meant that "the Italian Republic had now paid its debt to the Jews in full," betrays a certain defensive wish to consider closed a chapter of Italian history that so contradicts this part of the national imaginary. It is significant that the word Spadolini used throughout his speech to refer to the redemptive abrogation – *rimozione* – translates as both *removal* and *repression*.[44] For this purely juridical solution to Italy's "Jewish question" buries issues of Italian complicity in Jewish persecution during the war and the continuation of Fascist attitudes in the postwar period, as well as the persistence of the more ancient sentiment of anti-Judaism.

∗

I will conclude by returning to *Life Is Beautiful* which, I argue, makes manifest the legacies of all of these paradigms of popular memory and critical inquiry regarding the fate of Jews under Mussolini. Although the film reminds Italians of the costs and inhumanity of their past of racial persecution, it also offers hints of how the feelings of victimization among non-Jewish Italians that resulted from the war have continued to influence public and private memories of Fascism and Italian racism. Benigni's representations of Jews in the film are a case in point. Guido's Jewishness is a kind of secret, one which comes out only through the force of historical events. Throughout the film, it is alluded to rather than referred to explicitly, and even his son Joshua, who has a Christian mother and a tendentially anti-Semitic grandmother, seems to have been kept in the dark about his father's religion. Other family members seem to respect this code of disclosure as well. When Guido's uncle is beaten by Fascist thugs, he refuses to tell Guido why they are targets, nor does he lodge any protest, commenting only that "silence is the most powerful cry." An argument can certainly be made for the historical accuracy of such a "weak" or buried Italian Jewish identity, since that

Italian Jewish community was always marked by a high degree of assimilation. Moreover, as Maurizio Viano has written, this intentional concealment of Guido's Jewishness is necessary to the film's schizophrenic structure, which brilliantly disorients audiences by disarming them with slapstick comedy before they are exposed to a tragedy that culminates with the death of the comic protagonist.[45] Yet it is also true that the dialogue and behavior of the film's Jewish characters perfectly conform to Italian Catholic ideals of a disarmed Jewish population that accommodates and respects the hegemony of Christian society. The humorous and bittersweet tone of the grown Joshua's recollections serves in fact to blunt any anger he must have toward the Italian Catholic compatriots who made possible his father's deportation and demise.

It is this unique tone of bittersweet humor that brings us back to the film's own secret history, that of another paternal tragedy at the hands of the Germans whose Fascist origins Benigni, a man of the left, chose not to publicly narrate, perhaps out of respect for his father, perhaps out of fear that a film that showed Fascist soldiers as victims would give further fuel to historical revisionism. In any event, these two strands of storytelling, that of private memory and public history, come together in Guido, the film's protagonist. An innocent caught up in the cruel workings of history, the character of Guido works beautifully to maximize audience empathy but also reflects Benigni's understanding of his father's position during the war. Indeed, the inclusion in the narrative of a self-sacrificing Christian wife who volunteers to go to the Lager to remain with her family affirms that Jews have no monopoly in Italy on suffering and victimhood, even as they remain the most acceptable public symbols of Fascism's inhumanity.

In an interview soon after the release of his film, Benigni explained his unusual choice to narrate the Shoah through the lens of comedy as a means of helping people to "smile at the Holocaust" and place it behind them. "Even though I can't say if it is wrong or right to get over it, it has to be done somehow."[46] This desire for closure, which echoes Senator Spadolini's assurance that Italy "paid its debts in full" to Jewish victims of the Holocaust, is certainly not limited to Italians. It takes on special meaning, though, in a country that has been slow to acknowledge the consequences of its history as a Nazi ally and participant in state anti-Semitism.

For *Life Is Beautiful* is a film that lays bare the clash between private memory and public history: what is not represented, here is not so much the true Holocaust as the history of those Italian Fascist soldiers who fought alongside Hitler's armies, only to be deported to Mauthausen and other Lagers that also imprisoned Italian anti-Fascists and Italian Jews. In the slippage between Guido and Benigni's father – in that space created by the transmutation of a Fascist soldier to a disarmed Jew – lies the oblivion of the Italian past.

NOTES

1. This debate is discussed in Maurizio Viano, *"Life Is Beautiful:* Reception, Allegory, and Holocaust Laughter," *Jewish Social Studies,* no. 3 (1999), 47–66. See also Adrienne Kertzer, "Life a fable, not a pretty picture: Holocaust Representation in Roberto Benigni and Anita Lobel," *Michigan Quarterly Review,* 39, no. 2 (2000), 279–300; and Hilene Flanzbaum, "But wasn't it terrific?: A defense of liking *Life Is Beautiful,"* *Yale Journal of Criticism,* 14 (2001), 273–86. The different uses of humor the film engages in and the issue of using humor to represent moral issues is discussed in Millicent Marcus, "'Me lo dici babbo che gioco è?' The Serious Humor of *La vita è bella,"* *Italica,* 77, no. 2 (summer 2000), 153–70; and Casey Haskins, "Art, Morality, and the Holocaust: The Aesthetic Riddle of Benigni's *Life Is Beautiful,"* *Journal of Aesthetics and Art Criticism,* 59, no. 4 (fall 2001), 373–84. More general considerations on the issue of "Holocaust Laughter," as Terrence Des Pres has termed it in his essay of that name (published in his *Writing into the World: Essays, 1973–1987* [New York: Viking, 1991], 277–86), can be found in Sander Gilman, "Is Life Beautiful? Can the Shoah be Funny? Some thoughts on recent and older films," *Critical Inquiry,* 26, no. 2 (2000), 279–308.

2. On the changes in memory politics occasioned by Berlusconi's 1994 victory, see Ruth Ben-Ghiat, "Fascism, Writing and Memory," *Journal of Modern History,* 67, no. 3 (September 1995), 627–65.

3. The phrase "serious humor" is taken from Marcus' insightful essay, "Me lo dici babbo che gioco è?"

4. As Pamela Kroll has observed, the riddles posed throughout the film are "meta-texts intimately connected with the operation of the film." (See Kroll, "Games of Disappearance and Return: War and the Child in Roberto Benigni's *Life Is Beautiful,"* *Literature Film Quarterly,* 30, no. 1 (2002), 29–43, p. 41). On the role of riddles and games in the film, see also Steve Siporin, *"Life Is Beautiful:* Four riddles, three answers," *Journal of Modern Italian Studies,* 7, no. 3 (2002), 345–63, and Marcus, "Me lo dici babbo che gioco è?" My reference to the abolition of the question "why?" is to an episode recounted by Primo Levi in *Survival in Auschwitz,* trans. Stuart Woolf (New York: Macmillan, 1961). When the thirsty protagonist asks why he has been prevented from grabbing an icicle by an Auschwitz guard, the Nazi replies, "Hier ist kein warum" (There is no why here), 25.

5. The involvement and attitudes of the film's main historical consultant, Marcello Pezzetti of the Centro Documentazione Ebraica Contemporanea, is detailed in Celli, "Roberto Benigni's *Life Is Beautiful,"* 76, and especially in Celli, "Interview with Marcello Pezzetti," *Critical Inquiry,* 27 (2000), 149–57.

6. Erika Milvy, "The Beautiful Life and Art of Roberto Benigni," *Indie* (September/October 1998), 21. Celli examines the filmmakers' reasons for avoiding a

realist representation of the Holocaust in his "Roberto Benigni's *Life Is Beautiful*," 76–7.

7. The folklorist Siporin argues that the film's structure and mood better conform to the folktale genre. See his *"Life Is Beautiful,"* 348–9.

8. On the slippage between the roles of adult and child and the meanings and strategies inherent in Benigni's uses of a child's perspective see Kroll, "Games of Disappearance and Return."

9. Marcus, "Me lo dici babbo che gioco è," esp. 153–4. On the problematics of testimony, with particular reference to Holocaust witnesses, see Shoshana Felman and Dori Laub, *Testimony: Crises of Witnessing in Literature, Psychoanalysis, and History* (New York: Routledge, 1995); Lawrence Langer, *Holocaust Testimonies: The Ruins of Memory* (New Haven: Yale University Press, 1991); and Henry Greenspan, *Listening to Holocaust Survivors* (Westport, CT: Praeger, 1998).

10. Guido's fascination with the power of the will is presented in the film as a result of hearing a popularized version of Schopenhauer's philosophy from his friend Ferruccio. As Maurizio Viano points out, Benigni is here making an ironic point by placing a philosopher whose thought was appropriated by the Nazis (through the mediation of Nietzsche's will to power) in the service of humanism and individual fantasy – both things the Nazis sought to suppress. Viano, *"Life Is Beautiful,"* 59–60.

11. Statements by Benigni from Milvy, "The Beautiful Life and Art of Roberto Benigni," 21, and Alessandra Stanley, "The Funniest Italian You've Probably Never Heard Of," *The New York Times Magazine*, October 11, 1998, 44–5.

12. The growing literature on Italian prisoners of war in German hands includes Gabriele Hammermann, *Zwangarbeit für den "Verbündeten". Die Arbeits-und Lebensbedingungen der italienischen Militärinternierten in Deutschland 1943–1945* (Tübingen: Niemeyer, 2002); Gerhard Schreiber, *Italienischen Militarinternierten im deutschen Machtbereich 1943 bis 1945: verraten, verachtet, vergessen* (Munich: R. Oldenbourg, 1990); Nicola Della Santa, *I militari italiani internati dai tedeschi dopo l'8 settembre* (Florence: Le lettere, 1986); Nicola Labanca, ed., *Fra sterminio e sfruttamento. Militari internati e prigionieri di guerra nella Germania nazista, 1939–1945* (Florence: Le lettere, 1992); Lutz Klinkhammer, "Leben im Lager. Die italienischen Kriegsgefangenen und Deportierten im zweiten Weltkrieg," *Quellen und Forschungen aus italienischen Archiven und Bibliotheken* (Tubingin, 1987), 489–520, and Giorgio Rochat, "Die italienischen Militarinternierten im zweiten Weltkrieg," in ibid., 336–420.

13. The role Italian military men played in rescuing the Jewish populations of Italian occupied territories in the Balkans and in France is highlighted in Ivo Herzer, ed., *The Italian Refuge* (Washington, DC: Catholic Press, 1990). More balanced and contextualized views of these rescues are espoused in Jonathan Steinberg, *All of Nothing: The Axis and the Holocaust* (New York: Routledge, 1990); and Daniel Carpi, *Between Mussolini and Hitler. The Jews and Italian Authorities in France and Tunisia* (Hanover, NH: University Press of New England, 1994). On the Italian military refusal to collaborate with Nazis in the Lagers, which involved between 10 and 25 percent of captives, see Giuseppe Caforio and Marina Nuciari, *No! I soldati italiani internati in Germania. Analisi di un rifiuto* (Milan: Franco Angeli, 1994).

14. David Bidussa, *Il mito del bravo italiano* (Milan: Il Saggiatore, 1993); Filippo Focardi, "'Bravo italiano è 'cattivo tedesco': riflessioni sulla genesi di due immagini incrociate," *Storia e memoria*, 1 (1996), 55–83, and his "La memoria della guerra e il mito del 'bravo italiano': origine ed affirmazione di un autoritratto collettivo," *Italia contemporanea* (September–December 2000), 393–9. For the historiographical consequences of this trope see Ruth Ben-Ghiat, "A Lesser Evil? Italian Fascism and/in the Totalitarian Equation," in Helmut Dubiel and Gabriel Motzkin, eds., *The Lesser Evil: Moral Approaches to Genocide Practices* (London: Frank Cass, 2003): 137–153.

15. I am referring here to Mussolini's use of the trope of the "proletarian nation" to mobilize support against the "plutocratic" countries of England and France after World War I. Such rhetorics were especially prominent during the Ethiopian War, when Fascist propaganda presented League of Nations sanctions against Italy as confirmation of this victimization.

16. Adolfo Bandiera, *Io fui della IX Armata d'Albania* (Bologna: Massimilano Boni, 1982), 140; for similar sentiments expressed by those stationed in Russia and Greece, see Costantino Belluscio, *I giorni dell'orrore. Diario di guerra e di prigionia, 1943–45* (Cosenza: Effesette, 1991), 36; Mario Lerda, *Russia e Germania. Diario di guerra e di prigionia di un cappellano alpino* (Ravello: Nuova Stampa, 1974), 55. For German attitudes toward Italians in the period surrounding the Armistice, see Gerhard Schreiber, "Gli IMI ed i tedeschi," in *Fra sterminio e sfruttamento. Militari internati e prigionieri di guerra nella Germania nazista 1939–45*, Nicola Labanca, ed. (Florence: Le lettere, 1992), esp. 31–46.

17. See Schreiber, "Gli IMI e i tedeschi," for German attitudes toward Italians.

18. Giuseppe Lo Conte, *Vita nel lager 1243* (Milan: Todariana, 1978), 63.

19. On the difficult return of Italian POWs, see Nicola Labanca, "Il ritorno degli prigioneri," in *Internati, prigionieri, reduci*, Bendotti et al., eds. 207–19. See also the wonderful oral histories conducted among returnees from the German Lagers: Nicola Labanca, ed., *La memoria del ritorno. Il rimpatrio degli Internati militari italiani* (Florence: Giuntina, 2000); and Angelo Bendotti et al., *Prigionieri in Germania. La memoria degli internati militari* (Bergamo: Il filo di Arianna, 1990). This process of reintegration and the political and psychological legacies of this collective history of internment will be a main focus of Ruth Ben-Ghiat, *Italian Fascist Prisoners of War and the Transition from Dictatorship*, to be published by Princeton University Press.

20. R. S., interviewed in Bendotti et al., *Prigionieri in Germania*, 533.

21. In the daily *Roma*, one commentator singled out veterans as "those who are the most horrifying to us, reduced as they appear to be to mere shadows of human beings when they were for us symbols and paragons of physical performance." Mario Stefanile, "Hanno perduto il loro nome," *Roma*, September 23, 1946.

22. See Claudio Sommaruga, "Ritorno alla base. Dai quantativi sull'internamento in Germania," *Studi e ricerche di storia contemporanea* 51 (1999), 27–51.

23. The long silence maintained by Alessandro Natta, chief of the Italian Communist Party in the late 1980s, is symptomatic. Natta was captured by the Germans as a young soldier in Italian-occupied Greece and spent time in the Küstrin, Sandbostel, and

Wietzendorf camps. After his reflections on these years were rejected by one press in 1954, he did not publish them until 1997, although his prominent position would have ensured him a contract. Natta cannot explain exactly why he left them in his desk drawer for forty years, but assures readers that no "veterans' complex" was responsible for his "renunciation." Alessandro Natta, *L'altra resistenza* (Turin: Einaudi, 1997), xxviii. On the traumatic states that result from captivity and interpretations of the POW experience as a process that extends from initial capture to reintegration into community and family, see Judith Herman, *Trauma and Recovery* (New York: Basic Books, 1992), 74–95; and Col. Robert J. Ursano and Major James R. Rundel, "The Prisoner of War," *Military Medicine* (April 1990), 176–80.

24. Oddone Usai, *Kriegsgefangener 23533* (Genoa: Laterna, 1980), entry of June 16, 1945, 217. The oral history research group headed by Angelo Bendotti, which has studied POW repatriation and its memorialization, concludes that this group of Italians faced "delusion, bitterness, rejection, and incomprehension." Bendotti et al., *Prigionieri in Germania*, 500.

25. On the mechanisms of intergenerational transmission of traumatic experience, see Michelle R. Ancharoff et al., "The Legacy of Combat Trauma. Clinical Implications of Intergenerational Transmission," in *International Handbook of Multigenerational Legacies of Trauma*, Yael Danieli, ed. (New York and London: Plenum Press, 1998), 257–76; also Robert Rosenheck, "Impact of Posttraumatic Stress Disorder of World War II on the Next Generation," *The Journal of Nervous and Mental Disease* (June 1986), esp. 321–2.

26. Benigni, in Milvy, "The Beautiful Life and Art of Roberto Benigni," 21.

27. On the issue of ex-POWs' consistent elision of their precapture experiences as occupiers, see Angelo Bendotti, et al., "'Ho fatto la Grecia, l'Albania, la Jugoslavia...' Il disagio della memoria," in *Italia in guerra*, B. Micheletti, ed. (Brescia: Fondazione Micheletti, 1992), 964–79.

28. See Nicola Caracciolo, *Gli ebrei e l'Italia durante la guerra, 1940–45* (Rome: Bonacci, 1986); and above all Susan Zuccotti, *The Italians and the Holocaust* (New York: Basic Books, 1987), remains the best historical overview.

29. Corrado Alvaro, *Italia rinunzia?* (1944, reprint: Palermo: Sellerio, 1986), 40.

30. See on such issues the essays in Michele Sarfatti, *Il ritorno alla vita. Vicende e diritti degli ebrei in Italia dopo la seconda guerra mondiale* (Florence: Giuntina, 1998); and in Alberto Cavaglion, ed. *Il ritorno dai Lager* (Milan: Franco Angeli, 1993).

31. For a historiographical survey that focuses on the motivations for Fascist racism, see Meir Michaelis, "The Current Debate over Fascist Racial Policy," in *Fascist Antisemitism and the Italian Jews*, Robert S. Wistrich and Sergio Della Pergola, eds. (Jerusalem: Vidal Sassoon International Center for the Study of Antisemitism, 1995), 48–96. This tendency is reinforced in popular memory among both Jews and non-Jews as reported by Carla Forti, *Il caso Pardo Roques. Un eccidio del 1944 tra memoria e oblio* (Turin: Einaudi, 1998), 226.

32. I am referring here to works that detail the mobilization of the intellectuals for the formation of a racial bureaucracy and the consequences of racial policy in the academy: Roberto Finzi, *L'università italiana e le leggi antiebraiche* (Rome: Riuniti, 1997); Ruth

Ben-Ghiat, *Fascist Modernities: Italy, 1922–1945* (Berkeley: University of California Press, 2001), 148–57; Carl Ipsen, *Dictating Demography* (Cambridge: Cambridge University Press, 1996), esp. 185–94; Giorgio Israel and Piero Nastasi, *Scienza e razza nell'Italia Fascista* (Bologna: Il Mulino, 1998); and Giorgio Fabre, *L'elenco. Censura Fascista, editoria e autori ebrei* (Turin: Silvio Zamaroni, 1998).

33. The definitive work on the capture and deportation of Italian Jews, which gives the biographies of each known victim, is Liliana Picciotto Fargion, *Il libro della memoria* (Milan: Mursia, 1991).

34. See the articles by Monsignor Cazzani and Francesco Capponi in the *L'Osservatore Romano* of January 16–17, 1939 and August 14, 1938, respectively, both reproduced in *Le interdizioni del Duce*, Alberto Cavaglion and Gian Paolo Romagnoni, eds. (Turin: Albert Meynier, 1988), 139–45; on this issue, G. Miccoli, "Santa Sede e Chiesa italiana di fronte alle legge antiebraiche del 1938," in *La legislazione antiebraica in Italia e in Europa. Atti del Convegno nel cinquantenario delle leggi razziali* (Rome: Camera dei Deputati, 1989), 163–274; Susan Zuccotti, *Under His Very Windows: The Vatican and the Holocaust in Italy* (New Haven: Yale University Press, 2000); and David Kertzer, *The Popes and the Jews. The Vatican's Role in the Rise of Modern Anti-Semitism* (New York: Knopf, 2001).

35. See Ben-Ghiat, *Fascist Modernities*, 153.

36. Mussolini, "Il troppo storpia," *Il Popolo d'Italia*, December 31, 1936; Mussolini, interview with Yvon De Begnac, October 1941, in De Begnac, *Palazzo Venezia* (Rome, 1950), 643. For rates of abjurations, conversions, and Aryanizations among Italian Jews after 1938, see Renzo De Felice, *Storia degli ebrei sotto il fascismo* (Turin, 1993), 334, 346–9.

37. See on this issue Stephen Gundle, *I comunisti italiani tra Hollywood e Mosca* (Florence: Giunti, 1995); and David Kertzer, *Comrades and Christians: Religion and Political Struggle in Communist Italy* (Prospect Heights, IL: Waveland Press, 1980).

38. Woman interviewed for the documentary *A Debt to Honor* (Sy Rotter, 1995).

39. See Forti, *Il caso Pardo Roques*; Federica Barozzi, "L'uscita degli ebrei di Roma dalla clandestinita," in *Il ritorno alla vita* , Sarfatti, ed. 31–46, and Adriana Goldstaub, "Appunti per uno studio sui pregiudizi antiebraici nei primi anni del dopoguerra (1945–1955), in ibid. 139–50. As Forti tells it in her study of the memory of Fascist and Nazi persecution of the Jews of Pisa, this "protective" identity survived even the test of genocidal persecution; only further research will reveal if other Jewish communities were guided after the war by the triple mandate of ensuring continuity, community, and conciliation.

40. On this legislation see *L'Abrogazione delle leggi razziali in Italia 1943–87* (Rome: Servizio Studi del Senato della Repubblica, 1988), which reprints all postwar laws regarding the Jews. The citation is from the essay therein by Mario Toscano, "L'abrogazione delle leggi razziali e il reinserimento degli ebrei nella società italiana," 22. On Jews' struggles to reclaim their assets, see Fabio Levi, "La restituzione dei beni," in *Il ritorno alla vita*, Sarfatti, ed., 77–94.

41. On this issue see Finzi, *L'Università italiana e le leggi antiebraiche*, 89–106.

42. For this argument see Toscano, "L'abrogazione delle leggi razziali," and Finzi, *L'università italiana e le leggi antiebraiche*. On the theme of state continuities from fascism to the republic, see Claudio Pavone, *Alle origini della Repubblica. Scritti su*

fascismo, antifascismo e la continuità dello stato (Turin: Bollati Boringhieri, 1995), esp. 70–159.

43. On this point, see Toscano, "L'abrogazione delle leggi razziali," 61.

44. Senator Giovanni Spadolini, *L'Abrogazione delle leggi razziali in Italia 1943–87*, esp. 16–19.

45. Viano, "*Life Is Beautiful*," 54–5.

46. Benigni, in Stanley, "The Funniest Italian You've Probably Never Heard Of," 45.

INDEX

Italicized numbers indicate illustrations.

9 780521 145947